WILSON FAMILIES
IN COLONIAL VIRGINIA
AND
RELATED MASON, SEAWELL, GOODRICH, BOUSH FAMILIES

Ancestors and Kin of
Benjamin Wilson
1733-1814

Compiled by
Patti Sue McCrary

HERITAGE BOOKS
2007

HERITAGE BOOKS
AN IMPRINT OF HERITAGE BOOKS, INC.

Books, CDs, and more—Worldwide

For our listing of thousands of titles see our website
at
www.HeritageBooks.com

Published 2007 by
HERITAGE BOOKS, INC.
Publishing Division
65 East Main Street
Westminster, Maryland 21157-5026

Copyright © 2007 Patti Sue McCrary

Other books by the author:
Cumberland County, Virginia Historical Inventory, Subject and Owner Indexes
Cumberland County, Virginia Tithable Lists for 1759
Wilson Families in Cumberland County, Virginia and Woodford County, Kentucky with Correspondence and Other Papers, 1785-1849
Wilson Families: Descendants of Colonel Benjamin Wilson, 1733-1814

All rights reserved. No part of this book may be reproduced or transmitted in any form or by any means, electronic or mechanical, including photocopying, recording or by any information storage and retrieval system without written permission from the author, except for the inclusion of brief quotations in a review.

International Standard Book Number: 978-0-7884-4391-6

Dedication

To Paul

In our extensive RV travels, he drove to places that
gave me the opportunity
to gather a great deal of information about my ancestors
and to absorb a bit of the atmosphere of Colonial Virginia

Table of Contents

Introduction ix

Reading This Book xii

Glossary xiii

CHAPTER 1 - Wilson Families 1

CHAPTER 2 - Mason Families 79

CHAPTER 3 - Seawell Families 147

CHAPTER 4 - Goodrich Families 157

CHAPTER 5 - Boush Families 194

Appendix 211
    1679 Will of Thomas Goodrich 211
    1680 Morris Survey and Tappahannock Plat 214
    1680 Will of Margaret (Gancy) Cheesman 217
    1695 Will of Lemuel Mason 220
    1702 Will of Elizabeth (Mason) Thelaball 224
    1705 Will of Ann (Seawell) Mason 227
    1712 Will of James Wilson 229
    1812 Will of Benjamin Wilson 233
    1728 Marriage Bond of Willis Wilson and Elizabeth Goodrich 236
    1754 Marriage Bond of Benjamin Wilson and Anne Seay 237

Bibliography 239

Index of Names 255

Detailed Table of Contents

CHAPTER 1 - Wilson 1

1. ____[1] Wilson 1
   2. James[2] Wilson 2
      3. Thomas[3] Wilson 6
      5. James[3] Wilson 8
         6. Solomon[4] Wilson, ... 10
            7. Simon[5] Wilson 11
            13. Jane[5] Wilson 12
         14. Thomas[4] Wilson 12
         18. Willis[4] Wilson, Jr. 12
            19. Malachi[5] Wilson, Jr. 13
            20. John[5] Wilson 14
            21. Mary[5] Wilson 15
         24. Mary[4] Wilson 16
         28. Elizabeth[4] Wilson 16
            31. Elizabeth[5] Boush 18
            32. Frederick Wilson[5] Boush 19
         39. Caleb[4] Wilson 20
            40. James[5] Wilson, Sr. 21
         45. Josiah[4] Wilson 22
            48. Mary[5] Wilson 23
            49. Josiah[5] Wilson 23
            50. Charles[5] Wilson 24
            51. Euphan[5] Wilson 24
         53. William[4] Wilson 25
            54. Willis[5] Wilson 25
         55. Malachi[4] Wilson, Sr. 26
            59. Elizabeth[5] Wilson 27
         63. Prudence[4] Wilson 28
         66. ____[4] Wilson 29
         68. Dinah[4] Wilson 29
         72. Affiah[4] Wilson 29
         79. Euphan[4] Wilson 31
   85. Lemuel[3] Wilson 31
   91. John[3] Wilson 34
   96. Samuel[3] Wilson 36
      97. Willis[4] Wilson 38
         98. Benjamin[5] Wilson, Sr. 40
   104. Willis[3] Wilson 46
      105. Lemuel[4] Wilson 48
         107. Willis[5] Wilson 49

Table of Contents   v

  115. Euphan[4] Wilson 50
 121. Affiah[3] Wilson 50
  122. Elizabeth[4] Newton 51
  125. Thomas[4] Newton 52
  128. Wilson[4] Newton 52
   131. Rebecca[5] Newton 53
  134. Ann[4] Newton 53
  138. Frances[4] Newton 54
 141. Solomon[3] Wilson 54
  143. Tabitha[4] Wilson 56
  149. Mason[4] Wilson 57
 153. Mary[3] Wilson 57
162. William[2] Wilson 59
 163. Willis[3] Wilson 62
 167. Mary[3] Wilson 64
  170. William[4] Roscow 68
  175. Wilson[4] Cary 68
   177. Mary[5] Cary 69
   178. Wilson Miles[5] Cary 70
   179. Anne[5] Cary 70
   180. Elizabeth[5] Cary 71
  181. Mary[4] Cary 71
   182. Cary[5] Selden 71
   183. Samuel[5] Selden 72
   184. Miles[5] Selden 72
  187. John[4] Blair 72
 190. Jane[3] Wilson 73
  192. Wilson[4] Curle 76
   194. David Wilson[5] Curle 77
   198. William Roscow Wilson[5] Curle 77
   200. Mary Latham[5] Curle 78

CHAPTER 2 - Mason 79

1. Francis[1] Mason 79
 4. Lemuel[2] Mason 83
  5. Frances[3] Mason 90
   6. George[4] Newton 92
   9. Nathaniel[4] Newton 94
   10. Lemuel[4] Newton 95
   11. Thomas[4] Newton 96
  13. Thomas[3] Mason 97
   15. Anne[4] Mason 100
  18. Lemuel[3] Mason 101

Table of Contents

    19. Tabitha^4 Mason 103
    20. Elizabeth^4 Mason 104
    25. Mary^4 Chichester 104
  26. Alice^3 Mason 105
    27. Mary^4 Hodge 107
    28. Margaret^4 Porten 108
    29. Daniel^4 Porten 108
    31. Anne^4 Porten 109
    32. Samuel^4 Boush 109
  34. Elizabeth^3 Mason 110
    36. Mary^4 Cocke 111
  37. George^3 Mason 111
    38. Thomas^4 Mason 113
    40. Abigail^4 Mason 114
    41. Frances^4 Mason 115
  42. Anne^3 Mason 115
    44. William^4 Kendall 117
    47. Ann^4 Kendall 117
  49. Abigail^3 Mason 117
    51. Abigail^4 Crawford 118
  52. Mary^3 Mason 119
    53. Thomas^4 Cocke 121
  56. Dinah^3 Mason 121
    57. Thomas^4 Thorowgood 123
    60. Willis^4 Wilson 124
61. Elizabeth^2 Mason 124
  62. Francis^3 Thelaball 126
    63. James^4 Thelaball 128
  68. Margaret^3 Thelaball 128
    69. William^4 Langley 130
    70. Nathan^4 Langley 130
    71. James^4 Langley 131
    75. Margaret^4 Langley 132
    76. Joyce^4 Langley 133
    77. Elizabeth^4 Langley 134
  79. James^3 Thelaball 135
    80. Francis^4 Thelaball 136
    81. Lemuel^4 Thelaball 137
    82. Dinah^4 Thelaball 138
    83. Elizabeth^4 Thelaball 140
    84. Ann^4 Thelaball 140
  86. Elizabeth^3 Thelaball 141
    87. Thomas^4 Langley 142
    88. Lemuel^4 Langley 142

Table of Contents

  89. John[4] Langley 144
  92. Abigail[4] Langley 144
 93. Mary[3] Thelaball 145

CHAPTER 3 - Seawell 147

1. Henry[1] Seawell 147
2. Ann[2] Seawell 154

CHAPTER 4 - Goodrich 157

1. Thomas[1] Goodrich 157
 2. Benjamin[2] Goodrich 170
  3. Benjamin[3] Goodrich 175
   4. Anne[4] Goodrich 177
   5. Elizabeth[4] Goodrich 178
 14. Joseph[2] Goodrich 180
 17. Charles[2] Goodrich 183
  18. Edward[3] Goodrich 185
   21. Benjamin[4] Goodrich 186
   22. Edward[4] Goodrich 186
  24. Anne[3] Goodrich 187
34. Anne[2] Goodrich 187
 35. Goodrich[3] Lightfoot 190
  38. Goodrich[4] Lightfoot 191
 42. Sherwood[3] Lightfoot 192
  45. John[4] Lightfoot 192
  47. Elizabeth[4] Lightfoot 192
 48. Thomas[3] Lightfoot 193

CHAPTER 5 - Boush 194

1. ____[1] Boush. 194
 2. ____[2] Boush 194
  3. Maximillian[3] Boush 194
   4. Maximillian[4] Boush 195
    6. Mary[5] Boush 197
    8. Elizabeth[5] Boush 198
    9. Frederick Wilson[5] Boush 199
   15. Samuel[4] Boush 200
 26. Samuel[2] Boush 201
  27. Samuel[3] Boush 202
   28. Ann[4] Boush 204
    32. Elizabeth[5] O'Sheal 205

Table of Contents

33. Samuel[4] Boush 206
40. Goodrich[4] Boush 207
    44. Ann[5] Boush 208
49. Arthur[4] Boush 208
59. Margaret "Peggy"[4] Boush 209

Introduction

The ancestral lines of Benjamin Wilson (1733-1814) of Cumberland County, Virginia, include several immigrants to the colonial Virginia tidewater area in the 1600's: James Wilson (ca 1648-1712), Francis Mason (ca 1595-1648), Henry Seawell (-1644), and Thomas Goodrich (ca 1614-1679). In this project, a chapter is given for each surname, listing descendants for several generations and documenting some details of their lives. The Boush line in Norfolk County is included because of the intermarriages with some of the forementioned surnames and because some documentation supports details passed down in Wilson family stories.

Microfilms of the county court records at the Library of Virginia provide documentation of land transactions, marriages, wills, etc. Other information, such as scanned images of land patents, is available on their website, http://www.lva.lib.va.us/. The library at the Virginia Historical Society and the Library of Virginia both have large collections of books that contain abstracts of deeds, wills, marriages, church records, etc. Copies of family Bibles and other personal papers are also available at both libraries. Long lost records continue to be found in the attics and basements of court houses and private homes. Search for primary documentation becomes easier as more indexes and abstracts are published and more information is available on the internet.

Marshall Wingfield Butt wrote a very helpful, privately printed, book in 1968 on the Wilson family. Unfortunately he did not want to "clutter the text" with footnotes and references. His book will be cited when court documents were not located. He had access to research done by Elizabeth (Baum) Wingo, also a descendant of the Wilson and Mason lines, who published many books of abstracts of court records in the counties of Norfolk and Princess Anne. Copies of the two privately printed books by Mr. Butt are located in the Sargeant Memorial Room at the Kirn Norfolk Public Library.

Many of the names, dates and places in this book were taken from my PAF database (Personal Ancestral File, Church of Jesus Christ of Latter-day Saints in Salt Lake City). GenBook (copyrighted by Rex Clement) uses that data to produce a WordPerfect (Corel Corporation) document with identification numbers, cross reference and index markers. The word processing software allowed modifying and expanding the text and adding footnotes. Since each chapter was generated separately, the identification numbers begin with the numeral 1 in each chapter. Because some entries have been deleted, there are gaps in the numbering system. There is repetition of information and citations, because names occur in more than one chapter as a result of the marriages between the families. Index entries and cross references show these connections.

The marriage dates often apply to the date of the marriage bond, and the death place may be assumed because of the county in which the will was recorded. Many birth dates were estimated mainly to give a possible generation clue to persons with the same name. The order of birth of children when birth dates are not known is sometimes determined by the order in which the names occur in a will; sons were usually listed first, but other references sometimes suggested a different order for the sons and provided information allowing daughters to be merged into the list.

Spelling was not standard. Names and other words are usually spelled in this book as they are in the court documents and transcriptions . E.g., Francis (sometimes ffrancis) was sometimes used for females, Frances for males; surnames occurred in a variety of ways - Seawell/Sewell, Goodrich/Gutteridge, Ivey/Ivy, Triniman/Trueman.

Documents signed with signature and seal indicated literacy. There could have been some signed with a mark because of illness or some other physical problem, although it is usually interpreted to indicate that the person could not read or write. The mark was not always an "X"; some marks were quite elaborate.

Titles and relationships were used differently. Mrs. sometimes was used as the abbreviation for mistress, a single lady. "Cozen" often meant nephew or niece. Daughter could mean daughter-in-law; brother could mean brother-in-law. The term "in-law" sometimes referred to a step-son, step-daughter or step-mother.

The glossary should help with some of the terms in the documents not in use today. An appendix gives transcriptions and scans of some wills, marriage bonds and land surveys.

Short titles are given for footnotes, except for county records cited. The alphabetical bibliography gives full references.

As the text and references were proofed against the supporting documents, new descendants, information, and relationships became apparent. Most of this information was not included, since it would have involved a great deal of adjustment to the identification numbers and work in adding index

Introduction

entries. Very little information is given past the period of Revolutionary War.

Errors will be found, I am sure, in my references and analysis, as I disagree with some made in the third edition of Meyer and Dorman, *Adventurers of Purse and Person* and the two volumes that had been published so far (Jan 2007) of the fourth edition by Dorman. The footnotes given in those works give excellent sources of supporting documents and have helped me considerably in my research.

Two of the extensive text sections were done with a Wilson cousin, Maurice Leach. A Mason cousin, Beth Uiterwyk, has been an excellent source of information, analysis, and support. Other researchers have been very generous in sharing their work. My thanks to all.

Special thanks to my brother Dick Thomas for proofing the manuscript.

This book completes a trilogy of publications about the life of my ancestor, Benjamin Wilson: the letters exchanged between him and his children (*Wilson Families in Cumberland County Virginia and Woodford County Kentucky with Correspondence and Other Papers 1785-1849*), his descendants (*Wilson Families: Descendants of Colonel Benjamin Wilson (1733-1814)*), and now his ancestors.

Patti Sue (Thomas) McCrary
Gulf Shores, Alabama

Reading This Book

(The following is an extraction from the article which is generated, along with index and cross reference markers, by the software, GenBook. PSM)

If, while reading the following pages of this book, the reader will keep these few facts in mind, a much clearer understanding of the contents will result. The format or style used in this book is known as the **Modified Register System,** which has been refined by the National Genealogical Society.

Three types of numbers are used: one to uniquely identify the individual, one to indicate the generation into which that person falls, and one to denote his or her birth-order within the nuclear family. The identification numbering system used in this book is called **By Descendants, in Sequential Order**. The starting person is 1, his first child is 2, his first child's first child is 3, and so on. After all the descendants of the first child are listed, then the descendants of the second child are listed, and so on. The ID numbers are in sequential order.

When an individual is introduced in his/her separate sketch, the name appears in boldface letters. The name is preceded by the identification number. The last given name is followed immediately by a superscript number indicating the number of generations from the starting individual in this book. In parentheses following the name is a list of direct ancestors back to the starting individual. Only the given name is listed, preceded by his/her ID number, and followed by the generation number in superscript.

When the list of children is presented, the plus (+) sign indicates that more about this child will be presented in his/her separate sketch. The ID number is printed, followed by M/F indicating the sex. Next a small roman numeral in front of the name designates birth-order. Next the name is followed by the birth and death dates.

The index is arranged alphabetically by surname. Under each surname, the given names are alphabetically arranged. The name is followed by the year of birth and death in square brackets. The number to the right indicates the page where this name appears. The wife appears under her maiden name and under her married names with her maiden name in parentheses.

Glossary

Ancient planters - those who came to VA before the end of 1616, survived the 1622 Indian massacre, and appeared in the 1624/5 muster.[1]

Burgess - Two burgesses were elected from each county as representatives in the "lower house" of the General Assembly of Colonial Virginia.[2]

Council - The members of the upper house of the General Assembly of Colonial Virginia were "appointed by the Crown on the recommendation of the Governor."[3]

Court of Oyer and Terminer - "held for hearing serious criminal cases."[4]

Dates/Calendar - "Old Style" dates, used in the English colonies before 2 Sep 1752, began the new year on Mar 25.[5] The dates from Jan 1 - March 24 might be written, as an example, Feb 1, 1623/4.

Governor - appointed by the Crown.[6]

Headrights - The "London Company ordained that any person who paid his own way to Virginia should be assigned 50 acres of land 'for his owne personal adventure', and if he transported 'at his owne cost' one or more persons he should, for each person whose passage he paid, be awarded fifty acres of land." The claim for land was not necessarily done at the time of arrival(s).[7]

Justice, Justice of the Peace or Commissioner - The justices of the county court were appointed by the Governor, the first named in the court record being referred to as "presiding justice."[8]

Processioning - performed by the church to establish land boundaries.[9]

---

[1] Nugent, *Cavaliers and Pioneers*, 1:xxvii.
[2] Leonard, *General Assembly of Virginia*, x.
[3] Stanard, *Colonial VA Register*, 8.
[4] Cross, *County Court... Norfolk*, 5.
[5] Leonard, *General Assembly of Virginia*, xxxi.
[6] Stanard, *Colonial VA Register*, 5-6.
[7] Nugent, *Cavaliers and Pioneers*, 1:xxiv, xxv.
[8] Whichard, *History of Lower Tidewater VA*, 1:235.
[9] Chamberlayne, *Vestry Book and Register of St. Paul's Parish*, xv, xvi

Quit Rents - land tax, at one time 2 shillings per hundred acres, payable to the Crown.[10]

Sheriff - a county office of profit which required resigning a position as burgess.[11]

Tithable - "In colonial Virginia, a poll tax or capitation tax was assessed on free white males, African American slaves, and Native American servants (both male and female), all age sixteen or older. Owners and masters paid the taxes levied on their slaves and servants."[12]

"Ye" - "the"- thorn - "Despite almost universal belief, people never said the word 'ye'. This mistake results from an old letter that is no longer in our alphabet, called a thorn, which was used where 'th' is used today. A thorn looks a bit like a 'y' and this led to the confusion."[13]

---

[10] LVA - http://www.lva.lib.va.us/whatwehave/local/va20_coltax.htm.
[11] Stanard, *Colonial VA Register*, 9-10.
[12] *Colonial Tithables* (Research Notes Number 17), Library of Virginia.
[13] Moorshead, Halvor. "Reading Old Handwriting." *The Family Chronicle Collection* Sept 1996-Aug 1997, p. 62.

CHAPTER 1 - Wilson Families

1. ____¹ Wilson.

Family stories have named **Felix Wilson**, born in England, as the immigrant to colonial Virginia. Since one family story also stated that he was "solicitor to Queen Elizabeth",[14] wills were examined relating to a Felix Wilson who lived during her reign, 1558-1603. None showed any indication of a connection to this Wilson family.[15] A Felix Wilson was a 1609 subscriber to the second charter of the Virginia Company, "whether they go in their persons, to be planters there in the said plantation, or whether they go not, but adventure their monies, goods, or chattles."[16]

Another source gave the name **Thomas Wilson** as the immigrant; examination of a will showed no connection.[17] A search was also made for an intervening generation, perhaps Willis Wilson, since that given name was used so frequently for descendants, but again, no records in England were found to give a link to this Wilson family. An interesting speculation is that the immigrant was **James Wilson** who was hanged on the site of Yorktown in Jan 1677 for his participation in Bacon's Rebellion.[18]

The kinship of the two brothers, listed below, is proved by a deed made by William² Wilson, confirming land regarding his brother James² Wilson.[19]

ISSUE:
+ 2. m i. **James Wilson**, born about 1648, died before 19 Dec 1712 <See pg. 2>.
+ 162. m ii. **William Wilson**, born 1646, died 17 Jun 1713 <See pg. 59>.

---

[14] McLean, *Wilson Family*, 8.

[15] PROB 11/195, 1646 will of Felix Wilson, and PROB 11/307, 1662 will of his son Felix, Public Records Office, Records of the Prerogative Court of Canterbury, transcriptions done by Simon Neal, records agent, e-mail sn014i4785@blueyonder.co.uk.

[16] Hening, *Statutes*, 1:85, 87.

[17] "Wilson Family", *VA Mag Hist*, 25:199. PROB 11/247, 1655 will of Thomas Wilson.

[18] Wertenbaker, *Torchbearer of the Revolution*, 198-9.

[19] Norfolk Co VA Deed Book 9:254.

2. James² Wilson <See pg. 1> (1. ____ Wilson¹) was born about 1648, probably in England. He married **Elizabeth**. She was born about 1651. She may have been the daughter of **John Willis**.²⁰

ISSUE:

+ 3.   m   i.   **Thomas Wilson**, born about 1669, died before 15 Sep 1696 <See pg. 6>.
+ 5.   m   ii. **James Wilson**, born 1671, died before Feb 1756 <See pg. 8>.
  84. f   iii. **Elizabeth Wilson**, born about 1673. She married **Henry Tregany, Jr.** He was the son of **Henry Tregany**.²¹ On 16 Mar 1701/2 Lemuel Wilson bought land from **Joel Martin**. On 17 Aug 1703 Lemuel assigned it to Henry Tregany Jr., Gent.²² Henry Trigoney was listed with 200 acres in Norfolk County in the 1704 quit rents.²³ On 17 Oct 1712 Henry Tregeny Jr. of Philadelphia, mariner, was indebted to James Wilson regarding the land he bought from Lemuel Wilson.²⁴ The 12 Nov 1712 will of Elizabeth's father stated, "I give to my daughter Elizabeth the wife of Mr. Henry Tregany of Philadelphia, five pounds current money, in full of her part of my estate, she have had her part before."²⁵ Henry was buried 17 Oct 1715 at Christ Church in Philadelphia, Pennsylvania. Elizabeth was buried there 25 May 1741.²⁶
+ 85. m   iv. **Lemuel Wilson**, born about 1675, died 1731 <See pg. 31>.
+ 91. m   v.   **John Wilson**, born about 1677, died before 4 Jun 1728 <See pg. 34>.
+ 96. m   vi. **Samuel Wilson**, born about 1680, died before 3 Jan 1710/11 <See pg. 36>.
+ 104. m vii. **Willis Wilson**, born about 1683, died before Sep 1760 <See pg. 46>.
+ 121. f viii. **Affiah Wilson**, born 1689, died after 30 May 1753 <See pg. 50>.
+ 141. m ix.   **Solomon Wilson**, born about 1694, died before Feb 1775 <See pg. 54>.
+ 153. f   x.   **Mary Wilson**, born about 1697, died before May 1772 <See pg. 57>.

---

²⁰ Boddie, *Historical Southern Families*, 3:61.
²¹ Abstracts of Philadelphia Co PA Wills, 1682-1726, B:388, 1704 will of Henry Tregeny.
²² Norfolk Co VA Deed Book 6:285.
²³ Smith, *Quit Rents of Virginia, 1704*, 90.
²⁴ Norfolk Co VA Deed Book 9:213.
²⁵ Norfolk Co VA Deed Book 9:220-2. (See appendix).
²⁶ Hildeburn, ... *Christ Church*, 220. The name was spelled "Traganey, Triganey."

James[2] Wilson was in Norfolk County, Virginia, before 1673 as shown by a 12 Jun 1713 deed in which his brother "**William Wilson** Gent. of Elizabeth City County" confirmed his prior sale of 300 acres on the Southern branch of the Elizabeth River in Norfolk County to "my deceased brother James" who "dwelt upon same upwards of forty years."[27]

On 20 Oct 1688 James received a patent for 1083 acres in Lower Norfolk County for transporting 22 persons. This land was described as on the branches of Cypress Swamp running to the head of "Northwest River of Currituck."[28] In 1693 he submitted an application for a patent, 120 acres at the "head of Southward Creek of Southern Branch to the mouth of Gilliam Neck Run" which did not pass seal, because it named the county as Lower Norfolk, "not being any such county."[29] In 1691 Lower Norfolk was divided into Norfolk and Princess Anne counties. The patent was granted in 1694 with the correct county name, noting that of the three headrights, two were for transporting **Willis**[3] **Wilson** for two crossings.[30] This was probably his nephew.

On 29 Apr 1693, for importing 12 persons, James was granted 600 acres on the branches of the Northwest River "crossing the Cypress Swamp to the Green Sea."[31] He and his wife Elizabeth signed, with their seals, a deed selling 300 acres of this land on 14 Mar 1693/4 to **Henry Butt**.[32]

In Dec 1701 Major James Wilson purchased land from **John Fulford**,[33] and on 28 Oct 1703 he was granted 211 acres adjacent to his own land, a place called the Cow Pen.[34] He had many more land transactions recorded in the Norfolk County deed books. In the 1704 quit rents, he was listed with 2800 acres.[35]

On 13 Jul 1710, James purchased about 8 acres of land which had been part of a 50 acre plot that **Walter Costen** had given **Walter**, **Thomas** and **Costen Sikes**. This was called Costens Island at the head of the South

---

[27] Norfolk Co VA Deed Book 9:254-6.
[28] Nugent, *Cavaliers and Pioneers*, 2:330 (Patent Book 7:694).
[29] Nugent, *Cavaliers and Pioneers*, 2:380 (Patent Book 8:256).
[30] Nugent, *Cavaliers and Pioneers*, 2:390 (Patent Book 8:354).
[31] Nugent, *Cavaliers and Pioneers*, 2:379 (Patent Book 8:250).
[32] Norfolk Co VA Deed Book 5:214a.
[33] Norfolk Co VA Deed Book 6:226a.
[34] Nugent, *Cavaliers and Pioneers*, 3:63 (Patent Book 9:477).
[35] Smith, *Quit Rents of Virginia, 1704*, 98.

Branch of the Elizabeth River, beginning at the foot of Great Bridge.[36] Walter Costen's will, written in 1688 and proved in 1694, named his "cozen" (probably nephew) Walter Sickes Senr. and his children.[37] James "built some 'storehouses' on this land and, like other merchants, probably engaged in trading by sea to and from the West Indies."[38]

After Lower Norfolk County was divided into Norfolk County and Princess Anne County in April 1691, Mr. James Wilson was seated as one of the justices for Norfolk County.[39] On 15 Dec 1709, Col. James Wilson was listed as presiding justice.[40]

On 19 Nov 1695 Mr. James Wilson as high sheriff was ordered to collect levies, 59 lbs of tobacco for every tithable,[41] and on 15 May 1696 Mr. James Wilson presented to the court a commission from the governor to be high sheriff for the year 1696 with his son Lemuel Wilson to be under sheriff.[42] Later that year Mr. James Wilson, high sheriff was paid for arranging for boats, etc. to carry the burgesses to and from James Town, and he was ordered to collect 59 lbs of tobacco per pole for the annual levy.[43]

James Wilson was elected burgess to the General Assembly, representing Norfolk County in 1698, 1703-5, and 1710-12.[44] For his service in the 1703 session Col. James Wilson was paid 3600 pounds of tobacco, 30 days at 120 lbs. per day.[45]

Among those listed in the 1698 militia, the officers and troops from Norfolk County were Lt. Coll. **Lemll² Mason** and Capt. James² Wilson.[46] In 1699 James was commissioned major of the Norfolk County militia.[47] In an

---

[36] Norfolk Co VA Deed Book 9:1.
[37] McIntosh, *Norfolk Co Wills 1637-1710*, 151-2 (Book 5:220).
[38] Butt, *Col James Wilson*, 8.
[39] Hening, *Statutes*, 3:95. Norfolk Co VA Deed Book 5, pt. 2 Orders:225. Whichard, *History of Lower Tidewater VA*, 1:286-7.
[40] Norfolk Co VA Deed Book 8:103.
[41] Norfolk Co VA Deed Book 6:9.
[42] Norfolk Co VA Deed Book 6:30.
[43] Norfolk Co VA Deed Book 6:64.
[44] Leonard, *General Assembly of Virginia*, 58, 62, 65.
[45] Norfolk Co VA Deed Book 7:15.
[46] Bockstruck, *Virginia Colonial Soldiers*, 231-2 (Manuscript Division, Library of Congress).
[47] McIlwaine, *Executive Journals - Colonial VA*, 1:443. Crozier, *VA Colonial Militia*, 105.

abstract of militia for Norfolk County between September 1701 and July 1702, an entry states, "Names of officers lately commissioned: Coll' Ja: Wilson."[48] At court on 16 Feb 1701/2 Col. James Wilson was present as a justice.[49]

On 16 July 1701 Majr. James Wilson was appointed by the court as a "feeofee" (trustee) for the sale of lands in Norfolk Town in place of **Anthony Lawson**, deceased.[50] James Wilson and **Samuel Boush**, as feofees in trust of lots sold in Norfolk Town, sold one lot to **Joseph Lee** on 20 Jul 1711.[51]

Coll. James Wilson was named an overseer of the 1708 will of **Roger Kelsall**. The inventory and appraisement of the estate, which was ordered 15 May 1710, was sworn to on July 8 before Col. James Wilson "one of her majesties justices."[52]

In 1712 Col. James Wilson and Majr. Sam'll Boush were named churchwardens of Elizabeth River Parish.[53]

The last appearance of James as a justice of the Norfolk County court was 15 Aug 1712. He died between 19 Sep 1712, when he was appointed surveyor of highways of Southern Branch, and 19 Dec 1712, when the following was recorded: "Its ordered that Mr. **Matthew Godfrey** be Surveyor of the heighways in the head of the Southern branch above the grate bridge in the room of Corll. James Wilson Dec'd."[54]

The will of James Wilson, dated 12 Nov 1712, was presented for probate by the executors, his widow Elizabeth and son Willis, at the court held 16 Jan

---

[48] London, Public Record Office, C.O. 5/1312, part 2, folios 277-278, no. 587 or 40. Transcription done by Simon Neal, records agent, e-mail sn014i4785@blueyonder.co.uk. (Bockstruck, *Virginia Colonial Soldiers*, 215, 218, 223).
[49] Norfolk Co VA Deed Book 6:230.
[50] Norfolk Co VA Deed Book 6:212a.
[51] Norfolk Co VA Deed Book 9:42.
[52] Norfolk Co VA Deed Book 9:32. McIntosh, *Norfolk Co Wills 1637-1710*, 1:194-5 (Book 8:51).
[53] Norfolk Co VA Deed Book 9:170.
[54] Norfolk Co VA Deed Book 9, pt. 2 Orders:37, 39, 43.

1712/3.[55] An inventory of Colonel James Wilson's moveable estate was dated **7 April 1713** and totaled more than 574 pounds sterling.[56]

In his will, he named his sons John and Willis, wife Elizabeth, grandson James, son of son Thomas deceased, grandson Willis, son of son Samuel deceased, sons Solomon and James, Capt. George Newton (his son-in-law, but not naming daughter Affiah as his wife), son Solomon age less than 21, daughters Affiah, Mary and Elizabeth, wife of Mr. Henry Trigany of Philadelphia, and son Lemuel.

James's wife **Elizabeth** died after 18 Feb 1714/5, when she was recorded in court as executrix of her husband.[57]

- - - - - - - - - - -

3. Thomas³ Wilson <See pg. 2> (2.James², 1. ____ Wilson¹) was born about 1669. He married **Isabella Burgess** about 1690. She was born about 1675. She was the daughter of **Robert Burgess** and **Anne** ____.[58]
                      ISSUE:
4. m i. **James⁴ Wilson**, born about 1691. Thomas³'s father's 1712 will stated, "I give and bequeath unto my Grandson James Wilson Son of my Son Thomas Wilson Dec'd the plantation whereon my Negro Sambo lives ... beginning on the south side of Sambo's plantation at the swamp called the Cypress Swamp ...." In the will of James⁴, dated 7 Apr 1718 and proved 18 Sep 1718, he named his uncles **Lemuel³ Wilson**, **Willis³ Wilson**, **Emanuel Burgess**, and aunt **Sarah Malbone** among others. James⁴ named his mother and uncle **Solomon³ Wilson**, executrix and executor. The will was signed James Wilson Junr. with his seal.[59]

Thomas³ died before 15 Sep 1696, when upon a petition at Court, Isabella Wilson was granted administration on the estate of her late husband Thomas Wilson. The appraisal of his estate was ordered Sep 16, and the appraisers

---

[55] Norfolk Co VA Deed Book 9:220-2. (See appendix). Norfolk Co VA Deed Book 9, pt. 2 Orders:45-6.
[56] Norfolk Co VA Deed Book 9:278-9. Butt, *Col. James Wilson*, 10.
[57] Norfolk Co VA Deed Book 9, pt. 2 Orders:111.
[58] Norfolk Co VA Deed Books 8:40a, 9:292, Robert Burgiss 1709 and 1714 gifts to his other children. Isabella's will named sisters that were named in their father's deeds of gift.
[59] Norfolk Co VA Deed Book 10:18/35.

were to meet Oct 1 at the house of Mr. James Wilson, and the inventory was entered and sworn to by Isabella Wilson on 17 Nov 1696.[60]

Isabella married (2) **Mathew Godfrey**. On 15 Jan 1703/4 Matthew and Isabella Godfrey sold 100 acres of land to **John Godfrey**. The deed was acknowledged in court by Matthew Godfrey and **George Burgess**, attorney for Mrs. Isabella Godfrey.[61] Isabella's son James[4] Wilson was named as son-in-law (step-son) in the will of Matthew Godfrey, which was dated 13 Mar 1715/6 and proved 17 May 1717.[62] Isabella was named executrix of Matthew Godfrey's estate 2 Nov 1717.[63]

On 13 May 1718 Isabella Godfrey gave slaves, household goods, and stock to her son James[4] Wilson.[64]

Isabella married (3) **Edward Moseley** between 13 May 1718 and 17 Jul 1718.[65] He was born about 1661, the son of **William Moseley** and **Mary Gookin**.[66]

On 19 Feb 1719/20 Solomon[3] Wilson, executor of the will of James[4] Wilson, entered a suit against Col. Edward Moseley and Isabella his wife, admx. of Thomas[3] Wilson deceased.[67]

The will of Col. Edward Moseley, which named wife Isabella and his grandson **Edward Hack Moseley**, was written 6 Mar 1735/6 and proved 7 Apr 1736.[68]

Isabella Moseley's will, dated 8 Mar 1739, named cousins (nephews and nieces) **James Ives, Robert Burgess, Robert Hodges, Ann Fazakerly, Emanuel Burgess, Thomas Burgess, Mary Hodges,** sister **Rachel Ives,** sister **Elizabeth Hodges,** and left to Edward Hack Moseley one large punch bowl formerly his grandfather's. Robert Burgess and Robert Hodges were named executors. Her will was proved 3 Apr 1740.[69]

---

[60] Norfolk Co VA Deed Book 6:48, 49, 69.
[61] Norfolk Co VA Deed Book 7:22a.
[62] Norfolk Co VA Deed Book 9:591-6.
[63] Norfolk Co VA Deed Book 10:15a/30.
[64] Norfolk Co VA Deed Book 10:25/49.
[65] Norfolk Co VA Deed Book 10:24/47.
[66] Dorman, *Adventurers of Purse and Person*, 2:107-8.
[67] Norfolk Co VA Orders, Appraisements & Wills: 14-14a.
[68] Princess Anne Co VA Deed Book 5:59.
[69] Princess Anne Co VA Deed Book 5:451.

5. James³ Wilson <See pg. 2> (2.James², 1. ____ Wilson¹) was born about 1671. He married (1) **Prudence Butt** about 1692. She was born about 1678. She was the daughter of **Thomas Butt** and **Elizabeth** ____, shown in a 1712 action brought by James Wilson Junr. and Prudence his wife, legatee of Thomas Butt.[70]

ISSUE:

+ 6. m i. **Solomon Wilson, Sr.** born about 1693, died after 19 Feb 1754 <See pg. 10>.
+ 14. m ii. **Thomas Wilson**, born about 1694, died 1724 <See pg. 12>.
  16. f iii. **Ann Wilson**, born about 1695, died after 1750. In his 1750 will, Maj James Wilson left Ann 60 acres near Great Bridge, slaves, bed, etc..[71]
  17. m iv. **James Wilson**, born about 1696. He appears to have married (1) **Sarah** ____ before 19 Aug 1725, when James Wilson Jr. and Sarah his wife sold property to **William Butt**.[72] James married (2) **Grace Duke** 16 Dec 1743. His brother Willis Wilson made oath that Grace was nearly 22 years of age.[73] In his 1750 will, Maj. James² Wilson left James³ a plantation bought of **John Coats**.[74] In the will of James⁴, dated 9 Jun 1759 and proved Feb 1761, this land was bequeathed to his cousin **Caseby Coats** after her father's decease.[75] The abstract does not name his wife Grace. Grace Wilson died in 1795 leaving all to "cousin Sarah Duke."[76]
+ 18. m v. **Willis Wilson, Jr.**, born about 1687, died before 19 Apr 1750 <See pg. 12>.
+ 24. f vi. **Mary Wilson**, born about 1700, died after 1760 <See pg. 16>.
+ 28. f vii. **Elizabeth Wilson**, born about 1704, died 20 Apr 1783 <See pg. 16>.
+ 39. mviii. **Caleb Wilson**, born about 1706, died after 28 May 1754 <See pg. 20>.
+ 45. m ix. **Josiah Wilson**, born 1708, died 12 May 1795 <See pg. 22>.

---

[70] Norfolk Co VA Deed Book 9, pt. 2 Orders:26. Butt, *An Account .... Robert Butt*, 10.
[71] Norfolk Co VA Will Book 1:7a-9.
[72] Norfolk Co VA Wills & Deeds F:172a.
[73] Wingo, *Marriages of Norfolk Co VA, Vol 1*, 74.
[74] Norfolk Co VA Will Book 1:7a-9.
[75] Wingo, *Norfolk Co VA Will Book 1*, 36 (f 55).
[76] Butt, *Col James Wilson*, 24.

52. m x. **Nathaniel Wilson**, born about 1714.[77] In his father's 1750 will he was given "the two plantations I bought of **Richard Ellerson** and **Walter Sikes**..[78]
+ 53. m xi. **William Wilson**, born about 1715, died 1752 <See pg. 25>.
+ 55. m xii. **Malachi Wilson, Sr.**, born about 1716, died before 18 Oct 1787 <See pg. 26>.
+ 63. f xiii. **Prudence Wilson**, born after 1722 <See pg. 28>.
+ 66. f xiv. ____ **Wilson**, died before 13 Jan 1749/50 <See pg. 29>.

James[3] made a deposition in 1700 that he was about age 29.[79]

James[3] Jr. appeared as a justice in the Norfolk County court from 1702[80] until 1756.[81] On 16 Apr 1705 James Wilson Junr. was sworn in as high sheriff of Norfolk County.[82] In the Norfolk County militia James Wilson was "commissioned captain ... by 1725 and major before 1742."[83]

On 16 Jul 1701, for love and affection, Major James[2] Wilson of the Southern Branch of the Elizabeth River deeded 85 acres of land to son James Wilson Jr.[84] The 1704 quit rents show James Wilson Jr. with 200 acres in Norfolk County, so he evidently had started accumulating more land.[85]

On 12 Sep 1712 **John** and **Isabel Coats** sold 100 acres to Mr. James Wilson, high sheriff.[86] In the 1712 will of his father, James[3] was given "one hundred acres of land lying and being over the Gumme swamp in the back woods."[87] James[3] had more land transactions in the Norfolk County deed books.

Prudence died before 20 Jul 1724, when James married (2) **Grace Phillips**.[88] James married (3) **Dinah Nicholson** 20 Aug 1725. She was the daughter of

---

[77] Butt, *Col James Wilson*, 28.
[78] Norfolk Co VA Will Book 1:7a-9.
[79] Butt, *Col James Wilson*, 11.
[80] des Cognets, *English Duplicates*, 11, 16.
[81] Butt, *Col James Wilson*, 20.
[82] Norfolk Co VA Deed Book 7:74.
[83] Butt, *Col James Wilson*, 20.
[84] Norfolk Co VA Deed Book 6:210.
[85] Smith, *Quit Rents of Virginia, 1704*, 98.
[86] Norfolk Co VA Deed Book 9:205-8.
[87] Norfolk Co VA Deed Book 9:220-2. (See appendix).
[88] Wingo, *Marriages of Norfolk Co VA, Vol 1*, 74.

Wilson Families

William Nicholson and **Alice** ____; she was named Dinah Wilson in her father's 1728 will.[89]

ISSUE:
+ 68. f xv. **Dinah Wilson**, born about 1727, died before 17 Apr 1762 <See pg. 29>.
+ 72. f xvi. **Affiah Wilson**, born about 1729, died after 24 Dec 1767 <See pg. 29>.
+ 79. f xvii. **Euphan Wilson**, born after 1734 <See pg. 31>.

The will of James[3] Wilson, dated 13 Jan 1749/50 and proved Feb 1756, named wife Dinah, son Solomon, grandson Jeremiah son of Thomas deceased, sons James, Willis, Caleb, Josiah, Nathaniel, William and Malachi, daughter Mary Butt, grandson William Nicholson, daughters Elizabeth Thelaball, Prudence Tatem, Dinah Nicholson, Affiah Langley, Ann Wilson and Uphan Wilson.[90]

Dinah Wilson's will dated 17 Apr 1762 and proved Nov 1771 named daughters Affiah Langley and Uphan Corprew, grandsons William Nicholson, James Nicholson and John Nicholson - youngest not 18, granddaughters Letice Langley and Sally Corprew, grandsons Willis Langley, James Langley, Josiah Langley, John Corprew and James Corprew and granddaughter Elizabeth Corprew. Her executors were her three sons-in-law, William Nicholson, Willis Langley and John Corprew.[91]

- - - - - - - - - - -

6. Solomon[4] Wilson, Sr. <See pg. 8> (5.James[3], 2.James[2], 1. ____ Wilson[1]) was born about 1693. He married (1) **Elizabeth Holstead**. She was the daughter of **Henry Holstead**. In a 7 Apr 1730 deposition Solomon Wilson age about thirty odd stated that he and his wife were at the house of her father Henry Holstead about the last of June or July 1729.[92]

ISSUE:[93]
+ 7. m i. **Simon Wilson**, died before 21 Sep 1801 <See pg. 11>.
   8. m ii. **Caleb Wilson**.
   9. m iii. **Henry Wilson**, born about 1738.
  10. f iv. **Sarah Wilson**. She married **James Butt (See number 156)**.
  11. f v. **Abiah Wilson**.
  12. f vi. **Elizabeth Wilson**.

---

[89] Wingo, *Marriages of Norfolk Co VA, Vol 1*, 74. McIntosh, *Norfolk Co Wills 1710-1753*, 118.
[90] Norfolk Co VA Will Book 1:7-9.
[91] Norfolk Co VA Will Book 1:209-210.
[92] Norfolk Co VA Wills, 1722-1736, 18.
[93] Butt, *Col James Wilson*, 23-4.

+ 13. f   vii. **Jane Wilson** <See pg. 12>.

Solomon[4] was older than his uncle **Solomon**[3] **Wilson**.[94] On 11 Aug 1736, it was ordered that "Solomon Wilson the Elder" be added to the Norfolk County justices.[95]

In his father's 1750 will he was given the plantation his father bought from **Henry Tregany** in 1712.[96] In 1712 Colonel James[2] Wilson had bequeathed to his grandson Solomon[4], son of his son James, 200 acres called "Canoe Neck."[97]

Elizabeth died before 1754, and Solomon, Sr. married (2) **Frances** ____ widow of **Richard Hodges**.[98]

In Solomon's will, dated 19 Feb 1754 and proved May 1754, he named his wife Frances, son Simon, to whom he left the "Canoe Neck" plantation, sons Caleb, Henry and daughters Sarah, Abiah, Elizabeth and Jane.[99]

- - - - - - - - - - -

7. **Simon**[5] **Wilson** <See pg. 10> (6.Solomon, Sr[4], 5.James[3], 2.James[2], 1. ____ Wilson[1]). He married **Sarah** ____.
ISSUE:
f   i.   **Deborah Wilson**.
m ii. **William Wilson**, died 1815.[100]
f   iii. **Winnie Wilson**.

Simon's will, dated 10 May 1801 and proved 21 Sep 1801, named his wife Sarah, daughter Deborah, son William, daughter **Wenny Slack**, and grandchildren.[101]

- - - - - - - - - - -

---

[94] Butt, *Col James Wilson*, 22.
[95] McIlwaine, *Executive Journals - Colonial VA*, 4:373.
[96] Norfolk Co VA Deed Book 9:213. Norfolk Co VA Will Book 1:7a-9.
[97] Norfolk Co VA Deed Book 9:220-2. (See appendix).
[98] Butt, *Col James Wilson*, 22.
[99] Wingo, *Unrecorded Wills Norfolk Co VA*, 123-4. Butt, *Col James Wilson*, 22 - states proved May 1754.
[100] Butt, *Col James Wilson*, 23.
[101] Brewster, *Norfolk Co VA Will Book 3*, 173.

13. Jane⁵ Wilson <See pg. 11> (6.Solomon, Sr⁴, 5.James³, 2.James², 1. ____ Wilson¹). She married **Nathaniel Butt (See number 154)**.¹⁰²

ISSUE:

   f   i. **Jane Butt**.¹⁰³

- - - - - - - - - - -

14. Thomas⁴ Wilson <See pg. 8> (5.James³, 2.James², 1. ____ Wilson¹) was born about 1694. He married **Elizabeth** ____.

ISSUE:

15. m   i. **Jeremiah Wilson**.

Thomas died before 18 Dec 1724, the date of the court order for the inventory of his estate; the inventory was presented by Elizabeth Wilson, his widow.¹⁰⁴ In his 1750 will, Maj. James Wilson left to grandson Jeremiah⁵ Wilson, son of Thomas, the 100-acre plantation Thomas had lived on.¹⁰⁵

- - - - - - - - - - -

18. Willis⁴ Wilson, Jr. <See pg. 8> (5.James³, 2.James², 1. ____ Wilson¹) was born about 1687. He married **Mary** ____ about 1730.

ISSUE:

+ 19. m   i. **Malachi Wilson, Jr.**, born about 1736, died 19 May 1794 <See pg. 13>.
+ 20. m   ii. **John Wilson**, born about 1737, died before Feb 1780 <See pg. 14>.
+ 21. f   iii. **Mary Wilson**, born about 1739, died after 17 Aug 1778 <See pg. 15>.

He was called Willis Wilson Jr. to distinguish him from his uncle.

On 12 Mar 1745/6 a verbal will of **Joseph Russell** was made before Capt. Willis Wilson Jr.¹⁰⁶ The Jan 1747 will of **Moses Prescott** mentions land of Major Wilson and witness Willis Wilson Jr.¹⁰⁷ Capt. Willis⁴ Wilson Jun: was a vestryman of Elizabeth River Parish 18 Oct 1749.¹⁰⁸

---

¹⁰² Butt, *Col James Wilson*, 19, 24.
¹⁰³ Butt, *An Account .... Robert Butt*, 16.
¹⁰⁴ Butt, *Col James Wilson*, 24.
¹⁰⁵ Norfolk Co VA Will Book 1:7a-9.
¹⁰⁶ McIntosh, *Norfolk Co Wills 1710-1753*, 195 (Book H:170).
¹⁰⁷ McIntosh, *Norfolk Co Wills 1710-1753*, 271-2.
¹⁰⁸ Walter, *Vestry Book of Elizabeth River Parish*, 1.

In his 1750 will, Maj. James Wilson left Willis the tract of land James bought of **Joseph Church** adjoining the land his Grandfather Butt gave him.[109]

The will of Willis[4] Wilson Jun[r], written 10 Jan 1749/50 and proved 19 Apr 1750, named his son Malachi to whom he gave the land that had been given Willis by his grandfather **Thomas Butt**. He also named his son John, daughter Mary, his wife Mary and brother Josiah executors.[110]

Willis's wife Mary married (2) **William Bradley** whose will, dated 23 Apr 1768 and proved 17 Feb 1785, named his wife Mary, her first husband Mr. Willis Wilson and their children Mary Boush, John Wilson, excluding their son Malachi Wilson. He named **Goodrich Boush** and John Wilson executors.[111]

- - - - - - - - - - -

19. **Malachi[5] Wilson, Jr.** <See pg. 12> (18.Willis, Jr[4], 5.James[3], 2.James[2], 1. ____ Wilson[1]) was born about 1736. He married **Lydia** ____ about 1760.
ISSUE:[112]
   m i. **John Wilson**, may have been administrator of his brother Robert's estate.
   m ii. **Willis Wilson**, born about 1770.
   m iii. **Malachi Wilson**.
   m iv. **Robert Wilson**, died 14 Jan 1793.[113]
   m v. **Frederick Wilson**, died after 1819.
   m vi. **Samuel Wilson**.
   m vii. **Miles Simmons Wilson**, born about 1781.
   m viii. **Amsey White Wilson**, born about 1783, died 1824.
   f ix. **Lydia Wilson**.
   f x. **Mary Wilson**, died before 1803.

In 1761 Malachi[5] Wilson Jr. was elected vestryman for St. Brides Parish.[114]

Malachi[5] died 19 May 1794.[115] In his will, dated 8 Jan 1785 and proved 22 Jul 1794, he named his wife Ledy, sons John, Willis, Malachi, Robert,

---

[109] Norfolk Co VA Will Book 1:7a-9.
[110] McIntosh, *Norfolk Co Wills 1710-1753*, 272-3 (Book I).
[111] Norfolk Co VA Will Book 2:208-9/252-3.
[112] Butt, *Col James Wilson*, 33-5.
[113] Headley, *18th-Century Newspapers*, 372.
[114] James, *Lower Norfolk Antiquary*, 1:19-20.
[115] Headley, *18th-Century Newspapers*, 372.

Frederick, Samuel, Miles Simmons, and Amsey White Wilson and daughters Mary and Ledy.[116]

Lydia's 1803 will named all the children except Robert amd Mary.[117]

- - - - - - - - - - -

20. John[5] Wilson <See pg. 12> (18.Willis, Jr[4], 5.James[3], 2.James[2], 1. ____ Wilson[1]) was born about 1737. He married (1) **Mary Happer** 29 Dec 1760.[118] She was the daughter of **William Happer** and **Sarah** ____.[119]

ISSUE:[120]

- m i. **William Wilson**, born 1761, died 18 Jul 1838.
- f ii. **Sarah Wilson**, born about 1763, died 1803.
- f iii. **Mary Wilson**, born about 1765, died 1799.
- f iv. **Ann Wilson**, born about 1767, died 1824.
- f v. **Charlotte Happer Wilson**, born about 1769.

Col. John[5] Wilson was born about 1737.[121] In 1761 John was elected vestryman for St. Brides Parish.[122] He was burgess for Norfolk County from 1769 to 1771.[123]

Mary died before 17 Sep 1772 when John married (2) **Margaret Bruce**.[124] She was born 1755. She was the daughter of **Alexander Bruce** and **Sarah Tucker**.[125]

ISSUE:

- m vi. **John Wilson**, born 1776, died 26 Sep 1843.[126]
- m vii. **Holt Wilson**, born 19 May 1779, died 24 Mar 1845.[127]

---

[116] Brewster, *Norfolk Co VA Will Book 3*, 60-1.
[117] Butt, *Col James Wilson*, 34.
[118] Wingo, *Marriages of Norfolk Co VA, Vol 1*, 74.
[119] Wingo, *Norfolk Co VA Will Book 1*, 10-11 (f 19a), 77 (f 120), wills of William and Sarah Happer.
[120] Butt, *Col James Wilson*, 43, 44.
[121] Butt, *Col James Wilson*, 36-43.
[122] James, *Lower Norfolk Antiquary*, 1:19-20.
[123] Leonard, *General Assembly of Virginia*, 97-101
[124] Wingo, *Marriages of Norfolk Co VA, Vol 1*, 74.
[125] Butt, *Col James Wilson*, 36.
[126] Butt, *Col James Wilson*, 47-8.
[127] Butt, *Col James Wilson*, 50-5. This is an ancestral line of Marshall Wingfield Butt (1896-1974).

During the Revolutionary War John[5] was a captain in the militia; in 1775 he was at the Battle of Great Bridge, and by 1777 he advanced to the rank of colonel.[128] He wrote a letter to Patrick Henry in 1778 concerning the bravery and death of his cousin, Captain **Josiah Wilson**.[129]

The will of John[5], dated 1 Sep 1779 and proved Feb 1780, named his wife Margaret, his sons William, John, Holt, daughters Sarah, Molley, Nancy and Charlotte H. and also **Susanna Tucker**, daughter of **Robert** and **Elizabeth Tucker**, provided she not marry "an Enemy to the Independence of America."[130]

The Virginia Gazette reported the death of John Wilson Esq. of Norfolk County 2 Oct 1779.[131]

Margaret died 1827.[132]

- - - - - - - - - - -

21. Mary[5] Wilson <See pg. 12> (18.Willis, Jr[4], 5.James[3], 2.James[2], 1. ____ Wilson[1]) was born about 1739. She married **Goodrich Boush** 25 Jan 1759.[133] **(See number 40 - pg. 207).**

ISSUE:[134]

m   i.   **Wilson Boush**, born about 1761, died 1 Dec 1829.
m   ii.   **Samuel Boush**, born about 1763.
m   iii.   **James Boush**, born about 1765.
f   iv.   **Ann Boush**, born 1762, died 1835.
f   v.   **Mary Boush**, born about 1769.
f   vi.   **Elizabeth Boush**, born about 1771.

Mary[5] and Goodrich Boush were witnesses to a deed made by his father and step-mother, Samuel and Frances Boush in 1759.[135] In the will of Goodrich Boush, dated 17 Aug 1778 and proved Dec 1782, he named his wife Mary,

---

[128] Butt, *Col James Wilson*, 37.
[129] Wirt, *Patrick Henry*, 235-6.
[130] Norfolk Co VA Will Book 2:129/157.
[131] Headley, *18th-Century Newspapers*, 372.
[132] Butt, *Col James Wilson*, 47. Henley, *Marriage/Obituary Index* states that Mrs. Margaret Martin died at the home of her son, Holt Wilson, 1828.
[133] Wingo, *Marriages of Norfolk Co VA, Vol 1*, 6.
[134] Dorman, *Adventurers of Purse and Person*, 2:606
[135] Norfolk Co VA Deed Book 19:3

sons Wilson, Samuel, James, and daughters Ann, Mary, and Elizabeth. One of his executors was his brother-in-law, Malachi Wilson.[136]

- - - - - - - - - - -

24. Mary⁴ Wilson <See pg. 8> (5.James³, 2.James², 1. ____ Wilson¹) was born about 1700. She married **William Butt** about 1726. He was born about 1699 and died 1751. He was the son of **Richard Butt** and **Sarah Sayer**.[137]

ISSUE:[138]

25. m i. **Caleb Butt**, born about 1728.
26. f ii. **Sarah Butt**, born about 1730. She married **Henry Holstead** 1753.
27. m iii. **Edward Butt**, born about 1732.

In his 1750 will, her father named his daughter, Mary Butt. Mary died after 1760.

- - - - - - - - - - -

28. Elizabeth⁴ Wilson <See pg. 8> (5.James³, 2.James², 1. ____ Wilson¹) was born about 1704. She married (1) **Lazarus Sweny** 14 Feb 1728/9.[139]

ISSUE:

29. m i. **Daniel Sweny**, born about 1730. In his will, dated 25 Oct 1761 and proved Nov 1761, he divided his estate into 5 parts, 3 to go to his mother Elizabeth Thelaball, the other two to be divided between his brother (half-brother) Frederick Boush and sister (half-sister) Elizabeth Nimmo, naming Frederick Boush and Gershom Nimmo executors.[140]
30. m ii. **James Sweny**, born about 1732, died before 25 Oct 1761.

The will of Lazarus Sweny, dated 21 Oct 1732 and proved 15 Dec 1732, named his brother **Samuel**, wife Elizabeth, and sons Daniel and James.[141] Elizabeth Sweny was listed with three tithables in 1733.[142]

Elizabeth married (2) **Maximillian Boush** after 1733. **(See number 4 - pg. 195)**.

ISSUE:

---

[136] Norfolk Co VA Will Book 2:206/176-8.
[137] Butt, *An Account .... Robert Butt*, 8- 9.
[138] Butt, *Col James Wilson*, 24-5. All dates on parents and children.
[139] Norfolk Co VA Marriage Bonds 1706-1768.
[140] Norfolk Co VA Will Book 1:72.
[141] McIntosh, *Norfolk Co Wills 1710-1753*, 129-30.
[142] Wingo, *Norfolk Co VA Tithables 1730-1750*, 83.

+ 31. f vi. **Elizabeth Boush**, born about 1734, died before 7 Jan 1811 <See pg. 18, 198>.
+ 32. m vii. **Frederick Wilson Boush**, born before 2 Feb 1736/7, died before 1 Dec 1806 <See pg. 19, 199>.

The 2 Feb 1736/7 division of the estate of Maximillian named his widow Elizabeth, children from his first marriage and the children of Elizabeth and Maximillian, Elizabeth and Frederick.[143]

Elizabeth married (3) **Thomas Thelaball** about 1744. He was born 30 Mar 1718.[144] **(See pg. 136).**

ISSUE:[145]

36. f viii. **Abigail Thelaball**, born Jan 1745/6. She married **Matthew Godfrey** 24 Feb 1784.[146] He was the son of **Matthew Godfrey** and **Abigail Porter**.[147] Abigail died before 26 Mar 1805[148].
37. f ix. **Prudence Thelaball**, born 25 Nov 1747. She married **Charles Sayer Boush** 14 Jul 1796.[149] **(See number 58 - pg. 203).** Charles died before 25 Apr 1809.[150] Prudence died 22 Dec 1807.
38. m x. **Lemuel Thelaball**, born 22 Dec 1749, died young.

She was named Elizabeth Thelaball 18 Jan 1749/50, the date her father's will was written.[151] Thomas died before Jun 1751 when "Elizabeth Tenaball, Thomas's widow", was listed with two tithables. In 1753, she was named with her son Frederick Boush.[152]

The will of Elizabeth[4] Thelaball, dated 1 Jan 1778 and proved Jul 1783, named son Frederick Boush, daughters Elizabeth Hunter, Abigail Thelaball, Prudence Thelaball, grandson Gershom Nimmo, and granddaughter Elizabeth Jacomine Boush.[153]

---

[143] Princess Anne Co VA Deed Book 5:169, 201.
[144] Thelaball Family Bible, Accession 35231, LVA.
[145] Dorman, *Adventurers of Purse and Person*, 2:620.
[146] Wingo, *Marriages of Norfolk Co VA, Vol 1*, 26.
[147] Dorman, *Adventurers of Purse and Person*, 2:622-3
[148] Maling, *Princess Anne Co VA, Wills*, 92 - will of Frederick Boush.
[149] Wingo, *Marriages of Norfolk Co VA, Vol 2*, 16.
[150] Dorman, *Adventurers of Purse and Person*, 2:609.
[151] Norfolk Co VA Will Book 1:7a-9.
[152] Wingo, *Norfolk Co VA Tithables 1751-1765*, 16, 70.
[153] Norfolk Co VA Will Book 2:212-3/181-2.

Elizabeth died 20 Apr 1783.[154]

- - - - - - - - - - -

31. Elizabeth[5] Boush <See pg. 17, 196> (28.Elizabeth[4], 5.James[3], 2.James[2], 1. ____ Wilson[1]) was born about 1734. She married (1) **Gershom Nimmo**. He was the son of **James Nimmo** and **Mary Johnson**.[155]

ISSUE:[156]
- m i. **James Nimmo**.
- m ii. **William Nimmo**.
- m iii. **Gershom Nimmo**, born before 17 Sep 1764, died 5 Jul 1817.[157]

Elizabeth[5] was named as sister Elizabeth Nimmo in the 1761 will of Daniel Sweny.[158] Her mother, in her 1778 will, named her daughter Elizabeth Hunter and grandson Gershom Nimmo.[159]

The will of Gershom Nimmo, dated 17 Sep 1764 and proved 20 Nov 1764, named his sons James, William and Gershom, and mentioned his wife, but did not name her.[160]

Elizabeth Nimmo married (2) **Jacob Hunter** 5 Dec 1766.[161] He was born about 1715. He was the son of **John Hunter** and **Jacomine Johnson**.[162]

ISSUE:
- m iv. **James Hunter**, born about 1767.
- m v. **Jonathan Hunter**, born about 1769.
- m vi. **Josiah Wilson Hunter**, born about 1770.
- m vii. **William Hunter**, born about 1775. His will, dated 4 Apr 1803 and proved 4 Jul 1803, named his mother Elizabeth, brothers Jonathan and Josiah Hunter and Gershom Nimmo.[163]

---

[154] Boush Family Bible, Accession 22246, LVA.
[155] Maling, *Princess Anne Co VA Deed Books 1-7*, 95 (7DB448) - will of James Nimmo.
[156] Maling, *Princess Anne Co VA Deed Books 8-18*, 26 (9DB430) - will of Gershom Nimmo.
[157] Boush Family Bible, Accession 22246, LVA.
[158] Wingo, *Norfolk Co VA Will Book 1*, 48 (f 72).
[159] Norfolk Co VA Will Book 2:212-3/181-2.
[160] Maling, *Princess Anne Co VA Deed Books 8-18*, 26 (9DB430).
[161] Wingo, *Marriages of Princess Anne Co VA*, 2:1.
[162] Maling, *Princess Anne Co VA Deed Books 1-7*, 95. Walter, *Princess Anne Co VA Deed and Minute Books*, 7DB449 - will of John Hunter.
[163] Maling, *Princess Anne Co VA, Wills*, 77.

In the will of Jacob Hunter, dated 24 Jan 1780 and proved 11May 1780, he named his wife Elizabeth, requesting that she educate the four youngest sons, James, Jonathan, Josiah Wilson, and William.[164]

Elizabeth Hunter's will, dated 8 Jun 1809 and proved 7 Jan 1811, named her sons Gershom Nimmo, Jonathan Hunter and Josiah Wilson Hunter.[165]

- - - - - - - - - - -

32. Frederick Wilson^5 Boush <See pg. 17, 196> (28.Elizabeth^4, 5.James^3, 2.James^2, 1.____ Wilson^1) was born before 2 Feb 1736/7, the date of the division of his father's estate.[166] He married (1) **Jacomine Hunter**.[167] She was the daughter of **John Hunter** and **Jacomine Johnson**.[168]

ISSUE:
- m i. **William Boush**, died before 3 Feb 1834.[169]
- m ii. **Caleb Boush**, born after 1765.[170]
- f iii. **Elizabeth Jacomine Boush**, born 9 Jan 1775, died 13 Aug 1861.[171]

Jacomine died 7 Nov 1791.[172]

Frederick married (2) **Elizabeth Wilson (See number 59)** 14 May 1795.[173]

ISSUE:[174]
- f iv. **Jacomine Boush**, born 23 Mar 1796, died 5 Mar 1797.

The will of Frederick, dated 26 Mar 1805 and proved 1 Dec 1806, named his wife Elizabeth, sons William and Caleb, and daughter Elizabeth Jacomine Smith.[175]

---

[164] Princess Anne Co VA Deed Book 17:1.
[165] Maling, *Princess Anne Co VA, Wills,* 101.
[166] Princess Anne Co VA Deed Book 5:169, 201.
[167] Boush Family Bible, Accession 22246, LVA.
[168] Maling, *Princess Anne Co VA Deed Books 1-7*, 95. Walter, *Princess Anne Co VA Deed and Minute Books,* 7DB449 - will of John Hunter.
[169] Maling, *Princess Anne Co VA, Wills*, 177.
[170] Wingo, *Marriages of Princess Anne Co VA 1749-1821*, 10.
[171] Boush Family Bible, Accession 22246, LVA.
[172] Boush Family Bible, Accession 22246, LVA.
[173] Wingo, *Marriages of Princess Anne Co VA*, 2:2.
[174] Boush Family Bible, Accession 22246, LVA.
[175] Maling, *Princess Anne Co VA, Wills*, 92.

Wilson Families

Elizabeth died 30 Jan 1816.[176]

- - - - - - - - - - -

39. Caleb⁴ Wilson <See pg. 8> (5.James³, 2.James², 1. ____ Wilson¹) was born about 1706. He married (1) **Love Tatem** after 18 Oct 1737, the date of her father's will.[177] She was the daughter of **Nathaniel Tatem** and **Anne Godfrey**.[178]

ISSUE:

+ 40. m i. **James Wilson, Sr**, born 4 Sep 1742, died 18 Nov 1820 <See pg. 21>.
 41. m ii. **Tatem Wilson**. He married **Charity** ____. Charity died Feb 1797. Tatem died 23 Apr 1795.[179]
 42. f iii. **Love Wilson**, died after 17 Mar 1787.[180]

On 11 Aug 1736, Caleb Wilson was named a justice for Norfolk County.[181]

Caleb married (2) **Ann** ____ 1738. Ann married (1) ____ **Church**.[182]

Caleb married (3) **Sarah** ____. Sarah also married (1) ____ **Swann**.

ISSUE:

 43. m v. **William⁵ Wilson, Jr**. In 1771 William⁵ was named as an orphan of Caleb Wilson, his half-brother James Wilson his guardian.[183] In his will, dated 17 Mar 1787 and proved 20 Apr 1787, William Wilson, Jr., of St. Brides Parish, Norfolk County, named his (half) brothers James and Tatem Wilson, (half) sister Love Wilson. He also named his (half) brother Samuel Swann, deceased.[184]

Caleb had 1 stepchild:
 44. m iv. **Samuel Swann**. He was the son of ____ **Swann** and **Sarah** ____, died before 17 Mar 1787.

---

[176] Wilson Bible 1742-1896, Accession 29076, LVA.
[177] Wingo, *Unrecorded Wills Norfolk Co VA*, 108-9.
[178] McIntosh, *Norfolk Co Wills 1710-1753*, 83 (OAW:38) - will of Mary Godfrey.
[179] Wilson Bible 1742-1896, Accession 29076, LVA.
[180] McVey, *Norfolk Co VA Will Book 2*, 208 - will of William Wilson Jr.
[181] McIlwaine, *Executive Journals - Colonial VA*, 4:373.
[182] James, *Lower Norfolk Antiquary*, 3:78.
[183] Wingo, *Guardian Bonds of Norfolk Co VA*, .84-5.
[184] McVey, *Norfolk Co VA Will Book 2*, 208-9.

Caleb[4] died after 28 May 1754, the date of his will in Currituck County North Carolina.[185] He named his eldest son James Wilson, son Tatem Wilson, daughter Lovey Wilson, son William Wilson, his wife Sarah, his nephews Daniel Sweeny and Malachi Wilson, and his brothers Josiah and Malachi Wilson.[186]

- - - - - - - - - - -

40. James[5] Wilson, Sr. <See pg. 20> (39.Caleb[4], 5.James[3], 2.James[2], 1.____ Wilson[1]) was born 4 Sep 1742. He married (1) **Mary Wilson (See number 48)** 10 Aug 1770.[187] She was born 16 Apr 1749. She was the daughter of **Josiah Wilson** and **Frances Langley**.[188]

ISSUE:[189]

- m i. **Caleb Wilson**, born 1 May 1771, died after 27 Sep 1817.
- f ii. **Frances Wilson**, born Jan 1773.
- m iii. **Tatem Wilson**, born 27 Mar 1774, died 30 Oct 1831.
- m iv. **James Wilson**, born 11 Jan 1776, died 24 Jun 1801.
- f v. **Mary Wilson**, born 6 Mar 1778.
- f vi. **Love Wilson**, born Sep 1779.
- f vii. **Euphan Wilson**, born 12 May 1782, died 14 Oct 1810.
- f viii. **Peggy Wilson**, born 20 Apr 1784.
- m ix. **Charles Wesley Wilson**, born 24 Mar 1787, died 23 Aug 1817.
- m x. **Josiah Ashbury Wilson**, born 18 Feb 1789, died 18 Dec 1801.
- m xi. **Nathaniel Wilson**, born 18 Mar 1790, died after 27 Sep 1817.

Mary died 17 Jan 1805.

James, Sr. married (2) **Elizabeth Wilson (See number 59)** 3 Nov 1808.

ISSUE:

- m xii. **William Wilson**.[190]

Elizabeth died 30 Jan 1816.

---

[185] Butt, *Col James Wilson*, 25-6.
[186] Butt, *Col James Wilson*, 26.
[187] Wingo, *Marriages of Norfolk Co VA, Vol 1*, 74. This is an ancestral line of Mrs. Elizabeth (Baum) Wingo. Butt, *Col James Wilson*, 26.
[188] Brewster, *Norfolk Co VA Will Book 3*, 77-9 - will of Josiah Wilson.
[189] Wilson Bible 1742-1896, Accession 29076, LVA. This also has the dates or the parents.
[190] Wilson Bible 1742-1896, Accession 29076, LVA - he is named a half-brother.

James, Sr. died 18 Nov 1820 in St. Brides Parish, Norfolk County, Virginia. His will, dated 27 Sep 1817 and proved 19 Dec 1820, named his sons Nathaniel, Caleb, Tatem, and William.[191]

- - - - - - - - - - -

45. Josiah⁴ Wilson <See pg. 8> (5.James³, 2.James², 1. ____ Wilson¹) was born 1708.[192] He married **Frances Langley** before 10 Dec 1748. She was born about 1718. She was the daughter of **Lemuel Langley** and **Margaret** ____. She was named Frances Wilson in her father's will.[193] **(See pg. 143)**.

ISSUE:

  46. m i. **Lemuel Wilson**, executor of his father's will, was guardian of his brother Josiah's sons Josiah and Christopher 15 Oct 1792 and of his brother Charles's son Josiah 18 Dec 1797.[194]
  47. f ii. **Peggy Wilson**.
+ 48. f iii. **Mary Wilson**, born 16 Apr 1749, died 17 Jan 1805 <See pg. 23>.
+ 49. m iv. **Josiah Wilson**, died 1778 <See pg. 23>.
+ 50. m v. **Charles Wilson**, died before 1794 <See pg. 24>.
+ 51. f vi. **Euphan Wilson** <See pg. 24>.

In the 1750 will of Josiah's father, he received the plantation and land bought of **William Howson**, 200 acres at Long Ridge and a lot at Great Bridge adjoining his brother Caleb Wilson.[195]

He was named in the 1759 Norfolk County tithables list and was commissioned lieutenant colonel 18 March 1768.[196]

Mrs. Frances Wilson, spouse of Col. Josiah Wilson of Norfolk County, died by 16 Feb 1775.[197]

In the will of Josiah Wilson of St. Brides Parish, dated 14 Oct 1794 and proved 20 Jul 1795, he named son Lemuel Wilson, daughters Peggy Wilson, Mary Wilson, grandson Josiah Wilson son of Josiah, grandson Christopher Wilson son of Josiah, grandson Josiah Wilson son of Charles, granddaughter **Prudence Harrison**, granddaughter **Frances Matthias**, grandson Josiah

---

[191] Crozier, *Williamsburg Wills*, 64.
[192] Headley, *18th-Century Newspapers*, 372 - states that he died 1795 at age 87.
[193] McIntosh, *Norfolk Co Wills 1710-1753*, 220-1 (Book H:245).
[194] Wingo, *Guardian Bonds of Norfolk Co VA*, 83, 84.
[195] Norfolk Co VA Will Book 1:7a-9.
[196] Butt, *Col James Wilson*, 26.
[197] Headley, *18th-Century Newspapers*, 371.

Wilson Hunter son of John Hunter, grandsons Caleb Wilson and Tatem Wilson, nephew/son-in-law James Wilson Sr., brother Malachi, grandsons Josiah Ashberry and Nathaniel, sons of James and Mary Wilson.[198]

Col. Josiah Wilson of St. Bride's Parish died 12 May 1795, age 87.[199]

- - - - - - - - - - -

48. Mary⁵ Wilson <See pg. 22> (45.Josiah⁴, 5.James³, 2.James², 1.____ Wilson¹) was born 16 Apr 1749. She married **James Wilson, Sr. (See number 40)** 10 Aug 1770.[200]

ISSUE:[201]

m i. **Caleb Wilson**, born 1 May 1771, died 15 Feb 1835.
f ii. **Frances Wilson**, born Jan 1773.
m iii. **Tatem Wilson**, born 27 Mar 1774, died 30 Oct 1831.
m iv. **James Wilson**, born 11 Jan 1776, died 24 Jun 1801.
f v. **Mary Wilson**, born 6 Mar 1778.
f vi. **Love Wilson**, born Sep 1779.
f vii. **Euphan Wilson**, born 12 May 1782, died 14 Oct 1810.
f viii. **Peggy Wilson**, born 20 Apr 1784.
m ix. **Charles Wesley Wilson**, born 24 Mar 1787, died 23 Aug 1817.
m x. **Josiah Ashbury Wilson**, born 18 Feb 1789, died 18 Dec 1801.
m xi. **Nathaniel Wilson**, born 18 Mar 1790, died after 27 Sep 1817, the date of his father's will.

Mary died 17 Jan 1805.

- - - - - - - - - - -

49. Josiah⁵ Wilson <See pg. 22> (45.Josiah⁴, 5.James³, 2.James², 1.____ Wilson¹). He married **Margaret Cawson** 4 Dec 1771.[202] She was born May 1749. She was the daughter of **Christopher Cawson** and **Margaret** ___.[203]

ISSUE:

---

[198] Brewster, *Norfolk Co VA Will Book 3*, 77-9.

[199] Headley, *18ᵗʰ-Century Newspapers*, 372.

[200] Wingo, *Marriages of Norfolk Co VA, Vol 1*, 74.

[201] Wilson Bible 1742-1896, Accession 29076, LVA. This also has the dates for the parents.

[202] Wingo, *Marriages of Norfolk Co VA, Vol 1*, 74.

[203] Wingo, *Norfolk Co VA Will Book 1*, 9 (f 16). McVey, *Norfolk Co VA Will Book 2*, 154 - wills of Christopher and Margaret Cawson.

Wilson Families

  m i. **Josiah Wilson**, born about 1772. He may have died about 1809, naming in his will, his brother-in-law Tatem Wilson.[204]
  f ii. **Frances Wilson**, born about 1774, her guardian, **John Portlock**, was appointed 16 Jul 1792 [205] Frances married 28 Jul 1792 **Joshua Matthias**, who became guardian of her brother Christopher 4 Jul 1794.[206] Frances married (2) **Tatem Wilson** 18 Dec 1804. She died 5 Jun 1833.[207]
  m iii. **Christopher Wilson**, born about 1776.

Josiah[5] died 1778, murdered by Tory outlaws, told in a letter written by his cousin John to Patrick Henry.[208] He was survived by his sons Christopher and Josiah Wilson and his daughter Frances. All three children were mentioned in their grandfather's 1774 will and named in guardian bonds.[209]

- - - - - - - - - - -

50. Charles[5] Wilson <See pg. 22> (45.Josiah[4], 5.James[3], 2.James[2], 1. ____ Wilson[1]).
        ISSUE:
  m i. **Josiah Wilson**, guardian appointed 18 Dec 1797.[210]

Charles Wilson died before 1794, the date of his father's will.[211]

- - - - - - - - - - -

51. Euphan[5] Wilson <See pg. 22> (45.Josiah[4], 5.James[3], 2.James[2], 1. ____ Wilson[1]). She married **John Hunter** 14 Jan 1783.[212] He was born about 1758. He was the son of **Jacob Hunter** and **Susannah Moore**.[213]
        ISSUE:
  m i. **Josiah Wilson Hunter**, born about 1785.

---

[204] Butt, *Col James Wilson*, 27-8. It appears that Mr. Butt mixed up the cousins.
[205] Wingo, *Guardian Bonds of Norfolk Co VA*, 83.
[206] Wingo, *Marriages of Norfolk Co VA, Vol 1*, 43. Wingo, *Guardian Bonds of Norfolk Co VA*, 82.
[207] Wilson Bible 1742-1896, Accession 29076, LVA.
[208] Wirt, *Patrick Henry*, 235-7.
[209] Brewster, *Norfolk Co VA Will Book 3*, 77-9. Wingo, *Guardian Bonds of Norfolk Co VA*, 82-3.
[210] Wingo, *Guardian Bonds of Norfolk Co VA*, 84.
[211] Brewster, *Norfolk Co VA Will Book 3*, 77-9.
[212] Wingo, *Marriages of Norfolk Co VA, Vol 1*, 35.
[213] Walter, *Princess Anne Co VA Deed and Minute Books*, 33, 110 (6DB390/7MB249).

Euphan evidently died before 14 Oct 1794, the date of her father's will, in which her husband John and son Josiah Wilson Hunter, less than age 21, were named.[214]

- - - - - - - - - - -

53. William[4] Wilson <See pg. 9> (5.James[3], 2.James[2], 1. ____ Wilson[1]) was born about 1715. He married **Sarah** ____.
ISSUE:
+ 54. m i. **Willis Wilson**, born about 1744, died 1804 <See pg. 25>.

In his father's 1750 will, William received the land bought of **Eleanor Leachley** together with other land.[215]

In William's will, dated 14 October 1752 and proved 21 Dec 1752, he named his son Willis, his wife Sarah, and his brother Josiah.[216]

Sarah married (2) **Joseph Church** 25 Oct 1753.[217] He was the son of **Richard Church** and **Abiah Corprew**.[218] Joseph's will was dated 5 Jul 1756 and named his wife Sarah.[219]

Sarah married (3) **Butts Roberts** 7 Feb 1759.[220]

- - - - - - - - - - -

54. Willis[5] Wilson <See pg. 25> (53.William[4], 5.James[3], 2.James[2], 1. ____ Wilson[1]) was born about 1744. He married **Martha** ____.
ISSUE:[221]
f i. **Sarah Wilson**, born 26 Mar 1780.
m ii. **William Wilson**, born 29 Jan 1782.

Willis[5] Wilson was a minor in 1752 when his father died. Simon Wilson submitted a petition in 1755 which stated that Sarah had married Joseph Church, who had died. He petitioned the court in 1762 saying Sarah's third husband Butts Roberts was wasting the estate of her first husband, William

---

[214] Brewster, *Norfolk Co VA Will Book 3*, 77-9.
[215] Norfolk Co VA Will Book 1:7a-9.
[216] McIntosh, *Norfolk Co Wills 1710-1753*, 298 (Book I:294).
[217] Wingo, *Marriages of Norfolk Co VA, Vol 1*, 14.
[218] McIntosh, *Norfolk Co Wills 1710-1753*, 173-4 (Book H:72 - will of Richard Church). Maling, *Princess Anne Co VA Deed Books 1-7*,45 (3DB448 - will of Thomas Corprew).
[219] Wingo, *Norfolk Co VA Will Book 1*, 108 (f 174a).
[220] Wingo, *Marriages of Norfolk Co VA, Vol 1*, 56.
[221] Bell, *Charles Parish, York Co VA*, 195.

Wilson.[222] Simon Wilson was appointed guardian of Willis Wilson on 17 Jun 1762.[223]

Willis took the oath as a Lt. in the York County militia 20 Oct 1777 and was recommended as 1st Lieut. 18 Sep 1780.[224]

In a 16 Jan 1786 deed, Willis Wilson of the Parish of Charles, County of York, and Martha his wife, sold 137 acres on Northwest River, St. Brides Parish, Norfolk County. The land had been bought by Major James^3 Wilson and descended to his son William^4 Wilson and then to said Willis^5, son and heir of William.[225]

Willis's will was dated 27 Feb 1804.[226]

- - - - - - - - - - -

55. Malachi^4 Wilson, Sr. <See pg. 9> (5.James^3, 2.James^2, 1. ____ Wilson^1). He married **Lydia Carron**.[227]

ISSUE:

   56. m   i. **Nathaniel Wilson**, died 1803.[228]

   57. m   ii. **Caleb Wilson**, died after 3 May 1796, the date of his brother's will.

   58. m   iii. **Thomas Wilson**, married **Nancy Happer** 12 Apr 1791.[229] She was born about 1770. In his will, dated 3 May 1796 and proved 18 Jul 1797, he named brothers Caleb, Nathaniel, his mother Lydia Wilson, sisters Rebecca Bartee and Lydia Bartee, his nephew **Thomas Bartee**, son of William, and niece Elizabeth Smith, daughter of Solomon Smith.[230]

+ 59. f   iv. **Elizabeth Wilson**, born 5 Jul 1749, died 30 Jan 1816 <See pg. 27>.

   60. f   v. **Alice Wilson**, married **William Reid** 21 Aug 1790.[231]

---

[222] Butt, *Col James Wilson*, 28.
[223] Wingo, *Guardian Bonds of Norfolk Co VA*, 85.
[224] Gwathmey, *Historical Register*, 837.
[225] Norfolk Co VA Deed Book 29:227-8.
[226] Gardner, *Index* .... *York Co VA*, 110 (York W&I #26:637).
[227] Butt, *Col James Wilson*, 29.
[228] Butt, *Col James Wilson*, 29.
[229] Wingo, *Marriages of Norfolk Co VA, Vol 1*, 74.
[230] Brewster, *Norfolk Co VA Will Book 3*, 111-2.
[231] Wingo, *Marriages of Norfolk Co VA, Vol 1*, 55.

61. f   vi. **Lydia Wilson**. She married **Lemuel Bartee** before 1785, the date of her father's will. He was the son of **William Bartee** and **Letitia Butt**.[232]

62. f   vii. **Rebecca Wilson**. She married **William Bartee** before 1785, the date of her father's will. He was the son of **William Bartee** and **Letitia Butt**.[233]

In 1750 Malachi[4] inherited from his father a plantation bought of **James Smith**, land at Mossy Point, and 200 acres at Long Ridge.[234]

In the will of Malachi Wilson Sr., dated 12 July 1785 and proved 18 Oct 1787, he named his sons Nathaniel, Caleb, Thomas, and daughter Elizabeth[5] Smith, her husband Solomon Smith deceased. He named his granddaughter Elizabeth[6] Smith and her sisters and brothers: John[6], James[6], Charles[6] Mary[6], and Elice[6] Smith. He also named his daughters Alice Wilson, Ledy Bartee, Rebecca Bartee and wife Ledy, who with son-in-law, Lemuel Bartee, were named executors.[235]

Lydia died after 3 May 1796 when she was named in the will of her son Thomas.[236]

- - - - - - - - - - -

59. Elizabeth[5] Wilson <See pg. 26> (55.Malachi, Sr[4], 5.James[3], 2.James[2], 1. ____ Wilson[1]) was born 5 Jul 1749.[237] She married (1) **Solomon Smith** 30 Sep 1765.[238]

ISSUE:

m   i.   **John Smith**, born about 1766.
m   ii. **James Smith**, born about 1770.
f   iii. **Elizabeth Smith**, born about 1772.
f   iv. **Mary Smith**, born about 1774.
m   v.   **Charles Smith**, born about 1776.
f   vi. **Alice Smith**, born about 1780.

In his will, dated 3 Nov 1784 and proved 20 Jan 1785, Solomon named his wife Elizabeth and their six children John, James, Elizabeth, Mary, Charles

---

[232] Butt, *An Account .... Robert Butt*, 15.
[233] Butt, *An Account .... Robert Butt*, 15.
[234] Norfolk Co VA Will Book 1:7a-9.
[235] McVey, *Norfolk Co VA Will Book 2*, 211.
[236] Brewster, *Norfolk Co VA Will Book 3*, 111-2.
[237] Wilson Bible 1742-1896, Accession 29076, LVA.
[238] Wingo, *Marriages of Norfolk Co VA, Vol 1*, 61.

and Alice. He also named a daughter **Prudence Smith**, evidently his child from a prior marriage.[239]

Elizabeth married (2) **Frederick Wilson Boush (See number 32)** 14 May 1795.[240]

ISSUE:

f iv. **Jacomine Boush**, born 23 Mar 1796, died 5 Mar 1797.[241]

Elizabeth married (3) **James Wilson, Sr. (See number 40)** 3 Nov 1808.[242]

ISSUE:

m xii. **William Wilson**.

Elizabeth died 30 Jan 1816.

- - - - - - - - - - -

63. Prudence⁴ Wilson <See pg. 9> (5.James³, 2.James², 1. ____ Wilson¹) was born after 1722. She married **Nathaniel Tatem** 13 Dec 1743, the consent of her father given.[243] He was the son of **Nathaniel Tatem** and **Anne Godfrey**.[244]

ISSUE:

64. m i. **James Tatem**.

In her father's 1750 will, Prudence was given land bought of **John Fife**.[245]

Nathaniel married (2) **Dinah Nash** 12 Feb 1755. She was the daughter of **Thomas Nash**.[246]

In his will, dated 21 May 1771 and proved Jul 1771, Nathaniel named his wife Dinah, son James and other children.[247]

- - - - - - - - - - -

---

[239] McVey, *Norfolk Co VA Will Book 2*, 171-2. Wingo, *Marriages of Norfolk Co VA, Vol 1*, 61 - gives a 1762 marriage, Solomon Smith and Prudence Wilson.

[240] Wingo, *Marriages of Princess Anne Co VA 1749-1821*, 10.

[241] Boush Family Bible Accession 22246, LVA.

[242] Wilson Bible 1742-1896, Accession 29076, LVA.

[243] Wingo, *Marriages of Norfolk Co VA, Vol 1*, 63.

[244] Wingo, *Unrecorded Wills Norfolk Co VA*, 108-9 (will of Nathaniel Tatem). McIntosh, *Norfolk Co Wills 1710-1753*, 83 (OAW:38 - will of Mary Godfrey).

[245] Norfolk Co VA Will Book 1:7a-9.

[246] Wingo, *Marriages of Norfolk Co VA, Vol 1*, 63.

[247] Wingo, *Norfolk Co VA Will Book 1*, 125 (f 205).

Wilson Families

66. ____⁴ **Wilson** <See pg. 9> (5.James³, 2.James², 1. ____ Wilson¹). She married ____ **Nicholson**.
ISSUE:
67. m   i. **Wilson Nicholson**, born about 1735, died after 1780.

Wilson Nicholson was named in his grandfather's 1750 will, receiving two cows and calves, "in full of his mother's portion."²⁴⁸ This implies that his mother had died.

Wilson was listed with **Joshua Nicholson** in the Norfolk County tithables lists from 1751-1754. Wilson was listed along with his own tithables from 1757-1780.²⁴⁹ He was not named in the 1767 will of Joshua Nicholson.²⁵⁰ Nor was he listed in the 1762 will of Dinah Wilson, in which she named all her grandchildren, but did not name her husband's grandchildren from his first marriage.²⁵¹

- - - - - - - - - - -

68. Dinah⁴ Wilson <See pg. 10> (5.James³, 2.James², 1. ____ Wilson¹) was born about 1727. She married **William Nicholson**. He may have been the son of **William Nicholson** and **Prudence** ____.²⁵²
ISSUE:
69. m   i. **William Nicholson**, born about 1745, died after 1762.
70. m   ii. **James Nicholson**, born about 1747, died after 1762.
71. m   iii. **John Nicholson**, died after 1762.

She was named Dinah Nicholson in her father's 1750 will.²⁵³ Dinah⁴ was not named in the 1762 will of her mother Dinah Wilson, who named her grandsons, William, James and John Nicholson and executor William Nicholson.²⁵⁴

- - - - - - - - - - -

72. Affiah⁴ Wilson <See pg. 10> (5.James³, 2.James², 1. ____ Wilson¹) was born about 1729. She married (1) **Willis Langley** before 13 Jan 1749/50, the

---

²⁴⁸ Norfolk Co VA Will Book 1:7a-9.
²⁴⁹ Wingo, *Norfolk Co VA Tithables 1751-1765*, 15, 31, 68, 93, and 121, 144, 157. Wingo, *Norfolk Co VA Tithables 1766-1780*, 42, 62, 101, 139, 179, 257, 277.
²⁵⁰ Wingo, *Norfolk Co VA Will Book 1*, 104 f 169a).
²⁵¹ Wingo, *Norfolk Co VA Will Book 1*, 128 (f 209).
²⁵² McIntosh, *Norfolk Co Wills 1710-1753*, 127.
²⁵³ Norfolk Co VA Will Book 1:7a-9.
²⁵⁴ Wingo, *Norfolk Co VA Will Book 1*, 128 (f 209).

date of her father's will.[255] He was the son of **Lemuel Langley** and **Mary Nicholson.**[256] (See pg. 143).

ISSUE:

73. f   i. **Letitia Langley**, born after 1750. She was less than 16 in her father's will. She married **James Pasteur** 20 Dec 1770.[257]
74. m ii. **Willis Wilson Langley**, born about 1753. He married **Susanna Bruce** 9 Nov 1779.[258]
75. m iii. **James Langley**, born about 1756; his will dated 17 Dec 1776 and proved 16 Sep 1785 named his brother Willis Langley and sister Letitia Pasteur.[259]
76. m iv. **Josiah Langley**, born about 1760, died before 25 Nov 1766, the date of his father's will.
77. f   v. **Mary Langley**, born about 1762.
78. f vi. **Euphan Langley**, born about 1764.

The will of Mary Langley, dated 11 Sep 1761, named her son Willis, daughter-in-law Affia Langley and grandchildren Letitia, Willis Wilson, James and Josiah Langley, children of her son Willis Langley.[260] In the will of her mother Dinah Wilson, dated 17 Apr 1762 she named her daughter Affia Langley and grandchildren Letice, Willis, James and Josiah Langley.[261]

Affiah's husband Willis Langley died before 19 Mar 1767. In his will dated 25 Nov 1766 he named his wife Affia, sons Willis and James, daughters Letitia, Mary and Euphan.[262]

Affiah married (2) **James Webb** 24 Dec 1767.[263]

- - - - - - - - - - -

---

[255] Norfolk Co VA Will Book 1:7a-9.

[256] McIntosh, *Norfolk Co Wills 1710-1753*, 118 (will of William Nicholson), 220 (will of Lemuel Langley).

[257] Wingo, *Marriages of Norfolk Co VA, Vol 1*, 51.

[258] Wingo, *Marriages of Norfolk Co VA, Vol 1*, 39.

[259] McVey, *Norfolk Co VA Will Book 2*, 191.

[260] Wingo, *Norfolk Co VA Will Book 1*, 49 (f 74).

[261] Norfolk Co VA Will Book 1:209.

[262] Wingo, *Norfolk Co VA Will Book 1*, 97-8 (f 154).

[263] Wingo, *Marriages of Norfolk Co VA, Vol 1*, 69.

79. Euphan⁴ Wilson <See pg. 10> (5.James³, 2.James², 1. ____ Wilson¹) was born after 1734. She was less than age 16 in her father's 1750 will.²⁶⁴ She married **John Corprew** 3 May 1756.²⁶⁵

ISSUE:
- 80. f i. **Sally Corprew**, born before 1762.
- 81. m ii. **John Corprew**, born before 1762.
- 82. m iii. **James Corprew**, born before 1762.
- 83. f iv. **Elizabeth Corprew**, born before 1762.

In the will of her mother, Dinah Wilson, dated 1762, she named daughter Uphan Corprew and grandchildren Sally, John, James and Elizabeth Corprew.²⁶⁶

- - - - - - - - - - -

85. Lemuel³ Wilson <See pg. 2> (2.James², 1. ____ Wilson¹) was born about 1675. He married **Katherine** ____ before 20 Apr 1710.²⁶⁷

ISSUE:
- 86. f i. **Mary Wilson**, born about 1711. She married **Gilbert MacNary** 22 Jul 1732.²⁶⁸
- 87. m ii. **Lemuel Wilson**, born 7 Apr 1713, written on the page preceding page 1 of Norfolk County Deed Book 9. He died before 16 May 1719. He was not named when his father made a deed of gift to his children and step-son.²⁶⁹
- 88. f iii. **Luce Wilson**, born about 1716.
- 89. m iv. **Samuel Wilson**.

Lemuel had 1 stepchild:
- 90. m v. **John Kelsall**, born after 1698. He was the son of **Roger Kelsall** and **Katherine** ____.

Katherine married (1) **Roger Kelsall**, whose will was dated 14 Sep 1708 and proved 15 Feb 1708/9.²⁷⁰

---

²⁶⁴ Norfolk Co VA Will Book 1:7a-9.
²⁶⁵ Wingo, *Marriages of Norfolk Co VA, Vol 1*, 16.
²⁶⁶ Wingo, *Norfolk Co VA Will Book 1*, 128 (f 209).
²⁶⁷ Norfolk Co VA Deed Book 9:33.
²⁶⁸ Wingo, *Marriages of Norfolk Co VA, Vol 1*, 45.
²⁶⁹ Norfolk Co VA Deed Book 10:70/143.
²⁷⁰ McIntosh, *Norfolk Co Wills 1637-1710*, 194-5 (Book 8:51).

On 15 May 1696 Mr. James[2] Wilson received a commission from the governor to be high sheriff, and his son Lemuel Wilson was named under sheriff.[271]

On 23 August 1699 Lemuel[3] was sworn in as clerk of Norfolk County Court.[272] Lemuel Wilson's petition 15 Feb 1704/5 to the court, to move the clerk's office to his dwelling house on the Southern Branch near the Great Bridge, was approved by the court over the objection of Major **Samuel Boush**, one of the justices.[273] Lemuel was succeeded in this office by his younger brother Solomon on 22 Nov 1718.[274]

The militia named in Norfolk County 4 Apr 1702 included Lemuel Wilson, Capt. of Foot.[275]

Joel Martin sold to Capt. Lemuell Wilson 270 acres on the Southern Branch toward the Northwest River on 16 Mar 1701/2. This was confirmed by a deed in which Lemuel assigned this property to **Henry Tregany Jr.** 17 Aug 1703.[276] On 16 Aug 1703, James Wilson Sr. deeded to his son Lemuel land that he'd bought from **Henry Smith** 17 Nov 1701. The tract was made up of 232 acres of land by Cypress Swamp, which included 100 acres on the northwest side of Beaver Dam.[277]

On 1703 Aug 16 Lemuel Wilson was awarded a certificate for 3 headrights.[278] The 1704 quit rents listed Lemuell with 300 acres in Norfolk Co.[279]

Lemuel Wilson's mark for hogs and cattle was recorded 11 Aug 1705.[280]

---

[271] Norfolk Co VA Deed Book 6:30.
[272] Norfolk Co VA Deed Book 6:157.
[273] Norfolk Co VA Deed Book 7:71a.
[274] Norfolk Co VA Deed Book 10:35.
[275] London, PRO, CO 5/1312, part 2, folios 277-278 (or 256-7), no. 587 or 40 (Transcription done by Simon Neal, records agent, e-mail sn014i4785@blueyonder.co.uk). (Bockstruck, *Virginia Colonial Soldiers*, 215, 218. "Samuel" Wilson, Capt. of Foot, is a transcription error).
[276] Norfolk Co VA Deed Book 6:231, 284-5.
[277] Norfolk Co VA Deed Books 6:283, 7:1-2a.
[278] Norfolk Co VA Deed Book 7:11a.
[279] Smith, *Quit Rents of Virginia, 1704*, 98.
[280] Norfolk Co VA Deed Book 7:84.

Wilson Families

In 1708/9 Coll James[2] Wilson was named overseer of the will of Roger Kelsall, minister of Elizabeth River Parish. The witnesses were Lemll Wilson and Willis Wilson.[281] Lemuel[3] married the widow Katherine ( ) Kelsall after 16 Nov 1709 and before 14 May 1710 when she was named wife of Lemuell Wilson, executrix of Roger Kelsall.[282] Lemuel and Katherine signed, with their seals, the 6 Dec 1710 deed to **William Southerland** for 220 acres which Mr. Roger Kelsall, minister, left to his wife Katherine "which is now wife of said Lemll Wilson." Katherine Wilson accepted an addition to the appraisal of the estate of Roger Kelsall 6 Dec 1711.[283] **Ruth Willoughby** orphan, daughter of **Thomas**, was bound out to Lemuel and Katherine Wilson until age 18 on 20 Jul 1711. The court ordered that they "learn her to Read."[284]

In the 1712 will of his father, Lemuel received five shillings "in full of his portion, he having had a sufficient part already."[285]

In Norfolk County VA Deed Book 9, before the first page, when Lemuel Wilson was clerk of court, he wrote, "Lemll Wilson son of Leml Wilson was borne the 7th day of April Ano 1713 between Twelve and one o Clock."

On 16 Nov 1715 to "my well beloved brother Lemuel Wilson" John Wilson deeded a thirty foot square parcel on Costins Island on the western side of Solomon Wilson, which was devised to John by their father's will.[286] This area at Great Bridge was apparently developed and divided into lots appropriate for warehouses, to be used for the transfer of goods to and from vessels at the head of the Southern branch of the Elizabeth River.

Lemuel[3] Wilson made a deed of gift 16 May 1719 to his children Mary and Luce Wilson under age 16, Samuel Wilson, no age stated, and John Kelsall, son-in-law (step-son) less than 21. His son Lemuel[4] had apparently died by that date.[287]

Captain Lemuel Wilson died intestate probably in February 1731.[288]

---

[281] McIntosh, *Norfolk Co Wills 1637-1710*, 194-5 (Book 8:51).
[282] Norfolk Co VA Deed Book 8:91, 149.
[283] Norfolk Co VA Deed Book 9:32-4.
[284] Norfolk Co VA Deed Book, pt. 2 Orders:9:14.
[285] Norfolk Co VA Deed Book 9:220-2. (See appendix).
[286] Norfolk Co VA Deed Book 9:478.
[287] Norfolk Co VA Deed Book 10:70/143.
[288] Butt, *Col James Wilson*, 12.

91. John³ Wilson <See pg. 2> (2.James², 1. ____ Wilson¹) was born about 1677. He married **Margaret** ____ before 14 Nov 1715.[289]

ISSUE:[290]

92. m i. **John Wilson**, born about 1716. He was shown only in the 1734 tithable list with his mother.[291] A suit after 1730 suggests a transaction between John Wilson Jr. and **James Cumming**, which may have been part of the settlement of his father's estate.[292] On 29 Jan 1745 John⁴ Wilson sold **Samuel Smith** 100 acres, as son of John³ Wilson whose father James² Wilson left him the land in his will.[293] John was said to have "moved up the Chesapeake bay and most likely settled on the waters of the Potomac."[294] He may have been the John Wilson who died after 1763 in Romney, Hampshire County, Virginia (now West Virginia), leaving land to his heirs, John Wilson and Priscilla, his wife.[295] This" heir" John was referred to as a "kinsman" of the Benjamin Wilson family in Cumberland County, Virginia, in 1798.[296]

93. f ii. **Margaret Wilson**. She married **John Cheshire**.[297] The following documents show a Margaret, wife of John Cheshire: John and Margaret Cheshire deed to **John Tucker**, ½ lot in Norfolk Town 20 Dec 1733, and 20 Nov 1734 Jno and Margaret Cheshire to **Edward Thruston** 1 lot.[298] He may have been the son of **Richard Cheshire** and **Sarah Thruston**.[299]

94. f iii. **Jane Wilson**.

95. f iv. **Elizabeth Wilson**.

In 1705 John Wilson bought 200 acres from **Richard Bolton** and his wife **Jane**, relict and coexecutor of Capt. **Hugh Campbell**.[300] In 1711 John

---

[289] Norfolk Co VA Deed Book 9:443-4.
[290] Butt, *Col James Wilson*, 13.
[291] Wingo, *Norfolk Co VA Tithables 1730-1750*, 6, 128, 175.
[292] Walker, *General Index .... 1646-1780, Norfolk*, Grantee:7 (11:39).
[293] Norfolk Co VA Deed Book 13:265-6.
[294] "Wilson Family", *VA Mag Hist*, 25:199.
[295] Hampshire Co VA (WV) Deed Book 5:39 or 391.
[296] McCrary, *Wilson Families ... Correspondence .... 1785-1849*, 13-17, etc.
[297] Butt, *Col James Wilson*, 13.
[298] Norfolk Co VA Deed Book 11:141, 168-170.
[299] Maling, *Princess Anne Co VA Deed Books 1-7*, 59 (4DB461).
[300] Norfolk Co VA Deed Book 7:79.

Wilson Gent' of Norfolk County sold 12 acres of Ward's Island, at the head of the Southern Branch of the Elizabeth River, and in November of the same year he sold a parcel at the head of the Southern Branch of the Elizabeth River, part of the divident he had purchased from Richard Bolten and Jane his wife, executrix of Capt. Hugh Campbell, dec'd, known as Ward's Island.[301]

The 1712 will of his father stated, "I give to my Son John Wilson two hundred acres of land which land I bought of **John Fulford**. I give to my Said Son all my Land and crops being and lying on the westernmost side of the land at the bridge at the head of the Southern branch. I give and bequeath unto my son John Wilson one hundred acres of land lying and being over the Gumme Swamp in the back woods."[302]

Typical of the day, folks seemed to love to be in court. Perhaps the term "sue" was not as harsh a legal term then as it is taken today. On 20 Mar 1712/3 John[3] filed a suit against Mrs **Elizabeth Wilson** and Mr. **Willis Wilson** executors of the last will and testament of Col. James Wilson, for his full legacy.[303]

At a Princess Anne County, Virginia, court before 23 Jan 1713/4, John[3] Wilson was named guardian of his nephew Willis[4] Wilson, son of his brother Samuel[3].[304]

By 1715 he had married Margaret, shown by their 14 Nov 1715 deed: John Wilson Gent and Margarett his wife sold to **Jonas Cawson** a 60' x 50' lot on Costin's Island, the land given by last will and testament of Coll James[2] Wilson to John[3] Wilson.[305]

There were many other land transactions concerning the property at Great Bridge, which was a place for warehouses and wharves for items shipped to and from the Southern Branch of the Elizabeth River,[306] to name a few:

> **1715** Nov 17 John Wilson of Norfolk County merchant to **Samuel Boush** 10' x 6' on Hickory Nowle near Grate Bridge by Boushes house.

---

[301] Norfolk Co VA Deed Book 9:142-6.
[302] Norfolk Co VA Deed Books 6:226a, 9:220-2. (See appendix).
[303] Norfolk Co VA Deed Book 9, pt. 2 Orders:50.
[304] Princess Anne Co VA Minute Book 2:145.
[305] Norfolk Co VA Deed Book 9:443-4.
[306] Wertenbaker, *Norfolk*, 34.

1715 Nov 17 John Wilson and wife Margaret to **William Roe** a lot on Costin's Island which was given to John Wilson by the last will and testament of Col. James Wilson.

1715 Nov 14 John and Margaret to **William Miller** 30'x30'.

1716 Jul 19 John and Margaret more to Jonas Cawson 30'x50'.[307]

In the 1719 will of William Miller, he gave his son Willis land that he bought from John Wilson, Costin's Island.[308]

On 22 Jun 1719, Mr. John Wilson was commissioned high sheriff of Norfolk County.[309] He was also a captain in the Norfolk County militia in 1719[310] and appeared in Norfolk County court as a justice 19 Jul 1723.[311]

In 1725/6 John Wilson sold to "the Worshipfull Vestry of Norfolk County" for 1000 pounds of tobacco, about two acres of land near Great Bridge, "up New Mill road, on which the Chapple now stands."[312]

On 1 Dec 1725, John Wilson, Gent of Norfolk County, sold to **Thomas Sikes** property at the "head of the Cosesay, formerly called Costings Island now Bridgetown."[313]

Margaret Wilson was granted a certificate of administration on 17 May 1728, and the estate of Capt. John Wilson was inventoried and appraised on 4 Jun 1728.[314]

- - - - - - - - - - -

96. Samuel³ Wilson <See pg. 2> (2.James², 1. ____ Wilson¹) was born about 1680. He married **Dinah Mason. (See number 56 - pg. 121).**
ISSUE:
+ 97.   m   i.   **Willis Wilson**, born about 1707, died about 1740 <See pg. 38, 124>.

---

[307] Norfolk Co VA Deed Book 9:447-9, 454, 475-7, 508-10.
[308] McIntosh, *Norfolk Co Wills 1710-1753*, 80-3 (Book 10:76).
[309] Norfolk Co VA Deed Book 10:71/145.
[310] Butt, *Col James Wilson*, 13.
[311] Norfolk Co VA Orders, Appraisements, Wills, pt. 3:61a.
[312] Norfolk Co VA Wills & Deeds G:28-9.
[313] Norfolk Co VA Wills & Deeds G:27a-28.
[314] Butt, *Col James Wilson*, 13. Norfolk Co VA Wills & Orders 1723-1734:44.

Dinah married (1) **Robert Thorowgood**.
ISSUE:*³¹⁵*
99. m ii. **Thomas Thorowgood**.
103. m iii. **Robert Thorowgood**.

Samuel³ Wilson married Dinah³ Mason after 4 Jul 1706 when Dinah Thorowgood was ordered to make payments as executrix of Robert Thorowgood.*³¹⁶*

He may have been the Samuel Wilson named as one of the Virginia executors of the will of his cousin, **Willis Wilson (See number 163)**, concerning affairs in England.*³¹⁷* Samuel may have made a trip to England, being claimed as a headright on the 1711 patent of **Evan Jones**, who also claimed **Maximillian Boush** and **Nathaniel Newton**.*³¹⁸*

Samuel³ Wilson has been mistakenly called Capt. Samuel Wilson, because of a transcription error of the 1702 Norfolk County militia. The correct name is Capt. Lemuel Wilson.*³¹⁹*

Samuel³ was listed in several suits in the Norfolk County court from 1705-1709: Samuel Wilson sueing **Jnº Branton**, Mr. Samuel Wilson suing **James Cummings**, and Samuell Wilson against **Benjamin Barrington**.*³²⁰*

In Jul 1709 Mr. Samuel Wilson appeared in the Princess Anne County court concerning a debt owed him by **Basil Barrett**.*³²¹* Samuel³ served as a justice in Princess Anne County in the "Court held the 8ᵗʰ of September 1709: Present **Colº Edw: Moseley**, ..., Mr. Samuel Wilson - Justices ..... above mentioned gentlemen ...... have taken oaths ..... of allegiance and

---

³¹⁵ Princess Anne Co VA Deed Book 2:195.

³¹⁶ Princess Anne Co VA Order Book 1, pt. 2:443-4.

³¹⁷ London Public Record Office C 11/767/68. Transcription done by Simon Neal, records agent, e-mail sn014i4785@blueyonder.co.uk.

³¹⁸ Nugent, *Cavaliers and Pioneers*, 3:116 (Patent Book 10:20).

³¹⁹ London, PRO, CO 5/1312, part 2, folios 277-278 (or 256-7), no. 587 or 40 (Transcription done by Simon Neal, records agent, e-mail sn014i4785@blueyonder.co.uk). (Bockstruck, *Virginia Colonial Soldiers*, 215, 218. "Samuel" Wilson, Capt. of Foot, is a transcription error). Dorman, *Adventurers of Purse and Person*, 2:576.

³²⁰ Norfolk Co VA Deed Book 7: 93, 97, 111. Norfolk Co VA Deed Book 8:13, 17a, 81.

³²¹ Princess Anne Co VA Minute Book 2:2.

supremacy." Justices named at the Princess Anne County court 2 Mar 1709/10 were Col° Edward Moseley, ..., Mr. Samuel Wilson.[322]

Samuel[3] died before 3 Jan 1710/11 when "On the petition of Mrs. Dinah Wilson a Commission of Administration ...... is granted her on the Estate of her dec'd Husband Mr. Samuell Wilson"; appraisers were named "to meet at the Late Dwelling house of Mr. Samuell Wilson dec'd on the 11th Instant & appraise his estate ....."[323]

The inventory of Mr. Samuel Wilson was signed by the appraisers 12 Jan 1710/11, sworn to be a true inventory 8 Feb 1710/11 by Dinah[3] Wilson with a value of 280:7:6, "an old maire" being added 2 Apr 1711.[324] The estates of Captain **Robert Thorowgood** and Mr. Samuel Wilson were settled on 12 Jan 1713/4 in Princess Anne County, Virginia, portions going to **Thomas** and **Robert Thorowgood**, Willis[4] Wilson and Mr. **William Trevethan**, who had married Mrs. Dinah Wilson.[325]

The 1712 will of Samuel's father named ".... Grandson Willis Wilson son of my dec'd son, Samuel Wilson ....."[326]

Dinah[3] Mason died before 23 Jan 1713/4, the date of the audit of the Thorowgood and Wilson estates. The document mentioned the orphans of the two estates, "Dinah their late dec'd mother" and William Trevethan, "his proportioned part of the said Dinah his late wife's share of her decd Husbands estates due unto him by virtue of his intermarriage." John Wilson was named guardian of Willis Wilson.[327]

- - - - - - - - - - -

97. Willis[4] Wilson <See pg. 36, 123> (96.Samuel[3], 2.James[2], 1. ____ Wilson[1]) was born about 1707. He married **Elizabeth Goodrich**. She was born about 1707. **(See number 5 - pg. 178).** She was the daughter of **Benjamin Goodrich**.

ISSUE:

+ 98. m i. **Benjamin Wilson, Sr.**, born 6 Jan 1733, died 27 Oct 1814 <See pg. 40>.

---

[322] Princess Anne Co VA Minute Book 2:4, 23.
[323] Princess Anne Co VA Minute Book 2:45.
[324] Princess Anne Co VA Deed Book 2:67.
[325] Princess Anne Co VA Deed Book 2:195.
[326] Norfolk Co VA Deed Book 9:220-2. (See appendix).
[327] Princess Anne Co VA Minute Book 2:145.

Willis⁴ Wilson was born about 1707. The inventory of the estate of his father, Samuel³ Wilson was ordered on 3 Jan 1710/11 in Princess Anne County, Virginia.³²⁸ His mother, Dinah³ Mason was named 12 Jan 1713/4 when settlement was made of the estates of her first two husbands in favor of their respective orphans, Thomas and Robert Thorowgood and Willis⁴. Willis received "one Negro man called Sambo and 28:12:07 ½."³²⁹ Dinah³ died by 23 Jan 1713/4 when Willis's uncle John³ Wilson was appointed his guardian.³³⁰

Willis⁴ was named in the 1712 will of his grandfather, Col. James² Wilson: "I give and bequeath unto my Grandson Willis Wilson Son of my dec'd Son, Sam^ll Wilson four hundred acres of land known by the name of poplar Neck beginning at the Northerly Line of James Wilson and running Such a Course that shall Include the Land whereon the poplars Grow and thence to the Cypress Swamp to him and the heirs of his body lawfully begotten for Ever, to be Delivered Into his possession at the age of twenty one years and in Default of Such heirs then I Give and bequeath the said Land unto my Loveing Son Solloman Wilson and his heirs for Ever.

"I Give to my Grandson Willis, Son of my Dec'd on Sam^ll Wilson one Negro man & Stock that Shall be on the aforesd plantation to be Delivered to him, my Said Grandson at the age of Twenty one years."³³¹

Willis⁴ married Elizabeth Goodrich after their 7 Jun 1728 marriage bond. Since consents were not required of either, they both were evidently age 21.³³² Elizabeth was probably living with her sister **Anne (Goodrich) Boush**, wife of Colonel **Samuel Boush (See number 27 - 202)** in Norfolk when the marriage bond was issued. Anne and Elizabeth were daughters of Benjamin Goodrich of James City County, named his orphans in a 1719 lawsuit.³³³

At the time of their marriage, Willis⁴ may have been a "sea captain", however they soon settled on land near the mouth of the Chickahominy River in James City County, the home of Elizabeth's father.³³⁴

---

³²⁸ Princess Anne Co VA Minute Book 2:45.
³²⁹ Princess Anne Co VA Deed Book 2:195.
³³⁰ Princess Anne Co VA Minute Book 2:145.
³³¹ Norfolk Co VA Deed Book 9:220-2. (See appendix).
³³² Norfolk Co VA Marriage Bonds 1706-1768. (See appendix).
³³³ Lee Family Papers (1638-1867), Mss1:L51:f:65,66. 1719 Ravenscraft next friend.
³³⁴ "Wilson Family", *VA Mag Hist*, 25:200.

Willis was appointed a Justice of the Peace for James City County on 24 Apr 1731 and served again 15 Dec 1737. He was sheriff of James City County in 1732-33.[335]

On 18-20 January 1731/2 Willis[4] and Elizabeth sold to his uncle, **Solomon**[3] **Wilson, Jr.**, the 400 acre plantation which Willis had inherited from his grandfather, Colonel James[2] Wilson. In the deeds Willis[4] was described as a gent. of Chickahominy and Solomon[3] as of the town and county of Norfolk, merchant.[336] Willis and Elizabeth signed with their seals.

Willis[4] Wilson died "the representative of his county at Williamsburg in the year 1740."[337] It is not known whom his widow, Elizabeth (Goodrich) Wilson, married second nor when and where she died.[338]

Willis[4] and Elizabeth Wilson's known child was Benjamin[5] Wilson born 26 Dec 1733 in James City County. He settled in Cumberland County, Virginia. It is thought that Willis[4] and Elizabeth may have had more children between their 1728 marriage and his 1740 death. Family stories tell of **Richard Wilson** (1752-1827) of Cumberland county being reared by his uncle Benjamin[5] Wilson. Richard was the son of **Richard Willson** of Amelia Co. whose wife Ann may have been a sister of Benjamin.[339]

- - - - - - - - - - -

98. Benjamin[5] **Wilson, Sr.** <See pg. 38> (97.Willis[4], 96.Samuel[3], 2.James[2], 1. ____ Wilson[1]) was born 6 Jan 1733 in James City County, Virginia. He married **Anne Seay**. She was born 6 Mar 1735. She was the daughter of **James Seay, Sr.**[340]

ISSUE:[341]
- f i. **Mary Wilson**, born 23 Dec 1754, died 1787.[342]
- f ii. **Elizabeth Wilson**, born 17 Oct 1756, died 1808.[343]

---

[335] McIlwaine, *Executive Journals - Colonial VA*, 4:236, 413, 273, 297.
[336] Norfolk Co VA Deed Book 11:15-16
[337] Woodson Family, *Papers, 1740-1945*, Accession 29437-40, LVA. He was probably Justice in the county court.
[338] "Wilson Family", *VA Mag Hist*, 25:199-200.
[339] Amelia Co VA Will Book 2-X:229/231.
[340] Will of James Seay, LVA.
[341] Woodson Family, *Papers, 1740-1945*, Accession 29437-41, LVA. Item 41 is a copy of the prayer book of Anne (Seay) Wilson, giving birth dates for parents and children. McCrary, *Wilson Families: Descendants of Col Benjamin Wilson*.
[342] Wise, *Amelia Co VA Will Book 4*, 3 (WB 4:21).
[343] *Wm & M Qrtrly*, 20(2)433.

m iii. **Willis Wilson**, born 22 Apr 1758, died 10 Feb 1822.[344]
m iv. **Benjamin Wilson, Jr.**, born 24 Oct 1759, died 8 Sep 1839.[345]
f v. **Anne Wilson**, born 10 Sep 1762, died 1786.[346]
m vi. **James Wilson**, born 6 Feb 1765, died 5 Jun 1847.[347]
f vii. **Mason Wilson**, born 21 Dec 1768, died 1837.[348]
m viii. **Samuel Wilson**, born 30 Mar 1770, died before 24 Jan 1842.[349]
m ix. **Matthew Wilson**, born 25 Mar 1772, died before 18 Nov 1833.[350]
m x. **Alexander Wilson**, born 1 Apr 1774, died after 1850.[351]
m xi. **Goodridge Wilson**, born 26 Mar 1776, died 30 Sep 1849.[352]
f xii. **Martha Wilson**, born 1 Jun 1778, died before 22 Apr 1849.[353]
f xiii. **Unita Wilson**, born 22 Feb 1783, died before Feb 1852.[354]

(The following is a revision/update of an article by Maurice D. Leach Jr. and Patti Sue McCrary, "The Colonel Benjamin Wilson Family, 1754-1814" published in *Cumberland County Virginia and its people*, Fourth Supplement, 1999, by the Cumberland County Historical Society, unfortunately without the footnotes and references included in the submitted article).

Colonel Benjamin[5] Wilson, affectionately called Col. Ben, was born 26 Dec 1733 in James City County, Virginia, "at or near the mouth of the Chickahominy River."[355]

---

[344] McCrary, *Cumberland County ... Historical Inventory*, 4 - cemetery. Gwathmey, *Historical Register*, 838 - Lieut., Cumberland pension.
[345] McCrary, *Wilson Families ... Correspondence .... 1785-1849*, 270-1.
[346] *Wm & M Qrtrly*, 20(2)433.
[347] DAR - Meredith Family Bible.
[348] Rosen, *History of Maysville Presbyterian Church*, 15.
[349] Littleton Parish, Accession 29330, LVA.
[350] Pittsylvania Co VA Will Book 1:250-2.
[351] Woodson Co KY 1850 census.
[352] Boddie, *Historical Southern Families*, 3:65.
[353] Webster, *Rockingham Co NC Will Abstracts*, 73 (C:294).
[354] Webster, *Rockingham Co NC Will Abstracts*, 61 (C:131).
[355] Willis Wilson Bible.

He settled in Cumberland County, Virginia, by 25 Mar 1754, the date of his marriage bond.[356] His wife was Anne Seay; James Seay gave his consent to the marriage without stating his relationship.[357]

The home of Benjamin[5] and Anne was Somerset Plantation which was located on the west side of Willis River then a "main street" of the county, as the Willis provided easy access to the James River. The land was originally a part of a patent granted to **William Mayo** 25 Aug 1731.[358] Benjamin first purchased 200 acres for 80 pounds "currant money of Virginia" from **Robert Burton** on 15 Dec 1755. The tract was described as beginning at **Leonard Keeling**'s lower corner "on Willises River" near the mouth of Cat Branch, up his line to **Drury Scrugg**'s line over to **Job Thomas**'s line, etc.[359] Benjamin acquired 200 more acres of the Mayo tract in 1765 and bought 324 acres adjoining in 1784.[360] The location of Somerset was given in an interview with Mr. **Ray Watson** Sep 1992, owner of Bonbrook farm, the former home of Benjamin's son Willis Wilson. Mr. Watson who had recently retired from his position with Cumberland County was responsible for the names on the road signs - Hwy 696 Bonbrook Rd, Hwy 671 Summerset Rd, etc.

Benjamin was listed with nine tithables in 1759.[361]

Benjamin[5] was active in early Cumberland County affairs. He was plaintiff in a suit against **James Holloway** in the July 1755 court[362] and served on a jury with **John Wilson** and others 27 Jan 1756.[363] On 28 June 1757 he was assignee of **Len: Keeling** in his case against **John Cook**,[364] was sworn in as a member of the grand jury with **Daniel Coleman** on 22 May 1758,[365] served as executor of **John Holland**'s estate in 1763, **Daniel Coleman Jr.**'s estate in 1772, and **Edward Mathias**'s estate in 1775, among others.[366]

---

[356] Cumberland Co VA Marriage Bonds 1749-1788. (See appendix).
[357] Will of James Seay, LVA (1752 - King William Co VA - in a 1757-8 bundle).
[358] Goochland Co VA Deed Book 1:359-60.
[359] Cumberland Co VA Deed Book 2:260. Trout, *Slate and Willis Rivers*, 29 - map showing Willis River and Cat Branch.
[360] Cumberland Co VA Deed Books 4:82, 6:204-5.
[361] Cumberland Co 1759 Tithe list, vertical files, Cumberland County VA Library. McCrary, *Cumberland County Tithable Lists for 1759*.
[362] Cumberland Co VA Order Book 1752-1758, 296.
[363] Fretwell, *Cumberland Co VA Order Books from 1749-1756*, 195.
[364] Fretwell, *Cumberland Co VA Order Books from 1756-1762*, 28.
[365] Cumberland Co VA Order Book 1752-1758, 69.
[366] Reynolds, *Cumberland Co VA Will Books 1 & 2*, 22, 50, 62, 67, 83.

In 1763 **Ben Bryan** assigned land in James City County to Mr. **Leonard Keeling**. On 12 Dec 1766 Benjamin Wilson assigned a lease for this land to **Cary Wilkinson**.[367] In articles in the *Virginia Gazette*, 4 Dec 1766 and 22 Sep 1768, Benjamin Wilson, as executor of Leonard Keeling, was to sell Keeling's land in James City County and some of his property in Cumberland County.[368]

Benjamin[5] was chosen by **Mary, John** and **Richard Wilson** as guardian in 1769.[369] On the 1772 marriage bond of John Wilson, Ben: Wilson, surety, signed with his seal.[370] John Wilson was referred to as "kinsman" in family letters.[371] Descendants of Richard Wilson have a tradition that he was raised by his uncle Benjamin Wilson.[372] The exact kinship of John and Richard has not yet been determined.

In 1755 and 1765 Benjamin was listed as a processioner for Southam Parish; he was elected a vestryman in 1771.[373] Benjamin was a member of the vestry of Littleton Parish, which was separated from Southam, in 1772 serving with **Alexander Trent, Daniel Coleman** and **Nathan Glenn** all having close ties with the Wilson-Seay family.[374] This responsibility was enhanced with the appointment of the Rev. **Christopher McRae** as Rector, in that they became close friends, and the Rev. McRae influenced the educational development of the Wilson sons. To wit, Colonel Benjamin's son James[6] in a letter dated 10 Sep 1808 to his brother Benjamin[6] who lived in Woodford County, Kentucky, stated: ".......... Our parents settled at this place, poor strangers, little improved and unsupported by connections; their acquaintance and friendship with the Rev. Mr. McRae was certainly the most lucky occurrence in life; from his attention have their sons become learned and pious, possessing correct knowledge of both men and things-- that such an event may take place with you is much our wish."[375]

---

[367] Lee Family Papers (1638-1867), Mss1:L51:f672-3 (frames, 610, 614). Lease, 1672 land in Passbehay.
[368] Headley, *18th-Century Newspapers*, 190. Miscellaneous Reels 162, 163 LVA. Further research on the Keelings may indicate a second marriage for Benjamin's mother and give background for Benjamin's move to Cumberland County.
[369] Cumberland Co VA Order Book 1767-1770, 273, 376.
[370] Cumberland Co VA Marriage Bonds 1749-1788.
[371] McCrary, *Wilson Families ... Correspondence .... 1785-1849*, 13-17.
[372] McRee, Johnson. *Wilson-Sale Genealogy*. Richmond: before 1958. Tindall, Henry C. *Daniel Allen's Family Register*. Fayette MO: 1914.
[373] Blomquist, *Vestry Book of Southam Parish*, 82, 180-1, 217.
[374] *Today and Yesterday*, 230.
[375] McCrary, *Wilson Families ... Correspondence .... 1785-1849*, 130.

Another son was Dr. Samuel[6] Wilson, who earned a medical degree at the University of Edinburgh in 1792[376] and practiced in Buckingham and Cumberland Counties. He eventually became the owner of the 870 acre Somerset Plantation when he bought out the heirs in 1815;[377] he was buried there in the family cemetery on 11 Jan 1842.[378]

Benjamin[5] became Justice of Peace and a Commissioner of Oyer and Terminer on 28 Jul 1777[379] and served as "Gentlemen Justice" on the county court as late as 23 Feb 1807.[380]

His military service began with his membership in the Cumberland County Committee of Safety. On 18 Feb 1775 the committee wrote to delegates of the Continental Congress "Resolved, ... we shall be ready to risk our lives and fortunes", then later, "Resolved, ...members of the committee ... will give ..... three shillings per pound to ... persons ... who ... produce to the said committee ... fifty pounds weight of good gunpowder, manufactured in America ...", also that "whenever a suspicion shall arise of any merchant in this county having infringed the association of the late Continental Congress, ... do make information thereof ....to ... the committee."[381] On 17 Oct 1775 Benjamin Wilson was appointed a Captain in the Militia replacing **John Burton**. His Lieutenant was **Robert Anderson** and his Ensign was **George Keeling**.[382] On 26 Mar 1781 **George Carrington, Jr.** was appointed Colonel and Benjamin was appointed Lieutenant Colonel in the county Militia; at the same court Benjamin showed a receipt for providing "the publick" of the county a wagon, team of four horses and a driver for a month.[383] He signed a petition dated 10 Nov 1780 which asked the House of Delegates to reject a bill forbidding the use of depreciated currency in payment of debts.[384] By Aug 1781 he was appointed a Commissioner for the State for Public Service Claims whereby he certified claims made by the citizens of the county for property used in the Revolutionary War. Among the items Benjamin[5] provided were wheat, beef, and bacon.[385]

---

[376] "List of the American Graduates", *NEHGR*, 42:162.
[377] Cumberland Co VA Deed Book 13:148-9.
[378] Littleton Parish, Accession 29330, LVA.
[379] Cumberland Co VA Order Book 1774-1778, 408-9.
[380] Cumberland Co VA Order Book 1803-1807, 467.
[381] *Virginia Gazette* 25 Mar 1775, page 1, Film 11 Reel 5, LVA.
[382] McIlwaine, *Committee of Safety Cumberland Co*, 7-9, 19-20.
[383] Cumberland Co VA Order Book 1779-1784, 152-3.
[384] Hall, "Legislative Petitions", 30:88-89.
[385] Abercrombie, *VA Publick Claims*, 1:284, 297, 298. Cumberland Co VA Order Book 1779-1784, 182, etc..

Following the Revolution he was appointed coroner in 1784[386] and sheriff on 24 Nov 1787 with his son Willis Wilson and **Joseph Carrington** as his under sheriffs.[387] In 1785 it was "ordered that Benjamin Wilson and Cary Harrison Gentlemen agree with some person to repair the prison of this County",[388] and in 1786 he and **Archer Allen** were appointed to "let the rebuilding or replacing and receiving of Horn Quarter Bridge."[389]

Colonel Ben[5] was appointed on 26 Sep 1774 with **Cary Harrison**, **Stephen Woodson** and others " ... to raise the clearing of Willis Creek ..."[390] Thirteen years later on 10 Dec 1787 he, **Joseph Carrington**, **Mayo Carrington**, **Alexander Trent, Jr.** and **George Anderson**, gentlemen, were appointed " ... trustees for clearing, improving and extending the navigation of the Willis River, as far up the same as the Fork Plantation ...." His son Willis succeeded him as trustee soon after on 24 Dec 1787.[391] In 1818 subscribers to the Willis Navigation Company were Col. Benjamin's sons Goodrich[6], James[6], Matthew[6] and Willis[6]; also **Daniel Allen Wilson** who may have been a cousin of the brothers.[392]

His last governmental appointments were in 1797; on Feb 27 when Col. Benjamin[5] and **Joseph Carrington**, gentlemen, became Commissioners to inspect tobacco at Woodson's Warehouse in Cartersville,[393] and Benjamin, **William Powell, James Deane, Thomas Randolph, Ben Allen** and **Joseph Carrington** were charged with carrying out the act to establish public schools in the county.[394]

A letter to his son Benjamin[6] in Kentucky, dated 10 Oct 1801, shows fond parental concern: "I am desirous that you would be more frequent in your letters: for I suppose it is a part of the infirmities of age to be more desirous to hear of the welfare of those we are nearly bound to."[395]

The will of Benjamin Wilson, written 1 Feb 1812 and proved 28 Nov 1814, named his wife, his sons Willis, Benjamin, James, Samuel, Matthew,

---

[386] Hall, *Journals of the Council of the State of Virginia*, 3:378.
[387] Cumberland Co VA Order Book 1788-1792, 37.
[388] *Cumb Co VA and Its People*, 7.
[389] *Cumb. Co VA Hist Bulletin*, 3-2, p.14.
[390] Cumberland Co VA Order Book 1774-1798 or 1772-1774, 47.
[391] Hening, *Statutes*, 12:483-7.
[392] Trout, *Slate and Willis Rivers*, 32, 38.
[393] *Calendar of Virginia State Papers*, 8:452.
[394] *Cumb Co VA and Its People*, 7.
[395] McCrary, *Wilson Families ... Correspondence .... 1785-1849*, 92-3.

Wilson Families

Alexander and Goodrich, his daughters Mason, Martha, and Unity and his granddaughters (Mary) Hobson, Maria Willis (Wilson) and Ann (Wilson).[396]

Anne (Seay) Wilson died 25 Apr 1814, and Colonel Benjamin[5] Wilson died 27 Oct 1814.[397] Benjamin and Anne are believed to be buried on the Somerset Plantation, as their bachelor son Samuel[6] was and most likely the spinster daughters Elizabeth[6] and Anne[6].[398]

- - - - - - - - - - -

104. Willis[3] Wilson <See pg. 2> (2.James[2], 1. ____ Wilson[1]) was born about 1683. He married **Mary Chichester.** (See number 25 - pg. 104).

ISSUE:

+ 105. m i. **Lemuel Wilson**, born about 1713, died 1765 <See pg. 48>.

   112. m ii. **James Wilson**. He married **Elizabeth** ____ before 17 Jan 1743/4, when James Wilson, Planter, and Elizabeth, his wife, of Norfolk County sold **John Wickens** of Princess Anne County 50 acres upon the Cypress Swamp.[399] From his father's 1758 will, he received several tracts of land. James died after 21 Mar 1766, the date of the will of his brother Thomas.

   113. m iii. **Robert Wilson** was named in the 1736 and 1750 tithables with his father.[400] He died before 28 Apr 1758 the date of his father's will.

   114. m iv. **Thomas Wilson** received land from his father's 1758 will. In Thomas[4]'s will, dated 21 Mar 1766 and proved 19 Jun 1766, he gave his brother James among other tracts of land, "my part of land we heired from our father." Thomas also named his cousin (nephew) Willis Wilson, cousin (niece) Ann Wilson, cousin James Wilson Senr, and cousin Malachi Wilson Junr.[401]

+ 115. f v. **Euphan Wilson**, died after 1758 <See pg. 50>.

Two contemporary Willis Wilsons in Norfolk County were Major Willis[3] Wilson (1683-1760) son of Col. James[2] Wilson, and his nephew Capt.

---

[396] Will of Benjamin Wilson, LVA. (See appendix). Cumberland Co VA Order Book 1811-15, 464.

[397] McCrary, *Wilson Families ... Correspondence .... 1785-1849*, 167. Willis Wilson Bible.

[398] Littleton Parish, Accession 29330, LVA.

[399] Walter, *Princess Anne Co VA Deed and Minute Books*, 24 (6DB255).

[400] Wingo, *Norfolk Co VA Tithables 1730-1750*, 175, 212.

[401] Wingo, *Norfolk Co VA Will Book 1*, 91-2 (f 145).

Wilson Families

Willis⁴ Wilson Jr. (1687-1750), son of Major James³ Wilson. In general the younger used the title Jr.[402]

By 15 Feb 1711/2 Willis³ Wilson had married Mary⁴ Chichester shown in the settlement of the estate of her father William Chichester.[403]

The 1712 will of Willis's father, Col. James Wilson, stated, "I give to my Son Willis Wilson all the land and the New Store standing the easternmost side of the wroade by the bridge..... I give and bequeath to my said son Willis Wilson my plantation where on I now live being about four hundred acres..... And the rest of my land not already bequeathed, I give and bequeath unto my son, Willis Wilson." James named his wife Elizabeth and son Willis executors.[404] On 12 Jun 1713 Willis's uncle William² Wilson confirmed the 1672 sale of land to his brother James² who left it in his will to his son Willis³.[405]

On 19 Mar 1712/3 Mr. Willis³ Wilson sold 200 acres of land of his inheritance to his brother James³ Wilson, high sheriff.[406] His brother Solomon³ selected him as guardian 15 May 1713.[407] The 7 Apr 1718 will of James⁴ Wilson named his uncle, Willis³ Wilson.[408]

Willis first appeared as a justice of the Norfolk County court on 19 May 1713,[409] and he was high sheriff in the county for the years 1724 and 1732.[410] He served in the House of Burgesses from Norfolk County for the sessions of 1718, 1720-1722, and probably 1728-1734, 1748-1749.[411]

Willis³ was commissioned a captain in the Norfolk County militia by 1728 and major by 1750.[412] Major Willis Wilson's land was processioned 5 Apr 1752.[413]

---

[402] Butt, *Col. James Wilson*, 13, 24, 32.
[403] Norfolk Co VA Deed Book 9:154.
[404] Norfolk Co VA Deed Book 9:220-2. (See appendix).
[405] Norfolk Co VA Deed Book 9:254-5.
[406] Norfolk Co VA Deed Book 9:242-5.
[407] Norfolk Co VA Deed Book 9, pt. 2 Orders:59.
[408] McIntosh, *Norfolk Co Wills 1710-1753*, 69-70 (Book 10:18).
[409] Norfolk Co VA Deed Book 9, pt. 2 Orders:60.
[410] Butt, *Col James Wilson*, 13.
[411] Leonard, *General Assembly of Virginia*, 69, 70, 75, 82.
[412] Butt, *Col James Wilson*, 13.
[413] Walter, *Vestry Book of Elizabeth River Parish*, 12.

The will of Willis³ was dated 28 Apr 1758 and proved Sep 1760. His wife Mary and son Robert must have died. He named son Lemuel⁴ with his children Mary⁵, Willis⁵, Anne⁵, and Charles⁵. The section in the will regarding James⁴ named **Sarah**⁵ as a child of Lemuel in addition to the other children. Willis also named son Thomas⁴ and daughter Euphan⁴ Alston, wife of Joseph John Alston and their children Willis⁵, Henry⁵ and Mary⁵ Alston.⁴¹⁴

- - - - - - - - - - -

105. Lemuel⁴ Wilson <See pg. 46> (104.Willis³, 2.James², 1. ____ Wilson¹) was born about 1713. He married (1) **Sophia Lowery. (See pg. 140).**
ISSUE:⁴¹⁵
106. f   i.   **Mary Wilson**, born about 1746.
+ 107. m ii. **Willis Wilson**, born 1748, died 11 Sep 1798 <See pg. 49>.
108. f   iii. **Anne Wilson**, born about 1750.
109. m iv. **Charles Wilson**, born before Jan 1752.

Lemuel⁴ married (1) Sophia Lowery, before 20 May 1741, shown in a document that named Mr. Lemuel Wilson and Sophia his wife, concerning the estate of James Lowery.⁴¹⁶

In 1742 Lemuel and his father built a warehouse at Great Bridge, and in 1748 Lemuel Wilson was a justice in the Norfolk County Court.⁴¹⁷

Sophia died before 29 Jan 1752, when Lemuel married (2) **Martha Alston** in Chowan County, North Carolina.⁴¹⁸ She was the daughter of **John Alston**, and a sister of **Joseph John Alston**.

Martha died before 1755 when Lemuel married (3) **Winifred Pilkinton**. She was born about 1730. She was the daughter of **Seth Pilkinton** and **Sarah Porter**.⁴¹⁹
ISSUE:
110. f   v.   **Sarah Wilson**, born 21 Feb 1756, died 8 Nov 1779.

---

⁴¹⁴ Norfolk Co VA Will Book 1:50.
⁴¹⁵ Norfolk Co VA Will Book 1:50.
⁴¹⁶ Norfolk Co VA Deed Book 13:29.
⁴¹⁷ Butt, *Col James Wilson*, 14.
⁴¹⁸ Chowan Co NC Marriage Bond, 29 Jan 1752.
⁴¹⁹ Most information on the Alstons and Pilkintons is from correspondence, papers, and copies from Doris Wilson of Robersonville NC, citing Beaufort Co NC and NC Archives documents. Note that Sarah Wilson was named in the 1758 VA will of her grandfather Willis Wilson in the portion regarding his son James.

111. m vi. **Seth Pilkinton Wilson**, born 1761, died 1790 in Beaufort County, North Carolina.

Lemuel died 1765 in Beaufort County, North Carolina.

- - - - - - - - - - -

107. Willis⁵ Wilson <See pg. 48> (105.Lemuel⁴, 104.Willis³, 2.James², 1. ____ Wilson¹) was born 1748. He married **Mary Thorowgood**. She was born 1753. She was the daughter of **Adam Thorowgood** and **Mary Thelaball**.[420] (See pg. 138).

Mary Thorowgood married (1) **Hugh Craigdallie** whose 1774 will named his wife Mary and daughter **Janet**, executor **Lemuel Thorowgood**.[421] Mary's brother Lemuel Thorowgood in his will, dated 9 Oct 1785, named his sister Mary Wilson.[422]

Willis⁵ Wilson was appointed Captain of the galley *Caswell* in 1776 and was appointed to command the *Jefferson* 1 Dec 1780.[423] On 21 Apr 1785 he was commissioned Colonel of the Norfolk County militia.[424]

In 1787 he was listed in the census as non-tithable but with a four-wheeled post chaise, his slaves and horses.[425]

The will of Willis Wilson of Portsmouth was dated 2 Dec 1796 and probated 17 Dec 1798. He left his estate, which included four acres known as Gosport and lot at Great Bridge, to wife Mary; no children were named.[426]

On the grave stone of Willis Wilson, which was first at his home in Gosport, but was moved to Trinity Churchyard, was written that he died 11 Sep 1798, age 50. The stone was next to that of his step-daughter Janet Craigdallie, and near Mary's, which recorded that she died 14 Feb 1819, age 66.[427]

---

[420] Creecy, "Thorowgood Family." *Virginia Genealogist* 17:280.
[421] Maling, *Princess Anne Co VA Deed Books 8-18*, 66 (14DB82).
[422] Maling, *Princess Anne Co VA, Wills*, 12.
[423] Gwathmey, *Historical Register*, 837-8.
[424] Butt, *Col James Wilson*, 14-17.
[425] Schreiner-Yantis, *1787 census of Virginia*, 2:859.
[426] Brewster, *Norfolk Co VA Will Book 3*, 127.
[427] Butt, *Col James Wilson*, 15-17. Headley, *18ᵗʰ-Century Newspapers*, 373.

Mary's niece **Jacomine N. Thorowgood** married **Richard Holstead**, and her niece **Elizabeth T. Moseley** married **James Cornick**.[428] From 1834 to 1840 they applied, as heirs of Mary Thorowgood, for the land grants awarded Willis Wilson for his service in the Revolutionary War.[429]

- - - - - - - - - - -

115. Euphan⁴ Wilson <See pg. 46> (104.Willis³, 2.James², 1.____ Wilson¹). She married **Joseph John Alston** before 28 Apr 1758, the date of her father's will. He was the son of **John Alston**.[430]

ISSUE:[431]

116. m i. **Willis Alston**, born 1752. He married **Elizabeth Wright**. Elizabeth died 23 Mar 1823 in Edenton, North Carolina. Willis died 31 Oct 1819.
117. m ii. **Henry Alston**, born 1753. He married **Sarah Hill**.
118. f iii. **Mary Alston**, born 1756. She married **William Palmer**.
119. f iv. **Euphan Alston**, born 1761. She married **John Cooper**.
120. m v. **Joseph John Alston**, born 15 Mar 1767. He married **Martha Kearny** 1 Jun 1791. She was born 22 Feb 1771. Martha died Apr 1852. Joseph died 29 Apr 1841.

Her father's 1758 will named Euphan Alston, wife of Joseph John Alston and three of their children, Willis, Henry, and Mary Alston.[432]

Joseph died before Aug 1781 in Halifax County, North Carolina.

- - - - - - - - - - -

121. Affiah³ Wilson <See pg. 2> (2.James², 1.____ Wilson¹) was born 1689. She married **George Newton** in 1706.[433] **(See number 6 - pg. 92)**.

ISSUE:[434]

---

[428] Creecy, "Thorowgood Family." *Virginia Genealogist* 17:280. Walter, *Genealogical chart of... Thorowgood*, sheet 2. Dumont, "Some Virginia Revolutionary Veterans", *Virginia Genealogist* 1:47, 2:115. beth@TidewaterTapestry.com, e-mail (marriage records).

[429] Revolutionary War Records, Rejected Claims, Revolutionary Bounty Warrants, and Revolutionary War Land Office Military Certificates, Library of Virginia (http://www.lva.lib.va.us/whatwehave/mil/index.htm).

[430] Correspondence from Doris Wilson of Robersonville NC.

[431] Dorman, *Adventurers of Purse and Person*, 2:635. Gives Alston dates and marriages.

[432] Norfolk Co VA Will Book 1:50.

[433] Newton, "Newton Family of Norfolk", 4:539.

[434] Newton, "Newton Family of Norfolk", 4:542-3. Dorman, *Adventurers of Purse and Person*, 2:581.

Wilson Families

+ 122. f   i.   **Elizabeth Newton**, born 22 Jul 1707 <See pg. 51>.
  124. m   ii. **George Newton**, born 26 Feb 1711/2, died 17 May 1719.
+ 125. m   iii. **Thomas Newton**, born 14 Mar 1713/4, died 13 Dec 1794 <See pg. 52>.
  127. m   iv. **Lemuel Newton**, born 22 Jun 1715, died as an infant.
+ 128. m   v. **Wilson Newton**, born 9 Apr 1718, died before 18 Nov 1762 <See pg. 52>.
+ 134. f   vi. **Ann Newton**, born 17 Feb 1720/1, died Apr 1749 <See pg. 53>.
  136. m vii. **George Newton**, born 4 Mar 1722/3.
  137. mviii. **William Newton**, born 7 Dec 1726.
+ 138. f   ix. **Frances Newton**, born 24 Feb 1728/9, died 5 Jan 1793 <See pg. 54>.

Affiah, sometimes spelled Apphia, etc., was named in her father's 1712 will to receive a portion of his personal estate, her husband receiving 100 acres of land "called the Cowpens."[435]

In March 1728 when Colonel **William Byrd** was in Norfolk, he was a guest of Captain and Mrs. Newton and wrote in his diary: "Mrs. Newton provided a clean supper without any luxury about 8 o'clock, and appear'd to be one of the fine ladies of the town, and like a true fine lady to have a great deal of contempt for her husband." [436]

The will of George Newton, dated 30 May 1753 and proved Jul 1762, named wife Aphia, sons Thomas, Wilson, William, daughters Frances Loyal (wife of Paul Loyall), Elizabeth Benbow in England and grandson George Cook.[437]

- - - - - - - - - - -

122. Elizabeth[4] Newton <See pg. 51> (121.Affiah[3], 2.James[2], 1. ____ Wilson[1]) was born 22 Jul 1707. She married (1) **James Faulconer**. James died before 20 May 1728 in York County, Virginia. Elizabeth married (2) **Edward Benbow** Dec 1728 in Norfolk County, Virginia.[438]

- - - - - - - - - - -

---

[435] Norfolk Co VA Deed Book 9:220-2. (See asppendix). Nugent, *Cavaliers and Pioneers*, 3:156 (Patent Book 10:188).
[436] Wright, *Prose of William Byrd*, 51.
[437] Wingo, *Norfolk Co VA Will Book 1*, 57-8 (f 86).
[438] Dorman, *Adventurers of Purse and Person*, 2:601.

125. Thomas[4] **Newton** <See pg. 51> (121.Affiah[3], 2.James[2], 1. ____ Wilson[1]) was born 14 Mar 1713/4. He married **Amy Hutchings**. She was the daughter of **John Hutchings** and **Amy Godfrey**.[439]

ISSUE:[440]

126. m i. **Thomas Newton, Jr.**, born 15 May 1742. He married **Martha Tucker** 7 Oct 1767 in Norfolk County, Virginia. She was born 1748. She was the daughter of **Robert Tucker** and **Joanna Corbin**. Martha died 16 Nov 1816. Thomas, Jr. died 11 Sep 1807.

Thomas[4] died 13 Dec 1794.[441]

- - - - - - - - - - -

128. Wilson[4] **Newton** <See pg. 51> (121.Affiah[3], 2.James[2], 1. ____ Wilson[1]) was born 9 Apr 1718. He married **Rebecca Ellegood** 1742.[442] **(See pg. 114)**.

ISSUE:[443]

129. m i. **George Newton**, died before 27 Aug 1762.
130. f ii. **Frances Newton**. She married **John Esten**. John died before 16 Oct 1788 in Norfolk County, Virginia.
+ 131. f iii. **Rebecca Newton**, born 1749, died 1794 <See pg. 53>.
132. f iv. **Ann Newton**. She married **John Hodgson** 31 Aug 1775. John died before 10 Jul 1777 in Princess Anne County, Virginia.
133. f v. **Elizabeth Newton**, born 1761. She married **Jonathan Calvert** 2 May 1783 in Norfolk County, Virginia. He was born 1 Jan 1752 in Norfolk, Virginia. Jonathan died 17 Dec 1792 in Norfolk, Virginia. Elizabeth died Dec 1791.

In his will, dated 27 Aug 1762 and proved 18 Nov 1762, Wilson named his wife Rebecca, son George, daughters Frances, Rebecca , Ann, and Elizabeth Newton.[444]

---

[439] McIntosh, *Norfolk Co Wills 1710-1753*, 57-61 (Book 9:591 - will of Mathew Godfrey). Wingo, *Norfolk Co VA Will Book 1*, 106-7 (f 172a - will of John Hutchings).

[440] Dorman, *Adventurers of Purse and Person*, 2:601-2.

[441] Headley, *18th-Century Newspapers*, 250.

[442] McIntosh, *Norfolk Co Wills 1710-1753*, 236-7 (Book I:23 - will of John Ellegood). Wingo, *Norfolk Co VA Will Book 1*, 30 (f 47), 106 (f 171a) -wills of John and Jacob Ellegood.

[443] Dorman, *Adventurers of Purse and Person*, 2:601-2.

[444] Wingo, *Norfolk Co VA Will Book 1*, 59 (f 90).

Rebecca died before 11 Feb 1779 in Princess Anne County, Virginia. In her will dated 14 Jul 1775 and proved 11 Feb 1779, she named her daughters Frances, Ann and Elizabeth. She also named her daughter Rebecca Moseley, granddaughters Mary, Rebecca and Frances Moseley and son-in-law Bassett Moseley.[445]

- - - - - - - - - - -

131. Rebecca⁵ Newton <See pg. 52> (128.Wilson⁴, 121.Affiah³, 2.James², 1. ____ Wilson¹) was born 1749. She married **Bassett Moseley** 27 Jan 1768.[446] He was born 1745 in Princess Anne County, Virginia. He was the son of **Edward Hack Moseley** and **Mary Bassett**.[447]

ISSUE:[448]
- f i. **Mary Bassett Moseley**.
- f ii. **Rebecca Moseley**, born 1769, died 29 May 1812.
- f iii. **Frances Moseley**, born 1776, died 1836.

In his will, dated 24 May 1782 and proved 10 Apr 1783, Edward Hack Moseley named his granddaughters Mary Bassett, Rebecca and Frances, daughters of Bassett.[449]

In his will, dated 11 Apr 1782 and proved Dec 1782, Bassett named his wife Rebecca.[450] She may have died around 1794.[451]

- - - - - - - - - - -

134. Ann⁴ Newton <See pg. 51> (121.Affiah³, 2.James², 1. ____ Wilson¹) was born 17 Feb 1720/1 and died Apr 1749.[452] She probably married ____ **Cook**.

ISSUE:[453]
135. m i. **George Cook**.

- - - - - - - - - - -

---

[445] Headley, *18ᵗʰ-Century Newspapers*, 249. Maling, *Princess Anne Co VA Deed Books 8-18*, 81 (15DB135).
[446] Wingo, *Marriages of Norfolk Co VA, Vol 1*, 47.
[447] Dorman, *Adventurers of Purse and Person*, 2:110.
[448] Records of Sarah Johnson, 1999.
[449] Maling, *Princess Anne Co VA Deed Books 8-18*, 102 (18DB186).
[450] McVey, *Norfolk Co VA Will Book 2*, 140.
[451] Records of Sarah Johnson, 1999.
[452] Newton, "Newton Family of Norfolk", 4:543.
[453] The 1753 will of George Newton named a grandson George Cook.

Wilson Families

138. Frances⁴ Newton <See pg. 51> (121.Affiah³, 2.James², 1. ____ Wilson¹) was born 24 Feb 1728/9. She married **Paul Loyall**. He was born 1722.

ISSUE:[454]

139. f   i.   **Frances Loyall**. She married **Wilson Boush** 18 Sep 1794 in Norfolk County, Virginia. He was born about 1761. He was the son of **Goodrich Boush** and **Mary Wilson**. **(See number 21 - pg. 15)**. Wilson died 1 Dec 1829. **(See number 41 - pg. 207)**.

140. m   ii.   **George Loyall**.

Paul died 31 Jan 1807 in Norfolk, Virginia. Frances died 5 Jan 1793.

- - - - - - - - - - -

141. Solomon³ Wilson <See pg. 2> (2.James², 1. ____ Wilson¹) was born about 1694. He married **Tabitha Mason (See number 19 - pg. 103)**. She was born about 1699. She was the daughter of **Lemuel Mason** and **Mary Thelaball**.

ISSUE:[455]

142. f   i.   **Ann Wilson**, died after 20 Aug 1771.

+ 143. f   ii.   **Tabitha Wilson**, born after 1728, died after 22 Jan 1789 <See pg. 56>.

148. m   iii.   **Lemuel Wilson**, died after 20 Aug 1771.

+ 149. f   iv.   **Mason Wilson**, born before 1737, died before 20 Oct 1794 <See pg. 57>.

152. f   v.   **Elizabeth Wilson**, died after 20 Aug 1771.

Solomon³ Wilson was born about 1694. His nephew, Solomon Wilson Sr., son of his brother James, was about a year older.

In the 1712 will of his father, Solomon³ received the land bought of **Henry Bright**, about two hundred acres, and the land called the western Ridge, when age 21.[456]

At court on 15 May 1713, Solomon selected his guardian: "Whereas Solomon Wilson pet to this court to have his brother Mr. Willis Wilson Elected his Gardian and haveing Sett forth in his pet that he hath arrived of full age to Elect his Gardian according to Law and Likewise made the same

---

[454] Dorman, *Adventurers of Purse and Person*, 2: 603, 606.

[455] Bertie Co NC Wills 1749-1897 (B:19) - will of Solomon Wilson dated 20 Aug 1771.

[456] Norfolk Co VA Deed Book 9:220-2. (See appendix).

Wilson Families

appear to the court it is therefore Thought fitt that he the said Willis be Elected his gardian according to Law."[457]

Solomon was a witness to the 14 Nov 1715 deed when John Wilson Gent and Margarett his wife sold to **Jonas Cawson** a 60' x 50' lot on Costin's Island, and soon after, 18 Nov 1715, John Wilson gave to his "well beloved brother Solomon Wilson" 30' square on Costin's Island.[458]

On 22 Nov 1718 Solomon Wilson was sworn in as clerk of the Norfolk County Court,[459] serving until 18 Jun 1742.[460] On 15 May 1719, "On motion of Majr Saml Boush its by this court ordered that the clerk of the court bring to his office the records to Norfolke Towne as sone as conveniently may be."[461] In 1705 the records had been taken home by clerk Lemuel Wilson, Solomon's brother.[462] On 15 Feb 1719/20 Solomon bought lot 22 on the Market Place in Norfolk Town almost opposite the Court House.[463]

The 7 Apr 1718 will of James[4] Wilson named his uncles Lemuel, Willis, Solomon Wilson.[464] Solomon Wilson Jr. was a witness to the 3 Apr 1719 will of **William Miller**, who named sons **Willis, William, Solomon, Lemuel Miller.**[465]

At court 17 Jun 1720 **Elizabeth Mason** selected Mr. Solomon Wilson as her guardian. Solomon was married to Elizabeth's sister Tabitha, both heirs of Mr. Lemuel Mason, dec'd, shown when Solomon petitioned for the sisters to receive their portions of the estate.[466]

By 1727 Solomon had been commissioned captain in the Norfolk County Militia and was advanced to major before 1739.[467] On 18 Jan 1731/2 **George Mason** sold to **John Ellegood** the lot next to Capt. Solomon Wilson

---

[457] Norfolk Co VA Deed Book 9, pt. 2 Orders:59.
[458] Norfolk Co VA Deed Book 9:443-4, 453-4.
[459] Norfolk Co VA Deed Book 10:35/70.
[460] Cross, *County Court... Norfolk*, 34-6.
[461] Norfolk Co VA Deed Book 10:52a/103.
[462] Norfolk Co VA Deed Book 7:71a.
[463] Whichard, *History of Lower Tidewater VA*, 1:360.
[464] Norfolk Co VA Deed Book 10:18/35.
[465] McIntosh, *Norfolk Co Wills 1710-1753*, 81-2 (Book 10:76).
[466] Norfolk Co VA Orders, Appraisals & Wills, Pt 1:21a.
[467] Butt, *Col James Wilson*, 18. Dorman, *Adventurers of Purse and Person*, 2:579.

in Norfolk Town.[468] The 1740 will of John Ellegood mentioned a lot bought of Capt. Solomon Wilson.[469]

In a deed dated 19 Jan 1731/2, Willis Wilson Jr. of James City County of Chickahominy, Gent, and Elizabeth his wife sold to Solomon Wilson Jr. of the town and county of Norfolk, merchant, 400 acres bequeathed to Willis by his grandfather Col. James Wilson.[470]

On 23 Jul 1736 Solomon Wilson Jr. and Tabitha his wife sold John Ellegood a lot on the Southwest side of the maine Street of Norfolk Town next to Capt. George Mason's lot.[471]

Tabitha was not named in the 1738 deed when Solomon Wilson Junr. Gent of the County of Norfolk sold **Samuel Smith** a 1200 acre plantation in the Northwest Woods of Norfolk County.[472]

Solomon may have been the witness to the wills of **Thomas Langley**, 1746, **Lemuel Langley**, 1748, and **Thomas Langley**, 1750.[473]

The will of Solomon Wilson was dated 20 Aug 1771 and proved Feb 1775. After stating that he was "late of Norfolk Town in Virginia", he said that he had entered a suit that continued for eleven years, which suit was dismissed and "this was the reason for my leaving Virginia" for Carolina. He named daughters Ann (an executor), Tabitha, son Lemuel, and daughters Mason and Elizabeth.[474]

- - - - - - - - - - -

143. Tabitha^4 Wilson <See pg. 54> (141.Solomon^3, 2.James^2, 1. ____ Wilson^1) was born after 1728, her father's consent being given on the marriage bond. She married **William Freeman** 7 Feb 1748/9.[475]
ISSUE:[476]
  144. f   i.   **Mary Freeman**. She married **Thomas Burke** 28 Mar 1770 in Norfolk County, Virginia.

---

[468] Norfolk Co VA Deed Book 11:9.
[469] McIntosh, *Norfolk Co Wills 1710-1753*, 236-7 (Book I:23).
[470] Norfolk Co VA Deed Book 11:15-16.
[471] Norfolk Co VA Deed Book 12:133.
[472] Norfolk Co VA Deed Book 12:207.
[473] McIntosh, *Norfolk Co Wills 1710-1753*, 211-2, 220-1, 270.
[474] Bertie Co NC Wills 1749-1897 (B:19).
[475] Wingo, *Marriages of Norfolk Co VA, Vol 1*, 25.
[476] Dorman, *Adventurers of Purse and Person*, 2:592-3.

145. f ii. **Frances Freeman**. She married **John McCariel** 13 Apr 1769 in Norfolk County, Virginia.
146. m iii. **John Freeman**.
147. m iv. **Robert Freeman**. His mother deeded land in Bertie County, North Carolina, to him 22 Jan 1789.

William died before Feb 1782 in Bertie County, North Carolina.

- - - - - - - - - - -

149. Mason[4] Wilson <See pg. 54> (141.Solomon[3], 2.James[2], 1. ___ Wilson[1]) was born before 1737. She married **Robert Waller** 3 Jun 1758.[477]
ISSUE:[478]
150. f i. **Ann Waller**. She married **William Ronald** 1 Mar 1785 in Norfolk County, Virginia. William died before 3 Feb 1793 in Cumberland County, Virginia. Ann died before 27 Mar 1788.
151. f ii. **Martha Waller**. She married (1) ___ **Hicks**. Martha married (2) **Henry Kean** 1790 in Norfolk County, Virginia. Martha married (3) **Lewis Dey** 18 Apr 1796 in Norfolk County, Virginia.

Robert died before 20 Sep 1787. Mason died before 20 Oct 1794.

- - - - - - - - - - -

153. Mary[3] Wilson <See pg. 2> (2.James[2], 1. ___ Wilson[1]) was born about 1697. She married **Nathaniel Butt** about 1717. He was born about 1695. He was the son of **Thomas Butt** and **Elizabeth** ___.[479]
ISSUE:[480]
154. m i. **Nathaniel Butt**, born about 1721. He married **Jane Wilson** (See number 13). She was the daughter of **Solomon Wilson, Sr.** and **Elizabeth Holstead**. Nathaniel died 1788.
156. m ii. **James Butt**, born about 1723. He married **Sarah Wilson** (See number 10). She was the daughter of **Solomon Wilson, Sr.** and **Elizabeth Holstead**. James died 1762.
157. f iii. **Mary Butt**, born about 1725. She married **Maximillian Murden**. He was probably the son of **Edward Murden** and **Mary** ___.[481]

---

[477] Wingo, *Marriages of Norfolk Co VA, Vol 1*, 68.
[478] Dorman, *Adventurers of Purse and Person*, 2:593.
[479] Butt, *An Account .... Robert Butt*, 11.
[480] Butt, *Col James Wilson*, 19, 24.
[481] McIntosh, *Norfolk Co Wills 1710-1753*, 164 (Book 12:83 - will of Edward Murden).

158. f iv. **Theresa Butt**, born about 1730. She married ____ **Wallace**.
159. m v. **Thomas Butt**, born about 1735.
160. m vi. **Wilson Butt**, born about 1737.
161. m vii. **John Butt**, born about 1739. He married **Elizabeth Fairfield** 29 Jul 1765.[482]

Mary³ was named in her father's 1712 will, all personal estate not before given was to be equally divided among sons: Willis, John, and Solomon, and daughters Affiah and Mary.[483]

Nathaniel's will, dated 2 Jan 1749/50 and proved 6 Apr 1750, named sons Nathaniel, James, Thomas, Wilson, John, daughters Teresa Butt, Mary Murden, and wife Mary[484]

Mary's will, dated 17 Mar 1772 and proved May 1772, named executor son John Butt, sons Josiah, Nathaniel, Wilson, John, daughter Treshia Wallis, and granddaughter Jeen Bel (torn).[485]

Josiah Butt was named as a son in the 1772 will of Mary Butt but not in the abstract of the 1750 will of Nathaniel Butt. The full will of Nathaniel Butt should be examined.

Josiah Butt, born about 1719-1720, married **Mary Boush**, **(See number 6 - pg. 197)**. daughter of Maximillian Boush, Jr., and his wife Elizabeth Wilson, daughter of Major James Wilson.[486] **(See number 28 - pg. 16)**.

A land transaction was recorded 22 Jun 1772 between Josiah and Mary Butt and **Daniel Curling**. This land adjoined that of Wilson Butt. In 1782 a deed that had not been recorded was confirmed to Josiah Butt's heir, his daughter **Prudence Butt**.[487]

The will of Josiah Butt, dated 16 May 1780 and proved Dec 1781, named daughters **Sarah Murden**, **Olive Tooley**, grandson **Horatio Boush Butt**, son **Nathaniel Butt**, and his wife Mary; at her death, the 150 acres called Curlings was to go to daughter Prudence.[488]

---

[482] Wingo, *Marriages of Norfolk Co VA, Vol 1*, 10.
[483] Norfolk Co VA Deed Book 9:220-2. (See appendix).
[484] McIntosh, *Norfolk Co Wills 1710-1753*, 258-9 (Book I:154).
[485] McVey, *Norfolk Co VA Will Book 2*, 3.
[486] Butt, *Col James Wilson*, 19.
[487] Norfolk Co VA Deed Books 26:50, 27:173. Transcriptions by James Curlin, http://ftp.rootsweb.com/pub/usgenweb/va/norfolk/deeds/deeds1.txt.
[488] Norfolk Co VA Will Book 2:142-3/175.

162. William² Wilson <See pg. 1> (1. ____ Wilson¹)
ISSUE:
+ 163. m   i.   **Willis Wilson**, born aft 5 Apr 1671, died 19 Nov 1701 <See pg. 62>.
+ 167. f   ii. **Mary Wilson**, born Oct 1675, died 11 Jan 1741/2 <See pg. 64>.
+ 190. f   iii. **Jane Wilson**, died before 2 May 1758 <See pg. 73>.

William² Wilson was born around 1646. He married **Jane** ____ who was born about 1655. It has been suggested that he married Jane Willis,[489] but no proof has been found for that surname. Jane's birth and death dates were taken from the tombstone inscription.[490] It has also been suggested that he married Jane Davis in 1698. This probably refers to another William Wilson in Elizabeth City County.[491]

The first patent found for William Wilson was dated 28 Mar 1672 for 300 acres in Lower Norfolk County, at the head of a branch of the Elizabeth River. Six headrights were listed.[492] He sold this to his brother James, confirmation of which was shown in a 1713 deed.[493] In 1691 and 1695 William acquired the land in Elizabeth City County called Ceeleys, located on the banks of the James River to the mouth of Saltford Creek.[494] He accumulated other land adjoining and nearby. By 1704 he owned 1024 acres of land.[495]

In Apr 1691 affirmation was given for the port for Elizabeth City County to be located on the west side of Hampton River on the land of Mr. William Wilson, several houses and warehouses already built.[496] In 1693 Major William Wilson of Elizabeth City County appointed his son Capt. Willis Wilson as his attorney in all matters.[497]

---

[489] Hutton, *Colonial Dames XVII Century*, 283.
[490] Stauffer, "The Old Farms ....", 5:825-6.
[491] Chapman, *Wills ... Elizabeth City*, 161, 107, 105 (1720 will of William Wilson).
[492] Nugent, *Cavaliers and Pioneers*, 2:125 (Patent Book 6:453).
[493] Norfolk Co VA Deed Book 9:254-6.
[494] Hening, *Statutes*, 3:59. Neal, *Elizabeth City Co VA, Deeds,..... 1702*, 42-3.
[495] Smith, *Quit Rents of Virginia, 1704*, 99.
[496] Hening, *Statutes*, 3:58-9. Chapman, *Wills ... Elizabeth City*, 165.
[497] Neal, *Elizabeth City Co VA, Deeds,..... 1702*, 42.

William Wilson served as a burgess representing Elizabeth City County from 1684-1695 and 1700-02.[498] He attended only the first session in 1692 because of his being appointed sheriff in that year.[499]

In the 1698 Elizabeth City County militia, Major William Wilson was the first officer listed,[500] and by 1699 he was named Lt. Col. and Commander in Chief of the militia.[501] As justice of the county court the same titles were given: 10 Nov 1698 court Major Wm. Wilson, 14 Nov 1699 court Col. Wm. Wilson.[502] In 1704/5 Col. William Wilson was one of the vestrymen signing a letter to Governor Nicholson regarding their minister.[503]

In 1699 William was named as one of the owners of the ship *Harrison* of London and in 1703-4, one of the owners of *William* of Virginia.[504] On 8 Jun 1699 William Wilson was appointed Naval officer and Receiver of the Virginia duties for the Lower District James River.[505] He served in these positions for over ten years and was also a "Member of the Committee to Try Pirates."[506]

On 5 May 1700 he wrote to **Gov. Nicholson** concerning a brigantine and French prisoners.[507] In a 1709 letter to **Edmund Jennings**, acting governor of Virginia, William[2] described the outfitting and piloting of a sloop "to the Rock .... to Corituck, there to wait for Captain Cook"; it also told of his problems with a crew of sailors who rudely demanded "Vitules" or they would pull the houses down.[508]

His health was failing by 24 Oct 1710 as shown in Gov. Spotswood's letter stating that Collo. Wilson had resigned from his appointment as Naval Officer of the Lower District of the James River. William[2] recommended that his son-in-law Mr. **Nicholas Curle** replace him.[509]

---

[498] Leonard, *General Assembly of Virginia*, 47-54, 60.
[499] Chapman, *Wills ... Elizabeth City*, 155.
[500] Bockstruck, *Virginia Colonial Soldiers*, 231.
[501] Chapman, *Wills ... Elizabeth City*, 155.
[502] Neal, *Elizabeth City Co VA, Deeds,..... 1702*, 276-7.
[503] Neal, *Elizabeth City Co VA, Deeds,..... 1721*, xiii.
[504] des Cognets, *English Duplicates*, 323, 307.
[505] Fleet, *VA Col Abs, King & Queen Co*, 2:231-2.
[506] Stauffer, "The Old Farms ....", 5:825.
[507] VA Colonial Records Project, Survey Report 07275.
[508] *Calendar of Virginia State Papers*, 1:136. This states that the letter bore a handsome private seal in wax.
[509] Brock, *Official Letters of Alexander Spotswood*, 1:29-33.

William[2] Wilson died testate 20 Aug 1713. His will is not extant, but later actions by his heirs, confirm their relationships and the property inherited.[510]

"The Wilson family arms was carved on the stone which covered the graves of Colonel William, his wife Jane, and their son Captain Willis, in St. John's churchyard in Hampton, Virginia. The stone was destroyed by Federal troops during the Civil War but the blazoning and inscription were fortunately recorded earlier.

Confirmation of the Wilson arms ..... was ..... found in the Virginia State Library by **Mrs. William B. Wingo** in the form of a wax seal affixed to a 1709 document signed by Colonel William Wilson."[511]

"ARMS OF WILSON

[As described in Burke, *General Armoury.* "Sa. on a cross engr. between four cherubim or, a human heart of the first, wounded on the left side ppr. and crowned with a crown of thorns, vert."]

UNDER THIS STONE LYES THE BODY OF CAPT. WILLIS WILSON, WHO DEPARTED THIS LIFE THE 19TH DAY OF NOVEMBER, IN THE YEAR 1701: IT BEING THE 28TH YEAR OF HIS AGE. THE MEMORY OF THE JUST IS BLESSED. PROV. 10. MAY HIS MEMORY BE RECORDED IN EVERLASTING REMEMBRANCE.

UNDER THIS ALSO LYES THE BODIES OF COLONEL WILLIAM WILSON & OF JANE, HIS WIFE, PARENTS OF THIS BEFORE-MENTIONED CAPT. WILSON. THE SAID COLONEL WILSON DIED JUNE 17, 1713, AGED ABOUT 67 YEARS, & HIS SAID WIFE, MAY 5, 1713, AGED ABOUT 58 YEARS, & LEFT AN ONLY DAUGHTER SURVIVING."[512]

The inscription has been misinterpreted to mean that William had only one daughter, but it applies to the one daughter of Willis. It is not known when the stone was placed nor by whom.

- - - - - - - - - -

---

[510] Chapman, *Wills ... Elizabeth City*, 105. Elizabeth City Co VA Deeds, Wills & Orders, 1723-1730, Pt. 1, pp. 15-20 (follow p. 192 & include years 1741). Neal, *Elizabeth City Co VA, Deeds,......1721*, 27, 85-91.
[511] Butt, *Col James Wilson*, 6-7. Probably the letter above, *Calendar of Virginia State Papers*, 1:136.
[512] Harrison, *The Virginia Carys*, 102.

Wilson Families

163. Willis³ Wilson <See pg. 59> (162.William², 1. ____ Wilson¹) was born about 1673. He married **Jane Lane** about 1695. She was the daughter of **John Lane** and **Mary** ____.[513]

ISSUE:

164. f   i. **Jane Wilson**, born about 1700. Jane⁴ was named an heir to her uncle **Henry Fielding**[514] in his 1704 will, in which he named his mother-in law Madam **Mary Lane**, his sister-in-law and her husband Col. **Gawin Corbin** and Madam **Jane Corbin**, and his niece "Jane Wilson, daughter of Madam Jane Corbin." Evidently his wife, Mary Lane, had died, so he left the residue to his daughter **Frances Fielding** "unless she dies before 21" in which case some would go to his step-children, **John** and **Mary Howell**, children from Mary's first marriage.[515] Jane⁴ married **James Roscow (See number 169)** in 1717. **William Byrd** II wrote to **John Custis** 30 Mar 1717, "As for news, James Roscoe has marryd the great fortune Jenny Willson with the comfort £3500 ... Her mother died of measles .. the girl came to her aunt, Roscoes mother; Roscoe persuades the girl to choose him her guardian; and then immediately marries her. Poor **Tom Lee** will bee disappointed who was engaged to her."[516] Jane⁴ had chosen James Roscow as her guardian 18 Mar 1716/7.[517]

In Apr 1692, though Willis³ Wilson was named as a burgess from Elizabeth City County; it was determined that since he was under age 21, he was "uncapable" of serving,[518] but he was a burgess in the 1693, 1696-7, 1698, and 1699 sessions.[519] On 24 Aug 1694 Willis³ Wilson was a witness to the will of **George Bradley**.[520]

Around 1695 he married Jane Lane, daughter of John Lane of Laneville plantation in King and Queen County.[521] In 1695 Maj. William Wilson of Elizabeth City County appointed his son Capt. Willis Wilson as his attorney

---

[513] Harris, *Old New Kent Co .... Planters*, 342.
[514] Harris, *Old New Kent Co .... Planters*, 303-4.
[515] VA Colonial Records Project, Survey Report 04361.
[516] Tinling, *Correspondence of Three Wm Byrds*, 1:297-8.
[517] *Wm & M Qrtrly*, 26(1)286.
[518] McIlwaine, *Journals .... Burgesses 1660-93*, 382. McIlwaine, *Legislative Journals*, 1:159.
[519] Leonard, *General Assembly of Virginia*, 52, 56-9.
[520] McIntosh, *Norfolk Co Wills 1637-1710*, 156-7 (Book 5:247).
[521] Harris, *Old New Kent Co .... Planters*, 303, 342.

in all matters.⁵²² The 1698 Elizabeth City County militia listed Capt. Willis Wilson, 36 men.⁵²³ On 25 Feb 1699 Willis³ Wilson was listed in the quorum of justices for King and Queen County with **William Leigh**, who also held the position of colonel and commander in chief of the county militia.⁵²⁴

On 8 Mar 1697/8, the new owners of the ship *William* registered at James City were **William Byrd** Esq, Captain Willis Wilson, and Mr. **Thomas Ward** of Barbados.⁵²⁵ The list of ships entering the lower district of James River from 25 Dec 1699 to 6 Jun 1701 included the *Jane & Margaret* of London, Captain Willis Wilson, **Roger Jones**, **Benja: Harrison**, owners; the *William* of Virginia, and the *Prize of Harwich*, Capt. Willis Wilson, Mr. **William Roscow**, owners.⁵²⁶

Willis³ was listed as an owner of the *Harrison* of London in the collector's certification from 29 Sep to 25 Dec 1701, but Mme. Jane Wilson and Tho: Ward were owners of the *William* in the Mar 25-Jul 16, 1702 list.⁵²⁷ A letter written 2 Dec 1701 from the Royal African Company of London to Mr. **Edward Hill**, the company's factor, mentioned Mr. Willis Wilson of York River. In a 16 Dec 1701 letter to Mr. Henry Fielding, York River, Virginia, who had been appointed the Company's agent, the Company had sent the *Lusitania* to Angola for 360 Negroes (consigned to Mr. Willis Willson, deceased), whom Fielding was instructed to sell for the Company.⁵²⁸

Willis³ died 19 Nov 1701.⁵²⁹ The errors in the appraisal of the estate of Mr. Williss Wilson were excepted by Jane Wilson, one of his executors, on 6 Nov 1703.⁵³⁰

A 21 Oct 1719 bill of complaint at the Public Record Office in London, claimed that Willis Wilson left a legacy to **Lucy Halbert**, possibly an illegitimate child of his. His executors Jane Wilson, Coll. Wm Wilson, Col. **Wlllliam Leigh**, **James Wallace** and **Samuel Wilson** of Virginia empowered **Micajah Perry**, **Richard Perry** and **Thomas Lane** of London

---

⁵²² Neal, *Elizabeth City Co VA, Deeds,......1702*, 42.
⁵²³ Bockstruck, *Virginia Colonial Soldiers*, 231.
⁵²⁴ *VA Mag Hist*, 1:234. Fleet, *VA Col Abs, King & Queen Co*, 2:231.
⁵²⁵ Lawrence-Dow, *Autographs*, 126.
⁵²⁶ des Cognets, *English Duplicates*, 284, 290.
⁵²⁷ des Cognets, *English Duplicates*, 295.
⁵²⁸ VA Colonial Records Project, Survey Reports. 05753, 05759.
⁵²⁹ Stauffer, "The Old Farms ....", 5:825.
⁵³⁰ Fleet, *VA Col Abs, Essex Co*, 2:103.

to pay the legacy when Lucy reached the age of 21.⁵³¹ This document erroneously dated the will of Willis Wilson 1706. William Leigh was a burgess from King & Queen County 1691-1704. Willis Wilson was burgess from Elizabeth City County in some of those years.⁵³² James Wallace may be the Rev. James Wallace, minister of Elizabeth City Parish.⁵³³ Samuel Wilson may have been the cousin of Willis.

An 8 Jul 1702 account of the arms and ammunition in King and Queen County listed Mrs Jane Wilson - 12 lb of powder, 7 swords and belts, 2 guns, 2 cases of pistols and holsters.⁵³⁴ By 26 Oct 1704 Jane married (2) **Gawin Corbin**,⁵³⁵ who was burgess from Middlesex County from 1698-1705 and other sessions.⁵³⁶

Jane died before 18 Mar 1716/7, when her daughter chose a guardian.⁵³⁷

- - - - - - - - - - -

167. Mary³ Wilson <See pg. 59> (162.William², 1. ____ Wilson¹) was born Oct 1675.⁵³⁸ She married (1) **William Roscow** 1695.⁵³⁹ He was born 30 Nov 1664 in Chorley, Lancashire, England.⁵⁴⁰
ISSUE:
168. m i. **Willis Roscow**, died in infancy.⁵⁴¹
169. m ii. **James Roscow**. He married **Jane Wilson (See number 164)** 1717.⁵⁴² On 26 Mar 1716 James⁴ Roscow was named receiver general (treasurer) of Virginia in place of **William**

---

⁵³¹ VA Colonial Records Project, Survey Reports Nos. 10627-9. London Public Record Office C 11/767/68. Transcription done by Simon Neal, records agent, e-mail sn014i4785@blueyonder.co.uk.
⁵³² Leonard, *General Assembly of Virginia*, 50-62.
⁵³³ "Old Kecoughtan", *Wm & M Qrtrly* 9(1)130. des Cognets, *English Duplicates*, 250.
⁵³⁴ Fleet, *VA Col Abs, King & Queen Co*, 2:235.
⁵³⁵ VA Colonial Records Project, Survey Report No. 04361, will of Henry Fielding. Harris, *Old New Kent Co .... Planters*, 303, 337.
⁵³⁶ Leonard, *General Assembly of Virginia*, 58-62, 68-.
⁵³⁷ Tinling, *Correspondence of Three Wm Byrds*, 1:297. *Wm & M Qrtrly*, 26(1)286.
⁵³⁸ *VA Mag Hist*, 7:285-6.
⁵³⁹ Brock, *Official Letters of Alexander Spotswood*, 1:30.
⁵⁴⁰ *VA Mag Hist*, 7:285-6.
⁵⁴¹ Brock, *Official Letters of Alexander Spotswood*, 1:31.
⁵⁴² Tinling, *Correspondence of Three Wm Byrds*, 1:297.

Byrd.[543] In a letter written 2 Oct 1716 by William Byrd II from London to **John Custis**, he calls it a great surprise and seems to have mixed feelings about not being chosen for the office.[544] On 30 Apr 1719 in Chancery Court in Virginia, a case concerning land in Virginia, **Gawin Corbin** vs. James Roscow and Jane his wife, was found in favor of Roscow.[545] James[4] was named burgess from Warwick County in the 1720 session, but he died before the opening of the 1722 session.[546] On 17 Jan 1721/2 **John Grymes** was appointed receiver general in succession to James Roscow, and on 26 Feb 1722/3 William Roscow, as brother and executor to will of James Roscow esq., late receiver-general of Virginia, submitted a petition regarding money for quit rents received by his brother's deputy.[547]

+ 170. m iii. **William Roscow**, born about 1695, died 1752 <See pg. 68>.
 174. m iv. **Wilson Roscow**. He married **Euphan Wallace**. She was born 1695. She was the daughter of **James Wallace** and **Anne Sheppard**.[548] Wilson Roscow died 2 Feb 1713/4 with a will dated 26 Aug 1713.[549] Euphan Roscow was a witness to the 19 Mar 1713/4 will of **Sarah Curle**.[550] Euphan married (2) **William Dandridge** before 17 Aug 1715.[551] On 19 Sep 1717 William Dandridge and the others of Elizabeth City County put up one thousand pounds as bond regarding the following estates: "Whereas Coll. William Wilson Died Possest of a Considerable Estate, sufficient to Sattisfie and pay his Debts and Legacies and Wilson Roscow late of the said County was one of his Executors and did possess himselfe the greatest part of that Estate and Died alsoe Possest of a Considerable Estate Sufficient to Satisfie and pay his Debts and Legacies to which Wilson Roscow, Euphan his widdow was executrix, the above bound William Dandridge Did Intermarrie and thereby become possest thereof, ...", the obligation to

---

[543] VA Colonial Records Project, Survey Report 04296.
[544] Tinling, *Correspondence of Three Wm Byrds*, 1:292-3.
[545] VA Colonial Records Project, Survey Report 03922.
[546] Leonard, *General Assembly of Virginia*, 70-1.
[547] VA Colonial Records Project, Survey Report, 04299, 05095.
[548] beth@TidewaterTapestry.com (Kennedy, *Seldens of Virginia*, 2:13-15).
[549] Chapman, *Wills ... Elizabeth City*, 78, 109.
[550] Chapman, *Wills ... Elizabeth City*, 29.
[551] beth@TidewaterTapestry.com (Elizabeth City County VA Chancery suit). Cary, "The Dandridges of Virginia", *Genealogies, Wm & M Qrtrly*, 2:118.

remain in full force until the debts and legacies were paid and delivered.[552] Wilson Roscow's will described a legacy for his cousin/godson **Pasco Curle**, who died under age. In Aug 1745 **Merritt Sweny** received funds from William Dandridge for payment of Pasco's schooling in London and other debts.[553] Euphan died 22 Apr 1717.[554]

Mary[3] Wilson was described as an especially attractive young lady.[555] In 1687 **Sarah Harrison** made a vow to marry William Roscow, though she ended up marrying Mr. **James Blair**, perhaps because William had married Mary Wilson.[556]

William Roscow was a burgess from Warwick County in 1693 and in 1696, when he had to resign because of his appointment as county sheriff. He again was burgess in 1699.[557] William died 2 Nov 1700 at Blunt Point, Warwick County, Virginia.[558]

Before the marriage of Mary and Miles Cary, Capt. **James Moodie** caused quite a commotion in demanding the hand of Mary, though he had a wife and children in London.[559]

Mary married (2) **Miles Cary** 13 Apr 1702.[560] He was born 27 Oct 1655.[561] He was the son of **Miles Cary** and **Anne Taylor**.[562]

ISSUE:

+ 175. m vi. **Wilson Cary**, born 1702, died 28 Nov 1772 <See pg. 68>.
+ 181. f vii. **Mary Cary**, born 1704, died before 25 Mar 1775 <See pg. 71>.

---

[552] Elizabeth City Co VA Deeds, Wills, Inventories and Orders 1715-1721, pt. 1, p. 106 (Reel 3, LVA).
[553] Chapman, *Wills ... Elizabeth City*, 28, 109.
[554] Cary, "The Dandridges of Virginia", *Genealogies, Wm & M Qrtrly*, 2:118.
[555] Stauffer, "The Old Farms ....", 5:828-9.
[556] Stanard, "Harrison", *Genealogies, VA Mag Hist*, 3:692.
[557] Leonard, *General Assembly of Virginia*, 53-55, 59.
[558] *VA Mag Hist*, 7:285-6 - epitaph.
[559] Stauffer, "The Old Farms ....", 5:828.
[560] Chapman, *Wills ... Elizabeth City*, 161. Elizabeth City Co VA Deeds, Wills, Inventories, Orders & Settlements 1684-1699, 218, 413.
[561] Stauffer, "The Old Farms ....", 5:829.
[562] Harrison, *The Virginia Carys*, 34-56, 100-1.

185. f viii. **Anne Cary**, born 1706. She married **Peter Whiting** about 1724.[563]

186. m ix. **Miles Cary**, born 1708, died 8 Sep 1756.[564] His will, dated 11 Oct 1752, estate appraised 2 Nov 1756, named sister Mary Selden, nephews Cary, Samuel and Miles Selden, brother Wilson Cary, nieces Mary, Elizabeth and nephew Wilson Miles Cary, nieces Sarah Fairfax and Ann Nicholas, brother (half-brother) William Roscow, deceased, and his sons James and Wilson Roscow.[565]

Miles Cary was a burgess from Warwick County in 1682, 1684, 1688-1692, etc.[566] He held numerous other public offices.[567] Miles Cary had married (1) **Mary Milner** and was buried by her at Rich Neck in Warwick County. The headstone of Col. Miles Cary reads: Mary Cary ... wife of Miles Cary, daughter of **Thomas Milner** and **Mary**, born 6 Aug 1667, died 27 Oct 1700, issueless, Col'o Miles Cary, husband of the said Mary, died Feb 17, 1708 and "left 2 sons Wilson & Miles & 2 Daughters Mary & Ann by Mary the Daughter of Col'o W'm Wilson of Hampton."[568]

Mary married (3) **Archibald Blair** about 1720. He was born in Scotland. Archibald Blair was the burgess from James Town or James City County for sessions from 1718 until his death in 1734.[569] He had children from prior marriages.[570]

+ 187. m v. **John Blair**, born 1687, died 1771 <See pg. 72>.

Mary was buried at Blunt Point in Warwick County, Virginia, with her first husband. Their tombstone records: William Roscow Gentleman born at Chorley, county of Lancashire (England) 30 Nov 1661, died at Blunt Point Warwick County (Virginia) 10 Nov 1700, Mary wife of William Roscow

---

[563] Harrison, *The Virginia Carys*, 103. Meyer and Dorman, *Adventurers of Purse and Person*, 605-6, 672.

[564] Harrison, *The Virginia Carys*, 103-4.

[565] Cary, "Wilson Cary", *Genealogies, VA Mag Hist*, 1:696 has the correct names for his half brother William Roscow, deceased, and nephews Wilson Roscow and James Roscow. Chapman, *Wills ... Elizabeth City*, 21-2 mistakenly names "father" Wilson Cary and adds the surname Cary to the Roscows.

[566] Leonard, *General Assembly of Virginia*, 45-7, 49-51, -64.

[567] Stauffer, "The Old Farms ....", 5:829-830. Harrison, *The Virginia Carys*, 100-.

[568] *Wm & M Qrtrly*, 14(1)167.

[569] Leonard, *General Assembly of Virginia*, 69-74.

[570] Stauffer, "The Old Farms ....", 5:829.

and daughter of Col. Wm. Wilson of Elizabeth City County, born Oct 1675, died 11 Jan 1741/2.[571]

----

170. **William**[4] **Roscow** <See pg. 65> (167.Mary[3], 162.William[2], 1. ____ Wilson[1]) was born about 1695. He married **Lucy Bassett**.[572] She was born 24 May 1699. She was the daughter of **William Bassett, III** and **Joanna Burwell**.[573]

ISSUE:[574]

171. m i. **James Roscow**.
172. m ii. **Wilson Roscow**.
173. f iii. **Mary Roscow**. She married **William Cole**. He was born about 1692. He was the son of **William Cole** and **Martha Lear**.[575] William died 1729. Mary died 1752.[576]

John Allen, who married Lucy's sister **Elizabeth**, in his 1741 will, gave a gold watch to Mary[5] Roscow, daughter of Col. William[4] Roscow.[577]

William was a burgess from Warwick County from 1723 to 1740, except for a time in 1732 when he served as sheriff.[578]

William died before 11 Oct 1752.[579] Lucy died after 4 Sep 1755.[580]

----

175. **Wilson**[4] **Cary** <See pg. 66> (167.Mary[3], 162.William[2], 1. ____ Wilson[1]) was born about 1702. He married (2) **Sarah Pate** before 20 Jan 1728/9. She was born about 1710. Sarah died Sep 1783.[581]

---

[571] *VA Mag Hist*, 7:286.

[572] *VA Mag Hist*, 7:286. Torrence, *Winston of Virginia*, 330, 350.

[573] *VA Mag Hist*, 7:286. Meyer and Dorman, *Adventurers of Purse and Person*, 145, 604.

[574] Cary, "Wilson Cary", *Genealogies, VA Mag Hist*, 1:695-6.

[575] Torrence, *Winston of Virginia*, 317-8.

[576] Hopkins, "Selected Wills from the Burned Record Counties", 31:353-4.

[577] *Genealogies, Wm & M Qrtrly*, 1:59 ("Allen Family of Surry County").

[578] Leonard, *General Assembly of Virginia*, 72-77.

[579] Cary, "Wilson Cary", *Genealogies, VA Mag Hist*, 1:696.

[580] Hiden, *Genealogies, Wm & M Qrtrly*, 1:406.

[581] Cary, "Wilson Cary", *Genealogies, VA Mag Hist*, 1:691-3. Stauffer, "The Old Farms ....", 5:831-2.

ISSUE:[582]

176. f i. **Sarah "Sally" Cary**, born 1730. She married **George William Fairfax** 12 Dec 1748. He was born 1724. He was the son of **William Fairfax**. George died 1787 in Bath, England. Sarah died there 1811.
+ 177. f ii. **Mary Cary**, born 1732, died 1781 <See pg. 69>.
+ 178. m iii. **Wilson Miles Cary**, born 1734, died 1817 <See pg. 70>.
+ 179. f iv. **Anne Cary**, born 1735, died 1786 <See pg. 70>.
+ 180. f v. **Elizabeth Cary**, born 1738, died 1778 <See pg. 71>.

Wilson married (1) **Mary** ____. He married Sarah (probably) Pate before 20 Jan 1728/9.[583] In his will, dated 10 Oct 1772 and proved 25 Feb 1778, he named his wife Sarah, granddaughters Sarah Cary and Mary Munro Cary, son Wilson Miles Cary and his wife Sarah, daughters Sarah, Mary, Anne, and Elizabeth, wife of Bryan Fairfax and their son William Fairfax. He also named his nephew Col. Cary Selden, sister (Mary) Selden, sister Anne Whiting and son-in-law Robert Carter Nicholas. He mentions the husbands of his daughters, but the only name specified was Bryan Fairfax.[584]

Col. Wilson Cary died 28 Nov 1772 at Ceelys, Virginia.[585]

- - - - - - - - - - -

177. **Mary⁵ Cary** <See pg. 69> (175.Wilson⁴, 167.Mary³, 162.William², 1. ____ Wilson¹) was born 1732. She married **Edward Ambler** 1754. He was born 1732. He was the son of **Richard Ambler** and **Elizabeth Jaquelin**.[586]

ISSUE:[587]
m i. **Edward Ambler**, born 1758, died 1775.
f ii. **Sarah Ambler**, born 1760, died 1782.
m iii. **John Ambler**, born 1762, died 1836.

Edward died 30 Oct 1768. Mary died 1781.

- - - - - - - - - - -

---

[582] Stauffer, "The Old Farms ....", 5:832. Harrison, *The Virginia Carys*, 106-7. Cary, "Wilson Cary", *Genealogies, VA Mag Hist*, 1:693-4.
[583] Cary, "Wilson Cary", *Genealogies, VA Mag Hist*, 1:692.
[584] Chapman, *Wills ... Elizabeth City*, 22. Cary, "Wilson Cary", *Genealogies, VA Mag Hist*, 1:696-700.
[585] Meyer and Dorman, *Adventurers of Purse and Person*, 605. Headley, *18th-Century Newspapers*, 59.
[586] Pecquet du Bellet, *Some Prominent Virginia Families*, 23.
[587] Cary, "Wilson Cary", *Genealogies, VA Mag Hist*, 1:693 - all dates for family.

178. Wilson Miles⁵ Cary <See pg. 69> (175.Wilson⁴, 167.Mary³, 162.William², 1. ____ Wilson¹) was born 1734. He married (1) **Sarah Blair (See number 189)** 1759. She was born 1739. She was the daughter of **John Blair** and **Mary Monro**.⁵⁸⁸

ISSUE:⁵⁸⁹

- m   i. **Wilson Cary**, born 1760, died 1793.
- f   ii. **Sally Cary**, born 1762, died 1779.
- f   iii. **Mary Monro Cary**, born 1764, died 1836.
- m   iv. **Miles Cary**, born about 1766.
- f   v. **Elizabeth Blair Cary**, born about 1770.

Sarah died 28 Feb 1799 at Ceelys.⁵⁹⁰

Wilson married (2) **Rebecca Dawson**. She was born 1755. She was the daughter of **Thomas Dawson** and **Priscilla Bassett**. Rebecca died 1823.⁵⁹¹ Col. Wilson Miles Cary, formerly a resident of Hampton, died 1817.⁵⁹²

- - - - - - - - - - -

179. Anne⁵ Cary <See pg. 69> (175.Wilson⁴, 167.Mary³, 162.William², 1. ____ Wilson¹) was born 1735. She married **Robert Carter Nicholas** 1751. He was born 1728.

ISSUE:⁵⁹³

- f   i. **Sarah Nicholas**, born 1752.
- f   ii. **Elizabeth Nicholas**, born 1753, died 1810.
- m   iii. **George Nicholas**, born 1754, died 1799.
- m   iv. **John Nicholas**, born about 1756, died 1819.
- m   v. **Wilson Cary Nicholas**, born 1761, died 1820.
- f   vi. **Judith Nicholas**, born 1765.
- m   vii. **Lewis Nicholas**.
- m   viii. **Robert Nicholas**, born 1768.
- f   ix. **Mary Nicholas**, born about 1772.
- m   x. **Philip Norborne Nicholas**, born 1775, died 1849.

Robert died 1780. Anne died 1786.

- - - - - - - - - - -

---

⁵⁸⁸ "Blair", *Genealogies, Wm & M Qrtrly*, 1:361-2.
⁵⁸⁹ Harrison, *The Virginia Carys*, 109-111.
⁵⁹⁰ Headley, *18ᵗʰ-Century Newspapers*, 59. Henley, *Marriage/Obituary Index*.
⁵⁹¹ Harrison, *The Virginia Carys*, 110.
⁵⁹² Henley, *Marriage/Obituary Index*.
⁵⁹³ Cary, "Wilson Cary", *Genealogies, VA Mag Hist*, 1:693 - has all names and dates for this family.

Wilson Families

180. Elizabeth⁵ Cary <See pg. 69> (175.Wilson⁴, 167.Mary³, 162.William², 1. ____ Wilson¹) was born 1738. She married **8th Lord Bryan Fairfax** 1759. He was born 1736. He was the son of **William Fairfax**.⁵⁹⁴

ISSUE:⁵⁹⁵
- f   i.   **Sally Fairfax**, born 1760, died before 1779.
- m ii. **9th Lord Thomas Fairfax**, born 1762, died 1846.
- m iii. **William Fairfax**, born 1765, died about 1782.
- m iv. **Ferdinando Fairfax**, born 1766, died 1820.
- m v.   **Robert Fairfax**, died after 1787.
- m vi. **Henry Fairfax**.
- f   vii. **Elizabeth Fairfax**, born about 1770.

Bryan died 1802. Elizabeth died 1778.

- - - - - - - - - - -

181. Mary⁴ Cary <See pg. 66> (167.Mary³, 162.William², 1. ____ Wilson¹) was born 1704. She married **Joseph Selden** about 1720. He was the son of **Samuel Selden** and **Rebecca Yeo**.⁵⁹⁶

ISSUE:
- + 182. m   i.   **Cary Selden**, born about 1723 <See pg. 71>.
- + 183. m ii. **Samuel Selden**, born about 1725 <See pg. 72>.
- + 184. m iii. **Miles Selden**, born about 1726, died 1785 <See pg. 72>.

Joseph's will, filed 21 Jun 1727, named his wife Mary, sons Samuel, Miles, and Cary, his mother Rebecca, his brother John Selden, and his brothers-in-law Wilson Cary and Miles Cary.⁵⁹⁷

Mary's will, dated 5 Oct 1773 and proved 25 Mar 1775, named sons Cary, Samuel and Miles.⁵⁹⁸

- - - - - - - - - - -

182. Cary⁵ Selden <See pg. 71> (181.Mary⁴, 167.Mary³, 162.William², 1. ____ Wilson¹) was born about 1723. He married **Elizabeth Jennings**.

ISSUE:⁵⁹⁹
- m   i.   **Joseph Selden**.
- f   ii. **Mary Selden**.

---

⁵⁹⁴ Meade, *Old Churches*, 2:281-3.
⁵⁹⁵ Cary, "Wilson Cary", *Genealogies, VA Mag Hist*, 1:693-4 - names and dates.
⁵⁹⁶ Kennedy, *Seldens of Virginia*, 1:19, 56-7.
⁵⁹⁷ Chapman, *Wills ... Elizabeth City*, 81.
⁵⁹⁸ Chapman, *Wills ... Elizabeth City*, 82 - the date 1723 is obviously an error. Meyer and Dorman, *Adventurers of Purse and Person*, 605.
⁵⁹⁹ Kennedy, *Seldens of Virginia*, 1:57-61, 74-80 - names and dates for this family.

- f   iii. **Elizabeth Selden**, born 1761, died 28 Jun 1815.
- m iv. **Wilson Cary Selden**, born 1761, died 14 Mar 1835.
- f   v. **Rebecca Selden**.
- f   vi. **Ann Selden**.
- m vii. **Miles Selden**.
- f   viii. **Sarah Selden**.

- - - - - - - - - - -

183. Samuel^5 Selden <See pg. 71> (181.Mary^4, 167.Mary^3, 162.William^2, 1. ____ Wilson^1) was born about 1725. He married **Mary Mason**.

ISSUE:^{600}

- m i. **Cary Selden**, died 1822.
- f   ii. **Mary Mason Selden**, born 1754, died 17 Sep 1787.

- - - - - - - - - - -

184. Miles^5 Selden <See pg. 71> (181.Mary^4, 167.Mary^3, 162.William^2, 1. ____ Wilson^1) was born about 1726. He married **Rebecca Cary** about 1747. She was born 1728. She was the daughter of **Miles Cary** and **Hannah Armistead**.

ISSUE:^{601}

- m i. **Joseph Selden**, died 1 Jan 1807.
- f   ii. **Mary Selden**.
- m iii. **Miles Cary Selden**, died before 2 Apr 1833.
- f   iv. **Hannah Selden**, born 7 Feb 1762, died 18 Sep 1813.
- f   v. **Rebecca Selden**, died before 1833.
- m vi. **Nathaniel Selden**, died before 1833.
- f   vii. **Elizabeth Selden**, died 9 Dec 1825.

Miles died 1785.

- - - - - - - - - - -

187. John^4 Blair <See pg. 67> (stepchild of 167.Mary^3, 162.William^2, 1. ____ Wilson^1) was born 1687. He was the son of **Archibald Blair**.cf He married **Mary Monro**. She was born 1708. Mary died about 1768. John died 1771.^{602}

ISSUE:

---

^{600} Kennedy, *Seldens of Virginia*, 1:57, 110-113. Cary, "Wilson Cary", *Genealogies, VA Mag Hist*, 1:694.

^{601} Kennedy, *Seldens of Virginia*, 1:57, 122-143.

^{602} "Blair", *Genealogies, Wm & M Qrtrly*, 1:361-2. Cary, "Wilson Cary", *Genealogies, VA Mag Hist*, 1:695.

189. f ii. **Sarah Blair**, born 1739. She married **Wilson Miles Cary** (**See number 178**) 1759. Sarah died 1799.[603]

- - - - - - - - - - -

190. **Jane³ Wilson** <See pg. 59> (162.William², 1. ____ Wilson¹). She married (1) **Nicholas Curle** about 1705. He was the son of **Pasco Curle** and **Sarah ____**.[604]

ISSUE:

191. f i. **Jane Curle**. She married **George Walker** after 5 Feb 1733/4, when she was named Jane Curle as a witness to **Susanna Alkin**'s will.[605] He was born about 1698. He was the son of **George Walker** and **Ann Keith**. George died 1773.[606]

+ 192. m ii. **Wilson Curle**, born 18 Dec 1709, died before 4 Jun 1748 <See pg. 76>.

201. m iii. **Pasco Curle**. Wilson Roscow died 2 Feb 1713/4 without issue and left a legacy to his cousin/godson, Pasco Curle.[607] Wilson Roscow's widow **Euphan Wallace** married (2) **William Dandridge**. Pasco⁴ died before 16 Feb 1731/2.[608] On 21 Aug 1745 Merritt Sweeney received funds from Dandridge to pay for Pasco's debts and schooling in England out of Pasco's legacies from his cousin's and father's estates.[609]

202. f iv. **Mary Curle**, born after 12 Aug 1714. Her father's will named an unborn child. She married (1) **Alexander Hamilton** before 5 Feb 1733/4, when she was named Mary Hamilton, witness to **Susanna Alkin**'s will.[610] Alexander died before 16 Jul 1646 when his will was probated. He left his wife Mary his whole estate.[611] Mary married (2) **John Nash**. John died 1776. Mary died before Dec 1775.[612]

---

[603] Harrison, *The Virginia Carys*, 109.

[604] Chapman, *Wills ... Elizabeth City*, 29 - 1713 will of Sarah ( ) Curle). "Elizabeth City County Families", *Genealogies, Wm & M Qrtrly*, 5:655-6.

[605] Chapman, *Wills ... Elizabeth City*, 1.

[606] Boddie, *Historical Southern Families*, 20:112, 114-5.

[607] Chapman, *Wills ... Elizabeth City*, 78, 109.

[608] beth@TidewaterTapestry.com (Elizabeth City Co VA Order Book 1731-1747, 19).

[609] Chapman, *Wills ... Elizabeth City*, 28.

[610] Chapman, *Wills ... Elizabeth City*, 1.

[611] Chapman, *Wills ... Elizabeth City*, 37.

[612] beth@TidewaterTapestry.com (e-mail, Prince Edward Co VA records).

Nicholas married (1) **Elizabeth Gutherick** 14 Jun 1700 in Elizabeth City County, Virginia. She was the daughter of **Quintillian Gutherick** and **Anne Sheppard**.[613]

Jane³ married Nicholas Curle around 1705. He was a burgess from Elizabeth City County in 1705 and 1710 through 1713.[614] Sarah Curle, in her 1714 will, named her son Nicholas Curle executor.[615]

The will of Nicholas Curle of Elizabeth City County, Gent., dated 12 Aug 1714 and proved 15 Sep 1714, named his wife Jane, son Pasco Curle, daughter Jane Curle, an unborn child, and son Wilson Curle under age, mentioning land given to Wilson by his grandfather Col. William Wilson.[616]

Jane married (2) **James Ricketts** before 21 Sep 1715, the date of a lawsuit against the Curle estate.[617]

ISSUE:

203. f   v.   **Elizabeth Ricketts**. She married ____ **Cullington**.[618]

James was a burgess from Elizabeth City County from 1720-1723.[619] James Ricketts and his wife Jane Ricketts, late Jane Curle, were ordered to make an inventory of Nicholas Curle's estate 21 Mar 1715/6.[620] James died before 24 Mar 1724/5, the date of the appraisal of his estate.[621]

Jane married (3) **Merritt Sweny** before 5 Feb 1733/4, when she was named Mrs. Jane Sweny in **Susanna Alkin**'s will.[622]

ISSUE:

204. m   vi.   **Roscow Sweny**, died after 23 Aug 1765, when he was listed in a poll for the election of burgesses.[623]

---

[613] Chapman, *Wills ... Elizabeth City*, 161, 37, 83. "Ancestry of George Wythe, LL. D.", *Genealogies, Wm & M Qrtrly*, 5:612.
[614] Leonard, *General Assembly of Virginia*, 62-67.
[615] Elizabeth City Co VA Deeds, Wills, Inventories & Orders 1715-1721, 11-12.
[616] Will of Nicholas Curle, Accession 30881, LVA. Chapman, *Wills ... Elizabeth City*, 28.
[617] beth@TidewaterTapestry.com (Elizabeth City Co VA Deeds, Wills, Inventories & Orders 1715-1721, Orders: 9).
[618] Chapman, *Wills ... Elizabeth City*, 89 - will of Jane Sweny.
[619] Leonard, *General Assembly of Virginia*, 70-72.
[620] Elizabeth City Co VA Deeds, Wills, Inventories & Orders 1715-1721, 27-8.
[621] Chapman, *Wills ... Elizabeth City*, 74.
[622] Chapman, *Wills ... Elizabeth City*, 1.
[623] Chapman, *Wills ... Elizabeth City*, 146-7.

207. f vii. **Priscilla Sweny**, died before 2 Nov 1756, when administration of the estate of **Priscilla Kirkpatrick** was granted to Augustine Moore and others.[624]

209. f viii. **Ann Sweny**, married **Augustine Moore**. She died after 9 Feb 1801, the date of her will, as **Ann Moore**.[625]

217. f ix. **Sarah Sweny**, died before 3 Nov 1768, the date of her husband's will, in which **James Westwood** named wife **Elizabeth**.[626]

221. f x. **Martha Sweny**. Her will, dated 30 May 1757, named brother-in-law Augustine Moore, brother Roscow Sweny, late sister Priscilla Kirkpatrick, and brother-in-law **George Walker**, executor.[627]

222. f xi. **Mary Sweny**, married **John Parsons**. She died after 6 Apr 1787, the date of her husband's will.[628]

Merritt Sweny was a burgess from Elizabeth City County from 1732-1747.[629]

On 17 Jul 1745, the estate of James Ricketts dec'd, with amounts due Nicholas Curle's children, was in account with Major Merrit Sweny, and on 21 Aug 1745 he received part of Pasco Curle's estate from William Dandridge to pay the debts of the estate, including Pasco's schooling in England.[630]

In a lawsuit, *Armistead vs. Swiney and his wife ex'rs of N. Curle*, it was recorded that Jane, widow of Nicholas Curle of Elizabeth City County who died "being possessed of a considerable estate", married secondly James Ricketts who "wasted Curles Estate." She married third a Mr. Swiney. She had to pay the plaintiff, being responsible for Ricketts wasting Curles's estate by her "folly in Marrying such a Husband."[631]

The will of Merritt Sweny, dated 28 Dec 1751 and proved 3 Sep 1752, named his son Roscow, daughters Priscilla Kirkpatrick, Ann Moore, Sarah

---

[624] Chapman, *Wills ... Elizabeth City*, 50.
[625] beth@TidewaterTapestry.com (Elizabeth City Co VA Loose Wills 1701-1859, item 366).
[626] Chapman, *Wills ... Elizabeth City*, 101.
[627] Chapman, *Wills ... Elizabeth City*, 89.
[628] Chapman, *Wills ... Elizabeth City*, 67.
[629] Leonard, *General Assembly of Virginia*, 74-78.
[630] Chapman, *Wills ... Elizabeth City*, 28.
[631] Barton, *VA Colonial Decisions*, 1:R97-102.

Westwood, Martha and Mary, granddaughter **Sarah Sweny** and wife Jane. Equal payments from his estate were made 4 Dec 1764 to **Augustine Moore**, Martha Sweny, Roscow Sweny and **John Parsons**.

Jane's will, dated 31 Jul 1757 named son Roscow, granddaughter **Jane Sweny**, and daughter Elizabeth Cullington and her son-in-law **George Walker**, executor. He refused, and Augustine Moore qualified as executor.[632]

- - - - - - - - - - -

192. Wilson⁴ Curle <See pg. 73> (190.Jane³, 162.William², 1. ____ Wilson¹) was born 18 Dec 1709.[633] He married **Priscilla Meade**. She was the daughter of **Andrew Meade** and **Mary Latham**.[634]

ISSUE:

 193. m i. **Wilson Curle**. He may have been a witness to his mother's 6 Oct 1784 will.[635]
+ 194. m ii. **David Wilson Curle**, died about 1767 <See pg. 77>.
 195. m iii. **Nicholas Wilson Curle**. He married **Mary** ____. Nicholas died about 1771.[636]
 196. m iv. **Andrew Curle**. He married **Ann** ____. Andrew died after 27 Mar 1762.[637]
 197. m v. **Hamilton Curle**, died before 2 Jan 1760.[638]
+ 198. m vi. **William Roscow Wilson Curle**, born after 1729, died before 30 Mar 1782 <See pg. 77>.
 199. f vii. **Jane Curle**.
+ 200. f viii. **Mary Latham Curle**, died after 23 Aug 1799 <See pg. 78>.

The will of Wilson Curle, dated 15 Dec 1746 and proved 7 Jun 1748, named his wife Priscilla, sons Wilson, David, Hamilton, Nicholas, Andrew, William Roscow Curle and daughters Jane and Mary Curle.[639]

---

[632] Chapman, *Wills ... Elizabeth City*, 89.
[633] Elizabeth City Co VA Deeds, Wills & Orders, 1723-1730, Pt. 1:15-20 (follows p. 192 and includes year 1741). *Wm & M Qrtrly*, 26(1)286.
[634] Meade, *Old Churches*, 1:291-2.
[635] Chapman, *Wills ... Elizabeth City*, 21.
[636] beth@TidewaterTapestry.com, (Elizabeth City Co VA Wills 1701-1859, item 152).
[637] beth@TidewaterTapestry.com, (Elizabeth City Co VA Wills 1701-1859, item 125).
[638] beth@TidewaterTapestry.com, (Elizabeth City Co VA Deeds & Wills, Vol E, 1758-1764, 143-4).
[639] Chapman, *Wills ... Elizabeth City*, 29.

Wilson Families

Priscilla married (2) **John Campbell**.[640] In her will, dated 6 Oct 1784 and proved 22 Dec 1785, she named her daughter Mary, wife of **William Armistead**.[641]

- - - - - - - - - - -

194. David Wilson^5 Curle <See pg. 76> (192.Wilson^4, 190.Jane^3, 162.William^2, 1. ____ Wilson^1). He married **Mary Armistead**. She was the daughter of **Robert Armistead** and **Ann Wallace**.[642]

ISSUE:[643]

 f i. **Priscilla Curle**.
 f ii. **Mary Curle**.

The appraisal of the estate of David Wilson Curle was ordered Jun 1767.[644]

Mary married (2) **Joseph Selden** after 1769. He was the son of **John Selden** and **Grace Boswell**.[645] Joseph died before 28 Mar 1776 in Elizabeth City County, Virginia.[646]

- - - - - - - - - - -

198. William Roscow Wilson^5 Curle <See pg. 76> (192.Wilson^4, 190.Jane^3, 162.William^2, 1. ____ Wilson^1) was born after 1729. He married (1) **Euphan Wallace**. She was the daughter of **James Wallace** and **Martha ____**.[647]

ISSUE:[648]

 m i. **Wilson Curle**.

William Roscow Wilson^5 Curle was stated as under age 21 in a lawsuit 2 Oct 1750.[649]

Euphan died before 7 Apr 1774.[650]

---

[640] beth@TidewaterTapestry.com (Elizabeth City Co VA Minutes 1760-9, 4).
[641] Chapman, *Wills ... Elizabeth City*, 21.
[642] Kennedy, *Seldens of Virginia*, 1:38.
[643] Chapman, *Wills ... Elizabeth City*, 82 (will of Mary Selden referring to marriage contract with Joseph Selden).
[644] Chapman, *Wills ... Elizabeth City*, 27.
[645] Kennedy, *Seldens of Virginia*, 1:33-4, 37.
[646] Kennedy, *Seldens of Virginia*, 1:38.
[647] "Elizabeth City County Families", *Genealogies, Wm & M Qrtrly*, 5:656, 660.
[648] "Elizabeth City County Families", *Genealogies, Wm & M Qrtrly*, 5:656.
[649] Elizabeth City Co Order Book 1747-1755:191.
[650] Headley, *18th-Century Newspapers*, 82.

William married (2) **Sarah Hancock** before 6 Sep 1776. She was the widow of **Walter Lyon**.[651]

William married (3) **Mary** (possibly) **Kello** 1773.[652]
ISSUE:[653]
   f ii. **Elizabeth Kello Curle**.

William died before 30 Mar 1782.[654]

- - - - - - - - - - -

200. Mary Latham[5] **Curle** <See pg. 76> (192.Wilson[4], 190.Jane[3], 162.William[2], 1. ____ Wilson[1]). She married (1) **Robert Wallace**. He was the son of **James Wallace** and **Martha** ____.
ISSUE:[655]
   m i. **James Wallace**.
   m ii. **Wilson Wallace**.

The will of Martha Wallace, dated 10 Dec 1768, named her son Robert deceased and Robert's sons James and Wilson. The will of James Wallace, dated 31 Dec 1775, named James and Wilson, sons of his deceased brother Robert.

Mary married (2) **William Armistead**.[656] The will of William, dated 23 Aug 1799 and proved 26 Sep 1799, named his children and mentioned his wife's dower. The original will has the phrase "after the death of my wife."[657]

---

[651] Headley, *18th-Century Newspapers*, 82.
[652] "Elizabeth City County Families", *Genealogies, Wm & M Qrtrly*, 5:656.
[653] "Elizabeth City County Families", *Genealogies, Wm & M Qrtrly*, 5:656.
[654] Headley, *18th-Century Newspapers*, 82.
[655] Chapman, *Wills ... Elizabeth City*, 98 - wills of James and Martha Wallace.
[656] "Armistead Family", *Genealogies, Wm & M Qrtrly*, 1:150, 163-4.
[657] Chapman, *Wills ... Elizabeth City*, 8. beth@TidewaterTapestry.com (William Armistead, the Elder will, Elizabeth City Co VA Deeds & Wills, Vol 34, 1787-1800, 486-7).

CHAPTER 2 - Mason Families

1. **Francis¹ Mason**. He married (1) **Mary** ____ before 16 Feb 1623/4.
   ISSUE:
   2. f   i. **Ann Mason**, born in England.
   3. m ii. **Francis Mason**, born before Jan 1624/5 in Virginia.

Francis¹ Mason was born between 1585-1595 in England. Although his age was stated to be 40 in the 1624/5 muster,¹ he gave depositions in 1638 and 1641 giving his age as 42 and 46 respectively.²

He immigrated to Virginia in 1613 on the *John and Francis*³ under the charters of the Virginia Company of London 1609-1615.⁴

In spite of the peace treaty the King of England had made with Powhatan in 1614, Powhatan's successor **Opechancanough** led the Indians in a massacre on 22 Mar 1622, killing one-fourth of the colonists.⁵ A list of the living and dead dated 16 Feb 1623/4, showed living in Elizabeth City, Francis Mason, Mary Mason, **Anna Gany, Anna Gany "fillia", William** and **Henry Gany, John Robinson** and **William Querke**.⁶

By Francis's first wife Mary, he had a daughter Ann² as shown in the headrights of his 1642 patent where he claimed himself, "Mary Mason his wife, Ann his daughter, **Alice Ganey, Margery Ganey**" and 20 others.⁷ Francis and Mary also had a son Francis². Mary and Ann² had died by the February 1624/5 muster where Francis¹ was listed in Elizabeth City with his wife Alice age 26 who had come to America on the *Margett and John* in 1622, and his son Francis² who was born in Virginia. Also listed were servants **William Querke, Thomas Worthall, William Stafford, Henrie Gany** and **John Robinson**.⁸ The word "servant" was used as the term

---

¹ Dorman, *Adventurers of Purse and Person*, 1:58.
² Walter, *Book "A" Lower Norfolk Co VA 1637-1646*, 6, 67.
³ Dorman, *Adventurers of Purse and Person*, 1:58.
⁴ Brown, *First Republic*, 613.
⁵ Rountree, *Pocahontas's People*, 60, 73-5, 304.
⁶ Hotten, *Original Lists*, 169, 184, 187, 188.
⁷ Norfolk Co VA Min Bk 1637-1646, 165. Walter, *Book "A" Lower Norfolk Co VA 1637-1646*, 99. Patent Book 1:816.
⁸ Dorman, *Adventurers of Purse and Person*, 1:58.

"employee" is today. Many paid back their passage by working a few years.[9]

Francis married (2) **Alice Ganey** before Feb 1624/5.[10]

ISSUE:
+ 4. m iii. **Lemuel Mason,** born about 1629, died before Jul 1702 <See pg. 83>.
+ 61. f iv. **Elizabeth Mason,** born about 1630, died before 15 Mar 1706/7 <See pg. 124>.

Francis's wife Alice Ganey was claimed as a headright in the 1642 patent, as was Margery Ganey. In her 1680 will **Margaret (Ganey) Cheesman** named her "cozens" (nephew and niece) Lemuel Mason and Elizabeth Thelaball and left bequests to their children.[11] Lemuel's daughter Alice[3] listed gifts given to her by her "Aunt Margarett Cheesman" in her claims from the estate of her deceased husband William Porten.[12]

The minutes of the 25 Nov 1624 General Court refer to Mrs. **Ann Geyny** and her problems with a **Captain Whittakers**. The captain sent **Thomas Morys** to ffrancis Mason's to let Mrs. Geny know that the Captain was at her house to receive tobacco. She wanted to delay payment until her husband came home. Perhaps Mr. Ganey was in England. At the 13 Oct 1626 court Mr. **William Gainye** and ffrances Mason were granted passes to go to England.[13]

A patent was issued in 1626 to Francis Mason for 50 acres in the Corporation of Charles Cittie on the south side of the James River.[14] The November 1635 patent for **Thomas Willoughby** for 300 acres in Elizabeth City County was located "between Francis Mason & his own land",[15] and in July 1636 **William Julian**'s Elizabeth City County land was described as "land upon the entrance to the Eliz. Riv. ..... W. upon a Cr. joyning to Francis Mason."[16] Mason Creek is at Willoughby Bay on today's Norfolk map.

---

[9] Dorman, *Adventurers of Purse and Person*, 1:xxiv.
[10] Dorman, *Adventurers of Purse and Person*, 1:58.
[11] Will of Margaret Cheesman, PROB 11/363 [92 Bath]. (See appendix). Dorman, *Adventurers of Purse and Person*, 1:570.
[12] Norfolk Co VA Deed Book 5, Pt 1:197a.
[13] McIlwaine, *Minutes of Colonial VA*, 31-2, 121.
[14] Hotten, *Original Lists*, 266-8.
[15] Nugent, *Cavaliers and Pioneers*, 1:34 (Patent Book 1:312).
[16] Nugent, *Cavaliers and Pioneers*, 1:48-9 (Patent Book 1:388).

New Norfolk County was formed from Elizabeth City County in 1636, and it in turn was divided into Lower Norfolk and Upper Norfolk in 1637.[17] Francis Mason was named as one of the commissioners at the first court: "At a court houlden in the Lower County of New Norfolke the 15th of Mae 1637, Present: Capt. **Adam Thorowgood**, esq., Capt. **John Sibsey**, ... Mr. ffrancis Mason, Mr. Wm Julian, ..." Frances served regularly from 15 May 1637 until 15 Aug 1648 with court being held at his house several times.[18]

At a Grand Assembly 6 Jan 1639/40 "men of experience and integrity" were chosen as tobacco viewers, inspecting each man's crop for the quantity allowed and the quality expected. Lt. Frans. Mason, **Henry Cattelyn**, and **Thomas Wright** were appointed for the Western Branch to the Elizabeth River area in Lower Norfolk County.[19] Francis was assigned the same position "for the Tellinge of plants" 4 Oct 1641.[20]

At court on 6 July 1640 "Leftent ffrancis Massone" was appointed churchwarden, and on 4 Jan 1640/1 Mr. ffrancis Masson and Mr. **Henry Seawell** were churchwardens.[21] The names of the vestrymen for Elizabeth River Parish 1 Aug 1648 included Mr. ffrancis Mason.[22]

On 5 Jul 1642 Lieut. Francis Mason presented to the court the names of people he had transported: himself, his first wife Mary, his daughter Ann Mason, Alice Ganey, Margerie Ganey, etc.,[23] for which he received a patent for 1250 acres beginning at "Hoggpen Point, near land of Capt. Thomas Willoughbye."[24] He patented 200 acres in Lower New Norfolk County on 29 Sep 1643,[25] for transporting four persons[26] and repatented this same tract 22 Mar 1645 which consisted of 150 acres in Linnhaven at a creek to the west of **John Holmes**'s house, adjacent **Giles Collins** and 50 acres "being 3

---

[17] Robinson, *Virginia Counties*, 62, 59.

[18] Walter, *Book "A" Lower Norfolk Co VA 1637-1646*, iii, 1, Walter, B*ook "B" Lower Norfolk Co VA 1646-1651/2*, 76 (f 82a).

[19] Robinson, "Acts of the General Assembly, Jan. 6, 1639-40", *Wm & M Qrtrly* 4(2)16-25.

[20] Walter, *Book "A" Lower Norfolk Co VA 1637-1646*, 84.

[21] Walter, *Book "A" Lower Norfolk Co VA 1637-1646*, 31, 48.

[22] Walter, B*ook "B" Lower Norfolk Co VA 1646-1651/2*, 76 (f 82).

[23] Walter, *Book "A" Lower Norfolk Co VA 1637-1646*, 99.

[24] Nugent, *Cavaliers and Pioneers*, 1:134 (Patent Book 1:816).

[25] Nugent, *Cavaliers and Pioneers*, 1:151 (Patent Book 1:945).

[26] Walter, *Book "A" Lower Norfolk Co VA 1637-1646*, 138.

smaller hammocks of land joined together upon Hogg Island in Little Creek in Linn haven."[27]

On 16 May 1643 Lieut: Francis Mason was given custody of cattle which belonged to Mr. **William Ganey** deceased. The accompanying 1642 document to "cosen ffrancis Mason" from "your loving cosen ... **Tho: Hart**" suggests a Hart kinship.[28]

The family evidently survived the 18 Apr 1644 Indian massacre led by **Opechancanough**, during which around 500 settlers were killed.[29]

At a quarter court held at James Citty 5 Mar 1646/7 Mr. ffrancis Mason was selected High Sheriff of Lower Norfolke County "to be admitted and sworne at theire next Court."[30] He had the unpleasant job of trying to obtain an account of the estate of the first husband of **Sarah (Offley) Thorowgood Gookin**, who felt that she did not need to account to anyone but her children and to them only when they came of age.[31]

Mr. Francis Mason was present as a justice at the county court held 15 Aug 1648,[32] witnessed a document 16 Aug 1648,[33] but he died by 7 Nov 1648 when "Alice Mason vid & relict of Mr. ffrancis Mason deceased" and her son Lemuel Mason made an agreement with Mr. **James Thelaball** about the division of land on Hogg Island and other items Thelaball was to receive, apparently the legacy of his wife, Elizabeth (Mason) Thelaball.[34] Administration of his estate was requested on 15 Nov 1648 and granted on 22 Nov 1648 to Alice Mason, widow and relict of Francis Mason, and their son Lemuel.[35]

---

[27] Nugent, *Cavaliers and Pioneers*, 1:166 (Patent Book 2:88).
[28] Walter, *Book "A" Lower Norfolk Co VA 1637-1646*, 133.
[29] Noël Hume, *The Virginia Adventure*, 393.
[30] Walter, B*ook "B" Lower Norfolk Co VA 1646-1651/2*, 37 (f. 37).
[31] Walter, B*ook "B" Lower Norfolk Co VA 1646-1651/2*, 47-8 (f 48-9), 50-2 (f 51a-52a).
[32] Walter, B*ook "B" Lower Norfolk Co VA 1646-1651/2*, 76 (f 82a).
[33] Walter, B*ook "B" Lower Norfolk Co VA 1646-1651/2*, 97 (f 102).
[34] Norfolk Co VA Wills & Deeds C:1 - recorded 15 Jan 1651/2..
[35] Walter, B*ook "B" Lower Norfolk Co VA 1646-1651/2*, 80 (f 90), 89-90 (f 96a-97).

Alice was named in the 17 Nov 1653 Norfolk County will of **Daniell Tanner**.[36] She may have lived as late as 15 Aug 1655.[37]

- - - - - - - - - - -

4. Lemuel² Mason <See pg. 80> (1.Francis¹) was born about 1629 in Virginia. He married **Ann Seawell** before 27 Feb 1649/50 in Virginia.[38] She was born about 1635. She was the daughter of **Henry Seawell** and **Alice** ____. **(See number 2 - pg. 154)**.

ISSUE:

+ 5. f   i.   **Frances Mason**, born about 1650, died after 15 Jul 1708 <See pg. 90>.

12. f   ii.   **Margaret Mason**, born about 1652. On 15 Sep 1673 Margaret³ Mason, her sister Frances, and their aunt **Elizabeth (Mason) Thelaball** were witnesses to the will of **Sarah Willoughby**. "Mrs. Francis Mason and Mrs. Margrett Mason" proved the will 17 Feb 1673/4.[39] After 1674 she evidently went to St. Mary Magdalen Parish, Bermondsey, Surrey, England to live with her godmother, her grandmother's sister, **Margaret (Ganey) Cheesman**. In her grand aunt's will which was proved 21 Jul 1680 she gave, "unto my Godaughter Margarett Mason who lives with me the sum of one hundred and fifty pounds of good and lawfull Money of England and all my household Goodes Lynnen and Apparell and the lease of my house and all the plate I had of **John Harrison**....." She appointed Margaret³ as one of her overseers and as executor in trust in the absence of the Executor, nephew Lemuel² Mason in Virginia, until he or his Assignes come to England to receive the estate.[40] Margaret³ was named in her father's 1695 will: "my daughter Margaret ....wife of Mr. ...... in England."[41] She evidently married **William Marsh** 24 Dec 1682 in St. Mary Magdalen Parish, Bermondsey, Surrey, England. William also married (2)

---

[36] McIntosh, *Norfolk Co Wills 1637-1710*, 11 (Book C:65).
[37] Norfolk Co VA Wills & Deeds C:169.
[38] Walter, B*ook "B" Lower Norfolk Co VA 1646-1651/2*, 130-1 (f 137a-138).
[39] McIntosh, *Norfolk Co Wills 1637-1710*, 41 (Book E:163).
[40] Will of Margaret Cheesman, PROB 11/363 [92 Bath]. (See appendix).
[41] Norfolk Co VA Deed Book 6:258. (See appendix).

Susannah Thomas 24 Jun 1697.⁴² Margaret³ was not named in her mother's 1705 will.⁴³

+ 13. m iii. **Thomas Mason**, born about 1654, died before 15 Jun 1711 <See pg. 97>.
+ 18. m iv. **Lemuel Mason**, born about 1657, died before 15 Jun 1711 <See pg. 101>.
+ 26. f v. **Alice Mason**, born about 1659, died after 10 Jun 1735 <See pg. 105>.
+ 34. f vi. **Elizabeth Mason**, born about 1662, died before 20 Aug 1697 <See pg. 110>.
+ 37. m vii. **George Mason**, born about 1666, died before 16 Mar 1710/11 <See pg. 111>.
+ 42. f viii. **Anne Mason**, born about 1668, died before 30 Nov 1703 <See pg. 115>.
+ 49. f ix. **Abigail Mason**, born about 1671, died before 16 Jul 1691 <See pg. 117>.
+ 52. f x. **Mary Mason**, born about 1675, died before 1 Aug 1735 <See pg. 119>.
+ 56. f xi. **Dinah Mason**, born about 1678, died before 23 Jan 1713/4 <See pg. 121>.

Lemuel² Mason was born about 1627 according to a deposition he gave in a Norfolk County, Virginia, court on 16 Jan 1653/4 that he was age 25 or thereabouts.⁴⁴ He was the son of Francis¹ and Alice (Ganey) Mason, shown when he and his mother were granted administration of the estate of Francis Mason on 22 Nov 1648.⁴⁵ On 7 Nov 1648 Alice and Lemuell Mason made an agreement with **James Thelaball**, the son-in-law of Francis¹ Mason, regarding the land on Hogg Island, "sawen planke", glass and lead for windows, and silver spoons, evidently Elizabeth² (Mason) Thelaball's share of her father's estate.⁴⁶

By 27 Feb 1649/50 Lemuell² Mason married Ann² Seawell: "Att an Orphants Court held 27 Feb 1649/50 ... concerning the Estate of Hen: Sewell dec'd ..... Mr. Lemuell Mason who hath intermarried with Ann the daughter of the sd Sewell ...."⁴⁷ At the 15 Dec 1650 court Mr. Lemuell Mason was given full power and authority to handle legal matters, debts and

---

⁴² beth@TidewaterTapestry.com (Marriage registration, St. Mary Magdalen Church, Bermondsey, England).
⁴³ Norfolk Co VA Deed Book 7:117-8.
⁴⁴ Norfolk Co VA Wills & Deeds C:72.
⁴⁵ Walter, B*ook "B" Lower Norfolk Co VA 1646-1651/2*, 89 (f 96a-97).
⁴⁶ Norfolk Co VA Wills & Deeds C:1 - recorded 15 Jan 1651/2..
⁴⁷ Walter, B*ook "B" Lower Norfolk Co VA 1646-1651/2*, 130-1 (f 137a-138).

demands of **Henery Sewell**, orphan of Henery Sewell deceased.[48] In a 6 Dec 1653 letter to Capt. **Thomas Willoughby**, Mr. Lemuell Mason and Mr. **John Holmes, William Scapes** acknowledged tobacco received for the account of Henery[2] Seawell whom he proposed to take as an apprentice. The letter was accepted in court 22 Mar 1653/4.[49] On 25 Dec 1653 Lemuell Mason, guardian of Henry Sewell Jr., was ordered to pay a debt from the Seawell estate.[50] As one of the justices "of peace & court" on 15 Jun 1662, Lemuell Mason testified that henry Sewell was son and heir to henery Sewell the elder deceased, that he had been put out as apprentice to Mr. William Scapes in Yarmouth England and had served his time.[51]

On 14 May 1649 Mr. Lemuell Mason was nominated and elected as vestryman of Elizabeth River parish,[52] and at the quarter court held at James Citty on 3 Apr 1655, he was selected high Sheriff for the County of Lower Norfolk for the coming year, to be sworn at next court.[53]

At a quarter court in James City 16 Mar 1649/50 Lemuel Mason took the oath of supremacy and allegiance, being named a commissioner of the court of Lower Norfolk.[54] He was named as a justice/commissioner in many courts until his death, among them: 1 Jun 1652 "Mr. Lemuell Mason .... Mr. **Thomas Goodrich**",[55] 15 Oct 1656 "Major Lemuell Mason",[56] 16 Jun 1662 "Leift Coll: Lemuell Mason", 15 Jun 1663 presiding justice "Leift Coll: Lemuell Mason", and 17 Nov 1663 "Coll. Lemuel Mason."[57] After the April 1691 "Act for dividing Lower Norfolk " county into Norfolk and Princess Anne counties, the first court for Norfolk County listed Colo. Lemuel Mason .... Mr. **James Wilson**.[58]

At the 15 Nov 1650 Lower Norfolk court Mr. Lemuell Mason was appointed collector of tythes for the Little Creek 66 tytheable persons, his salary to be 250 pounds of tobacco. On 30 Oct 1651 Captain Lemuell

---

[48] Walter, B*ook "B" Lower Norfolk Co VA 1646-1651/2*, 153 (f 161a).
[49] Norfolk Co VA Wills & Deeds C:79-79a, 82.
[50] Norfolk Co VA Wills & Deeds C: 66.
[51] Norfolk Co VA Wills & Deeds D:347a.
[52] James, *Lower Norfolk Antiquary*, 2:63.
[53] Norfolk Co VA Wills & Deeds C: 142.
[54] Walter, B*ook "B" Lower Norfolk Co VA 1646-1651/2*, 133 (f 140).
[55] Fleet, *VA Col Abs, Lower Norfolk Co*, 3:428 (W&D C:10)
[56] Norfolk Co VA Wills & Deeds D:1.
[57] James, *Lower Norfolk Antiquary*, 3:140, 4:33, 79.
[58] Hening, *Statutes*, 3:95. Norfolk Co VA Deed Book 5, pt. 2 Orders:225. Whichard, *History of Lower Tidewater VA*, 1:286-7.

Mason was appointed collector for the Little Creek from 79 tytheable psons at 65 lb p poll.[59] On 21 Dec 1652 Mr. Lemuell Mason was collector of tythes from Daniell Tanner's Creek to Capt. Willoughbyes - 45 tithables. In 1653 payments in lbs. tobacco from the county levies included: Mr. Lemuell Mason for a "Woolfe and a Levye last year.[60] In 1646 the General Assembly had passed an act giving a reward of 100 pounds of tobacco for killing a wolf, "which do haunt and frequent ... plantations."[61]

Lemuell Mason was selected to handle the affairs of many of the local deceased. He, James Thelaball and others returned the inventory of the estate of **Richard Wake** on 13 Dec 1648, and **George Horner** chose Lemuell Mason and **John Holmes** as overseers for his 20 Aug 1650 will.[62] In the 17 Nov 1653 will of **Daniell Tanner**, he left to Mr. Lemuell Mason his estate on the south side of the James River and debts due. To Mrs. Anne Mason he bequeathed 3,000 lbs. of tobacco "for her great paynes & care & love towards me", to Mrs. Alice Mason 600 pounds of tobacco and Mrs. Elizabeth^2 Thelaball 600 pounds of tobacco. He named Lemuell Mason executor of his will which was probated 25 Dec 1653.[63]

Thomas Wright, in his 1654/5 will, asked friends Mr. Lemuell Mason, Mr. **Richard Conquest** and others to be his executors and overseers, and in the July 1655 will of **Henry Woodhouse**, he named his wife Maria, and friends Mr. Lemuel Mason and **Thomas Allen** as executors.[64] In the will of **William Jermy**, dated 23 Apr 1666, he left a bequest to his godson Lemuell^3 Mason and named his true friend Coll. Mason as overseer.[65] (**Trustram Mason** also wrote his will in 1666, leaving bequests to his children **Elizabeth** and **Thomas**.[66] Although Trustram is cited in many Lower Norfolk documents, no relationship has been found between him and this Francis Mason line).

Thomas Willoughby, who served as a justice with Lemuel^2 Mason and was a neighbor, died in 1672.[67] His wife **Sarah** named Lemuel Mason as an

---

[59] Walter, B*ook "B" Lower Norfolk Co VA 1646-1651/2*, 150 (f 159), 182 (f 200).
[60] Fleet, *VA Col Abs, Lower Norfolk Co*, 3:440, 456-7 (W&D C:32, 62, 64).
[61] Hening, *Statutes*, 1:328.
[62] Walter, B*ook "B" Lower Norfolk Co VA 1646-1651/2*, 90 (f 97a), 151 (f 159a).
[63] Norfolk Co VA Wills & Deeds C:65. Fleet, *VA Col Abs, Lower Norfolk Co*, 3:458.
[64] McIntosh, *Norfolk Co Wills 1637-1710*, 15 (Book C:133), 17-8 (Book C:181).
[65] McIntosh, *Norfolk Co Wills 1637-1710*, 22-3 (Book E:4).
[66] McIntosh, *Norfolk Co Wills 1637-1710*, 56 (Book 4:34).
[67] Meyer and Dorman, *Adventurers of Purse and Person*, 690.

overseer in her 1673 will. Witnesses to her will were Elizabeth[2] Thelaball, Frances[3] and Margaret[3] Mason.[68] In Jan 1679 **Frances Fowler**, wife of **George** dec'd, appointed Coll. Lemuell Mason as executor, and in May 1679 he was a witness to the nuncupative will of **Mary Fenwick** taken at the "late dwelling house of George Fowler on Little Creek."[69]

Adam Thorowgood of Linhaven wrote his will the "last day of October 1679." He asked his "loving friends" Coll Lemuell Mason, Major **Anthony Lawson**, **Malachy Thruston** and Mr. **William Porten** to be guardians of his children, seeing to their education and stated that if his wife should die before their majority that his land be divided between the children.[70] Lemuel's daughter Dinah[3] Mason married Adam's son **Robert Thorowgood**. William Porten was the second husband of Lemuel's daughter Alice[3].

In **Narthaniel Branker**'s 1685 will, he appointed Lemuel[3] Mason Esqr as an overseer and left Coll. Lemuel[2] Mason "one Ring of five pounds price."[71]

John Gooscott of Elizabeth River parish, before going on a voyage to "antegoe", wrote his will, dated 15 Mar 1688/9, at the house of Coll. Lemuel Mason who was named executor. He bequeathed his plantation to his wife, but after her death it was to go to George[3] Mason, son of Coll. Lemuell Mason. If he did not return from the trip, he wanted his sloope "I am now in" to go to Coll. Lemuell[2] Mason and to Thomas[3] Mason his son. He requested that his man **Thomas** be set free and have a "Sute of Clothes now in my chest in Virginia."[72]

James Thelaball's 1691 will was proved 15 Sep 1693 by Coll. Lemuell[2] Mason and Mr. Thomas[3] Mason. James was the husband of Lemuel's sister Elizabeth[2] who was named executrix. The witnesses were Lemuel[3] Mason, Thomas[3] Mason, and Mary[3] Mason.[73]

Lemuel[2] Mason inherited land from his father and accumulated a great deal on his own. At the 16 Apr 1649 county court Lemuel Mason "hath made it appear upon oath that there is due unto him 400 acres of land" for 8

---

[68] McIntosh, *Norfolk Co Wills 1637-1710*, 41 (Book E:163).
[69] McIntosh, *Norfolk Co Wills 1637-1710*, 69-70 (Book 4:58-9).
[70] McIntosh, *Norfolk Co Wills 1637-1710*, 96-7 (Book 4:217).
[71] McIntosh, *Norfolk Co Wills 1637-1710*, 97-8 (Book 4:218).
[72] McIntosh, *Norfolk Co Wills 1637-1710*, 133 (Book 5:155).
[73] Norfolk Co VA Deed Book 5:208.

headrights.[74] Since no corresponding grant has been located, it may be assumed that he sold those headrights. On 15 Dec 1653 Lemuell Mason gent. was granted 250 acres which he assigned to **George Kemp**.[75] "Lemll Mayson" received a grant 18 Feb 1653 of 200 acres in Linhaven parish in Lower Norfolk County which he sold to **Thomas Bridge**.[76] A 4 Oct 1671 patent for **Charles Grundy**, 366 acres on the north side of Daniel Tanner's Creek, was described as adjacent to Col. Mason.[77] Col. Lemuel Mason and Mr. **George Fowler** received a patent 9 Oct 1675 for 670 acres called Matchepongo lying easterly from the North River for transporting 14 persons, two of whom were **Richard Kemp** and **William Tanner**.[78] On 24 Apr 1679 Col. Lemuell Mason repatented the 1250 acres which had been granted to his father Lt. Fra. Mason in 1642. It was described as beginning at Hogpen Point on the SW side of a creek dividing this and the land of Mr. Tho. Willoughby.[79] **George Ivy**'s 1684 patent was described as on the north side of Tanner's Creek adjoining Col. Lemuell Mason.[80] (Tanner's Creek is present day Lafayette River in Norfolk).[81] Col. Lem. Mason, Mr. **Thomas Jarvis**, and Mr. **Thomas Willoughby** transported 52 persons and on 23 Apr 1688 were granted a patent for 2600 acres at Corrotuck commonly called White's Island, bounded on the east with Corrotuck Bay between the inlets of Roanoke and Curretuck, bounded on the north with Cowinjock Bay.[82]

Lemuell Mason served with **Bartholomew Hoskins** as burgess from Lower Norfolk County in the session assembled 20 Nov 1654.[83] He represented Lower Norfolk also from 1656-1662, 1671-1673 prior to Bacon's Rebellion and afterwards from 1680-1686. He was burgess from Norfolk County in 1693.[84]

---

[74] Walter, B*ook "B" Lower Norfolk Co VA 1646-1651/2*, 106 (f 113).
[75] Fleet, *VA Col Abs, Lower Norfolk Co*, 3:460 (W&D C:68).
[76] Nugent, *Cavaliers and Pioneers*, 1:518 (Patent Book 5:382).
[77] Nugent, *Cavaliers and Pioneers*, 2:100 (Patent Book 6:380).
[78] Nugent, *Cavaliers and Pioneers*, 2:169 (Patent Book 6:584). This land was described in 1695 as in Princess Anne Co VA 2:402. The North River gave access to Currituck Sound in what became North Carolina. Wertenbaker, *Norfolk*, 114, 185.
[79] Nugent, *Cavaliers and Pioneers*, 2:195 (Patent Book 6:674).
[80] Nugent, *Cavaliers and Pioneers*, 2:283 (Patent Book 7:411)
[81] Wertenbaker, *Norfolk*, 291.
[82] Nugent, *Cavaliers and Pioneers*, 2:324 (Patent Book 7:655).
[83] Stanard, *Colonial VA Register*, 71. (Hening 1:386 and Leonard p. 32 have error, Lyonell Mason)
[84] Leonard, *General Assembly of Virginia*, 33-39, 46-48, 52-53.

On 15 Sep 1663 Major Lem. Mason was appointed to be on the committee "to examine the business of the king of Potomack."[85] In March of 1675/6 the Grand Assemblie at James Cittie in an act for safeguard and defence of the country against the Indians, because of the "murthers, rapines and ... other depredations ... done by the Indians", authorized military leaders; "coll. Lemuell Mason and major **ffrancis Sawyer**, or one of them in Lower Norfolke .... to impresse (men) ... and .... boates."[86] By 1 Oct 1676, Bacon's Rebellion was in full swing. The *Young Prince* sailed to the mouth of the Elizabeth River, and a boat was sent ashore "with a message from Sir **William Berkeley** to Colonel Mason of the Lower Norfolk militia" to assist Admiral **Robert Morris**. "It was not clear whether Colonel Mason could obey. His countrymen were divided in their loyalty." They resented the decay of the forts, the cost of the Assembly, "and they disapproved of selling arms to the Indians", blaming these "evils on the Berkeleyans." On Oct 3 Col. Mason "sailed out to the English ships ... with his officers and forty impressed militiamen." Morris sent militia landing parties "to raid rebel-held plantations of the Elizabeth City region"; they were often "beaten off by the Baconian guards. Morris was disgusted by what he called the cowardice of the Lower Norfolk militia" and responded by torturing "rebellious" soldiers.[87]

On 15 Apr 1671 Lemuel Mason made out a "Competent settling" to his wife Ann in case she happened to survive him. It included 100 acres which his father Francis Mason had purchased, household goods, and two slaves.[88]

In the 1698 militia the officers and troops from Norfolk County were Lt. Coll Lemll[2] Mason - 110 men, Capt. Lemll[3] Mason - a troop of 56, Capt. **Tho: Hodges** Junr - 66, Capt. **James Wilson** - 99, and Capt. **Tho: Willowby** - 55.[89] On 3 Jun 1699 Lemuel was appointed Lt. Col. and Commander in Chief of the militia of Norfolk County.[90] **John Allit** submitted a request to the Com'tie of Publick Claimes for £ 333 for "watching and Looking out to Sea from 3'd of Jun 1700 to last of January ...... by the ord's of Lt. Co'll Lemuel Mason."[91]

---

[85] Hening, *Statutes*, 2:205.
[86] Hening, *Statutes*, 2:326-330.
[87] Webb, *1676, The End of Independence*, 90-93.
[88] Norfolk Co VA Wills & Deeds E:89.
[89] Bockstruck, *Virginia Colonial Soldiers*, 231-2.
[90] McIlwaine, *Executive Journals - Colonial VA*, 1:443.
[91] Fleet, *VA Col Abs, King & Queen Co*, 2:273.

Mason Families

In an abstract of militia for Norfolk County between September 1701 and July 1702, an entry states, "Coll' and field officers dead since last return: Lt. Coll' Lanll Mason dead."[92]

The will of Lemuel[2] Mason was written 17 Jun 1695 and probated 15 Sep 1702.[93] He named his wife Ann executrix, sons Thomas[3] and Lemuell[3] overseers, son George[3], and daughters Frances[3], Alice[3], Elizabeth[3], Margaret[3], Anne[3], Mary[3] and Dinah[3].

Lemuel's wife Ann's will, which was dated 30 Oct 1705 and proved 15 Mar 1705/6, lists their children living at that time, sons Thomas, Lemuel and George, daughters Frances Sayer, Alice Boush, Mary Cock and Dinah Thorowgood.[94]

- - - - - - - - - - -

5. Frances[3] Mason <See pg. 83, 154> (4.Lemuel[2], 1.Francis[1]) was born about 1650. She married (1) **George Newton** before 28 Sep 1675.[95]

ISSUE:

+ 6. m   i.   **George Newton**, born 1678, died 20 Jun 1762 <See pg. 92>.
   7. f   ii.   **Ann Newton**, born about 1680. Ann[4] Newton was named 17 Aug 1703 as an orphan of George Newton dec'd and of age 21,[96] but she must have died before the 1708 suits where her brothers and sister were named.[97]
   8. f   iii.   **Elizabeth Newton**, born about 1682. Elizabeth[4] Newton was named 17 Aug 1703 as an orphan of Geo Newton dec'd and age 21.[98] She was named in the suit against her mother Frances[3] Sayer 24 Jul 1708.[99]
+ 9. m   iv.   **Nathaniel Newton**, born about 1684, died before 23 May 1737 <See pg. 94>.
+ 10. m   v.   **Lemuel Newton**, born before 1687, died before 17 Nov 1721 <See pg. 95>.
+ 11. m   vi.   **Thomas Newton**, born after 1687 <See pg. 96>.

---

[92] London, PRO, CO 5/1312, part 2, folios 277-278, no. 587 or 40 - transcription 11 Jan 2002 by Simon Neal, records agent, e-mail sn014i4785@blueyonder.co.uk\. (Bockstruck, *Virginia Colonial Soldiers*, 215, 223).
[93] Norfolk Co VA Deed Book 6:258. (See appendix).
[94] Norfolk Co VA Deed Book 7:117-8. (See appendix).
[95] McIntosh, *Norfolk Co Wills 1637-1710*, 57 (Book 4:35 - will of Sarah Porten).
[96] Norfolk Co VA Deed Book 6:284.
[97] Norfolk Co VA Deed Book 8:15-17.
[98] Norfolk Co VA Deed Book 6:284.
[99] Norfolk Co VA Deed Book 8:16a.

Mason Families

Frances³ Mason was named first daughter, Frances Newton, in her father's will in 1695[100] and first daughter Frances Sayer in her mother's will in 1705.[101]

In a 15 Aug 1671 deposition concerning the noncupative will of **James Craig** it was stated, "after all his debts were paid, all the Remaynder of his estate hee did give to Mrs. frances Mason",[102] and Frances³ Mason was witness to and proved the will of **Sarah Willoughby** 17 Feb 1673/4.[103]

She married George Newton before 28 Sep 1675 when the will of **Sarah Porten** was witnessed by George Newton and Frances Newton.[104] George Newton was born about 1637 according to his deposition 15 May 1691.[105] He appeared in the Lower Norfolk court in Dec 1670[106] and was a justice in the court 15 Aug 1677.[107]

George and Frances³ sold part of a mill and 200 acres to **John Ferebee** in 1680.[108] In 1684 George Newton and **Richard Church** patented 1000 acres on the Southern Branch of Elizabeth River.[109]

At James City 15 May 1691 as High Sheriff "of the Court of Lower Norfolk", George described the commotion that had occurred in the May 7 county court where Capt. Jennings disrupted the Court.[110] After the division of Lower Norfolk County into Norfolk and Princess Anne in June 1691, George Newton "promised to lett the County have a 15 foot square house ... for a prison."[111] In 1694 George purchased property in the newly established Norfolk Town.[112]

---

[100] Norfolk Co VA Deed Book 6:258-260. (See appendix).
[101] Norfolk Co VA Deed Book 7:117-8. (See appendix).
[102] Norfolk Co VA Wills & Deeds E:99.
[103] McIntosh, *Norfolk Co Wills 1637-1710*, 41 (Book E:163).
[104] McIntosh, *Norfolk Co Wills 1637-1710*, 57 (Book 4:35).
[105] McIlwaine, *Executive Journals - Colonial VA*, 1:181.
[106] Newton, "Newton Family of Norfolk", 4:538.
[107] Norfolk Co VA Deed Book 4:29.
[108] Norfolk Co VA Deed Book 4:89.
[109] VA Land Office Patents No. 7 1679-1689, p. 398, George Newton, 26 April 1684, Library of Virginia. (http://www.lva.lib.va.us/)
[110] McIwaine, *Executive Journals - Colonial VA*, 1:181-2.
[111] Cross, C*ounty Court... Norfolk*, 58 (Order Book Dec 1686-Sep 1695, 227).
[112] Whichard, *History of Lower Tidewater VA*, 1:356.

He died intestate by 15 Jan 1694/5 when his wife was granted administration of his estate and the appraisal was ordered.[113] The inventory of his estate was taken 4 Mar 1694/5 by **Richard Butt, Alexander Foreman, John Corprew,** and **James Wilson** and sworn "just and true ... to the best of her knowledge" by Mrs. Frances Newton 15 May 1695. A note in the document states there was an addition presented at court 18 May 1696.[114]

Frances married (2) Major **Francis Sayer** after 16 Jul 1696[115] and before 19 Nov 1696.[116] He died by 11 May 1708 when debts due to the estate of George Newton were recorded. Frances was named as administratrix to both estates.[117]

Frances^3 died after 15 Jul 1708 when her children, George^4 Newton, Elizabeth^4 Newton, Nathaniel^4 Newton, Lemuel^4 Newton, and Nathaniel^4 Newton, guardian of Thomas^4 Newton, requested their shares of their father's estate.[118]

- - - - - - - - - - -

6. George^4 Newton <See pg. 90> (5.Frances^3, 4.Lemuel^2, 1.Francis^1). He married **Affiah Wilson. (See number 121 - pg. 50).**
                              ISSUE:[119]
   f   i. **Elizabeth Newton**, born 22 Jul 1707.
   m ii. **George Newton**, born 26 Feb 1711/2, died 17 May 1719.
   m iii. **Thomas Newton**, born 14 Mar 1713/4, died 13 Dec 1794.
   m iv. **Lemuel Newton**, born 22 Jun 1715.
   m v. **Wilson Newton**, born 9 Apr 1718, died before 18 Nov 1762.
   f   vi. **Ann Newton**, born 17 Feb 1720/1, died Apr 1749.
   m vii. **George Newton**, born 4 Mar 1722/3.
   m viii. **William Newton**, born 7 Dec 1726.
   f   ix. **Frances Newton**, born 24 Feb 1728/9, died 5 Jan 1793.

George^4 Newton was born in 1678 according to his deposition 21 Jul 1738, which also described his schooling in England.[120] He was named 17 Aug

---

[113] Norfolk Co VA Deed Book 5, pt. 2 Orders:341-2.
[114] Norfolk Co VA Deed Book 5:244a.
[115] Norfolk Co VA Deed Book 6:41.
[116] Norfolk Co VA Deed Book 6:67.
[117] Norfolk Co VA Deed Book 8:4a-5.
[118] Norfolk Co VA Deed Book 8:15-17.
[119] Newton, "Newton Family of Norfolk", 4:542-3.
[120] Norfolk Co VA Deed Book 12:202.

1703 as an orphan of George Newton dec'd and as at least age 21.[121] The following was recorded in Norfolk County court 15 Jul 1708: "Capt. Geo Newton, son of Mr. George Newton dec'd vs. Mrs. Frances Sayer adm'x of Major Francis Sayer dec'd who married Frances the adm'x of Mr. George Newton dec'd."[122]

George[4] purchased lot 25 in Norfolk Town in 1701/2[123] and by 1704 owned 1119 acres in Norfolk County.[124] About 1706 he married Aphia[3] Wilson daughter of Col. James Wilson.[125]

The militia list for Norfolk County 4 Apr 1702 records George Newton, Lt. of Horse.[126] In his 1711 Norfolk County will, **George Mason** named his "loveing kinsmen Capt. George Newton, Mr. Lemuell Newton ... to be Overseers."[127]

George[4] was appointed deputy clerk in Norfolk County in July 1699. Captain George[4] Newton was a justice in the Norfolk County court by 1708 and served until 1738.[128] He served as burgess for Norfolk County for the 1710-1712 session along with **James Wilson** and in the 1712-1714 and 1723-1726 sessions with **William Crawford**.[129] He and **Samuel Boush** were feofees (trustees) for Norfolk Town 17 Nov 1721.[130] George[4] was high sheriff of Norfolk County in 1728[131] and 1729.[132]

When **William Byrd** wrote of his experiences regarding the process of determining the dividing line between Virginia and North Carolina, he made an entry for 1 Mar 1728 about the home of Colonel Newton: "Mrs. Newton provided a clean supper without any luxury about eight o'clock and appeared to be one of the fine ladies of the town and, like a true lady, to have a great deal of contempt for her husband."[133]

---

[121] Norfolk Co VA Deed Book 6:284.
[122] Norfolk Co VA Deed Book 8:15-6.
[123] Whichard, *History of Lower Tidewater VA*, 1:326.
[124] Smith, *Quit Rents of Virginia, 1704*, 65.
[125] Newton, "Newton Family of Norfolk", 4:539.
[126] Bockstruck, *Virginia Colonial Soldiers*, 218.
[127] McIntosh, *Norfolk Co Wills 1710-1753*, 9 (Book 9:12).
[128] Newton, "Newton Family of Norfolk", 4:540-1.
[129] Leonard, *General Assembly of Virginia*, 65, 67, 72.
[130] Norfolk Co VA Wills & Deeds F:6a.
[131] Newton, "Newton Family of Norfolk", 4:541 (*Council Journal*).
[132] des Cognets, *English Duplicates*, 44, 50.
[133] Wright, *Prose of William Byrd*, 51.

Samuel Boush and George Newton were named trustees in Norfolk Town in a 1728 deed for erecting a school house.for the inhabitants of the town. On 19 Nov 1731 Lieutenant Colonel George Newton was named as one of the "Gentleman Justices."[134]

When Norfolk borough was chartered 15 Sep 1736 Samuel Boush was appointed Mayor, and George[4] Newton was appointed as one of the aldermen. As related in the *Virginia Gazette* 26 Nov 1736, "The first Mayor dying soon after the Grant of the said Charter, he is succeeded by G. Newton, Gent."[135]

The will of George[4] Newton, written 30 May 1753 and proved July 1762, named his wife Aphia, sons Thomas, Wilson, William, daughters Frances wife of Paul Loyall, Elizabeth Benbow in England and grandson George Cook.[136]

George died 20 Jun 1762.[137]

- - - - - - - - - - -

9. Nathaniel[4] Newton <See pg. 90> (5.Frances[3], 4.Lemuel[2], 1.Francis[1]) was born about 1684.

ISSUE:

f   i. **Mary Newton.** She married **Thomas Mason (See number 38 - pg. 113).** Mary died after 3 Nov 1740, when she was named Mary Mason, widow, in a deed..[138]

At the Norfolk County court 24 Jul 1708 Mr. Nathaniel Newton was named as one of the sons of Mr. George Newton suing his mother Mrs. Frances[3] Sayer for his share of his deceased father's estate.[139] On 13 Dec 1716 Capt. Nathaniel[4] Newton sold to his brother Capt. George[4] Newton his part of the Norfolk Town land they both bought from **Peter Malbone** in 1712.[140]

---

[134] James, *Lower Norfolk Antiquary*, 1:78-81.
[135] Forrest, *Historical ... Norfolk*, 51,53. Tarter, *Order Book ... Borough of Norfolk*, 45 58.
[136] Norfolk Co VA Will Book 1: 86-9.
[137] Newton, "Newton Family of Norfolk", 4:539.
[138] Norfolk Co VA Wills & Deeds I:106-7.
[139] Norfolk Co VA Deed Book 8:16.
[140] Norfolk Co VA Deed Book 9:545-7.

Major Nathaniel[4] Newton was commissioned a justice of Norfolk County about 1726[141] and was listed also in 1729.[142] He served as sheriff 1730-31.[143]

On 15 Jun 1708 Nathan: Newton petitioned the court for an ordinary (tavern) license.[144] He got involved in a suit in 1716 based on a party at **Richard Josslin**'s tavern. **Samuel Rogers**, Nathaniel[4] Newton, and others were enjoying themselves and encouraged **William Finiken** to dance. The party developed into some mock fighting and Finiken evidently was injured. The men checked to see that he was all right and put him to bed. The next morning Finiken was dead.[145]

Nathaniel[4] was a witness to the 1711 Norfolk County will of George[3] Mason.[146]

In 1728 Nathaniel[4] Newton along with **Samuel Boush** and **Samuel Smith** became school trustees authorized to hire a teacher and build a school.[147]

Nathaniel[4] Newton died by 23 May 1737 when Thomas[4] Mason of Norfolk Gent and Mary[5] his wife, sole Daughter and Heire of Capt. Nathl Newton dec'd, sold **John Ellegood** of the Borough of Norfolk, Merchant, 200 acres in Norfolk County.[148]

- - - - - - - - - - -

10. Lemuel[4] Newton <See pg. 90> (5.Frances[3], 4.Lemuel[2], 1.Francis[1]). He married (1) **Anne Lawson** before 2 Aug 1714. She was born about 1694. She was the daughter of **Thomas Lawson** and **Rose Thorowgood**.[149]
ISSUE:[150]
m i. **Nathaniel Newton**, born about 1714. He married **Elizabeth Sayer**, shown in the 18 Aug 1740 will of her father, **Charles Sayer**, where he named his daughter Elizabeth Newton and

---

[141] Cross, *County Court... Norfolk*, 145.
[142] des Cognets, *English Duplicates*, 44, 50.
[143] Dorman, *Adventurers of Purse and Person*, 2:581.
[144] Norfolk Co VA Deed Book 8:13a.
[145] Wertenbaker, *Norfolk*, 19 (Norfolk Co VA Deed Book 9, pt. 2 Orders::162-3).
[146] McIntosh, *Norfolk Co Wills 1710-1753*, 9 (Book 9:12).
[147] Wertenbaker, *Norfolk*, 6 (Whichard, *History of Lower Tidewater VA*, 1:350).
[148] Norfolk Co VA Deed Book 12:226-8.
[149] Princess Anne Co VA Minute Book 2:161, 165. Meyer and Dorman, *Adventurers of Purse and Person*, 620.
[150] Dorman, *Adventurers of Purse and Person*, 2:582.

Mason Families

son-in-law Nathaniel Newton and their children **Anne** and **Lemuel**.[151] Nathaniel died before 21 Apr 1767.[152]

m ii. **Anthony Newton**.

Lemuel[4] Newton was born about 1687 shown by his suit at Norfolk County court 24 Jul 1708 as one of the sons of Mr. George Newton suing his mother Mrs. Frances[3] Sayer.[153] He was surveyor for Norfolk and Princess Anne Counties 13 May 1708.[154] In his 1711 Norfolk County will, George Mason named his "loveing kinsmen Capt. George Newton, Mr. Lemuell Newton ... to be Overseers."[155] Mr. Lemuel[4] Newton was a justice in the county court of Norfolk by 1717.[156]

Before 2 Aug 1714 Lemuel married "Mris. Ann daughter of Thomas Lawson dec'd Gent."[157]

Lemuel married (2) **Margaret Porten (See number 28)** shown when administration of his estate was granted to Mrs. Margaret Newton, relict of Lemuel Newton deceased on 17 Nov 1721.[158]

On 3 Aug 1724 George[4] and Nathaniel[4] Newton, guardians of the orphans of Lemuel[4] Newton, signed a receipt for items they received from **John Haire** "who intermarried with Mrs. Margaret Newton."[159]

- - - - - - - - - - -

11. Thomas[4] **Newton** <See pg. 90> (5.Frances[3], 4.Lemuel[2], 1.Francis[1]) was born after 1687. He married (1) **Frances Love** 27 May 1719 in St. Michael Parish, Barbados.[160]

ISSUE:[161]

f   i.   **Mary Newton**, born Dec 1725.

---

[151] Princess Anne Co VA Deed Book 5:514-5.
[152] Dorman, *Adventurers of Purse and Person*, 2:603.
[153] Norfolk Co VA Deed Book 8:16a.
[154] Norfolk Co VA Deed Book 8:30a.
[155] McIntosh, *Norfolk Co Wills 1710-1753*, 9 (Book 9:12).
[156] Cross, *County Court... Norfolk*, 145.
[157] Princess Anne Co VA Minute Book 2:161, 165.
[158] Norfolk Co VA Orders, Appraisements, Wills 1719-1722, pt. 1:38a.
[159] Norfolk Co VA Wills & Deeds F:146a.
[160] Sanders, *Barbados Marriages*, 1:128.
[161] Sanders, *Barbados Baptisms*, 86.

Mason Families

Thomas[4] Newton was named in the suit against his mother Frances[3] Sayer 24 Jul 1708, his brother Nathaniel[4] Newton named as his guardian.[162] In a 19 May 1715 deed, **Lewis** and **Elizabeth Conner** of Norfolk County sold Captain Thomas[4] Newton of Barbadoes, gent. half a lot in Norfolk Borough.[163]

Thomas married (2) **Elizabeth Sims** 30 Nov 1730 in St. Michael Parish, Barbados, where their children were born.[164]

ISSUE:[165]

- m ii. **William Newton**, born 18 Sep 1731.
- f iii. **Katherine Newton**, born 2 Jun 1733.
- m iv. **George Newton**, born 8 Mar 1735.
- m v.   **Thomas Newton**, born 9 Jan 1737.
- f vi. **Frances Sims Newton**, born 8 Jul 1741.

On 4 Aug 1742 **Ruth Summersall** and **Susannah Patton** of the "Island of Bermudos" gave power of attorney to Capt. Thomas[4] Newton of Norfolk County.[166]

- - - - - - - - - - -

13. Thomas[3] Mason <See pg. 84, 154> (4.Lemuel[2], 1.Francis[1]) was born about 1654. He married **Elizabeth** ____.

ISSUE:

- 14. m i. **Lemuel Mason**, died before 19 Feb 1713/4, when in the audit of his father's estate, expenses for his schooling and funeral were listed.[167] In 1744 "Capt. Thomas Willoughby and Ann his wife" sold Capt. James Ivy 125 acres in Elizabeth River Parish "formerly belonging to Thomas Mason Father of the said Ann and which descended unto the said Ann as one of the sisters and co-heirs of Leml Mason deceased."[168]
- + 15. f ii. **Anne Mason**, died before Jul 1758 <See pg. 100>.

---

[162] Norfolk Co VA Deed Book 8:17.
[163] Newton, "Newton Family of Norfolk", 4:539.
[164] Sanders, *Barbados Marriages*, 1:151.
[165] Sanders, *Barbados Baptisms*, 96, 100, 103, 105, 111.
[166] Walter, *Princess Anne Co VA Deed and Minute Books*, 14 (6DB140-2).
[167] Norfolk Co VA Deed Book 9:515.
[168] Norfolk Co VA Deed Book 13:116-8.

16. f iii. **Mary Mason** married **Capt. William Ellison** before 9 Feb 1722/3.[169] On 17 Feb 1727/8 William Ellison "of the City of New York" appointed his friend (Mary's cousin) George Newton of Virginia to be his attorney for the division of the plantation of Mr. Thomas³ Mason deceased.[170] In 1730 Capt. William Ellison, Mariner, sold Capt. Tho Willoughby, Gent his portion of the Norfolk Town lot bought by his father-in-law Thos Mason deceased, naming "my sisters" Ann⁴ and Margaret⁴ and signed by W. Ellison and Mary Ellison.[171]

17. f iv. **Margaret Mason**. On 17 May 1728 she signed with Thomas Willoughby and George Newton, attorney of William Ellison, an agreement dividing the plantation of Mr. Thomas Mason deceased[172] and on 14 Jul 1730 sold her third to Capt. Thomas Willoughby.[173]

Thomas³ Mason was named first son in his father's 17 Jun 1695 will[174] and in his mother's will which was written 30 Oct 1705.[175] He was given power of attorney by his parents 5 Sep 1699, witnessed by his brothers George and Lemuel Jr.[176]

Michael Laurence wrote his will 16 Mar 1678/9, appointing Col. Lemuel² Mason, **William Narne**, Thomas³ Mason and **William Langley** overseers.[177] In his will dated 15 Mar 1688/9 **John Gooscott** stated, "... my will is that the Sloope I now am In and bound to antegee In if I neavor Returne ... unto Coll. Lemuell Mason and to Thomas Mason his Sonn....."[178] Thomas³ was executor with **Walter, William, Thomas** and **Christopher Cocke** of the Princess Anne County 1697 will of **Thomas Cocke**, the husband of Thomas Mason's sister Elizabeth³.[179] In the 1697/8 will of **William Chichester** he selected as overseers "cozens" Thos. Mason and

---

[169] Dorman, *Adventurers of Purse and Person*, 2:572 (Norfolk Co Record Bk F:76a).
[170] Norfolk Co VA Deed Book 11:22.
[171] Norfolk Co VA Deed Book 11:125-7.
[172] Norfolk Co VA Deed Book 11:22.
[173] Norfolk Co VA Wills & Deeds G:194a-195.
[174] Norfolk Co VA Deed Book 6:258-260. (See appendix).
[175] Norfolk Co VA Deed Book 7:117-8. (See appendix).
[176] Maling, *Princess Anne Co VA Deed Books 1-7*, 15 (1DB229).
[177] McIntosh, *Norfolk Co Wills 1637-1710*, 68-9 (Book 4:58).
[178] McIntosh, *Norfolk Co Wills 1637-1710*, 133 (Book 5:155).
[179] Maling, *Princess Anne Co VA Deed Books 1-7*, 12 (1DB154).

Lemuel Mason Jr.[180] William had married Thomas's cousin **Mary Thelaball**. Thomas's nephew **John Kendall**, son of his sister Anne[3], chose him as his guardian in 1704.[181]

On 16 Jan 1693/4 Mr. Thomas[3] Mason was coroner of Norfolk County,[182] and he was a Norfolk County burgess in the 1696-7 General Assembly.[183] In the list of county officers for Norfolk County 8 Jun 1699, Thomas was listed as one of the quorum.[184]

In 1696 he owned lot 27 in Norfolk Town.[185] The quit rents for 1704 show Thomas Mason with 653 acres in Norfolk County, 125 acres in Norfolk County and 140 acres in Princess Anne County [186] (Some of this land may have belonged to **Thomas Mason** son of **Trustram**.[187] Although some given names are common to both families, no kinship between them has been found yet).

In his will which was written 9 Jan 1710/11 and proved 15 Jun 1711, he stated, "I Thomas Mason of Elizabeth River Parrish in the County of Norfolk Gentleman .... I Give and Bequeath unto my son Lemuel Mason all my land and plantation ... only my will and desire is that my well beloved wife Elizabeth Mason shall have the manor plantation that I now Live on dureing her nattural life .... fifty pounds in good Spannish money be .... paid... for Son Lemuell at the Gramer Scoole at Williams Brough .... unto my son Lemuel ... my silver ... sword and ... pare of pistolls .... to be delivered to him when he comes to the age of twenty one ... or when he goes to house keeping......unto my four children Leml, Ann, Mary, Margaret ... when they come of age or when they marry......" Thomas[3] named his wife Elizabeth executrix, and his brother Capt. George[3] Mason and "cosen" (his nephew, son of his sister Frances) George[4] Newton overseers.[188]

---

[180] McIntosh, *Norfolk Co Wills 1637-1710*, 167 (Book 6:125 - torn)
[181] Marshall, *Wills ... Northampton Co VA*, 154.
[182] Norfolk Co VA Deed Book 5, pt. 2 Orders:311.
[183] Leonard, *General Assembly of Virginia*, 56.
[184] des Cognets, *English Duplicates*, 8.
[185] Whichard, *History of Lower Tidewater VA*, 1:326.
[186] Smith, *Quit Rents of Virginia, 1704*, 59.
[187] McIntosh, *Norfolk Co Wills 1637-1710*, 56. McIntosh, *Norfolk Co Wills 1710-1753*, 124. Norfolk Co VA Deed Book 5, pt 1:78a-79.
[188] Norfolk Co VA Deed Book 9:60-1.

Elizabeth married (2) **Richard Sanderson** before 19 Feb 1713/4.[189] On 20 Jul 1716 the court ordered "Capt. Richard Sanderson and Elizabeth his wife exrx of ... Thomas Mason dec'd" to pay Thomas Willoughby "who intermarried with Anne Mason one of the daughters ... of Mr. Thos Mason." his proportional part of the estate "in right of his wife."[190]

- - - - - - - - - - -

15. **Anne**[4] **Mason** <See pg. 97> (13.Thomas[3], 4.Lemuel[2], 1.Francis[1]). She married **Thomas Willoughby, IV**, the son of **Thomas Willoughby, III** and **Margaret** ____.[191]

ISSUE:
- m i. **John Willoughby**, died after 1776.[192]
- m ii. **Lemuel Willoughby**, died before Jan 1764, when his will was proved.[193]
- m iii. **Thomas Willoughby, V**, died 1784.[194]
- m iv. **William Willoughby**.
- f   v. **Elizabeth Willoughby**.
- m vi. **Allerton Willoughby**.[195]

At court on 20 Jul 1716, Thomas Willoughby "who intermarried with Anne Mason one of the daughters .... of Mr. Thomas Mason" entered a petition for her legacy.[196] Anne and Thomas Willoughby were witnesses to the 14 Mar 1753 will of **Samuel Sweny**.[197]

Thomas Willoughby's will, written 5 Sep 1752 and proved Jun 1753, named his eldest son John[5], sons Lemuel[5], Thomas[5], William[5], daughter Elizabeth[5] and wife Ann, the two youngest children not yet of age.[198]

---

[189] Norfolk Co VA Deed Book 9:291.
[190] Norfolk Co VA Deed Book 9, pt. 2 Orders:160.
[191] Meyer and Dorman, *Adventurers of Purse and Person*, 692.
[192] beth@TidewaterTapestry.com (McVey, *Norfolk Co VA Will Book 2*, 51).
[193] Wingo, *Norfolk Co VA Will Book 1*, 73 (f 114).
[194] beth@TidewaterTapestry.com, (McVey, *Norfolk Co VA Will Book 2*, 165).
[195] McIntosh, *Norfolk Co Wills 1710-1753*, 233 (Book I:20 -will of Sarah Willoughby named cousin Alderton).
[196] Norfolk Co VA Deed Book 9, pt. 2 Orders:160.
[197] McIntosh, *Norfolk Co Wills 1710-1753*, 317 (Book I:327).
[198] McIntosh, *Norfolk Co Wills 1710-1753*, 317-8 (Book I:328).

Mason Families

Anne's will, dated 23 May 1758 and proved Jul 1758, named only sons John[5], Thomas[5], and daughter Elizabeth[5]. She left Thomas[5] only some curtains and "any loose feathers."[199]

- - - - - - - - - - -

18. Lemuel[3] Mason <See pg. 84, 154> (4.Lemuel[2], 1.Francis[1]) was born about 1657 in Norfolk County, Virginia. He married **Mary Thelaball (See number 93).**

ISSUE:[200]

+ 19. f   i. **Tabitha Mason**, born about 1699, died after 23 Jul 1736 <See pg. 103>.
+ 20. f   ii. **Elizabeth Mason**, born 25 Apr 1701, died 10 Nov 1764 <See pg. 104>.

Mary married (1) **William Chichester** about 1678. William died before 17 May 1698, the date his will was proved.

ISSUE:[201]

21. m iii. **William Chichester**, born about 1679, died before 15 Feb 1711/2.
22. m iv. **James Chichester**, born about 1681, died before 15 Feb 1711/2.
23. m v. **John Chichester**, born about 1683.
24. m vi. **Thomas Chichester**, born about 1685.
+ 25. f vii. **Mary Chichester**, born about 1688, died before 28 Apr 1758 <See pg. 104>.

The will of William Chichester, dated 23 Mar 1697/8 and proved 17 May 1698, named wife Mary and sons William, James and John, then "my two Cozens Thomas Mason & Lemll Mason Junr Overseers." The witnesses were "Limuel Mason Junr and ffrancis Thelaball."[202]

Lemuel[3] was named in the 1680 will of his grand aunt **Margaret (Ganey) Cheesman** who left "to Lemuell Mason the younger my best greate Ring."[203] He was the second son named in his father's 1695 will[204] and was an executor with his two brothers of his mother's 1705 will.[205]

---

[199] Wingo, *Norfolk Co VA Will Book 1*, 17 (f 28)
[200] Norfolk Co VA Deed Book 9:366 - distribution of estate of Lemuel Mason.
[201] Norfolk Co VA Deed Book 9:154 - distribution of estate of William Chichester.
[202] McIntosh, *Norfolk Co Wills 1637-1710*, 167 (Book 6:125 - torn).
[203] Will of Margaret Cheesman, PROB 11/363 [92 Bath].
[204] Norfolk Co VA Deed Book 6:258. (See appendix).
[205] Norfolk Co VA Deed Book 7:117-8. (See appendix).

Mason Families

In his 1666 will **William Jermy** named "Lemuell Mason my God sonne",[206] and Lemuel[3] may have been a witness in 1678/9 to the will of **Michaell Laurence**.[207] **Narthaniel Branker**'s 1685 will listed Lemuel Mason Esqr as an overseer.[208] In 1686 a neighbor **Thomas Willoughby** for love and affection deeded 200 acres to "loveing friend Lemuel Mason Jr."[209] He was given a gold ring, in the 1688/9 will of **John Gooscott**.[210]

The 1695 patent for **Robert Vaughan** in Princess Anne County was described as on the East side of the North River adjoining Col. Mason's land at Matchepongo and Lemuel Mason's land.[211] In the 1704 quit rents there were entries for Lemuel Mason, 400 acres in Norfolk County, and Coll Lemuel Mason, 650 acres in Princess Anne County, possibly land not yet settled from his estate.[212]

In 1698 the officers and troops from the Norfolk County militia were "Lt. Col. Lemuel Mason 110 men; Capt. Lemuel Mason a troop of 56 men .. "[213] In 1699 when his brother Thomas[3] was given power of attorney by their parents, Lemuel Mason Jr. was a witness.[214] He and his brother George[3] Mason were justices for Norfolk County in 1702.[215]

Lemuel[3] Mason married Mary[3] (Thelaball) Chichester after 1698 and before 28 Aug 1699.[216] The 1702 will of her mother Elizabeth[2] (Mason) Thelaball named her "daughter Mary Mason now wife of Lemuell Mason."[217]

On 19 Mar 1711/2 a distribution of William Chichester's estate was made to Mrs. Mary Mason widow, to Mr. Willis Wilson who married Mary the daughter of Mr. Wm. Chichester, to Thomas Chichester and to John Chichester.[218]

---

[206] McIntosh, *Norfolk Co Wills 1637-1710*, 22-3 (Book E:4).
[207] McIntosh, *Norfolk Co Wills 1637-1710*, 68-9 (Book 4:58).
[208] McIntosh, *Norfolk Co Wills 1637-1710*, 97-8 (Book 4:218).
[209] Norfolk Co VA Deed Book 5:26a.
[210] McIntosh, *Norfolk Co Wills 1637-1710*, 133 (Book 5:155).
[211] Nugent, *Cavaliers and Pioneers*, 2:402 (Patent Book 8:443).
[212] Smith, *Quit Rents of Virginia, 1704*, 59.
[213] Bockstruck, *Virginia Colonial Soldiers*, 231-2.
[214] Maling, *Princess Anne Co VA Deed Books 1-7*, 15 (1DB229).
[215] des Cognets, *English Duplicates*, 11, 16.
[216] Norfolk Co VA Deed Book 6:168-9.
[217] James, *Lower Norfolk Antiquary*, 3:144-5. (See appendix).
[218] Norfolk Co VA Deed Book 9:154.

Lemuel³ Mason died intestate before 15 Jun 1711 when Mary Mason was granted administration of the estate of her husband Lemuel Mason.²¹⁹ On 18 Jan 1711/2 an inventory and appraisal of his estate was ordered. The inventory was added to 22 Jan 1714/5 by Thomas Chichester.²²⁰

Mary Mason's will, dated 15 Apr 1714 and proved 19 Nov 1714, named her sons from her first marriage, Thomas and John Chichester. She gave her daughter Elizabeth⁴ Mason a seal skin trunk and asked that her clothes be divided between her three daughters, with only daughter Elizabeth named.²²¹ The 10 Feb 1714/5 audit of Lemuel³ Mason's estate named Willis Wilson, who married Mary Chichester, Thomas and John Chichester and showed distributions to Mrs. Mary Mason, her daughter Elizabeth⁴ and her daughter Tabitha⁴. The portion due Mr. George Newton, administrator of the estate of Mr. Lemuel Mason, from Thomas Chichester, administrator of Mrs. Mary Mason, administratrix of Mr. Lem¹¹ Mason was recorded 18 Feb 1714/5.²²²

- - - - - - - - - - -

19. Tabitha⁴ Mason <See pg. 101> (18.Lemuel³, 4.Lemuel², 1.Francis¹) was born about 1699. She married **Solomon Wilson. (See number 141 - pg. 54).**

ISSUE:²²³
- f   i.   **Ann Wilson**, died after 20 Aug 1771.
- f   ii. **Tabitha Wilson**, born after 1728, died after 22 Jan 1789.
- m iii. **Lemuel Wilson**, died after 20 Aug 1771.
- f   iv. **Mason Wilson**, born before 1737, died before 20 Oct 1794.
- f   v.   **Elizabeth Wilson**, died after 20 Aug 1771.

On 17 Jun 1720 it was recorded that Mr. Solomon Wilson was married to Tabitha⁴ Mason, who was one of the co-heirs of Lemuel Mason deceased.²²⁴ Tabitha Wilson was a witness to the 1724 marriage bond of **Abigail Mason** and **John Ellegood**.²²⁵

Solomon Wilson Jr. and his wife Tabitha sold on 23 Jul 1736 a lot in the town of Norfolk to John Ellegood. Tabitha was not named in a deed dated

---

²¹⁹ Norfolk Co VA Deed Book 9, pt. 2 Orders:11-12.
²²⁰ Norfolk Co VA Deed Book 9:150-3, 364.
²²¹ Norfolk Co VA Deed Book 9:355-6.
²²² Norfolk Co VA Deed Book 9:366.
²²³ Dorman, *Adventurers of Purse and Person*, 2:579, 592-3.
²²⁴ Norfolk Co VA Orders, Appraisements, Wills 1719-1722, pt. 1:21a.
²²⁵ Wingo, *Marriages of Norfolk Co VA, Vol 1*, 22.

11 Dec 1738[226] nor in the 20 Aug 1771 will of Solomon in which he named his daughters Ann (an executor), Tabitha, son Lemuel, daughters Mason and Elizabeth.[227]

- - - - - - - - - - -

20. Elizabeth[4] **Mason** <See pg. 101> (18.Lemuel[3], 4.Lemuel[2], 1.Francis[1]) was born 25 Apr 1701. She married **Christopher Todd**. He was born 2 Apr 1690.

ISSUE:[228]

- f   i.   **Lucy Todd**, born 20 Nov 1721, died 18 Feb 1791.
- f   ii.   **Elizabeth Todd**, born 28 Jan 1723/4, died 9 Dec 1788.
- m   iii.   **Thomas Todd**, born 26 Dec 1728, died 22 Jul 1780.
- f   iv.   **Mary Todd**, born 15 May 1732, died 5 Jan 1805.

Elizabeth[4] Mason on 17 Jun 1720 declared that she was of age and selected as her guardian her brother-in-law, Solomon Wilson.[229]

She married Christopher Todd by 3 Sep 1722 when Christopher Todd of Gloucester County gent. and Elizabeth "his wife one of the daughters & copercorners of Lemuel Mason late of the county of Norfolk merchant" sold to **Maximillian Boush** land "on the western shore of Linhaven river in the above said county of Princess Anne, late the estate of the said Mr. Lemuel Mason" and 99 acres in Princess Anne County described in the 22 Jan 1718 patent granted Elizabeth and Tabitha her sister.[230]

Christopher died 26 Mar 1743. Elizabeth died by 10 Nov 1764.

- - - - - - - - - - -

25. Mary[4] **Chichester** <See pg. 101, 145> (stepchild of 18.Lemuel[3], 4.Lemuel[2], 1.Francis[1]) was born about 1688. She was the daughter of **William Chichester** and **Mary Thelaball**. She married **Willis Wilson**. **(See number 104 - pg. 46).**

ISSUE:

- m   i.   **Lemuel Wilson**, born about 1713, died 1765.[231]

---

[226] Norfolk Co VA Deed Book 12:133, 207.

[227] Bertie Co NC Will Book B:19.

[228] Dorman, *Adventurers of Purse and Person*, 1:264-5, 271 - gives all names and dates.

[229] Norfolk Co VA Orders, Appraisements, Wills 1719-1722, pt. 1:21a.

[230] Princess Anne Co VA Wills & Deeds 3:459-460. Nugent, *Cavaliers and Pioneers*, 3:210 (Patent Book 10:415).

[231] Doris Wilson of Robersonville NC, citing Beaufort Co NC and NC Archives documents.

Mason Families

    m ii. **James Wilson**, died after 21 Mar 1766. He was named in his brother Thomas's will.
    m iii. **Robert Wilson**, died before 28 Apr 1758, the date of his father's will.
    m iv. **Thomas Wilson**, died before 19 Jun 1766, the date his will was proved.[232]
    f v. **Euphan Wilson**.

By 1712 Mary^4 Chichester married Willis Wilson, shown in the distribution of William Chichester's estate, to Mr. Willis Wilson who married Mary the daughter of Mr. William Chichester.[233]

In his will dated 28 Apr 1758 and proved Sep 1760, Willis named his sons Lemuel, James and Thomas and daughter **Euphan Alston**, wife of **Joseph John Alston**.[234]

- - - - - - - - - - -

26. Alice^3 Mason <See pg. 84, 154> (4.Lemuel^2, 1.Francis^1). She married (1) **Robert Hodge**.

                             ISSUE:
+ 27. f i. **Mary Hodge**, born after 10 Sep 1681, died before 17 Mar 1743/4 <See pg. 107>.

Alice^3 Mason was born about 1659. Her grand aunt, **Margaret (Ganey) Cheesman** in her will dated 15 Jan 1679/80 left Alice, daughter of "cozen" Lemuell Mason "a greate Beaker."[235] Alice^3 was named second daughter in the 1695 will of her father[236] and as daughter Alice Boush in her mother's 1705 will.[237]

She married about 1680 Robert Hodge, who in 1670 was of Modbury, Devonshire.[238] His lengthy will, dated 10 Sep 1681 and proved 18 Oct 1681, named his "ffeather-in-law Coll. Lemuel Mason." He left estate to kin in Modbury, to his wife Alice Hodge and to their unborn child.[239]

---

[232] Norfolk Co VA Will Book 1:145.
[233] Norfolk Co VA Deed Book 9:154.
[234] Norfolk Co VA Will Book 1:50a.
[235] Will of Margaret Cheesman, PROB 11/363 [92 Bath].
[236] Norfolk Co VA Deed Book 6:258. (See appendix).
[237] Norfolk Co VA Deed Book 7:117-8. (See appendix).
[238] Stanard, *Some Emigrants to Virginia*, 44.
[239] McIntosh, *Norfolk Co Wills 1637-1710*, 79-80 (Book 4:106).

Alice married (2) **William Porten**.

ISSUE:

+ 28. f ii. **Margaret Porten**, born about 1682, died after 9 Sep 1740 <See pg. 108>.
+ 29. m iii. **Daniel Porten**, born about 1684, died 1714 <See pg. 108>.
   30. m iv. **William Porten**. In the 1694 will of **William Knott** he gave godson William Porten, son of Mr. William Porten, deceased, two lotts in the Towne of Norfolk.[240] William[4] sold land in 1720 as surviving brother of Daniel.[241] William died before 21 Dec 1722 the date of the inventory of his estate.[242]
+ 31. f v. **Anne Porten**, born about 1688, died before 21 Sep 1717 <See pg. 109>.

William Porten died before 15 Mar 1692/3 when Mrs. Alice Porten was granted administration on his estate.[243] On 18 May 1693 Alice Porten presented a petition to the Norfolk County court for support for herself and her five children.[244] In the account of the "goods in Mrs. Porten's chamber" she listed items given to her by her aunt **Margaret (Ganey) Cheesman** and her father.

Alice married (3) **Samuel Boush. (See number 26 - pg. 201)**.

ISSUE:

+ 32. m vi. **Samuel Boush**, born about 1694, died before Nov 1759 <See pg. 109, 202>.
   33. f vii. **Mason Boush**. On 15 May 1702 Samuel Boush Sr. gave his daughter Mason[4] Boush 2 negro boys, 1 negro girl, one new silver tankard, one silver ...., .. silver porringers marked in the bottom with her ... , one new silver salt .... & one new silver ......[245] She was not named in her father's 1733 will.

Alice[3] married Samuel Boush by 17 Jul 1694 as shown in the Boush vs. Danby, suit for goods due the estate of William Porten.[246] Samuell Boush and Alice Boush were witnesses to the 22 Aug 1697 will of **William Heslett**.[247]

---

[240] McIntosh, *Norfolk Co Wills 1637-1710*, 159 (Book 6:76).
[241] Norfolk Co VA Orders, Appraisements, Wills 1719-1722, pt. 2:137.
[242] Norfolk Co VA Wills & Deeds F:146a.
[243] Norfolk Co VA Deed Book 5, pt. 2 Orders:285.
[244] Norfolk Co VA Deed Book 5:197-199a.
[245] Norfolk Co VA Deed Book 6:244a.
[246] Norfolk Co VA Deed Book 5, pt. 2 Orders:328.
[247] McIntosh, *Norfolk Co Wills 1637-1710*, 163, (Book 6:105).

There are two wills for Samuel Boush. The first one was dated 18 Oct 1733 and was proved 17 Dec 1736.[248] In it he named his son Samuel[4] Boush and grandsons Samuel[5] Boush, Goodrich[5] Boush, and John[5] Boush. To his son Samuel[4] Boush, daughter (daughter-in-law) Anne Boush and grandson Samuel[5] Boush he gave each a suit of mourning clothes. His wife Alice Boush was to have good maintenance out of the estate and care was to be taken for the education of his grandson Samuel[5] Boush. The second will was written 10 Jun 1735 and was proved 16 Feb 1738/9. In it he mentioned care for his wife and named his son Major Samuel[4] Boush, Mrs. Mary[4] Miller, Mrs. Margaret[4] Haire, and grandsons Goodrich[5], William[5] and Samuel[5] Boush.[249]

Alice[3] Mason died after 10 Jun 1735, the date of Samuel Boush's second will.

- - - - - - - - - - -

27. Mary[4] Hodge <See pg. 105> (26.Alice[3], 4.Lemuel[2], 1.Francis[1]) was born after 10 Sep 1681, when an unborn child was referred to in her father's will.[250] She married **William Miller**.
                        ISSUE:[251]
m   i. **Mason Miller**, died before Aug 1775.
m ii. **Matthias Miller**, died before 15 Oct 1767.
f   iii. **Alice Miller**, died about 1772.
m iv. **Henry Miller**, died before 19 Mar 1741/2.

On 2 Sep 1707 Mary, only daughter of Robert Hodge deceased, and her husband William Miller sold 280 acres to **George Mason**.[252] In 1708/9 Dr. William Miller owned lot 29 in Norfolk Town;[253] in Jun 1711 he proved the will of Thomas Mason.[254] Mrs. Mary Miller was witness to the 1733 will of her mother's husband Samuel Boush and was left "a black suit of clothes" in 1735, his second will.[255] The will of Mary Miller, dated 22 Mar 1741/2 and

---

[248] McIntosh, *Norfolk Co Wills 1710-1753*, 139-40.
[249] Norfolk Co VA Wills & Deeds I:32.
[250] McIntosh, *Norfolk Co Wills 1637-1710*, 79-80 (Book 4:106).
[251] Dorman, *Adventurers of Purse and Person*, 2:582, 604, 629.
[252] Maling, *Princess Anne Co VA Deed Books 1-7*, 26 (1DB473).
[253] Whichard, *History of Lower Tidewater VA*, 1:326.
[254] Norfolk Co VA Deed Book 9:60-1.
[255] McIntosh, *Norfolk Co Wills 1710-1753*, 139-40. Norfolk Co VA Wills & Deeds I:32.

proved 17 Mar 1743/4, named her sons Mason, Matthais and Henry and daughter **Alice Ivy**.[256]

- - - - - - - - - - -

28. Margaret[4] **Porten** <See pg. 106> (26.Alice[3], 4.Lemuel[2], 1.Francis[1]) was born about 1682. She married (1) **Lemuel Newton (See number 10)** shown when she was granted administration of his estate 17 Nov 1721.[257]

Margaret married (2) **John Haire** before the court order 17 Jul 1724 concerning Lemuel Newton's estate.[258]

ISSUE:
- m i. **John Haire**.
- m ii. **Porten Haire**.
- m iii. **James Haire**.
- m iv. **Samuel Haire**.

Margaret[4] Haire was a witness to Samuel Boush's first will in 1733 and in his second will, 10 Jun 1735, she was given "a black suit of cloaths."[259]

Margaret probably married (3) **Peter Malbone** who named wife Margaret in his will. Peter died before 16 Jun 1738.[260] In Margaret Malbone's will, dated 9 Sep 1740 and proved 21 Nov 1740, she named her sons John[5], Porten[5], James[5] and Samuel[5] Hair and appointed her "loving brother Samuel Boush to be my Exer."[261]

- - - - - - - - - - -

29. Daniel[4] **Porten** <See pg. 106> (26.Alice[3], 4.Lemuel[2], 1.Francis[1]) was born about 1684. He married **Elizabeth Vaulx** before Feb 1712/3.[262]

ISSUE:
- m i. **Craddock Porten**, died young.

Daniel[4] Porten married Elizabeth (Vaulx) Craddock.[263] In his will, dated 31 Oct 1714 and proved 19 Nov 1714, he named Mary Furlong, daughter of his

---

[256] McIntosh, *Norfolk Co Wills 1710-1753*, 182 (Book H:95).

[257] Norfolk Co VA Orders, Appraisements, Wills 1719-1722, pt. 1:38a.

[258] Norfolk Co VA Wills & Deeds F:146.

[259] McIntosh, *Norfolk Co Wills 1710-1753*, 139-40. Norfolk Co VA Wills & Deeds I:32.

[260] Wingo, *Unrecorded Wills Norfolk Co VA*, 68-71.

[261] McIntosh, *Norfolk Co Wills 1710-1753*, 238 (Book I:24).

[262] Dorman, *Adventurers of Purse and Person*, 2:582-3.

[263] Fauntleroy, "Foxall-Vaulx-Elliott", 44:151-4.

sister **Ann⁴ Furlong**, son **Craddock⁵ Porten**, his wife Elizabeth executrix, and his step-father, "father in Law Majr Samuell Boush", his executor.²⁶⁴

- - - - - - - - - - -

31. Anne⁴ Porten <See pg. 106> (26.Alice³, 4.Lemuel², 1.Francis¹) was born about 1688. She married **Richard Furlong**.

ISSUE:²⁶⁵

  m i. **William Furlong**, born after 1691.
  f ii. **Mary Furlong**, born about 1705, died before 21 Oct 1737.

Anne⁴ Porten married Capt. Richard Furlong, whose will dated 5 Nov 1712 and proved 15 May 1713, witnessed by William Miller and Mary⁴ Miller, named his wife Anne⁴, son William⁵, and daughter Mary⁵.²⁶⁶ Anne's half-brother Samuel⁴ Boush Jr. was the administrator of Anne's estate,²⁶⁷ the inventory and appraisal of which was ordered 21 Sep 1717²⁶⁸ and audited 21 Feb 1717/8.²⁶⁹

- - - - - - - - - - -

32. Samuel⁴ Boush <See pg. 106, 201> (26.Alice³, 4.Lemuel², 1.Francis¹) was born about 1694. He married (1) **Anne Goodrich**. **(See number 4 - pg. 177). (See number 27. Samuel Boush - pg. 202).**²⁷⁰

ISSUE:

  f i. **Ann Boush**, born about 1721, died after 24 Mar 1779.
  m ii. **Samuel Boush**, born about 1722, died before 20 May 1784.
  m iii. **Goodrich Boush**, born about 1724, died before 22 May 1779.
  m iv. **John Boush**, born before 18 Oct 1733, died before 10 Jun 1735.
  m v. **William Boush**, born after 18 Oct 1733, died before 6 Nov 1756.

Anne died before 1735 in Norfolk County, Virginia.
Samuel married (2) **Frances Sayer**.

ISSUE:

---

²⁶⁴ Norfolk Co VA Deed Book 9:355.
²⁶⁵ Dorman, *Adventurers of Purse and Person*, 2:583, 629.
²⁶⁶ McIntosh, *Norfolk Co Wills 1710-1753*, 28-9 (Book 9:248).
²⁶⁷ Norfolk Co VA Deed Book 10:16a.
²⁶⁸ Norfolk Co VA Deed Book 9:630.
²⁶⁹ Norfolk Co VA Wills & Deeds F:145a.
²⁷⁰ References for the families of Samuel Boush are given in the Boush chapter. Charts which greatly added to research on these names are Boush, "Samuel Boush Family Chart", Misc Reel 520 and Boush, "The Identity of the 1st wife of Sam. Boush II, Norf. Co", Misc Reel 520.

m vi. **Arthur Boush**, born before 1740, died after Sep 1779.
f vii. **Mary "Molly" Boush**, born before 1740, died about 1763.
m viii. **Nathaniel Boush**, born after 1740, died 6 Jan 1813.
m ix. **Charles Sayer Boush**, born after 1740, died before 25 Apr 1809.
f x. **Margaret "Peggy" Boush**, born before 1754.

- - - - - - - - - - -

34. Elizabeth³ Mason <See pg. 84, 154> (4.Lemuel², 1.Francis¹) was born about 1662. She married **Thomas Cocke** about 1682. He was christened 6 Jul 1652 in Constantine, Cornwall, England. He was the son of **Thomas Cocke** and **Mary Pearse**.[271]

ISSUE:
35. f i. **Anne Cocke**, born before 15 Oct 1694 when she was named in the will of **William Ervin**.[272]
+ 36. f ii. **Mary Cocke**, born before 17 Jun 1695 <See pg. 111>.

Elizabeth³ was named in the 1680 will of her grand aunt **Margaret (Ganey) Cheesman**, who left her a tankard.[273] Her father's 1695 will states "I Give and Bequeath to Mr. T ..(torn).. Cocke, who married my daughter Elizabeth one Shill (torn) ..."[274]

Thomas Cocke patented 721 acres 21 Oct 1687 in Lynn Haven Parish of Lower Norfolk County,[275] and in the 16 Jan 1693/4 Norfolk County court Capt. Tho: Cock was listed as a justice.[276] In 1696 his brother **Walter** sold 225 acres in Princess Anne County to Thomas of Princess Anne County.[277]

The 15 Oct 1694 will of **William Ervin** stated that after the decease of his wife **Katherine** his estate should go to Anne⁴ Cocke daughter of Capt. Thos. Cocke.[278] Lemuel² Mason, Senr, in a deed 17 Jun 1695, referred to his son-in-law Thomas Cocke and his wife Elizabeth, "my daughter", and made a gift to his "two grandchildren Mary & Ann Cock."[279]

---

[271] Dorman, *Adventurers of Purse and Person*, 2:573.
[272] Maling, *Princess Anne Co VA Deed Books 1-7*, 11 (1DB136).
[273] Will of Margaret Cheesman, PROB 11/363 [92 Bath].
[274] Norfolk Co VA Deed Book 6:258. (See appendix).
[275] Nugent, *Cavaliers and Pioneers*, 2:311 (Patent Book 7:584).
[276] Norfolk Co VA Deed Book 5, pt. 2 Orders:311.
[277] Norfolk Co VA Deed Book 6:23.
[278] Maling, *Princess Anne Co VA Deed Books 1-7*, 11 (1DB136).
[279] Norfolk Co VA Deed Book 6:130.

Mason Families

Elizabeth evidently died before 20 Aug 1697. Thomas Cocke's will, written 20 Aug 1697 and proved 6 Oct 1697, named daughters Anne and Mary.[280] Of his four plantations, he left each daughter one and requested that the other two be sold. His executors were his brothers William and Walter Cocke, his nephew Thomas Cocke, his cousin Christopher Cocke and Thomas[3] Mason.[281]

----

36. Mary[4] Cocke <See pg. 110> (34.Elizabeth[3], 4.Lemuel[2], 1.Francis[1]) was born before 17 Jun 1695, when her grandfather named her in a deed of gift.[282] She married **John Simmons** of Surry County by 3 Jul 1706 when they sold 187 ½ acres in Princess Anne County to Lt. **Thomas Scott Sr**.[283]

ISSUE:[284]

m i. **William Simmons**.
m ii. **Benjamin Simmons**.
m iii. **Charles Simmons**, born 1722, died before 12 Dec 1771.
m iv. **Henry Simmons**, died before 28 Jul 1766.
f v. **Lucy Simmons**, died before 21 Oct 1799.
f vi. **Ann Simmons**, died 26 Oct 1749.
f vii. **Elizabeth Simmons**.
m viii. **John Simmons**, died before 19 Apr 1738.
f ix. **Sarah Simmons**.

John died before 14 Dec 1749 in Southampton County, Virginia.

----

37. George[3] Mason <See pg. 84, 154> (4.Lemuel[2], 1.Francis[1]) was born about 1666. He marriend **Phillis Hobson**. She was the daughter of **Peter Hobson** and **Elizabeth** ____.[285]

ISSUE:

+ 38. m i. **Thomas Mason**, died before 2 Nov 1740 <See pg. 113>.
 39. m ii. **George Mason**. On 18 Jan 1731/2 George[4] Mason sold **John Ellegood** a lot in Norfolk Town adjoining Capt. **Solomon Wilson**. He died after 15 Jun 1733 when he made another deed to Ellegood.[286]

---

[280] Maling, *Princess Anne Co VA Deed Books 1-7*, 12 (1DB154).
[281] Southall, "Genealogy of the Cocke Family ...", 2:185-6, 191.
[282] Norfolk Co VA Deed Book 6:130.
[283] Maling, *Princess Anne Co VA Deed Books 1-7*, 25 (1DB455).
[284] Dorman, *Adventurers of Purse and Person*, 2:580-1, 596–601.
[285] McIntosh, *Norfolk Co Wills 1637-1710*, 164 (Book 6:106a).
[286] Norfolk Co VA Deed Book 11:9, 83-4.

Mason Families

+ 40. f iii. **Abigail Mason**, died after 17 Mar 1757 <See pg. 114>.
+ 41. f iv. **Frances Mason** <See pg. 115>.

George[3] was named 3rd son in his father's 1695 will[287] and in his mother's 1705 will.[288] **John Gooscott** in his will dated 15 Mar 1688/9 specified that after the death of his wife his plantation should "fall and descend to George Mason Sonn of Coll. Lemuell Mason."[289]

After 25 Sep 1697 George[3] married Phillis Hobson, who was named as Phillis Hobson less than age 16 in the 1697 will of her father Peter Hobson.[290] She was also named as his daughter in a deed to her sons Thomas and George on 16 Feb 1710/11: "Phillis Mason widow and relict of Mr. George Mason & daughter of Mr. Petter Hopson .... "[291]

George[3] Mason was a witness with his brother Lemuel[3] on 5 Sep 1699 when their parents gave power of attorney to their brother Thomas.[292] In the militia lists for Norfolk County 4 Apr 1702 George[3] Mason was shown as "Capt. of Horse."[293] He served as a justice for Norfolk County with his brother Lemuel[3] in 1702[294] and represented Norfolk County as a burgess in the General Assembly which met 1705-1706.[295]

The 1704 quit rents show George[3] Mason owning 300 acres in Norfolk Co;[296] on 2 Sep 1707 **William Miller** and his wife **Mary (Hodge) Miller** sold 280 acres to George[3] Mason.[297]

George's will, dated 15 Jan 1710/11 and proved 16 Mar 1710/11, named his wife Phillis executrix, sons Thomas[4] less than age 21, George[4], daughters Abigail[4], Frances[4] less than age16, and kinsmen Capt. George Newton, Mr. Lemuel Newton, and Mr. **William Craford** as overseers.[298]

---

[287] Norfolk Co VA Deed Book 6:258-260. (See appendix).
[288] Norfolk Co VA Deed Book 7:117-8. (See appendix).
[289] McIntosh, *Norfolk Co Wills 1637-1710*, 133 (Book 5:155).
[290] McIntosh, *Norfolk Co Wills 1637-1710*, 164 (Book 6:106a).
[291] Norfolk Co VA Deed Book 9:14.
[292] Maling, *Princess Anne Co VA Deed Books 1-7*, 15 (1DB229).
[293] Bockstruck, *Virginia Colonial Soldiers*, 215, 218 (PRO, London, C. O. 5/1312 Part 2).
[294] des Cognets, *English Duplicates*, 11, 16.
[295] Leonard, *General Assembly of Virginia*, 64.
[296] Smith, *Quit Rents of Virginia, 1704*, 59.
[297] Maling, *Princess Anne Co VA Deed Books 1-7*, 26 (1DB473).
[298] Norfolk Co VA Deed Book 9:12-3.

Mason Families

Phillis married (2) **Samuel Rogers** before 20 Jun 1718 when they were named in a suit vs. **Richard** and **Elizabeth Sanderson**.[299]

Samuel Rogers will, dated 6 Jun 1719 and proved 21 Aug 1719, named his brother William and mentioned but did not name his wife.[300] A 22 Aug 1719 audit of Samuel Rogers's estate stated "......orphants portions of there fathers estate may be known .... paid by Mr. **William Rogers** and Mrs Phillis Roggers exr and extx of Samuel Rogers dec'd who Intermarryed with the sd Capt. Geo Masons Extx ...." .[301] On 8 Nov 1733, Phillis Rogers sold **John Ellegood** 300 acres called Jones Point.[302]

The will of Phillis Rogers, dated 14 Aug 1759 and proved Feb 1760, named her grandchildren Nathaniel[5] Mason, Rebecca[5] Newton, Fernelia[5] Ellegood, and Alice[5] Smith leaving each forty shillings. She named her son-in-law **John Phripp** executor.[303]

- - - - - - - - - - -

38. Thomas^4 Mason <See pg. 111> (37.George^3, 4.Lemuel^2, 1.Francis^1). He married **Mary Newton**. She was the daughter of **Nathaniel Newton**. (See pg. 94).

ISSUE:

m   i. **Nathaniel Newton Mason**. He married **Ann Snale** in 1758.[304]

Thomas^4 Mason may have been age 21 by 16 Feb 1710/11 when his mother, Phillis Mason, "for the natural love and motherly affection that I have for my son Thomas Mason" gave him her share of property in Norfolk Town, etc.[305] Thomas married Mary Newton shown by the deed 24 May 1737 when they sold **John Ellegood** of the Borough of Norfolk, merchant, 200 acres which Mary had inherited as sole heir of Capt. Nathaniel Newton.[306]

---

[299] Norfolk Co VA Deed Book 10:11/21.
[300] McIntosh, *Norfolk Co Wills 1710-1753*, 85 (OAW:42).
[301] Norfolk Co VA Deed Book 10:79/164. Norfolk Co VA Orders, Appraisements, Wills 1719-1722, pt. 3:59.
[302] Norfolk Co VA Deed Book 11:128.
[303] Norfolk Co VA Will Book 1:43.
[304] Wingo, *Norfolk Co VA Will Book 1*, 28 (f 43). Wingo, *Marriages of Norfolk Co VA, Vol 1*, 43.
[305] Norfolk Co VA Deed Book 9:13-14.
[306] Norfolk Co VA Deed Book 12:226-8.

Mary died after 3 Nov 1740, when she was named a widow selling a lot..[307]

- - - - - - - - - - -

40. Abigail[4] Mason <See pg. 112> (37.George[3], 4.Lemuel[2], 1.Francis[1]). She married (1) **John Ellegood** 13 Aug 1724.[308] He was probably the son of **William Ellegood** and **Mary Pallett**.[309]

ISSUE:[310]

f i. **Rebecca Ellegood**, married **Wilson Newton**,[311] died before 11 Feb 1779.[312] **(See number 126 - pg. 52)**.
m ii. **William Ellegood**, died after 21 Aug 1753.[313]
m iii. **John Ellegood**, died before Jun 1760.[314]
m iv. **Mason Ellegood**, died before 17 Jul 1753.[315]
m v. **Jacob Ellegood**, died before 17 Mar 1768.[316]
f vi. **Fernelia Ellegood** married **Neil Jamieson** 8 Sep 1761.[317]

John Ellegood was chosen alderman of Norfolk Borough from 1736 to 1741.[318]

In John's will, dated 30 Sep 1740 and proved 20 Nov 1740, he left to his son William[5] the 200 acre plantation he purchased from Thomas and Mary Mason which belonged to Major Newton. He also named sons John[5], Mason[5], Jacob[5] and daughters Rebecca[5] and Fernelia[5] and appointed his wife, his brother Jacob Ellegood and his friends Capt. **Edward Pugh** and Capt. **John Phripp** as executors.[319]

Abigail married (2) Rev. **Charles Smith**, minister of Portsmouth. The wills of her sons John and Jacob named "sister Alice Smith" in 1757 and "sister

---

[307] Norfolk Co VA Wills & Deeds I:106-7.
[308] Wingo, *Marriages of Norfolk Co VA, Vol 1*, 22.
[309] Maling, *Princess Anne Co VA Deed Books 1-7*, 38 (3DB228), 50 (4DB64), 58 (4DB435).
[310] Dorman, *Adventurers of Purse and Person*, 2:579-80, 593-4.
[311] Wingo, *Norfolk Co VA Will Book 1*, 30 (f 47 - will of brother John Ellegood).
[312] Maling, *Princess Anne Co VA Deed Books 8-18*, 81 (15DB135).
[313] Maling, *Princess Anne Co VA Deed Books 1-7*, 98 (7DB502).
[314] Wingo, *Norfolk Co VA Will Book 1*, 30 (f 47).
[315] Walter, *Princess Anne Co VA Deed and Minute Books*, 91 (7DB502).
[316] Wingo, *Norfolk Co VA Will Book 1*, 106 (f 171a).
[317] Wingo, *Marriages of Norfolk Co VA, Vol 1*, 36.
[318] Tarter, *Order Book ... Borough of Norfolk*, 45, 56.
[319] McIntosh, *Norfolk Co Wills 1710-1753*, 236-7 (Book I:23).

Alice Taylor" in 1768.[320] The will of Charles Smith, dated 30 Oct 1772 and proved Jan 1773, named granddaughters **Abigail** and **Margaret Taylor** and Mrs. Rebecca[5] Newton, Mrs. Fernelia[5] Jameson.[321]

ISSUE:[322]

 f vii. **Alice Smith**, born 1743, married **James Taylor**.[323] Alice died 21 Nov 1787.

Abigail died after 17 Mar 1757, when she was named in the will of her son John Ellegood.[324]

---

41. Frances[4] Mason <See pg. 112> (37.George[3], 4.Lemuel[2], 1.Francis[1]). She married **John Phripp** 25 Jul 1728.[325]

ISSUE:[326]

 m i. **John Phripp**, died Nov 1766.
 m ii. **Matthew Phripp**.
 f iii. **Ann Phripp**, died 14 Jun 1796.

John Phripp served as alderman or mayor in Norfolk Borough from 1736 until 1760.[327] Capt. John Phripp, late of Norfolk, died at age 93 in 1776.[328]

---

42. Anne[3] Mason <See pg. 84, 154> (4.Lemuel[2], 1.Francis[1]) was born about 1668. She married (1) **William Kendall**. He was the son of **William Kendall**.[329]

ISSUE:[330]

 43. f i. **Susanna Kendall**, born about 1683; she chose Lt. Col. **Nathaniel Littleton** as her guardian 28 Jan 1700/1.[331] She married **Devorax Godwin**. Devorax died before 14 Feb 1726/7 in Northampton County, Virginia.

---

[320] Wingo, *Norfolk Co VA Will Book 1*, 30 (f 47), 106 (f 171a).
[321] Norfolk Co VA Will Book 2:11/16.
[322] Dorman, *Adventurers of Purse and Person*, 2:594.
[323] Wingo, *Marriages of Norfolk Co VA, Vol 1*, 64.
[324] Wingo, *Norfolk Co VA Will Book 1*, 30 (f 47).
[325] Wingo, *Marriages of Norfolk Co VA, Vol 1*, 52.
[326] Dorman, *Adventurers of Purse and Person*, 2:580, 594-6.
[327] Tarter, *Order Book ... Borough of Norfolk*, 45, ..., 122.
[328] Henley, *Marriage/Obituary Index*.
[329] beth@TidewaterTapestry.com (Marshall, *Wills ... Northampton Co VA*, 126).
[330] Dorman, *Adventurers of Purse and Person*, 2:574-5, 583-6.
[331] Northampton Co VA Orders, Wills, Etc., No. 14:58.

+ 44. m ii. **William Kendall**, born Apr 1687, died before 20 Jul 1720 <See pg. 117>.
  45. m iii. **John Kendall**, born about 1689. On 28 Jul 1704 John[4] Kendall chose his uncle Thomas Mason of Elizabeth River in Norfolk County on the Western Shore as guardian.[332] He married (1) **Tabitha Watts**. John married (2) **Mary Taylor**. His will was dated 12 Mar 1738 and proved 6 Jun 1738.
  46. f iv. **Mason Kendall**, born about 1690. On 28 Jul 1704 Mason Kendall chose **Alexander Hamilton** for her guardian,[333] She married (1) **James Watt** 22 Mar 1709/10. James died before 2 Oct 1716 in Accomack County, Virginia. Mason married (2) **Samuel Welburn**. Samuel died before 8 May 1728.
+ 47. f v. **Ann Kendall**, born about 1692, died 18 May 1760 <See pg. 117>.

Anne[3] was named in the 1680 will of her grand aunt **Margaret (Ganey) Cheesman** who left her a tankard.[334] Her father's 1695 will states, "I Give and Bequeath ...(torn) .... my daughter Ann tenn sh.......(torn) ......" [335] Anne[3] died before 30 Oct 1705 the date of her mother's will.[336]

William's will was dated 29 Jan 1695/6 and proved 28 Jul 1696. He named his wife Ann and their children: William[4] age less than 21, Susanna[4], John[4], daughter Mason[4], and Ann[4] all less than age 16.[337]

Anne married (2) **Peter Collier** before 28 Feb 1699/1700.[338] The administration of his estate was recorded July 28, 1704.[339]

ISSUE:[340]

  48. f vi. **Mary Collier**.

- - - - - - - - - - -

---

[332] Northampton Co VA Orders, Wills, Etc., No. 14:213.
[333] Northampton Co VA Orders, Wills, Etc., No. 14:213.
[334] Will of Margaret Cheesman, PROB 11/363 [92 Bath].
[335] Norfolk Co VA Deed Book 6:258. (See appendix).
[336] Norfolk Co VA Deed Book 7:117-8. (See appendix).
[337] Northampton Co VA Orders & Wills No. 13:384-7.
[338] Northampton Co VA Orders, Wills, Etc., No. 14:36-7.
[339] Marshall, *Wills ... Northampton Co VA*, 176 (Orders, Wills, XVII, No. 14, 1698-1710 - p. 207).
[340] beth@TidewaterTapestry.com (Marshall, *Wills ... Northampton Co VA*, 235).

Mason Families 117

44. William⁴ Kendall <See pg. 116> (42.Anne³, 4.Lemuel², 1.Francis¹) was born Apr 1687.³⁴¹ He married **Sorrowful Margaret Custis**. She was the daughter of **John Custis, III** and **Margaret Michael**.³⁴²

ISSUE:³⁴³

- m i. **Littleton Kendall**.
- m ii. **Custis Kendall**.
- m iii. **William Kendall**.
- f iv. **Ann Kendall**.
- m v. **George Mason Kendall**.
- f vi. **Peggy Kendall**.
- f vii. **Leah Kendall**.

William died before 20 Jul 1720, the date his will was proved.³⁴⁴

- - - - - - - - - - -

47. Ann⁴ Kendall <See pg. 116> (42.Anne³, 4.Lemuel², 1.Francis¹) was born about 1692. She married (1) **Thomas Custis** 24 Jun 1717. He was the son of **Edmund Custis** and **Tabitha Scarburgh Whittington**.³⁴⁵

ISSUE:³⁴⁶

- f i. **Elizabeth Custis**.

Ann married (2) **Henry Custis**, and (3) **Edmund Allen** before 1738. Ann died 18 May 1760.

- - - - - - - - - - -

49. Abigail³ Mason <See pg. 84, 154> (4.Lemuel², 1.Francis¹) was born about 1671. She married **George Crawford** about 1688. He was the son of **William Crawford** and **Margaret** ____.³⁴⁷

ISSUE:

50. m i. **William Crawford**, born about 1689. In his will, dated 27 Jan 1762 and proved Apr 1762, he named his sister Abigail Conner and nephew William Conner.³⁴⁸

---

³⁴¹ Northampton Co VA Orders, Wills, Etc., No. 14:76-7.
³⁴² Meyer and Dorman, *Adventurers of Purse and Person*, 621-2.
³⁴³ Dorman, *Adventurers of Purse and Person*, 2:583-4.
³⁴⁴ Dorman, *Adventurers of Purse and Person*, 2:584 (Northampton Co Wills etc. 15:121).
³⁴⁵ Meyer and Dorman, *Adventurers of Purse and Person*, 622.
³⁴⁶ Dorman, *Adventurers of Purse and Person*, 2:584.
³⁴⁷ Norfolk Co VA Deed Book 5:185a-186. McIntosh, *Norfolk Co Wills 1637-1710*, 172-3 (Book 6:181).
³⁴⁸ Wingo, *Norfolk Co VA Will Book 1*, 53 (f 79).

+ 51. f   ii.   **Abigail Crawford**, born about 1690, died before Oct 1774 <See pg. 118>.

Abigail[3] was named in the 1680 will of her grand aunt **Margaret (Ganey) Cheesman**: "children of my said Cozen Lemuell Mason ..... Abigail Mary and Dynah all the rest of my plate to be equally divided among them."[349]

Abigail[3] married George Crawford about 1688. Her father made a deed 15 May 1690: "Lemuel Mason Senr .... for great love and nattural affection that I have to my well beloved children George Craford and Abigail his wife .... deed of gift ... one third part of an Island called Whites Island ... in Coratuck in North Carolina ...", etc. William Craford made a deed of gift to his son George Craford.[350]

Abigail[3] and George died before 16 July 1691 when the inventory of "what belonged to George and Abigail Craford dec'd" was given by William Craford.[351] In a deed 29 Oct 1692 regarding the land in North Carolina which had been deeded to George and Abigail, William Craford named his son George, George's marriage to Abigail[3] Mason daughter of Col. Lemuel[2] Mason, and William's grandchildren William[4] Craford Jr. and Abigail[4] Craford.[352]

The will of William Craford written 26 Sep 1699 and proved 16 Mar 1699/1700 named his grandchildren William[4] and Abigail[4]. It was proved by Mr. **Walter Cocke** and **Thomas Cocke**.[353]

- - - - - - - - - - -

51. Abigail[4] Crawford <See pg. 118> (49.Abigail[3], 4.Lemuel[2], 1.Francis[1]) was born about 1690. She married **Keader Conner** about 1705. He was the son of **Lewis Conner** and **Elizabeth Daines**.[354]

ISSUE:[355]

m   i.   **Lewis Conner**, born 22 Jun 1707, died before 1749, the date of his brother John's will.
f   ii. **Margaret Conner**, born 12 Mar 1710, died 27 Nov 1763.
m   iii. **William Conner**, born 26 Nov 1711, died 4 Jul 1775.

---

[349] Will of Margaret Cheesman, PROB 11/363 [92 Bath].
[350] Norfolk Co VA Deed Book 5:130a-131.
[351] Norfolk Co VA Deed Book 5:159a-160.
[352] Norfolk Co VA Deed Book 5:185a-186.
[353] McIntosh, *Norfolk Co Wills 1637-1710*, 172-3 (Book 6:181).
[354] McIntosh, *Norfolk Co Wills 1637-1710*, 165 (Book 6:111). beth@TidewaterTapestry.com, (Norfolk Co VA Deed Book 4:88a).
[355] Dorman, *Adventurers of Purse and Person*, 2:586-7, 617-8 (Conner Bible).

m iv. **John Conner**, born 5 Aug 1716, named his brothers and sisters William, Margaret, Elizabeth, and Craford in his will, which was dated 17 Jul 1749 and proved 19 Jul 1750.[356]

m v. **Crawford Conner**, born 6 Oct 1717. In his will, which was written 2 Aug 1757 and proved Oct 1757, he named brother William, sister Margaret and mother Abigail.[357]

f vi. **Elizabeth Conner**, born about 1717, died after 1766.[358]

Keador Conner's will was dated 19 Aug 1721 and named his wife Abigale Conner and brother-in-law William Craford.[359] The 1740 will of his mother, **Elizabeth (Daines) Connor Lawson**, named daughter-in-law Abigale Conner and among her grandchildren John and Lewis Conner, sons of Kedar.[360]

Abigail's will was dated 21 Sep 1771 and proved Oct 1774.[361]

- - - - - - - - - - -

52. Mary³ Mason <See pg. 84, 154> (4.Lemuel², 1.Francis¹) was born about 1675. She married **Walter Cocke**. He was christened 25 Jan 1657 in Constantine, Cornwall, England. He was the son of **Thomas Cocke** and **Mary Pearse**.[362]

ISSUE:
+ 53. m i. **Thomas Cocke**, died 2 Dec 1750 <See pg. 121>.
  54. m ii. **John Cocke**.
  55. f iii. **Anne Cocke**. She married ____ **Hamlin** before 1 Aug 1735, the date of her father's will.

Mary³ was named in the 1680 will of her grand aunt **Margaret (Ganey) Cheesman**: "children of my said Cozen Lemuell Mason ..... Abigail Mary and Dynah all the rest of my plate to be equally divided among them."[363] Her father's 1695 will states, " I give and Bequeath ...(torn) ...daughter Mary wife of Walter C.....one silver wine ..(torn) ...estate."[364] In her mother's

---

[356] McIntosh, *Norfolk Co Wills 1710-1753*, 262 (Book I:169).

[357] Wingo, *Norfolk Co VA Will Book 1*, 11 (f 21).

[358] Wingo, *Norfolk Co VA Will Book 1*, 94 (f 149a - will of Ann Southerland).

[359] Norfolk Co VA Wills & Orders 1723-1734, 7.

[360] McIntosh, *Norfolk Co Wills 1710-1753*, 103-4 (will of Lewis Connor), 144-5 (will of Elizabeth Lawson).

[361] McVey, *Norfolk Co VA Will Book 2*, 43-4.

[362] Dorman, *Adventurers of Purse and Person*, 2:575.

[363] Will of Margaret Cheesman, PROB 11/363 [92 Bath].

[364] Norfolk Co VA Deed Book 6:258. (See appendix).

Mason Families

1705 will she stated, "I give and bequeath unto my loving daughter Mary Cock the sum of seven pounds ten shillings in money to be paid her within two months after my decease and my will is that she dispose of the same at her own pleasure without being accountable to her husband for the same in any respect."[365]

On 3 Apr 1691 Mary[3] Mason was a witness to the will of **James Thelaball**.[366] She married Walter Cocke by 11 Jul 1692 shown when **William Cocke** gave power of attorney to his brother Thomas, witnesses Walter and Mary Cocke.[367] There was a Norfolk County deed 17 Mar 1695/6 from Walter and Mary[3] Cock of Surry County to his brother Thomas Cock of Princess Anne County.[368]

On 21 Oct 1687 Thomas Cocke received a patent for 721 acres Lower Norfolk County in Lynhaven on pocosan side of West's Creek for transporting Walter Cock 7 times and himself.[369] In 1704 Walter Cock was shown in the quit rent rolls with 875 acres and William Cock with 630 acres.[370] The 1707 records of Essex County show a debit report of Mr. **Joseph Groughere** of London that lists "Goods shipt on board the Corbin Cap't Walter Cocke,"[371] and also in 1707 Walter Cocke was a witness to a court document in Richmond County.[372] In 1714 William and Walter Cocke were justices in Surry Co.[373]

Evidently Mary[3] died before 1 Aug 1735 the date of her husband's will, which was proved 21 Mar 1738/9. He named two sons and one daughter, Thomas[4] Cocke, John[4] Cocke, and Anne[4] Hamlin.[374]

- - - - - - - - - -

---

[365] Norfolk Co VA Deed Book 7:117-8. (See appendix).
[366] Norfolk Co VA Deed Book 5:208-208a.
[367] Norfolk Co VA Deed Book 5:177a.
[368] Norfolk Co VA Deed Book 6:23.
[369] Nugent, *Cavaliers and Pioneers*, 2:311 (Patent Book 7:584).
[370] Smith, *Quit Rents of Virginia, 1704*, 19.
[371] Fleet, *VA Col Abs, Essex Co*, 2:39.
[372] Fleet, *VA Col Abs, Richmond Co*, 1:294.
[373] des Cognets, *English Duplicates*, 22, 28.
[374] Hart, *Surry Co VA Wills 1730-1800*, 22, 23 (Surry Co VA Deed & Will Book 1738-1754 pp. 35, 62).

Mason Families

53. Thomas⁴ Cocke <See pg. 119> (52.Mary³, 4.Lemuel², 1.Francis¹). He married **Hannah Hamlin**. She was the daughter of **John Hamlin** and **Elizabeth Taylor**.[375]

ISSUE:
- m   i. **Lemuel Cocke**, may have died before 20 Nov 1751.
- f   ii. **Elizabeth Cocke**.
- m iii. **Thomas Cocke**.
- m iv. **John Cocke**, born after 1729.

Thomas's will, dated 7 Jun 1750 and recorded 18 Dec 1750, named sons Lemuel⁵ and Thomas⁵ executors, his wife, Hannah, his son John⁵ age under 21, and daughter Elizabeth⁵.[376] Hannah's will, dated 20 Nov 1751 and recorded 16 Jun 1752, named sons Thomas⁵ and John⁵, Thomas⁵ executor.[377]

- - - - - - - - - - -

56. Dinah³ Mason <See pg. 84, 154> (4.Lemuel², 1.Francis¹) was born about 1678. She married (1) **Robert Thorowgood** about 1698. He was born about 1669. He was the son of **Adam Thorowgood** and **Frances Yeardley**.[378]

ISSUE:
- +57. m   i. **Thomas Thorowgood**, died before 1 Mar 1726/7 <See pg. 123>.
- 58. m ii. **Robert Thorowgood**. He married **Ann Keeling**. Ann died before 1744. Robert married (2) **Blandinah** ____.[379] Robert's will written, 17 Feb 1755 and proved 20 May 1755, named his wife Blandinah and son Robert⁵.[380]

Robert married (1) **Ann** ____.

ISSUE:
- 59. f iii. **Priscilla Thorowgood**, born about 1695, died before 12 Jan 1713/4.[381]

Dinah³ Mason was named in the 1680 will of her grand aunt **Margaret (Ganey) Cheesman**: "children of my said Cozen Lemuell Mason .....

---

[375] Hamlin, *They Went That Away*, 2:111.

[376] Hart, *Surry Co VA Wills 1730-1800*, 47 (Surry Co VA Deed & Will Book 1738-1754 p. 685).

[377] Hart, *Surry Co VA Wills 1730-1800*, 54, 55 (Surry Co VA Deed & Will Book 1738-1754 pp. 800, 815).

[378] Meyer and Dorman, *Adventurers of Purse and Person*, 610-1, 619-20.

[379] Meyer and Dorman, *Adventurers of Purse and Person*, 620.

[380] Maling, *Princess Anne Co VA Deed Books 1-7*, 105 (7DB702).

[381] Maling, *Princess Anne Co VA Deed Books 1-7*, 20 (1DB351). Princess Anne Co VA Deed Book, 2:195-6.

Abigail Mary and Dynah all the rest of my plate to be equally divided among them."[382] Her father's 1695 will states "I give and Bequeath.......(torn) ..to daughter Dinah..........20 shillings money and one small (torn) .... her estate as may Equa.............. her ....(torn) ...."[383] Her mother's 1705 will states "I give and bequeath unto my loving daughter Dinah Thorowgood seven pounds ten shill in money to be paid her within two months after my decease by my three sons ..... provided the said Dinah Thorowgood take nor receive anything more by virtue of the will of my dec'd husband Coll. Lemuel Mason than what is there directly mentioned in money it being 20 shillings. If claiming anything more by my husbands dec'd will than the twenty shill, my will is that she the said Dinah receive one shilling in full of her portion of my estate and noe more."[384]

On 17 Jun 1695 Dinah[3] Mason was a witness to her father's deed of gift to his granddaughters Mary and Ann Cocke, children of his son-in-law **Thomas Cocke** and his daughter Elizabeth[3].[385]

Dinah[3] Mason married first, before 6 Jul 1698 as his second wife, Captain Robert Thorowgood, shown by their deed to **George Moseley** and **John McCreife**.[386] Robert was justice of Princess Anne County in 1699 and coroner in 1702.[387] His receipt for a payment relating to the estate of **William Thorowgood** was dated 8 Jan 1701/2.[388] His will was undated but was proved 7 Jan 1702/3 and mentioned his "now wife" and three children Thomas, Robert, and Priscilla.[389]

Soon after 15 Jan 1702/3 Dinah[3] Thorowgood widow and relict of Capt. Robert Thorowgood dec'd late guardian of William Thorowgood, was ordered to deliver stock, etc. to Robert's brother **Adam Thorowgood**, guardian of William.[390] On 4 Jul 1706 Dinah Thorowgood was ordered to make payments as executrix of Robert Thorowgood.[391]

Dinah married (2) **Samuel Wilson. (See number 96 - pg. 36).**

---

[382] Will of Margaret Cheesman, PROB 11/363 [92 Bath].
[383] Norfolk Co VA Deed Book 6:258. (See appendix).
[384] Norfolk Co VA Deed Book 7:117-8. (See appendix).
[385] Norfolk Co VA Deed Book 6:130.
[386] Princess Anne Co VA Deed Book 1:184-5.
[387] Meyer and Dorman, *Adventurers of Purse and Person*, 619.
[388] Princess Anne Co VA Deed Book 1:302-3.
[389] Princess Anne Co VA Deed Book 1:351.
[390] Princess Anne Co VA Deed Book 1:354.
[391] Princess Anne Co VA Order Book 1, Part 2:443-4.

ISSUE:
+ 60. m iv. **Willis Wilson**, born about 1707, died about 1740 <See pg. 38, 124>.

Mr. Samuel Wilson was listed as a justice in Princess Anne County in the 8 Sep 1709 and 2 Mar 1709/10 courts.[392] Samuel died before 3 Jan 1710/11 when the appraisal/inventory of the estate of Mr. Samuel Wilson was ordered.[393] It was signed by the appraisers 12 Jan 1710/11, sworn to be a true inventory 8 Feb 1710/11 by Dinah[3] Wilson with a value of 280:7:6, "an old maire" being added 2 Apr 1711.[394]

Dinah married (3) **William Trevethan** before 12 Jan 1713/4. "In pursuance to an order bearing date the 4th day of this instant", there was found due to the only surviving orphans of Captain Robert Thorowgood sons Thomas and Robert "Nynty Nyne pounds fourteen shillings and two pence for them each party and have payed off the same in Negroes, plate, cattle, sheep and household goods ...." In respect to the estate of Mr. Samuel Wilson to "Willis his only surviving orphan one negro man called Sambo and 28:12:07 ½" the remainder to Mr. William Trevathan who married Mrs. Dinah[3] Wilson executrix of Robert Thorowgood and administratrix of Samuel Wilson her second husband. [395]

Dinah[3] died by 23 Jan 1713/4 when the audit of the settlement of the estates of Captain Robert Thorowgood and Mr. Samuel Wilson to their respective orphans was made and recorded "at the ....(blurred).... of William Trevathan who married Dinah their late deceased mother." The orphans named are Thomas and John Thorowgood and "Willis the only surviving orphant of Mr. Samuel Wilson it is ordered that Mr. John Wilson be guardian ..." The children's negroes and goods were put in care of the guardians while Mr. William Trevathan received "his proportioned part of the said Dinah his late wife's share of her dec'd Husbands and childrens estates ...."[396]

- - - - - - - - - - -

---

[392] Princess Anne Co VA Minute Book 2:4, 23.
[393] Princess Anne Co VA Minute Book 2:45.
[394] Princess Anne Co VA Deed Book 2:67.
[395] Princess Anne Co VA Deed Book 2:195-6.
[396] Princess Anne Co VA Minute Book 2:145.

Mason Families

57. Thomas⁴ Thorowgood <See pg. 121> (56.Dinah³, 4.Lemuel², 1.Francis¹) was born after 1695. He married **Mary Trevethan** 10 Feb 1724/5.³⁹⁷ She was the daughter of **Sampson Trevethan** and **Anne Church**.³⁹⁸

ISSUE:³⁹⁹

    f   i. **Mary Anne Thorowgood**.

The will of Thomas⁴, in which he named his wife Mary, "child wife goes with", and brother Robert⁴, was dated 3 Feb 1726/7 and proved 1 Mar 1726/7.⁴⁰⁰

Mary also married (2) **Stephen Wright** 4 Sep 1728.⁴⁰¹ Mary died before 7 Nov 1733.⁴⁰²

- - - - - - - - - - -

60. Willis⁴ Wilson <See pg. 36, 123> (56.Dinah³, 4.Lemuel², 1.Francis¹) was born about 1707 probably in Princess Anne County, Virginia. **(See number 97 - pg. 38)**. He married **Elizabeth Goodrich. (See number 5 - pg. 178)**.

ISSUE:

    m   i. **Benjamin Wilson, Sr.**, born 6 Jan 1733, died 27 Oct 1814.

Willis⁴ Wilson married Elizabeth⁴ Goodrich 7 Jun 1728, moved to James City County, was justice in 1731, 1737 and sheriff in 1721-3. Willis died about 1740 in James City County, Virginia.

- - - - - - - - - - -

61. Elizabeth² Mason <See pg. 80> (1.Francis¹) was born about 1630. She married **James Thelaball** about 1645.

ISSUE:

+ 62. m   i. **Francis Thelaball**, born about 1646, died before 15 Mar 1704/5 <See pg. 126>.
+ 68. f   ii. **Margaret Thelaball**, born about 1648, died before 12 May 1702 <See pg. 128>.
  78. m iii. **Lemuel Thelaball**, born about 1652. He was not named in his mother's gift to sons Frances and James 6 Jul 1677.⁴⁰³

---

³⁹⁷ Wingo, *Marriages of Princess Anne Co VA*, Vol II, 1.

³⁹⁸ McIntosh, *Norfolk Co Wills 1637-1710*, 191 (Book 7:106 - will of Richard Church). Meyer and Dorman, *Adventurers of Purse and Person*, 616.

³⁹⁹ Meyer and Dorman, *Adventurers of Purse and Person*, 619-620.

⁴⁰⁰ Maling, *Princess Anne Co VA Deed Books 1-7*, 52 (4DB100).

⁴⁰¹ Wingo, *Marriages of Princess Anne Co VA*, 2:1.

⁴⁰² Meyer and Dorman, *Adventurers of Purse and Person*, 620 (Princess Anne Co VA Minute Book 4:194).

⁴⁰³ Norfolk Co VA Deed Book 4:23.

+ 79. m iv. **James Thelaball**, born about 1655, died before 18 Jan 1711/2 <See pg. 135>.
+ 86. f v. **Elizabeth Thelaball**, born Aug 1660, died 19 Nov 1738 <See pg. 141>.
+ 93. f vi. **Mary Thelaball**, born about 1662, died before 19 Nov 1714 <See pg. 145>.

Elizabeth[2] was named as a "cozen" (niece) in the 1679/80 will of her aunt **Margaret (Ganey) Cheesman**.[404]

Before 7 Nov 1648 she had married Huguenot[405] James Thelaball, who made an agreement with his wife's mother and brother concerning her portion of the estate of her father Francis[1] Mason: 200 acres, ½ Hogg Iland, "two thousand foote of sawen planke", glass and lead for windows, and six silver spoons.[406] "Ja: The La Balle & Elizabeth his wife" were ordered to appear in the 10 Nov 1649 Lower Norfolk County court.[407]

In April of 1651 James Thelaball received a certificate for 500 acres for the transportation of ten persons,[408] and in Oct 1651 he patented 380 acres in Linhaven Parish adjoining Woolfs Neck for transporting 8 persons.[409] At the Jan 1652/3 court, he was named as seated on land at Woolves Neck.[410]

Mrs. Elizabeth[2] Thelaball was named in the 1653 will of **Daniel Tanner**, in which he left her 600 pounds of tobacco.[411]

James was a churchwarden in Elizabeth River parish in 1659 and 1660.[412]

Lemuel[2] Mason and his wife deeded 600 acres in Hogpen Neck to "Elizabeth Thelaball, my beloved sister and wife to Mr. James Thelaball" in

---

[404] Will of Margaret Cheesman, PROB 11/363 [92 Bath]. (See appendix). Dorman, *Adventurers of Purse and Person*, 1:570.
[405] "List of Qualified Huguenot Ancestors", The National Huguenot Society, http://www.huguenot.netnation.com/ancestor/default.htm (accessed 1 Feb 2007).
[406] Norfolk Co VA Wills & Deeds C:1 (recorded 15 Jan 1651/2).
[407] Walter, *Book "B" Lower Norfolk Co VA 1646-1651/2*, 117 (f 126).
[408] Walter, *Book "B" Lower Norfolk Co VA 1646-1651/2*, 170 (f 177).
[409] Nugent, *Cavaliers and Pioneers*, 1:221 (Patent Book 2:345).
[410] Fleet, *VA Col Abs, Lower Norfolk Co*, 3:442
[411] Norfolk Co VA Wills & Deeds C:65.
[412] James, *Lower Norfolk Antiquary*, 3:141.

1667.[413] On 15 Aug 1677 Elizabeth divided this land in a deed to her sons Francis and James.[414]

On 8 Nov 1683, King Charles II declared Mr. James Thelaball, who was born in France, professed the protestant religion and took the oath of Allegiance, "compleatly naturalized", granting him rights as if he had been "borne with In his Majesties Dominions."[415]

The will of James Thelaball was written 9 Apr 1691 and proved 15 Sep 1693. In it he named his sons Francis^3 and James^3 and his son Lemuel^3, deceased; also he named his daughters, Margaret^3 Langley, Elizabeth^3 Langley, Mary^3 Chichester and his wife Elizabeth, executor. He left his "coson", William Porten, all his "ffrench books."[416]

Elizabeth^2 was named in the 17 Jun 1695 will of her brother Lemuel^2 Mason: "If I ..... Die beefore my sister Elizabeth Thelaball then I Doe give & bequeath unto my said sister soe much good Black Serge as will make her a Morning Gowne."[417]

On 12 May 1702 Elizabeth wrote her will in which she named her sons Francis and James, her son-in-law William Langley "who formerly married my daughter Margaret", "daughter Elizabeth Langley, now wife of Thomas Langley", "daughter Mary Mason now wife of Lemuell Mason", grandson James Thelaball "Sonne to Francis Thelaball", grandson Thomas Langley "eldest son to Thomas Langley", and great grandson William Ivy "Sonn to George Ivey." She appointed her son Francis executor.[418]

The quit rents for 1704 show widow Thelaball with 600 acres in Norfolk County[419] Elizabeth^2 died before 15 Mar 1707, the date her will was probated.

- - - - - - - - - - -

---

[413] Norfolk Co VA Wills & Deeds E:19.
[414] James, *Lower Norfolk Antiquary*, 3:140. Norfolk Co VA Deed Book 4:23.
[415] James, *Lower Norfolk Antiquary*, 3:140. Hening, *Statutes*, 2:464-5.
[416] James, *Lower Norfolk Antiquary*, 3:142-4. Norfolk Co Deed Book 5:208.
[417] Norfolk Co VA Deed Book 6:258.
[418] James, *Lower Norfolk Antiquary*, 3:144-46. (See appendix).
[419] Smith, *Quit Rents of Virginia, 1704*, 88.

Mason Families

62. Francis³ Thelaball <See pg. 124> (61.Elizabeth², 1.Francis¹) born about 1646. He married (1) **Sarah Dyer** before 20 Apr 1682. She was the daughter of **Thomas Dyer**.[420]

ISSUE:

+ 63. m   i.   **James Thelaball**, born about 1677, died before 19 Feb 1767 <See pg. 128>.
  64. m   ii. **Dyer Thelaball**. His brother Lemuel was granted administration of his estate 19 Mar 1714/5.[421]
  65. m   iii. **Francis Thelaball**, born after 1684; he was bound until age 21 to **Thomas Mason** in 1704/5.[422]
  66. f   iv. **Sarah Thelaball**. She married **Alexander Gwyn** before 12 May 1708. Alexander died before 28 Jul 1721 in Norfolk County, Virginia.[423]
  67. m   v.   **Lemuel Thelaball**, died before 4 Jun 1718.[424]

Francis³ Thelaball was probably the witness, "Frances Thelaball" to the 24 Jul 1667 will of **Richard Russell**.[425]

Regarding 600 acres of land in Hogg Pen Neck given to Elizabeth² by her brother Lemuel Mason in 1667, Francis³ was deeded on 6 Jul 1677 by his mother, 400 acres, "the plantation whereon hee now Live."[426]

His parents made a deed 16 Oct 1690 in which Francis³, his wife Sarah and their children would move from their plantation to live with and take care of James and Elizabeth until their deaths, at which time their plantation would revert to "Sone francis thelaball."[427]

Francis married (2) **Margery** ____. Administration of the estate of **Alexander Ivy** was granted 17 Sep 1694 to Francis Thelaball, who had

---

[420] Nugent, *Cavaliers and Pioneers*, 2:234-5 (Patent Book 7:148).
[421] Norfolk Co VA Deed Book 9:425.
[422] Meyer and Dorman, *Adventurers of Purse and Person*, 439-40 (Norfolk Co VA Deed Book 7:70). Dorman, *Adventurers of Purse and Person* 2005 adds records to this Francis, which conflict with other documents.
[423] Dorman, *Adventurers of Purse and Person*, 2:576-7.
[424] Meyer and Dorman, *Adventurers of Purse and Person*, 440 (Princess Anne Co VA Minute Book 3:17).
[425] McIntosh, *Norfolk Co Wills 1637-1710*, 27-8 (Book E:29).
[426] James, *Lower Norfolk Antiquary*, 3:140. Norfolk Co VA Wills & Deeds E:19, Deed Book 4:23.
[427] James, *Lower Norfolk Antiquary*, 3:141. Norfolk Co VA Deed Book 5:146.

married Margery, widow of Alexander Ivy.[428] He was the son of **George Ivey** and **Hannah** ____.[429]

The will of Francis[3] Thelaball, which was dated 12 Dec 1702 and proved 15 Mar 1704/5, named his sons James executor, Dyer, Francis, Lemuel, his daughter Sarah, youngest son a cow when 21, and wife Margery. James was to pay his mother-in-law (step-mother) twenty shillings a year in her widowhood.[430] Margery petitioned 16 Apr 1705 as widow and relict of Francis Thelaball deceased for her third of his estate.[431]

- - - - - - - - - -

63. James[4] Thelaball <See pg. 126> (62.Francis[3], 61.Elizabeth[2], 1.Francis[1]).
ISSUE:[432]
- m i. **Francis Thelaball**, born before 1715,[433] died before 14 Aug 1758, the date of his father's will.
- m ii. **James Thelaball**.
- f iii. **Abigail Thelaball**, died before 8 Dec 1774.[434]
- f iv. **Elizabeth Thelaball**.
- f v. **Sarah Dyer Thelaball**.

James[4] Thelaball was born about 1677; on 21 Aug 1714 he, as constable, deposed that he was age 37 "or there abouts."[435]

He was named in his grandmother's 1702 will. In his father's will he was left the "plantation on which I live." On 18 Jan 1716/7 he deeded to Lemuel Thelaball, of Princess Anne Couty, 100 acres of land, part of the tract that his grandfather, James Thelaball lived on.[436]

His will, dated 14 Aug 1758 and proved 19 Feb 1767 named his son James[5], an executor, grandsons William[6] Thelaball, **James[6] Griffin**, daughter Abigale[5] Griffin, her four daughters and her husband **John Griffin** who was

---

[428] Norfolk Co VA Deed Book 5, pt. 2 Orders:331.
[429] Holtzclaw, "Ivey Family", Boddie, *Historical Southern Families*, 16:162-4.
[430] McIntosh, *Norfolk Co Wills 1637-1710*, 187 (Book 7:73).
[431] Norfolk Co VA Deed Book 7:74.
[432] Wingo, *Norfolk Co VA Will Book 1*, 97 (f 153).
[433] beth@TidewaterTapestry.com (Wingo, *Norfolk Co VA Tithables 1730-1750*, 43).
[434] Maling, *Princess Anne Co VA Deed Books 8-18*, 69 (14DB147).
[435] Norfolk Co VA Deed Book 9, pt. 2 Orders:92.
[436] Norfolk Co VA Deed Book 9:560-2.

also named an executor, daughters **Elizabeth⁵ Collins**, and Sarah Dyer⁵ Thelaball.⁴³⁷

- - - - - - - - - - -

68. Margaret³ Thelaball <See pg. 124> (61.Elizabeth², 1.Francis¹) was born about 1648. She married **William Langley** about 1664. He was born before 1650. He was the son of **William Langley** and **Joyce** ____. ⁴³⁸

ISSUE:⁴³⁹

+ 69. m   i.   **William Langley**, born about 1665, died after 27 Aug 1740 <See pg. 130>.
+ 70. m   ii. **Nathan Langley**, born about 1667, died before 19 Nov 1742 <See pg. 130>.
+ 71. m   iii. **James Langley**, born about 1669, died before 26 Sep 1752 <See pg. 131>.
  72. m   iv. **Abraham Langley**, born about 1671, died after 27 Aug 1740. He was named in his father's 1715 will and his brother Jacob's 1740 will.
  73. m   v.   **Jacob Langley**, born about 1673. His will, dated 27 Aug 1740 proved 3 Jun 1741, named all of his sisters and brothers and some "cousins" (nephews).⁴⁴⁰
  74. m   vi. **Jeremiah Langley**, born about 1675. His will, dated 9 Jun 1747 and proved 20 Jul 1749, named many family members.⁴⁴¹
+ 75. f   vii. **Margaret Langley**, born about 1677, died before 20 Mar 1749/50 <See pg. 132>.
+ 76. f   viii.**Joyce Langley**, born about 1680 <See pg. 133>.
+ 77. f   ix. **Elizabeth Langley**, born about 1682 <See pg. 134>.

Margaret³ died before 12 May 1702, the date of her mother's will.⁴⁴²

William was a justice in the Norfolk County court 16 Mar 1701/2, and as Captain William Langley, was a justice at court 16 Apr 1705; he served as a

---

⁴³⁷ Wingo, *Norfolk Co VA Will Book 1*, 97 (f 153).
⁴³⁸ "Langley Family", *Genealogies, Wm & M Qrtrly*, 3:303.
⁴³⁹ The approximate marriage date and birth dates are based on the youngest daughter having a son in 1702.
⁴⁴⁰ Maling, *Princess Anne Co VA Deed Books 1-7*, 72 (6DB49).
⁴⁴¹ McIntosh, *Norfolk Co Wills 1710-1753*, 222-3 (Book H:252).
⁴⁴² James, *Lower Norfolk Antiquary*, 3:144-6.

burgess in 1715.*443* He was listed with 1487 acres in Norfolk County in 1704.*444*

The will of William Langley, which was dated 19 Jul 1715 and proved 16 May 1718, named sons William, Nathan, James, Abraham, Jacob, Jeremiah, daughter Margaret Johnson, Leml Thelabald who married daughter Joyce, and George Ivy who married daughter Elizabeth.*445*

- - - - - - - - - - -

69. William⁴ Langley <See pg. 129> (68.Margaret³, 61.Elizabeth², 1.Francis¹) was born about 1665. He married **Sarah Vaughan**. She was the daughter of **William Vaughan** and **Elizabeth Purdy**.*446*

ISSUE:

- m i. **Jacob Langley**, died before 9 Jun 1747. He was not named in his uncle Jeremiah's will.
- m ii. **Joseph Langley**, died before 17 May 1750, the date his will was proved.*447*
- f iii. **Elizabeth Langley**.
- f iv. **Signa Langley**, died after 1771.*448*
- m v. **William Langley**, died before Feb 1755, the date his will was proved.*449*
- m vi. **Jonathan Langley**.

William⁴ died after 27 Aug 1740, the date of his brother Jacob's will, which named William and William's sons Jacob⁵ and Joseph⁵.*450* His brother Jeremiah's 1747 will listed the children of William⁴: Joseph⁵, William⁵, Jonathan⁵, Elizabeth⁵, and Signa⁵ who was married to **Samuel Bartee**.*451*

- - - - - - - - - - -

70. Nathan⁴ Langley <See pg. 129> (68.Margaret³, 61.Elizabeth², 1.Francis¹) was born about 1667. He married **Sarah ____**.

---

443 Norfolk Co VA Deed Books 6:231, 7:74. Leonard, *General Assembly of Virginia*, 68.
444 Smith, *Quit Rents of Virginia, 1704*, 54.
445 McIntosh, *Norfolk Co Wills 1710-1753*, 66-8 (Book 10:12).
446 beth@TidewaterTapestry.com (Norfolk Co CA Deed Book 4:94a. McIntosh, *Norfolk Co Wills 1637-1710*, 125).
447 McIntosh, *Norfolk Co Wills 1710-1753*, 259 (Book I:158).
448 beth@TidewaterTapestry.com (Wingo, *Norfolk Co VA Tithables 1766-1780*, 144).
449 Wingo, *Unrecorded Wills Norfolk Co VA*, 62.
450 Maling, *Princess Anne Co VA Deed Books 1-7*, 72 (6DB49).
451 McIntosh, *Norfolk Co Wills 1710-1753*, 222-3 (Book H:252).

ISSUE:[452]
- m i. **Absalom Langley**, died before 5 Apr 1760.[453]
- f ii. **Joyce Langley**, died before 19 Nov 1742, the date her will was proved. She left her sister Kezia property when she arrived at age 21.[454]
- m iii. **George Langley**.
- m iv. **James Langley**, died before May 1777.[455]
- f v. **Kezia Langley**, died before May 1753, the date her will was proved.[456]
- m vi. **Moses Langley**.

Nathan[4] Langley, in his will written 4 Aug 1742 and proved 19 Nov 1742, named wife Sarah, sons Absolom[5], George[5], James[5], Moses[5], and daughters Joyce[5] and Kesia[5].[457]

His wife Sarah, in her nuncupative will of 30 Dec 1742, "verbally ... signed on her dying bed", which was proved 21 Jan 1742/3, named son Moses[5] and daughter Kezia[5] evidently under age.[458]

Nathan's brother Jeremiah's 1747 will listed children of Nathan, Absolem[5], James[5], Moses[5], and Kezia[5].[459]

- - - - - - - - - - -

71. James[4] Langley <See pg. 129> (68.Margaret[3], 61.Elizabeth[2], 1.Francis[1]) was born about 1669. He married **Sarah Nicholson** 24 May 1731.[460]

ISSUE:[461]
- f i. **Anna Langley**, married **George Rouviere**. She died after 27 Jan 1768, the date of the will of her second husband, **Francis Moore**.[462]

---

[452] Dorman, *Adventurers of Purse and Person*, 2:590.
[453] Dorman, *Adventurers of Purse and Person*, 2:626.
[454] McIntosh, *Norfolk Co Wills 1710-1753*, 169 (Book H:9).
[455] Dorman, *Adventurers of Purse and Person*, 2:626.
[456] McIntosh, *Norfolk Co Wills 1710-1753*, 311 (Book I:317).
[457] McIntosh, *Norfolk Co Wills 1710-1753*, 169-70 (Book H:10).
[458] McIntosh, *Norfolk Co Wills 1710-1753*, 172 (Book H:18).
[459] McIntosh, *Norfolk Co Wills 1710-1753*, 222-3 (Book H:252).
[460] Wingo, *Marriages of Norfolk Co VA*, 1:39.
[461] Maling, *Princess Anne Co VA Deed Books 1-7*, 93 (7DB367).
[462] Maling, *Princess Anne Co VA Deed Books 8-18*, 8 (8DB355 - 1758 will of George Rouviere), 13 (8DB547 - 1761 - Francis Moore and wife Anna, daughter of James Langley), 35 (10DB220 - will of Francis Moore).

Mason Families

    f ii. **Frances Langley**.

James[4] was named in his brother Jacob's 1740 will.[463]

James[4]'s will, written 5 Dec 1751 and proved 26 Sep 1752, named his wife Sarah and his daughters Frances[5] and Anna[5], the wife of Dr. George Rouviere.[464]

Sarah died before 20 May 1755, when Dr. George Rouviere was named in a suit concerning the estates of both James and Sarah.[465]

- - - - - - - - - - -

75. Margaret[4] Langley <See pg. 129> (68.Margaret[3], 61.Elizabeth[2], 1.Francis[1]) was born about 1677. She married **Jacob Johnson**, Jr. about 1700.[466] He was the son of **Jacob Johnson** and **Mary Ashall**.[467]
                                  ISSUE:
    f i. **Mary[5] Johnson**, married before Mar 1723 Capt. **James Nimmo**,[468] whose will was dated 19 Mar 1753 and proved 17 Apr 1753.[469] Mary died before 20 Jan 1761, the date of the division of her estate.[470] Their son **Gershom[6] Nimmo**, married **Elizabeth Boush**.[471] **(See number 31 - pg. 18)**.
    f ii. **Jacomine[5] Johnson**, married **John Hunter**, both named in her mother's will. Jacomine died after 19 Jun 1753, the date of the inventory of her husband's estate.[472] **Jacob[6] Hunter** married (1) **Susannah Moore**, daughter of Capt. **Henry Moore**, before 21 Sep 1756.[473] On 5 Dec 1766 **Jacob[6] Hunter** married (2) **Elizabeth Boush**, the widow of

---

[463] Maling, *Princess Anne Co VA Deed Books 1-7*, 72 (6DB49).

[464] Maling, *Princess Anne Co VA Deed Books 1-7*, 93 (7DB367).

[465] Walter, *Princess Anne Co VA Deed and Minute Books*, 107 (7MB171).

[466] James, *Lower Norfolk Antiquary*, 1:85 (6 Mar 1722, Mrs Margaret Johnson, widow of Jacob Johnson Jr.). Maling, *Princess Anne Co VA Deed Books 1-7*, 72 (6DB49 Margaret Johnson, sister of Jacob Langley).

[467] James, *Lower Norfolk Antiquary*, 3:29-33 (1671 will of George Ashall and 1675 power of attorney, Mary Ashall, widow, to son-in-law Jacob Johnson).

[468] Dorman, *Adventurers of Purse and Person*, 2:627 (Princess Anne Co VA 3OB165).

[469] Maling, *Princess Anne Co VA Deed Books 1-7*, 95 (7DB448).

[470] Walter, *Princess Anne Co VA Deed and Minute Books*, 115 (7MB411).

[471] Dorman, *Adventurers of Purse and Person*, 2:627.

[472] Maling, *Princess Anne Co VA Deed Books 1-7*, 97 (7DB482).

[473] Walter, *Princess Anne Co VA Deed and Minute Books*, 33, 110 (6DB390/7MB249).

Mason Families 133

        Gershom⁶ Nimmo⁴⁷⁴ (See number 31 - pg. 18). **Jacomine⁶ Hunter** married Capt. **Frederick Wilson Boush** (See number 32 - pg. 19).⁴⁷⁵ **John⁷ Hunter** married **Euphan⁵ Wilson** 4 Jan 1783.⁴⁷⁶ (See number 51 - pg. 24).

m iii. **William Johnson**, died before 2 Aug 1727 when James Nimmo and his wife Mary obtained letters of administration on the estate of her brother William Johnson.⁴⁷⁷

m iv. **Jacob Johnson**.

Margaret⁴ Langley was named in her father's 1715 will and her brother Jacob Langley's 1740 will. She married Jacob Johnson Jr. whose will, written 12 Apr 1710 and proved 1 Nov 1710, named sons William⁵ and Jacob⁵, and daughters Mary⁵ and Jacomin⁵.⁴⁷⁸

Her will, dated 10 Mar 1749/50, named daughter Mary⁵ wife of Capt. James Nimmo and daughter Jacomine⁵ wife of John Hunter, and grandson Jacob Hunter⁶.⁴⁷⁹ **Edward Wilson James** (-1906), a descendant of this Mason line and also the Wilson and Boush lines, was the editor of *Lower Norfolk Antiquary*, a valuable resource on colonial Virginia.⁴⁸⁰

- - - - - - - - - - -

76. **Joyce⁴ Langley** <See pg. 129> (68.Margaret³, 61.Elizabeth², 1.Francis¹) was born about 1680. She married (1) **Lemuel Thelaball (See number 81)** before 19 Jul 1715, the date of her father's will.⁴⁸¹

                    ISSUE:⁴⁸²

m i. **Robert Thelaball**, died before 1 Feb 1737/8.

f ii. **Margaret Thelaball**.

f iii. **Keziah Thelaball**, died before 3 Jan 1774, the date of her husband's will.⁴⁸³

---

⁴⁷⁴ James, "Princess Anne Co Marriages", 529. Wingo, *Marriages of Princess Anne Co VA*, 2:1.

⁴⁷⁵ Dorman, *Adventurers of Purse and Person*, 2:627-8. Boush Family Bible, Accession 22246, LVA.

⁴⁷⁶ Wingo, *Marriages of Norfolk Co VA, Vol 1*, 35.

⁴⁷⁷ James, *Lower Norfolk Antiquary*, 1:86-7.

⁴⁷⁸ Maling, *Princess Anne Co VA Deed Books 1-7*, 29 (2DB38).

⁴⁷⁹ Maling, *Princess Anne Co VA Deed Books 1-7*, 87 (7DB166).

⁴⁸⁰ "James, Edward Wilson - In Memoriam."

⁴⁸¹ McIntosh, *Norfolk Co Wills 1710-1753*, 66-8 (Book 10:12).

⁴⁸² Dorman, *Adventurers of Purse and Person*, 2:588, 621.

⁴⁸³ Maling, *Princess Anne Co VA Deed Books 8-18*, 64 (14DB40).

Mason Families

  f iv. **Mary Thelaball**, died after 19 Sep 1758, when she and her sister Keziah were named with their husbands in a deed.[484]

Lemuel's will, dated 14 Feb 1726 and proved 3 May 1727, named his son Robert, wife Joyce, and daughters Margaret, Keziah and Mary.[485]

Joyce married (2) **John Wishart** 13 Sep 1732.[486] They were named in her brother Jacob's 1740 will.[487]

- - - - - - - - - - -

77. Elizabeth[4] **Langley** <See pg. 129> (68.Margaret[3], 61.Elizabeth[2], 1.Francis[1]) was born about 1682. She married **George Ivey** about 1698. He was born about 1669. He was the son of **George Ivey** and **Hannah** ____.[488]

      ISSUE:
  m i. **William Ivey**, born about 1700, died before 20 May 1769.[489]
  m ii. **James Ivey**, born about 1702, died before 16 Nov 1752.[490]
  m iii. **Joseph Ivey**, born about 1704, died about 1754.[491]
  f iv. **Margaret Ivey**, born about 1706.

George married (1) **Hannah** ____ shown when they sold land in 1694.[492]

Elizabeth[4] Langley married George Ivey around 1698. She signed the inventory of his estate in Dec 1710, excluding the increase of the two ewes given to William[5] in his great grandmother's 1702 will.[493] In Apr 1715 the estate was divided into five shares.[494]

In May 1714 William[5] Ivey chose Capt. Wm Langley as his guardian; in 1717 Elizabeth Ivey as next friend of James[5], Joseph[5] and Margaret[5] Ivey,

---

[484] Maling, *Princess Anne Co VA Deed Books 8-18*, 7 (8DB275).
[485] Maling, *Princess Anne Co VA Deed Books 1-7*, 52 (4DB115).
[486] Wingo, *Marriages of Princess Anne Co VA*, 2:1.
[487] Maling, *Princess Anne Co VA Deed Books 1-7*, 72 (6DB49).
[488] Holtzclaw, "Ivey Family", Boddie, *Historical Southern Families*, 16:162-4.
[489] Wingo, *Norfolk Co VA Will Book 1*, 115 (f 187a).
[490] Dorman, *Adventurers of Purse and Person*, 2:628-9.
[491] Dorman, *Adventurers of Purse and Person*, 2:629.
[492] Holtzclaw, "Ivey Family", Boddie, *Historical Southern Families*, 16:164-5 (Norfolk Co VA 6:22).
[493] Norfolk Co VA Deed Book 9:36.
[494] Norfolk Co VA Deed Book 9:384

all under the age of 21, sued William Ivey for their portions of property that George Ivey "there Deceased father Dyed Seised of."[495]

William[5] Ivey married **Ann[4] (Thelaball) Lowery (See number 84. - pg. 140)**, by 4 Apr 1744, shown when they consented for the marriage of Ann's daughter Tabitha Lowery.[496] James[5] Ivy married **Mary Furlong (See pg. 109)**, Nov 1728.[497] Joseph[5] Ivey married **Alice Miller (See pg. 107)** before 22 Mar 1741/2.[498]

The only explanation for the following statements in wills is that Elizabeth[4] married (2) another **George Ivey**. Her father's 1715 will states "I give and bequeath unto George Ivy who married my daughter Elizabeth one shilling in full of her portion of my estate." Her brother Jacob's 1740 will states "to Mr. George Ivy who intermarried with my sister Elizabeth Langley one shilling."[499]

- - - - - - - - - - -

79. James[3] Thelaball <See pg. 124> (61.Elizabeth[2], 1.Francis[1]) was born about 1655. He married **Ann** ____.

ISSUE:
+ 80. m   i.   **Francis Thelaball**, born 30 Jan 1684/5, died 17 Mar 1726/7 <See pg. 136>.
+ 81. m   ii. **Lemuel Thelaball**, born about 1686, died before 3 May 1726/7 <See pg. 137>.
+ 82. f   iii. **Dinah Thelaball**, born about 1688, died before 17 May 1765 <See pg. 138>.
+ 83. f   iv. **Elizabeth Thelaball**, born after 1691, died after 4 Feb 1722 <See pg. 140>.
+ 84. f   v.   **Ann Thelaball**, born after 1693, died after 8 Apr 1769 <See pg. 140>.
  85. f   vi. **Martha Thelaball**, born after 24 Dec 1707, the date of her father's will.

---

[495] Norfolk Co VA Deed Book 9, pt. 2 Orders:79, 196.
[496] Wingo, *Marriages of Norfolk Co VA, Vol 1*, 49.
[497] Wingo, *Marriages of Norfolk Co VA, Vol 1*, 35.
[498] McIntosh, *Norfolk Co Wills 1710-1753*, 182 (Book H:95 - will of Mary Miller).
[499] Norfolk Co VA Deed Book 10:12. Walter, *Princess Anne Co VA Deed and Minute Books*, 5 (6DB49).

Regarding 600 acres of land in Hogg Pen Neck given to Elizabeth² by her brother Lemuel Mason in 1667, James³ Thelaball was deeded on 6 Jul 1677 by his mother, 200 acres.⁵⁰⁰ He was named in the 1691 will of his father.⁵⁰¹

James³'s will, dated 24 Dec 1707 and proved 18 Jan 1711/12, named his wife Ann and son Francis⁴ executors, son Lemuel⁴, daughter Dinah⁴, and then daughters Elizabeth⁴ and Ann⁴ both under age 16.⁵⁰² Ann made a deed of gift to their daughters Martha, Elizabeth, and Ann in Jul 1711.⁵⁰³ The older children, Francis⁴, Lemuel⁴, Matthew Godfrey and Dinah⁴ his wife, Peter Godfrey and Elizabeth⁴ his wife, James Lowrey and Ann⁴ his wife, made a deed of gift in 1721 to their sister Martha⁴ who was born after their father wrote his will.⁵⁰⁴

Ann died after 4 Feb 1722/3, when she witnessed the will of Peter Godfrey.⁵⁰⁵

- - - - - - - - - - -

80. Francis⁴ Thelaball <See pg. 135> (79.James³, 61.Elizabeth², 1.Francis¹) was born 30 Jan 1684/5. He married **Abigail Butt**. She was born 8 Jan 1694/5.⁵⁰⁶

ISSUE:⁵⁰⁷

m   i.   **James Thelaball**, born 22 Aug 1714, died before 3 Feb 1741/2, when his will was proved.⁵⁰⁸

m   ii.   **Thomas Thelaball**, born 18 Mar 1716, died young.

m   iii.   **Thomas Thelaball**, born 30 Mar 1718, married **Elizabeth Wilson (See number 28 - pg. 16)** before 13 Jan 1749/50 when she was named Elizabeth Thelaball in her father's will.⁵⁰⁹ Thomas died before 18 Apr 1751, when administration of his estate was granted to his widow,

---

⁵⁰⁰ James, *Lower Norfolk Antiquary*, 3:140. Norfolk Co VA Wills & Deeds E:19, Deed Book 4:23.

⁵⁰¹ Norfolk Co VA Deed Book 5:208.

⁵⁰² McIntosh, *Norfolk Co Wills 1710-1753*, 19 (Book 9:124)

⁵⁰³ Norfolk Co VA Deed Book 9:313.

⁵⁰⁴ Norfolk Co VA Orders, Appraisements, Wills 1719-1722, pt. 2:140.

⁵⁰⁵ McIntosh, *Norfolk Co Wills 1710-1753*, 96.

⁵⁰⁶ Meyer and Dorman, *Adventurers of Purse and Person*, 440. Dorman, *Adventurers of Purse and Person* 2005 changed some descendant lines and assigns these records to another Francis Thelaball.

⁵⁰⁷ Thelaball Family Bible, Accession 35231, LVA - gives birth dates of the parents and children.

⁵⁰⁸ Maling, *Princess Anne Co VA Deed Books 1-7*, 73 (6DB101).

⁵⁰⁹ Wingo, *Norfolk Co VA Will Book 1*, 4 (f 71-9 - will of James Wilson).

Mason Families 137

    Elizabeth Thelaball.[510] Her will, written 31 Jan 1778 and
    proved Jul 1783,[511] named their daughters **Abigail**[6]
    Thelaball, (See number 36 - pg. 17) who in 1784[512] married
    Matthew Godfrey (See pg. 139), and **Prudence**[6] **Thelaball**
    (See number 37 - pg. 17) who in 1796[513] married **Charles**
    Sayer Boush (See number 58 - pg. 203).
m iv. **Lemuel Thelaball**, born 9 Sep 1720, "going to sea", named
    his brothers Lewis, Nathaniel and Thomas in his will written
    24 Mar 1745/6 and proved 17 Feb 1746/7.[514]
m v. **Lewis Thelaball**, born 17 Dec 1722, perhaps married **Mary**
    Ann Boush named in the 1769 will of **Samuel Boush**.[515]
    Lewis's will, dated 12 Jun 1766 and proved 21 May 1767,
    named his wife Mary and Elizabeth[6] Thelaball daughter of
    Nathaniel dec'd,.[516]
m vi. **Nathaniel Thelaball**, born 11 Dec 1724, died before 15 May
    1755.[517]

Francis[4] and Abigail made a deed to James Lowery 12 Oct 1719.[518] Francis was a witness to his brother Lemuel's will 14 Feb 1726/7.[519] His will, dated 17 Mar 1726 and proved 3 May 1727, named sons James[5], Lemuel[5], Thomas[5], Lewis[5] and his wife Abigail.[520]

Francis died 17 Mar 1726/7.[521]

Abigail married (2) **Anthony Moseley** before 4 Sep 1728.[522]

Abigail died after 31 Dec 1741, when she was named mother Abigail Moseley in the will of her son James.

---

[510] Dorman, *Adventurers of Purse and Person*, 2:620.
[511] Norfolk Co VA Will Book 2:212-3 (181-2).
[512] Wingo, *Marriages of Norfolk Co VA, Vol 1*, 26.
[513] Wingo, *Marriages of Norfolk Co VA, Vol 2*, 16.
[514] Maling, *Princess Anne Co VA Deed Books 1-7*, 81 (6DB634).
[515] Maling, *Princess Anne Co VA Deed Books 8-18*, 41 (11DB39).
[516] Wingo, *Norfolk Co VA Will Book 1*, 99 (f 157).
[517] Dorman, *Adventurers of Purse and Person*, 2:620-1.
[518] Norfolk Co VA Orders, Appraisements, Wills 1719-1722, pt. 2:2.
[519] Maling, *Princess Anne Co VA Deed Books 1-7*, 52 (4DB115).
[520] Maling, *Princess Anne Co VA Deed Books 1-7*, 52 (4DB115).
[521] Thelaball Family Bible, Accession 35231, LVA.
[522] Dorman, *Adventurers of Purse and Person*, 2:112, 587.

81. Lemuel⁴ Thelaball <See pg. 135> (79.James³, 61.Elizabeth², 1.Francis¹) was born about 1686. He married **Joyce Langley (See number 76)**. She was the daughter of **William Langley** and **Margaret Thelaball**.

ISSUE:[523]

m   i.   **Robert⁵ Thelaball**, died before 1 Feb 1737/8.[524]

f   ii.   **Margaret⁵ Thelaball**.

f   iii.   **Keziah⁵ Thelaball**, On 19 Sep 1758 **James Hunter** and wife Keziah and Adam Thorowgood and wife Mary (daughters of Lemuel Thelaball) made a deed to **Thomas Hunter**, land that Lemuel Thelaball left son Robert, who died intestate.[525] Keziah died before 3 Jan 1774, the date of her husband's will.[526]

f   iv.   **Mary⁵ Thelaball**, married **Adam Thorowgood** and died after 19 Sep 1758, as noted above in the deed with her sister Keziah. Their daughter **Mary⁶ Thorowgood** married (1) Dr. **Hugh Craigdallie**;[527] Mary⁶ married (2) after 1774 Capt. **Willis Wilson (See number 107 - pg. 49)**.[528] Mary⁶ was named Mary Wilson in the 1785 will of her brother **Lemuel Thorowgood**.[529] She died 14 Feb 1819 at the age of 66.[530]

Lemuel⁴ Thelaball married before 19 Jul 1715 Joyce Langley, shown when they were named in her father's will.[531] On 18 Jan 1716/7 James Thelaball deeded Lemuel 100 acres of land in Norfolk County, part of the tract that his grandfather lived on.[532]

Lemuel's will, written 14 Feb 1726 and proved 3 May 1727, named son Robert⁵, wife Joyce and daughters Margaret⁵, Keziah⁵ and Mary⁵. His brother Francis Thelaball was a witness.[533]

---

[523] Maling, *Princess Anne Co VA Deed Books 1-7*, 52 (4DB115 - will of Lemuel Thelaball).

[524] Dorman, *Adventurers of Purse and Person*, 2:588.

[525] Maling, *Princess Anne Co VA Deed Books 8-18*, 7 (8DB275).

[526] Maling, *Princess Anne Co VA Deed Books 8-18*, 64 (14 DB40).

[527] Maling, *Princess Anne Co VA Deed Books 8-18*, 66 (14DB82).

[528] Butt, *Col James Wilson,* 14-17. Creecy, "Thorowgood Family", *Virginia Genealogist* 17:280.

[529] Maling, *Princess Anne Co VA, Wills,* 12.

[530] Butt, *Col James Wilson,* 16-7.

[531] McIntosh, *Norfolk Co Wills 1710-1753*, 66-8 (Book 10:12)

[532] Norfolk Co VA Deed Book 9:560-2.

[533] Maling, *Princess Anne Co VA Deed Books 1-7*, 52 (4DB115).

Mason Families

82. **Dinah⁴ Thelaball** <See pg. 135> (79.James³, 61.Elizabeth², 1.Francis¹) was born about 1688. She married **Mathew Godfrey** about 1708. He was the son of **John Godfrey** and **Mary** ____.⁵³⁴

ISSUE:⁵³⁵

- f   i. **Anne Godfrey**, born about 1709, died before 3 Apr 1754, as shown in the will of her father.
- f ii. **Mary Godfrey**, born about 1711, died before 3 Apr 1754.
- f iii. **Elizabeth Godfrey**, born about 1713, died after 19 Mar 1741/2, the date that the will of her husband, **Henry Miller**, was proved. She was granted letters of administration. Henry named his father-in-law Matthew Godfrey in the will.⁵³⁶
- f iv. **Affiah Godfrey**, born about 1715, died after 21 Apr 1774, the date that the will of her husband, **Nicholas Woneycutt**, was written.⁵³⁷
- f v. **Keziah Godfrey**, died before Jul 1777.⁵³⁸
- m vi. **Matthew Godfrey** married **Abigail Porter** in 1756.⁵³⁹ Their son Col. **Matthew⁶ Godfrey** married **Abigail Thelaball (See pg. 17)**.⁵⁴⁰
- f vii. **Dinah Godfrey**, who married (1) ____ **Belgrove**, married in 1761 (2) **Edward Archer**.⁵⁴¹ She died after May 1772, the date of her petition, as relict of Edward Archer.⁵⁴²

Dinah⁴ was named wife of Matthew Godfrey and legatee of Mr. James Thelaball deceased in a 10 Mar 1720/1 document.⁵⁴³ In 1730 Matthew and Dinah Godfrey made gifts to their seven children.⁵⁴⁴ Anne and Mary died before Matthew's will, written 3 Apr 1754 and proved Nov 1755, which named wife Dinah, daughters Elizabeth⁵ Miller, Affiah⁵ Wonecutt, Keziah⁵ Godfrey, son Matthew⁵ Godfrey, and daughter Dinah⁵ Belgrove.⁵⁴⁵

---

⁵³⁴ McIntosh, *Norfolk Co Wills 1637-1710*, 200 (will of his father), McIntosh, *Norfolk Co Wills 1710-1753*, 57, 83 (wills of his uncle and mother).
⁵³⁵ Norfolk Co VA Deed Book 11:4-5 - deeds of gift to their seven children.
⁵³⁶ Wingo, *Norfolk Co VA Will Book 1*, 34 (f 51a).
⁵³⁷ McVey, *Norfolk Co VA Will Book 2*, 27.
⁵³⁸ beth@TidewaterTapestry.com (McVey, *Norfolk Co VA Will Book 2*, 72).
⁵³⁹ Wingo, *Marriages of Norfolk Co VA, Vol 1*, 26.
⁵⁴⁰ Dorman, *Adventurers of Purse and Person*, 2:622-3, 620.
⁵⁴¹ Wingo, *Marriages of Norfolk Co VA, Vol 1*, 1.
⁵⁴² McVey, *Norfolk Co VA Will Book 2*, 3.
⁵⁴³ Norfolk Co VA Orders, Appraisements, Wills 1719-1722, pt. 2:140.
⁵⁴⁴ Norfolk Co VA Deed Book 11:4-5.
⁵⁴⁵ Wingo, *Norfolk Co VA Will Book 1*, 3 (f 5a).

Dinah's will, dated 25 May 1759 and proved 17 May 1765, named son Matthew[5] Godfrey, daughters **Elizabeth[5] Cheshire**, Kezia[5] Godfrey, Affiah[5] Wonycutt, and Dinah[5] Belgrove.[546]

- - - - - - - - - - -

83. **Elizabeth[4] Thelaball** <See pg. 135> (79.James[3], 61.Elizabeth[2], 1.Francis[1]) was born after 1691. She was less than 16 in her father's 1707 will.[547] She married **Peter Godfrey** before 10 Mar 1720/1.[548] He was the son of **Warren Godfrey** and **Sarah ____**.[549]

ISSUE:
- m i. **Lemuel Godfrey**.
- f ii. **Leddy Godfrey**.

Peter married (1) **Abigail Cooper** before 13 Mar 1716. She was the daughter of **John Cooper** and **____ Wilder**.[550]

Peter's will, dated 4 Feb 1722/3 and proved 18 May 1723, named his son Lemuel Godfrey, daughter Leddy Godfrey, and wife Elizabeth.[551]

- - - - - - - - - - -

84. **Ann[4] Thelaball** <See pg. 135> (79.James[3], 61.Elizabeth[2], 1.Francis[1]) was born probably after 1693, named after her sister, both less than age 16, in their father's will.[552] She married (1) **James Lowery** before 10 Mar 1720/1, when they were named in a gift to her sister.[553] He was possibly the son of **James Lowery** and **Judith ____**.[554]

ISSUE:[555]

---

[546] Wingo, *Norfolk Co VA Will Book 1*, 86 (f 136a).
[547] McIntosh, *Norfolk Co Wills 1710-1753*, 19 (Book 9:124).
[548] Norfolk Co VA Orders, Appraisements, Wills 1719-1722, pt. 2:140-1.
[549] McIntosh, *Norfolk Co Wills 1710-1753*, 19-20 (Book 9:168). Norfolk Co VA Deed Book 9:266.
[550] McIntosh, *Norfolk Co Wills 1710-1753*, 63 (Book 9:666 - will of Michael Wilder), 64-5 (Book 10:7 - will of John Cooper)
[551] McIntosh, *Norfolk Co Wills 1710-1753*, 96.
[552] McIntosh, *Norfolk Co Wills 1710-1753*, 19 (Book 9:124).
[553] Norfolk Co VA Orders, Appraisements, Wills 1719-1722, pt. 2:140-1.
[554] McIntosh, *Norfolk Co Wills 1710-1753*, 75-6 (will of James Lowery).
[555] Dorman, *Adventurers of Purse and Person*, 2:589, 591, 623.

Mason Families

    f   i. **Sophia Lowery**, married **Lemuel Wilson (See number 105 - pg. 48)**. Sophia died before 1752, when Lemuel married **Martha Alston**.[556]
    f ii. **Tabitha Lowery**, died before 27 Aug 1762, the date of the second marriage of her husband, **Joshua Nicholson**.[557]
    f iii. **Ann Lowery**.
    f iv. **Sarah Lowery**, died before 20 May 1741. She was not named in the suit, which named her sisters, as described below.[558]

James died after 21 May 1736, when he and Ann gave gifts to their four daughters.[559]

Ann married (2) **William Ivey (See pg. 134)** before 20 May 1741, when Capt. William Ivy and Ann his wife, relict of Mr. James Lowery deceased were named in a suit. Mr. Lemuel Wilson and Sophia his wife, Capt. William Ivy and Ann his wife, relict of James Lowery deceased, Tabitha, second daughter of Mr. James Lowery, and Ann the youngest daughter were named concerning the estate of James Lowery.[560] On 4 Apr 1744 William and Ann Ivy consented to the marriage of Tabitha Lowery to Joshua Nicholson.[561]

                   ISSUE:[562]
    m v. **John Ivey**.
    f vi. **Elizabeth Ivey**, died before 8 Apr 1769, the date of her father's will.

William died before 20 May 1769, the date his will was proved. He named his wife Ann Ivy, son John Ivy and grandchildren George Ivy, **Ann Snale** and **William Ivy Snale**.[563]

- - - - - - - - - - -

---

[556] Chowan Co NC Marriage Bond 29 Jan 1752, Martha Alston and Lemuel Wilson of Virginia.
[557] Wingo, *Marriages of Norfolk Co VA, Vol 1*, 49.
[558] Norfolk Co VA Deed Book 13:29.
[559] Norfolk Co VA Deed Book 12:201-2.
[560] Norfolk Co VA Deed Book 13:29.
[561] Wingo, *Marriages of Norfolk Co VA, Vol 1*, 49.
[562] Dorman, *Adventurers of Purse and Person*, 2:623-4.
[563] Wingo, *Norfolk Co VA Will Book 1*, 115 (f 187a).

86. Elizabeth³ Thelaball <See pg. 124> (61.Elizabeth², 1.Francis¹) was born Aug 1660. She married **Thomas Langley** about 1680. He was born Dec 1654. He was the son of **William Langley and Joyce** ____. [564]

ISSUE:[565]

+ 87. m i. **Thomas Langley**, born about 1681, died before 21 Mar 1750/1 <See pg. 142>.
+ 88. m ii. **Lemuel Langley**, born about 1683, died before 16 Mar 1748/9 <See pg. 142>.
+ 89. m iii. **John Langley**, born about 1685, died Jun 1753 <See pg. 144>.
   90. m iv. **George Langley**, born about 1690, died after 7 Jun 1748.
   91. f v. **Mary Langley**, born about 1698. She married ____ **Millner**.
+ 92. f vi. **Abigail Langley**, born about 1702, died 1 Mar 1763 <See pg. 144>.

Thomas Langley's will, written 29 Aug 1746 and proved 15 Oct 1747, named sons Thomas, Lemuel, John, George, daughters Mary Millner, Abigail Hargrove, granddaughters **Margaret Smith**, and Abigail Langley.[566]

Thomas died 5 Oct 1747. Elizabeth died 19 Nov 1738.[567]

- - - - - - - - - - -

87. Thomas⁴ Langley <See pg. 141> (86.Elizabeth³, 61.Elizabeth², 1.Francis¹) was born about 1681. He married **Katherine** ____ about 1710.

ISSUE:[568]

m i. **Thomas Langley**, born about 1712, died before 16 Aug 1753.[569]
f ii. **Tabitha Langley**, born about 1714, died after 20 Jul 1750.
f iii. **Mary Langley**, born about 1716, died after 20 Jul 1750.
m iv. **John Langley**, born about 1718, died after 20 Jul 1750.
f v. **Katherine Langley**, born about 1720, died before 27 Jul 1750, the date of her father's will.[570]

Thomas⁴ Langley was named in his grandmother's 1702 will.[571] His will, dated 20 Jul 1750 and proved 21 Mar 1750/1, named sons Thomas, John,

---

[564] "Langley Family", *Genealogies, Wm & M Qrtrly*, 3:303, 306.
[565] Dorman, *Adventurers of Purse and Person*, 2:578.
[566] McIntosh, *Norfolk Co Wills 1710-1753*, 211-2 (Book H:215).
[567] Hargroves, *Commonplace Book, 1694-1818*. Gives birth and death dates.
[568] Dorman, *Adventurers of Purse and Person*, 2:591. The date of the marriage of his daughter Mary is 1738, not 1756. Wingo, *Marriages of Norfolk Co VA, Vol 1*, 9.
[569] Dorman, *Adventurers of Purse and Person*, 2:629.
[570] Dorman, *Adventurers of Purse and Person*, 2:629-30.
[571] James, *Lower Norfolk Antiquary*, 3:144-6. (See appendix).

daughters Tabitha, **Mary Briant**, grandchildren **Thomas Dunnock**, **Katherine Dunnock** and wife Katherine.[572]

- - - - - - - - - - -

88. Lemuel[4] Langley <See pg. 141> (86.Elizabeth[3], 61.Elizabeth[2], 1.Francis[1]) was born about 1683. He married (1) **Margaret** ____ before 20 Nov 1713.[573]

ISSUE:
- m   i.   **Thomas Langley**, born about 1714, died before 19 May 1761.[574]
- m ii.   **Lemuel Langley**, born about 1716, died before Jul 1772.[575]
- f iii. **Frances Langley**, born about 1718, died 16 Feb 1775. She married **Josiah Wilson (See number 45 - pg. 22)**. "Mrs. Frances Wilson, spouse of Col. Josiah Wilson of Norfolk County, died" 16 Feb 1775. "Col. Josiah Wilson of St. Bride's Parish, Norfolk County," died 12 May 1795.[576] Josiah Wilson's will, dated 14 Oct 1794, was proved 20 Jul 1795.[577]

On 15 Mar 1717/8 Lemuel[4] Langley, sloop carpenter, and Margaret signed a deed to **John Langley**.[578]

Lemuel married (2) **Mary Nicholson** before 24 Feb 1728, the date of her father's will.[579] She was the daughter of **William Nicholson** and **Alice** ____.

ISSUE:[580]
- m iv. **Willis Langley**, married before 13 Jan 1749/50 **Affiah Wilson, (See number 72 - pg. 29)** daughter of **James Wilson**, who named Affiah Langley in his will.[581] Willis's will, dated 25 Nov 1766 and proved 19 Mar 1767, named son **Willis Wilson Langley**.[582]

---

[572] McIntosh, *Norfolk Co Wills 1710-1753*, 270 (I:213).
[573] Norfolk Co VA Deed Book 9, pt. 2 Orders:74.
[574] Walter, *Princess Anne Co VA Deed and Minute Books*, 116 (7MB426).
[575] McVey, *Norfolk Co VA Will Book 2*, 3-4.
[576] Headley, *18th-Century Newspapers*, 371, 372.
[577] Brewster, *Norfolk Co VA Will Book 3*, 77-9.
[578] Norfolk Co VA Deed Book 10:6.
[579] McIntosh, *Norfolk Co Wills 1710-1753*, 118.
[580] Dorman, *Adventurers of Purse and Person*, 2:591-2, 631-2.
[581] Wingo, *Norfolk Co VA Will Book 1*, 4-5 (f 7a-9).
[582] Wingo, *Norfolk Co VA Will Book 1*, 97-8 (f 154).

m v. **Samuel Langley**, died before 27 Mar 1771.
m vi. **Nathaniel Langley**, died before 21 May 1752.[583]
f vii. **Mary Langley**, died after 22 Jan 1750/1, named in her brother Nathaniel's will.

The will of Capt. Lemuel Langley, dated 10 Dec 1748 and proved 16 Mar 1648/9, named sons Thomas, Lemuel, and daughter Frances Wilson from his first marriage and sons Willis, Samuel, Nathaniel, and daughter Mary and wife Mary from his second marriage.[584]

Mary Langley's will, dated 11 Sep 1761 and proved Dec 1761, named sons Willis, Samuel, daughter in-law Affia Langley, grandchildren **Letitia Langley, Lemuel Langley**, Willis Wilson Langley, **James Langley, Josiah Langley** all children of her son Willis Langley, and Nathaniel Langley, son of her son Samuel Langley.[585]

- - - - - - - - - - -

89. John[4] Langley <See pg. 141> (86.Elizabeth[3], 61.Elizabeth[2], 1.Francis[1]) was born about 1685.

ISSUE:[586]

f i. **Lydia Langley**.
f ii. **Betty Langley**.
f iii. **Abigail Langley**, born before 29 Aug 1746, the date of her grandfather's will.[587]

John died Jun 1753.

- - - - - - - - - - -

92. Abigail[4] Langley <See pg. 142> (86.Elizabeth[3], 61.Elizabeth[2], 1.Francis[1]) was born about 1702. She married (1) **John Granbery** 26 Feb 1722/3. He was born 1699.[588]

ISSUE:

m i. **Thomas Granbery**, born 24 Jun 1724, died before 1782.
f ii. **Mary Granbery**, born 8 Apr 1726, died 7 Jan 1814.
m iii. **Josiah Granbery**, born 14 Oct 1728, died Dec 1772.

---

[583] McIntosh, *Norfolk Co Wills 1710-1753*, 294-5 (Book I:255).

[584] McIntosh, *Norfolk Co Wills 1710-1753*, 220-1 (Book H:245).

[585] Wingo, *Norfolk Co VA Will Book 1*, 49-50 (f 74).

[586] beth@TidewaterTapestry.com (Langley et ux v. Guy, chancery case [1771], Norfolk Co VA chancery index no. 1771-006, LVA, Richmond VA).

[587] McIntosh, *Norfolk Co Wills 1710-1753*, 211-2 (Book H:215).

[588] Hargroves, *Commonplace Book, 1694-1818* - all dates in this family. Dorman, *Adventurers of Purse and Person*, 2:592.

  m iv. **John Granbery**, born 3 Oct 1730.
  m v. **William Granbery**, born 23 Mar 1731/2.
  f vi. **Margaret Granbery**, born 22 Sep 1733.

John died 25 Dec 1733.

Abigail married (2) **Robert Hargroves** after 1733.
         ISSUE:
  f vii. **Hilary Hargroves**, born 6 Mar 1736/7, died 2 Nov 1743.
  f viii. **Abigail Langley Hargroves**, born 20 Aug 1738, died 19 Oct 1747.
  f ix. **Margaret Hargroves**, born 5 Sep 1740, died 30 Oct 1740.
  m x. **Willis Hargroves**, born 10 Nov 1741.

Abigail died 1 Mar 1763.

Alice McAlpine (Granbery) Walter (1908-2003), who was the compiler of many of the books and charts used as references, descended from this Mason line and also the Wilson and Boush lines.

- - - - - - - - - - -

93. Mary³ Thelaball <See pg. 124> (61.Elizabeth², 1.Francis¹) was born about 1662. She married (1) **William Chichester** about 1678. **(See pg. 101).**
         ISSUE:[589]
  m i. **William Chichester**, born about 1679, died before 15 Feb 1711/2.
  m ii. **James Chichester**, born about 1681, died before 15 Feb 1711/2.
  m iii. **John Chichester**, born about 1683.
  m iv. **Thomas Chichester**, born about 1685.
  f v. **Mary Chichester**, born about 1688, died before 28 Apr 1758 <See pg. 104>.

William and Mary Chichester were witnesses to the 1685 will of **Narthaniel Branker**.[590] The will of William Chichester, dated 23 Mar 1697/8 and proved 17 May 1698, named wife Mary executrix, sons William⁴, James⁴, John⁴, Thomas⁴ and overseers "cozens" (nephews) Thomas Mason and Lemuel Mason Jr. Lemuel Mason Jr. and Francis Thelaball were witnesses.[591]

---

[589] Norfolk Co VA Deed Book 9:154.
[590] McIntosh, *Norfolk Co Wills 1637-1710*, 97-8 (Book 4:218).
[591] McIntosh, *Norfolk Co Wills 1637-1710*, 167 (Book 6:125 -The will is badly torn; the name of son Thomas barely legible, the name of daughter Mary missing).

Mary³ married (2) **Lemuel Mason (See number 18)** before 28 Aug 1699.[592] In the 1702 will of her mother, she was named "daughter Mary Mason now wife of Lemuell Mason."[593] On 15 Jun 1711 Mary Mason was granted administration of the estate of her husband Lemuel Mason. The inventory was added to in February 1712/3, signed by Thomas Chichester.[594]

On 19 Mar 1711/2 a distribution of William Chichester's estate was made to Mrs. Mary Mason widow, to Mr. **Willis Wilson** who married Mary⁴ the daughter of Mr. William Chichester, to Thomas Chichester and to John Chichester.[595]

The will of Mary³ Mason, dated 15 Apr 1714 and proved 19 Nov 1714, named sons Thomas and John Chichester and three daughters; the only daughter named was Elizabeth.[596]

An audit 15 Feb 1714/5 of Lemuel Mason's estate showed disbursements to Mrs. Mary Mason for her daughter Elizabeth Mason's part, and her daughter Tabitha Mason's part.[597]

---

[592] Norfolk Co VA Deed Book 6:168-9.
[593] James, *Lower Norfolk Antiquary*, 3:144-5. (See appendix).
[594] Norfolk Co VA Deed Book 9, pt. 2 Orders:11-12, Deed Book 9:364.
[595] Norfolk Co VA Deed Book 9:154
[596] Norfolk Co VA Deed Book 9:355-6, 424.
[597] Norfolk Co VA Deed Book 9:154, 366.

CHAPTER 3 - Seawell Families

1. **Henry**[1] **Seawell**. He married **Alice** ___.
   ISSUE:
   + 2. f   i. **Ann Seawell**, born about 1635, died before 15 Mar 1705/6
           <See pg. 154>.
     14. m   ii. **Henry Seawell**, born 1 May 1639 in Lower Norfolk County,
           Virginia, died before 16 Aug 1672. The details of his life are
           in the text below.

Henry[1] Seawell was born probably around 1600 in England and was in Virginia by 1629.[1] He married Alice, suggested to be the daughter of Thomas Willoughby.[2] Dates given for the descendants of **Thomas Willoughby** indicate that Alice, if a Willoughby, was more likely his sister.[3] Thomas Willoughby received a land patent for 2900 acres in 1654, which included 1500 acres for an earlier patent, for transporting 28 persons among whom were Alice, Thomas and Elizabeth Willoughby.[4] The relationships were not stated. Norfolk County's Books A and B name no Alice Willoughby, but Mrs. Seawell of Book A for the years 1642-1646 was shown to be Mrs. Alice Seawell in Book B in 1646.[5]

It is possible that **Thomas Seawell** who patented land in 1635 was a relative;[6] the given name Thomas was used for Henry Seawell's grandchildren and great-grandchildren. Some variations of the spelling of the surname - Seawell, Sewell, Sowell, etc. - are used in this narrative.

Henry Seawell settled 150 acres of land on the 650 acres that Capt. **William Tucker** patented in 1620, which Tucker later sold to Capt. **John Sibsey**. In a 1661 deed Elizabeth, the widow of John Sibsey, and her husband **John Triniman** confirmed the "tract or divident of Land called by the name of Sewell's Point" to Henry[2] Sewell son and heir of Henry[1] Sewell, deceased. It stated that Henry Seawell the elder "did in his lifetime many years prior

---

[1] Tucker, *Norfolk Highlights*, Chapter 3 (accessed 3 Feb 2007).
[2] Lee, *History of New Jersey*, Vol II:792. Boddie, *Historical Southern Families*, 3:59.
[3] Meyer and Dorman, *Adventurers of Purse and Person*, 688-91.
[4] Nugent, *Cavaliers and Pioneers*, 1:302 (Patent Book 3:321).
[5] Walter, *Books "A" and "B" Lower Norfolk Co VA*.
[6] Nugent, *Cavaliers and Pioneers*, 1:21 (Patent Book 1:164).

..... clear, seate, build, & plant uppon one parcel of the 650 acres."[7] Capt. John Sibsey's 1649 patent was described as "bounding on land of Mr. Sewell, dec'd."[8] Sewells Point, mentioned frequently in the Norfolk County court documents is still called by that name today, located on the Norfolk Naval Base, the point on the West side of Willoughby Bay. There is a historic marker there, not numbered, for the 1861 battle at Seawell's Point.[9]

Accounts in 1638 and 1639 show the credits and debits for Henry Seawell, prepared by **Robert Page**. His credits appear to be for tobacco and "one-half of a shallop lading of sassafras roots." His account as debtor included "two quarter cask of wine ... two adz, two coopers axe .... one drawinge knife, ½ a peece of silke mooehaire, 10 yards of silver lace .... one hatt casse, Coopers nayles," and charges in reference to the ships *Alexandria* and *Pellican*, totalling 321 pounds, 19 shillings, and 8 pence.[10]

Henry Seawell served as a burgess from Elizabeth City County, then later in 1639 and 1640 from Lower Norfolk County. At the Assembly held at James City 4 Sep1632, the Burgesses from the Upper Parish of Elizabeth City County were: Mr. Henry Seawell, Mr. John Sipsey, and Capt. Thos. Willoughby, absent.[11] New Norfolk County was created in 1636 from the part of Elizabeth City County that lay south of the James River, and Lower Norfolk was created from New Norfolk in 1637.[12]

On 15 May 1637 at the "Lower County of New Norfolke" court, Henry Seawell and others were ordered to appraise goods in custody of Capt. Sibsey.[13] In the Lower Norfolk Court 18 Oct 1639 in which Mr. Henry Seawell was present as a commissioner, the following was recorded: "Whereas by an act of Court made by the Sovereign and Council at James City the 10th of this present October, it is ordered the commissioners of every County with the consent of all the freemen should choose Burgesses for their county, it is therefore thought fit by this court, as also with the consent of the freemen therein that Mr. Henry Seawell and Mr. **John Hill** should be Burgesses for this county."[14]

---

[7] Norfolk Co VA Wills & Deeds D:348-348a. Whichard, *History of Lower Tidewater VA*, 1:106, 222.

[8] Nugent, *Cavaliers and Pioneers*, 1:179 (Patent Book 2:158).

[9] Salmon, *Historical Markers*, 202.

[10] Walter, *Book "A" Lower Norfolk Co VA 1637-1646*, 64.

[11] Hening, *Statutes*, 1:179. Leonard, *General Assembly of Virginia*, 11, 17, 18.

[12] Robinson, V*irginia Counties*, 165, 85-6.

[13] Walter, *Book "A" Lower Norfolk Co VA 1637-1646*, 2.

[14] Norfolk Co VA Minute Book 1637-1646, 36. Leonard, *General Assembly of Virginia*, 17.

Seawell Families

At a "Court houlden in the Lower County of New Norfolke" 21 Nov 1638, present ....., Capt. **John Sibsey**, ..., Mr. **ffrancis Mason**, Mr. Henery Seawell, those appointed to procure workmen for finishing the construction of a Church in the parish were Capt. John Sibsey and Henery Seawell.[15]

At the Assembly 6 Jan 1639/40 "men of experience and integrity" were chosen as tobacco viewers, inspecting each man's crop for the quantity allowed and the quality expected. In Lower Norfolk County, for the Little Creek and Eastern Shore area, Mr. Henry Sewell, **Robert Hayes**, and **Christopher Burrowes** were appointed. At the 4 Oct 1641 court Henry Seawell and **Thomas Meares** were appointed tobacco viewers.[16]

The commissioners at the 25 May 1640 Court, Capt. **Thos. Willoughbie** Esqr., Capt. John Sibsey, Lieut ffrans Mason, Mr. Henrie Sewell and Mr. **William Julian**, after settling payment from each of the three areas of the parish to the minister, Mr. **Thomas Harrison**, agreed that he should provide a certain amount of time "amongst the Inhabitants of Elizabeth River at the house of **Robert Glascocke**" teaching and instructing them as often as he did at the parish church at Mr. Sewell's Pointe.[17] On 4 Jan 1640/1 Mr. ffrancis Masson and Mr. Henry Seawell gave their report as church wardens.[18]

In the 1639/40 Norfolk will of Captain **Adam Thorowgood**, he stated, "My will and desire is that my beloved friends Captain Thomas Willoughbie and Mr. Henry Seawell, here in Virginia, ... shall be overseers of this my last will and testament."[19] By early 1640/1 Adam's widow **Sarah (Offley) Thorowgood** had married **John Gookin**,[20] and the overseers declined the honor.[21]

The court/church ordered punishments for what were considered crimes at the time. On 15 Nov 1641, a person was arrested for "divers defamations

---

[15] James, *Lower Norfolk Antiquary,* 1:82-83. Walter, *Book "A" Lower Norfolk Co VA 1637-1646*, 9-10.

[16] Robinson, "Acts of the General Assembly, Jan. 6, 1639-40", *Wm & M Qrtrly* 4(2)25. Walter, *Book "A" Lower Norfolk Co VA 1637-1646*, 84.

[17] James, *Lower Norfolk Antiquary,* 1:83-4. Walter, *Book "A" Lower Norfolk Co VA 1637-1646*, 27-8.

[18] James, *Lower Norfolk Antiquary,* 1:141. Walter, *Book "A" Lower Norfolk Co VA 1637-1646*, 48.

[19] Ellis, "Thorowgood Family", *Richmond Standard*, 26 Nov 1881.

[20] Dorman, *Adventurers of Purse and Person*, 2:103, 699. Turner, *Gateway to the New World,* 51-5.

[21] Walter, *Book "A" Lower Norfolk Co VA 1637-1646*, 45.

and slanderous speeches raysed upon the wife of **Richard ffoster** ....",
and if she continued to refuse to ask forgiveness would receive 30 lashes on
the bare back "at the howse of mr. Henry Seawell." Later it was reported
that the wife of Mr: Seawell had been "scandalously defamed."[22] In the
Lower Norfolk records on 15 May 1643 - "...... (adulterers) shall upon
Thursday next stand both in White sheets in the pish Church at Mr. Seawells
Poyn." to make public acknowledgment of their "sinne."[23]

The latest reference found so far showing Henry[1] Seawell alive is when he
was present as a justice at court on 15 Dec 1643.[24] He may have been killed
in the Indian massacre 18 Apr 1644, his wife dying later; the 15 Feb 1644/5
court refers to the estate and orphans of Mrs. Seawell deceased and Mr.
Matthew Phillips as guardian "unto the orphants." Unfortunately records
are missing between 16 Dec 1643 and Feb 1644/5.[25]

At the 14 Feb 1644/5 court - "The Court doth thinke fitt and order that Mr.
Mathew Phillipps the admor of Mrs. Seawell deceased shall within 10 dayes
sattisfy and pay unto Mr. Tho: Harrison, Clarke, 1000 lb Tob in
consideration and satisfaccon for the burial and preaching the funerall
sermon of Mr. Seawell and Mrs. Seawell deceased, and for breaking
grownde in the Channcell for them."[26]

It has been speculated that after the death of Henry, his widow **Alice** married
Matthew Phillips, who after Alice's death married **Anne ( ) Phillips**,
administrator of Matthew Phillips's estate, but she was never referred to as
Alice ( ) Seawell Phillips nor Alice Phillips, exx. of Henry Seawell.
Matthew Phillips was named often in the Lower Norfolk court records,
Books A and B 1645-1651/2 as shown in the following entries:

> 15 Feb 1644/5 - " .... estate of Mrs: Seawell deceased ..... paymt
> to bee made of the said tob unto Mr: Mathew Phillips guardian
> unto the orphants of the sd deceased...."[27]

> 15 Apr 1645 - "suite depending betweene Mr: Math: Phillipps
> guardian unto the orphants of Mrs: Seawell deceased plt" .....[28]

---

[22] James, *Lower Norfolk Antiquary*, 1:143-4. Walter, *Book "A" Lower Norfolk Co VA 1637-1646*, 82, 110.
[23] Walter, *Book "A" Lower Norfolk Co VA 1637-1646*, 132.
[24] Walter, *Book "A" Lower Norfolk Co VA 1637-1646*, 153, 155.
[25] Walter, *Book "A" Lower Norfolk Co VA 1637-1646*, 156-7.
[26] Walter, *Book "A" Lower Norfolk Co VA 1637-1646*, 164.
[27] Walter, *Book "A" Lower Norfolk Co VA 1637-1646*, 156.
[28] Walter, *Book "A" Lower Norfolk Co VA 1637-1646*, 167.

Seawell Families

15 Aug 1645 - "Land granted unto Mr. Math: Phillipps in the behalfe of Henry Seawell an orphant sonne and heire of Mrs: Seawell deceased for the transportation of ....." 21 persons.[29]

15 Dec 1645 - "Mr. Math: Phillipps shall pay 1000 lb tob for a fine for his act of incontinency with Mary......" Poor **Mary**, a servant at the Seawell house, besides having a child by Phillips, got 39 lashes on her bare back and was ordered to "depart ... nor frequent the howse belonging to the Orphants of Mrs. Seawell deceased ...." At least Mr. Phillips, who continued as a commissioner of the court, was ordered to support Mary's child.[30]

15 Dec 1646 - "Whereas: it appears unto the Court that **Thomas Smythairs** is indebted unto the estate belonging unto the orphants of Mrs: **Alice Seawell** decd: the summe of 550 pownds of tobacco and Caske due by bill. The Court doth order payment thereof with the Court Charges unto Mr. **Mathew Phillipps** guardian unto the orphants ...... within ten days."[31]

13 Jul 1647 - "The Comrs. doe appoynt at theire next session to pose and examine the accoumpts at this present produced and exhibited by Mr. Mathew Phillips concerning the estate of the orphants of Mrs. Alice Seawell deceased in his custody or protection."[32]

Matthew Phillips died intestate before the 12 Jan 1649/50 court.[33]

"Att an Orphants Court held 27 Feb 1649/50 att the House of Mris: **Ann Phillipps** ... concerning the Estate of Hen: Sewell dec'd ... consent of Jno: Holmes, Overseer, and Mr. **Lemuell Mason** who hath intermarried with Ann the daughter of the sd Sewell, it was agreed as foll: That the estate of Mr. Math: Phillipps late dec'd shall bee responsible & give security to make good the estate of the sd Hen: Sewell either in kind or vallew as it was left at the decease of Aloe (Alice) the wife of the sd Hen: Sewell by Inventory & if any difference arrise in the ..... of any of the goods which shall bee undelivered ... It shall bee determined by the Court & for any of the goods wanting or disposed of by the sd Mr. Phillipps. The valew of them shall bee

---

[29] Walter, *Book "A" Lower Norfolk Co VA 1637-1646*, 179. This should have been for 1050 acres.

[30] Walter, *Book "A" Lower Norfolk Co VA 1637-1646*, 208-9.

[31] Walter, B*ook "B" Lower Norfolk Co VA 1646-1651/2*, 15 (f 16).

[32] Walter, *Book "B" Lower Norfolk Co VA 1646-1651/2*, 48 (f 49).

[33] Walter, B*ook "B" Lower Norfolk Co VA 1646-1651/2*, 125 (f 132a).

praysed & stated by fower Indeffrent men chosen by & on behalf of the Orphants of the sd Lemuell (this should be Sewell) & Mris. **Anne Phillipps** aforesd administratrix of the sd Mr. **Math: Phillipps** ....."[34]

27 Feb 1649/50 - "...Ordered that 3 hh of good sound tob be provided to bee sent for Holland with Mr. Tho: Lee to bee sould there for the best advantage of Hen: Sewell who is to goe for Holland with the sd Mr: Lee .... being his kindsman & seeming to bee very desirous to have the young man with him .... It is also ordered that Mr. **Jno. Hill**, Mr. **Tho. Lambard**, **Jno. Holmes** & **Tho. Ivey** who are by the mutual consent of Mr. Lemuell Mason, who married Anne the daughter of the sd Hen: Sewell, and Mris: Anne Phillipps aforesd are to meete & arbitrate the busyness bee held on the 25 Mar next .... A Court to bee held for the County the 27th day ... for an outcry for the sale of the goods belonging unto the foresd Henery orphant of Hen: Sewell decd. Also ordered that Mr. Tho. Lee shall give good security for the return of the sd Henry Sewell ... when required."[35]

27 Mar 1650 - "Whereas at a Court hearing dated 27 Feb last past ...... by the mutual Consent of Mr. Lemuell Mason who intermarried with Ann the daughter of Mris. Aloe (Alice) Sewell decd & Mris. Ann Phillipps adm: of Mr. Math: Phillipps decd were appointed to be arbitrators to value that part of the Estate of the aforesaid Aloe (Alice) Sewell decd which could not be delivered in kind by the sd (Ann) Phillipps according to Inventory ..... if any difference should arrise concerning the decaye & Impairing of such goods (should) be undelivered in kind that they should make report thereof which order they have performed. In the difference between Mris. Ann Phillipps & Mr. Lemuel Mason concerning a wench named **Katherine** ... belonging to Capt. **Wm. Duglas** as by Inventory of Mris. Alice Sewell decd appeareth, the busyness is referred to the next Court. "[36]

28 Mar 1650 - "Delivered these following plate to Mr: Lemuel Mason & Mris. **Anne Phillipps** with the consent of the Court for the use of Henry Sewell, sonne of Henry Sewell decd... gold ring .... one Silver Wine Cuppe mrkd   S
               H: A:.
.... It is ordered that Mr: Lemuell Mason aforesd doe give with security that the plate & rings bee forthcoming .... It was agreed that Mris: **Anne Phillipps** shall have and Injoy the plantation & houses .... belonging unto Henry Sewell where shee now liveth, with all the preveleges thereunto belonging untill Christmas next .... for satisfaccon for the negroes &

---

[34] Walter, B*ook "B" Lower Norfolk Co VA 1646-1651/2*, 130 (f 137a).

[35] Walter, B*ook "B" Lower Norfolk Co VA 1646-1651/2*, 131 (f 138).

[36] Walter, B*ook "B" Lower Norfolk Co VA 1646-1651/2*, 134-5 (f 141a).

Seawell Families

Rent of the houses & land shee the sd Mris: Phillipps is then to pay unto the Comrs: 1200 lb tob........."[37]

15 Aug 1650 - "difference between ...... Mr. Lemuel Mason .... Phillipps concerning certain goods which were Mrs. Alice ..... it is... ordered the sd Lemuel Mason shall put in security ...."[38]

15 Dec 1650 - "Mr. Lemuel Mason shall have full power and authority ... debts and demands .... Henery Sewell, orphan of Henery Sewell deceased ....."[39]

In the Lower Norfolk County records of 6 Dec 1653, there was a letter addressed to Capt. **Thos. Willoughby**, Mr. **Lemuel Mason**, and Mr. **John Holmes**, who was overseer of Henry Seawell's estate, written by **Llilly (William) Scapes** of Yarmouth, giving an account of the tobacco received for Henery[2] Sewell, whom he received as an apprentice for "fower Yeeres, & seven yeeres of service", concerning the costs of Henry's schooling, diet, clothes, etc. and proposing payment due him. This was accepted by those to whom the letter was addressed.[40]

At Lower Norfolk court on 15 Jun 1662, the justices attested to the death of merchant Henery Sewell the elder in 1644, the age of Henery Sewell the younger, his being born 1 May 1639, his apprenticeship to Mr. William Scapes merchant in Yarmouth, England, and that Henry had served his 11 years. As mentioned earlier the 1661 deed from **Triniman** to Henry Seawell Jr. indicated his return from England, accepting the land his father lived on.[41] Henry[2] sold 150 acres of the land on 25 Aug 1665 to **James Wishard**.[42]

Henry[2] died by 16 Aug 1672 when depositions by **Ruth Hargrave** and **Simon Peeters**, former servants of Henry Seawell the elder, were given for Henry the younger's sister and heir, Anne, wife of Col. Lemuel Mason saying she was born "seven or eight & thirty years since" and that she was the sister of "Henry Saywell the younger late dec'd."[43] On 16 Feb 1674 Coll. Lemuell Mason and Ann his wife, heir to "our brother Henry Seawell

---

[37] Walter, B*ook "B" Lower Norfolk Co VA 1646-1651/2*, 135-6 (f 142a).
[38] Walter, B*ook "B" Lower Norfolk Co VA 1646-1651/2*, 143-4 (f 153).
[39] Walter, B*ook "B" Lower Norfolk Co VA 1646-1651/2*, 153 (f 161a).
[40] Norfolk Co VA Wills and Deeds C:79-79a, 82.
[41] Norfolk Co VA Wills & Deeds D:347a-348a.
[42] Whichard, *History of Lower Tidewater VA* 1:270. Norfolk Co VA Wills & Deeds D:428.
[43] Norfolk Co VA Wills & Deeds E:126, 127a.

Gent.", confirmed the sale of 100 acres in Elizabeth City County to **Mary Elcock** and her mother.[44]

In 1678 Lemuel and Ann (Seawell) Mason heirs of "our deare brother Henery Sewell merchant" sold his estate in Maryland to **Charles Egerton**.[45] Unfortunately the land was not described.

It has been suggested that Henry^2 was **Henry Sewell** of Maryland, perhaps losing contact with his family and they assuming he had died. Henry Sewell did a survey on the Severn River in 1661 and claimed 100 acres of land in 1662 for "service done." He married **Joanna Warner** and was named in her father's 1673 will. His will was written 1691 and was proved in 1700.[46] The coincidence of these dates with the end of the apprenticeship of Henry^2 in England is interesting.

2. Ann^2 Seawell <See pg. 147> (1.Henry^1). She married **Lemuel Mason. (See number 4 - pg. 83).**

ISSUE:
3. f i. **Frances Mason**, born about 1650, died after 15 Jul 1708 <See pg. 90>.
4. f ii. **Margaret Mason**, born about 1652, died before 24 Jun 1697 <See pg. 83>.
5. m iii. **Thomas Mason**, born about 1654, died before 15 Jun 1711 <See pg. 97>.
6. m iv. **Lemuel Mason**, born about 1657, died before 15 Jun 1711 <See pg. 101>.
7. f v. **Alice Mason**, born about 1659, died after 10 Jun 1735 <See pg. 105>.
8. f vi. **Elizabeth Mason**, born about 1662, died before 20 Aug 1697 <See pg. 110>.
9. m vii. **George Mason**, born about 1666, died before 16 Mar 1710/11 <See pg. 111>.
10. f viii. **Anne Mason**, born about 1668, died before 30 Nov 1703 <See pg. 115>.
11. f ix. **Abigail Mason**, born about 1671, died before 16 Jul 1691 <See pg. 117>.
12. f x. **Mary Mason**, born about 1675, died before 1 Aug 1735 <See pg. 119>.
13. f xi. **Dinah Mason**, born about 1678, died before 23 Jan 1713/4 <See pg. 121>.

---

[44] Norfolk Co VA Wills & Deeds E:182.
[45] Norfolk Co VA Deed Book 4:39a.
[46] Barnes, "Henry Sewell", 5:1. Sewell, *Sewell Families,* 40-4, 50, 54, 55.

Ann[2] Seawell was born about 1635, daughter of Henry[1] and Alice (Willoughby?) Seawell.[47] Her age was verified by the depositions in 1672 by **Ruth Hargrave** and **Simon Peeters**, former servants of Henry Seawell the elder, for Ann, wife of Col. Lemuel Mason, saying she was born "seven or eight & thirty years since." Simon swore that he was sent to get a midwife for "Mr. Saywell's wifes labour who was shortly after delivered of a daughter.... which daughter was baptised Ann ... and the sd daughter is now the wife of Collo. Lemuell Mason."[48]

By 15 Feb 1644/5 **Matthew Phillips** had been named guardian of the orphans of Henry[1] and Alice Seawell.[49] Before 27 Feb 1649/50 Phillips had died and Ann Seawell had married Lemuell Mason as shown at an orphans court held "att the House of Mris: Ann Phillipps - ... concerning the Estate of Hen: Sewell dec'd ... consent of Jno: Holmes, Overseer, and Mr. Lemuell Mason who hath intermarried with Ann the daughter of the sd Sewell. .... The estate of Mr. Math: Phillipps late decd shall be responsible & give security to make good the estate of the sd Hen: Sewell ..... Mris: **Anne Phillipps** ... administratrix of the sd Mr. Math. Phillipps."[50]

Lemuell Mason was given full power of attorney regarding the debts and demands of Henery[2] Sewell, orphan of Henery[1] Sewell deceased,[51] and he was described as Lemuell Mason, gent., guardian for Henery Sewell in the records of the 25 Dec 1653 court.[52]

In 1653 Ann was named in the will of **Daniell Tanner**. She must have been quite kind to him: "unto Mrs. Anne Mason, for her great paynes & care & love towards me Three Thousand pounds of tobacco to be paid her out of my Estate."[53]

Ann evidently had a bad accident or suffered a debilitating illness. On 17 April 1671 her husband Lemuel Mason made a "Competent settling" on her if she happened to survive him - "whereas it has pleased almighty god ... to visit my well beloved wife Anne ..... Lame ..... in her Limbs whereby she is altogether disabled to take any paynes of labour for a livelyhood." The

---

[47] Walter, B*ook "B" Lower Norfolk Co VA 1646-1651/2*, 134 (f 141a).
[48] Norfolk Co VA Wills & Deeds E:126, 127a.
[49] Walter, *Book "A" Lower Norfolk Co VA 1637-1646*, 156-7.
[50] Walter, B*ook "B" Lower Norfolk Co VA 1646-1651/2*, 130 (f 137a).
[51] Walter, B*ook "B" Lower Norfolk Co VA 1646-1651/2*, 153 (f 161a).
[52] Norfolk Co VA Wills & Deeds C:65a-66.
[53] Norfolk Co VA Wills & Deeds C:65.

settlement consisted of 100 acres which he had inherited from his father with houses, orchards, gardens, furnishings, and slaves.[54]

A 16 Aug 1672 deposition mentioned Henry[2] Seawell, the younger, as late deceased, and Ann, now wife of Colonel Lemuel Mason, as his sister.[55]

In a 1678 deed Lemuell and Ann Mason "right & lawfull heirs by the death of our deare brother Henery Sewell merchant" sold land in Maryland to **Charles Egerton**.[56]

Ann's will, dated 30 Oct 1705 and proved 15 Mar 1705/6, named her daughters Frances Sayer, Alice Boush, Mary Cock, and Dinah Thorowgood, her sons Thomas, Lemuel and George Mason executors.[57]

---

[54] Norfolk Co VA Wills & Deeds E:89.
[55] Norfolk Co VA Wills & Deeds E:127a.
[56] Norfolk Co VA Deed Book 4:39a.
[57] Norfolk Co VA Deed Book 7:117-8. (See appendix).

CHAPTER 4 - Goodrich Families

(Most of the text in this section is from an article written in 2000 with Maurice D. Leach Jr. It was never published).

1. **Thomas**[1] **Goodrich** was born about 1614 in England. He married **Anne Sherwood**. She may have been the daughter of **Philip Sherwood**.[1]

ISSUE:

+ 2. m i. **Benjamin Goodrich**, born about 1647, died before 27 Apr 1695 <See pg. 170>.
+ 14. m ii. **Joseph Goodrich**, born about 1650, died before 10 May 1694 <See pg. 180>.
+ 17. m iii. **Charles Goodrich**, born about 1652, died before 14 Jun 1726 <See pg. 183>.
+ 34. f iv. **Anne Goodrich**, born after 1658, died before 1707 <See pg. 187>.
  55. m v. **Peter Goodrich**, born about 1662. In his father's Mar 1679 will, he inherited 800 acres of land, part of the "foure thousand acres situate and being upon Hoskins Pocoson", six head of cattle, and two mulatto males "to be delivered when .... age... one and Twenty yeares."[2] Peter was given a cow called Dainty by **Katherine Gaines** on the 18 Dec 1679.[3] A record for 25 Oct 1695 shows Coll. **Edward Hill** received 5066 acres in King and Queen County for importing 102 persons. Two of the headrights named were Coll. Hill and Peter Goodrich, which implies that Peter may have accompanied his step-father on a trip to England.[4]
  56. f vi. **Katherine Goodrich**, born about 1663. Katherine was given half the increase of a mare given to her sister Ann² by their father 23 Apr 1673.[5] In her father's will she was given 800 acres, part of the 4,000 acres on Hoskins Pocoson, and two Negro boys "to be delivered ... upon her Marriage day or at the age of one and Twenty yeares ..."[6]

---

[1] Tyler, "The Goodrich Family", *Tyler's Quarterly*, 12:69.
[2] Sparacio, *Old Rappahannock Co VA - 1677-1682 (I) - RK.DW-09/90*, 36-7.
[3] Sparacio, *Old Rappahannock Co VA - 1677-1682 (II) - RK.DW-10/90*, 33.
[4] Fleet, *VA Col Abs, King & Queen Co*, 2:406.
[5] Sparacio, *Old Rappahannock Co VA - 1672-6 (I) - OR.DB-07/89*, 51.
[6] Sparacio, *Old Rappahannock Co VA - 1677-1682 (I) - RK.DW-09/90*, 36-7.

Thomas[1] Goodrich, was born about 1614, shown when he testified in Lower Norfolk County court in 1654 that he was 40 or thereabouts.[7] Research of many English wills has shown only one possibility for his parents. His father may have been **Thomas Goodridge**, gentleman of Saint Alvans, Hertfordshire, whose will dated 11 Jan 1628 and proved 16 Mar 1629, named his son Thomas who was less than age 21, his wife Mary, daughters Allice, Mary and Ann, wife of John Shedd.[8]

The earliest of the name to arrive in Virginia were possibly a Tho: Gudderidge listed at the age of 17 and transported on the *Assurance* 24 July 1635 and Ann Gudderidge age 23 on the *Transport* 4 July 1635.[9] Names associated with Thomas[1] and Anne Goodrich appearing in these passenger lists which will be mentioned later in this article are **Thomas Hobbs**, age 22, on the *Assurance* and **Peter Sexton**, age 20, on the *Transport*.

The name Goodrich was spelled in a variety of ways. **John Gutteridge**, who was in Lower Norfolk County as early as 15 Aug 1645, but reported "out of this Collony into Mariland" on 15 Feb 1646,[10] may be John Goodrich of Isle of Wight.[11] **Henry Goodricke** was in Lower Norfolk County before 1664, and in 1672 **Quintillian Goodrick** sold land in Lower Norfolk County that he had bought in 1670.[12] Quintillian Gutherick had land in Elizabeth City County before 1684 and served as a Justice in 1688. The administration of his estate was granted in 1689.[13] **Thomas Gottridge** was buried in St. Peter's Parish, Barbados in 1679.[14] No family connection has been found for these Goodriches.

It was the custom for men to marry around the age of 30 and women between 14 and 30 in those days. Probably around 1644 Thomas[1] Goodrich married Anne who may have been the daughter of **Philip Sherwood**.[15] There was a **Philip Sherwood**, possibly her brother, in Old Rappahannock County as early as 1657, whose estate in 1685 named, as heirs, his daughters

---

[7] McIntosh, "Ages of Lower Norfolk County People", *Wm & M Qrtrly* 25(1)36-8.
[8] Will of Thomas Goodridge, PROB 11/155.
[9] Hotten, *Original Lists*, 110-13, 101-2.
[10] Walter, *Book "A" Lower Norfolk Co VA 1637-1646*, 180, 216.
[11] Tyler, "The Goodrich Family", *Tyler's Quarterly*, 12:66.
[12] Norfolk Co VA Wills & Deeds Book D:421, E:64a, 145a.
[13] Chapman, *Wills ... Elizabeth City*, 139, 154, 37.
[14] Brandow, *Omitted Chapters from Hotten*, 87.
[15] Tyler, "The Goodrich Family", *Tyler's Quarterly*, 12:69.

Mary, Martha, Ann and Sarah.[16] A daughter of Thomas[1] and Anne Goodrich, Anne[2], named a son Sherwood[3] Lightfoot.[17]

Lower Norfolk County

The earliest record for Thomas[1] Goodrich being in Virginia appears to be at the 15 Apr 1651 court where Mr. **Lemuell Mason,** Thomas[1] Goodridge, **Thomas Ivey** and **Trusteram Mason** were ordered to appraise cattle at the house of Capt. **John Sibsey.**[18] In December 1651 Thomas Goodrich witnessed an agreement between **John Lownes** and Captain **Matthew Wood** whereby Lownes was to keep the stock Wood had just purchased from Lownes until his return from Barbados. Over a year later, on 16 Feb 1652/3, Thomas[1] Goodrich was administrator of Capt. Matthew Wood's estate.[19]

In the 12 Mar 1651/2 inventory of Capt. **John Gilham**, deceased, of Lynhaven, Lower Norfolk County, among his assets were debts due for tobacco, Mr. Tho: Goodrich - 250.[20]

By 1 Jun 1652 Thomas[1] was appointed to the important position of Commissioner of the Lower Norfolk Court. He served with **Lemuel**[2] **Mason** and **William Moseley**, and at least one session, on 13 Feb 1653, was to be held "at the house of Thomas Goodrich, gent."[21] He served as late as 15 Dec 1654.[22]

A certificate for 1250 acres was granted by the 17 Jan 1652/3 court of Lower Norfolk to Thomas[1] Goodrich, gent., for the transportation of thirteen persons into the Colony. Nine of these were assigned to **Peter Sexton**: himself, Anne his wife, and seven negroes.[23] Mr. Thomas Gutheridge was granted 700 acres in Lower Norfolk County up the South branch of the Elizabeth River in March 1652/3 for transporting 14 persons. The patent was assigned to Peter Sexton who used the rights for another tract.[24] Peter

---

[16] Essex Co VA Index to Wills & Deed A, Parts I & II, referring to Deed Book 8:7, Order Book 1:173.
[17] Harris, *Old New Kent Co .... Planters*, 122-3.
[18] Walter, *Book "B" Lower Norfolk Co VA 1646-1651/2*:166 (f 174).
[19] Fleet, *VA Col Abs, Lower Norfolk Co*, 3:422, 445 (Wills & Deeds C:1, 39).
[20] Fleet, *VA Col Abs, Lower Norfolk Co*, 3:426 (Wills & Deeds C:8).
[21] Fleet, *VA Col Abs, Lower Norfolk Co*, 3:428, 441 (Wills & Deeds C:10,33).
[22] James, *Lower Norfolk Antiquary*, 3:30.
[23] Norfolk Co VA Wills & Deeds Book C:34.
[24] Nugent, *Cavaliers and Pioneers*, 1:274 (Patent Book 3:178).

Sexton was granted 350 acres the last of March 1653 for the transportation of seven people: Thomas Goodrich, Anne Goodrich and five Negroes. This shows that Thomas[1] Goodrich evidently sold several of the passages due him to Peter Sexton.[25] Headrights were sold and bought regularly, were granted for subsequent passages to England and back, and often were claimed at a later date, therefore not showing the date of immigration.

Mr. Thomas[1] Goodrich was compensated 190 lbs. of tobacco from payments "to be made from the county levies" on 1 Nov 1653 "for his boate hire 19 dayes" for the use of the Burgesses.[26]

Captain Thomas Goodrich was named as an overseer of the 2 Nov 1654 will of **William Vincent**, merchant, which was recorded 15 Feb 1654/5, and he witnessed **Richard Starnell**'s will on 3 Oct 1655.[27]

(Old) Rappahannock County

On 1 Jan 1649 **Bartholomew Hoskins** patented 1,350 acres on the south side of the Rappahannock River, which he renewed 12 Aug 1651.[28] He was one of the land speculators who was attracted to Virginia's first real-estate boom in the 1650's. "By law no one could settle north of the York (River) until 1651, due to the Indian Treaty." The Rappahannock area was a prime attraction to settlers because of the open land and the accessibility which the Rappahannock River provided.[29] "Hoskins Pocosan" is used as a reference in many (Old) Rappahannock County deeds, pocosan an Indian word meaning wooded marsh or swamp. In 1692, Richmond and Essex counties were created from (Old) Rappahannock.[30]

Thomas[1] Goodrich was attracted to the opportunities open in the frontier and was shown there by 3 Nov 1656, when he was a witness to the deed between **John Weir** and **John Gillet**.[31] "Att a grand Assembly helde at James Cittie 11th Decemb[r], 1656" when the county of Rappahannock was organized, Major Tho. Goodrich was appointed a commissioner and a member of the County militia.[32] He was listed as a commissioner or justice of the court as

---

[25] Nugent, *Cavaliers and Pioneers*, 1:275 (Patent Book 3:185).
[26] Norfolk Co VA Wills & Deeds Book C:62, 63.
[27] McIntosh, *Norfolk Co Wills 1637-1710*:14, 16-7 (Book C:127, 179).
[28] Nugent, *Cavaliers and Pioneers*, 1:182, 219 (Patent Book 2:172, 338).
[29] Warner, *Hoskins of Virginia and Related Families*, 13. Slaughter, *Settlers .... of Essex Co VA*, 8.
[30] Robinson, *Virginia Counties*, 168, 86.
[31] Sparacio, *Old Rappahannock Co VA - 1656-64 (I) - RK.DB-01/89*, 3.
[32] "Organization of Rappahannock County, 1656", *VA Mag Hist* 8:176-7.

Major Thomas Goodrich in 1658 and as presiding justice, Lt. Coll. Tho Goodrich, in 1662.[33]

Major Thomas Goodrich patented 600 acres in 10 Jun 1657 on the south side of the Rappahannock River, 100 acres for transporting two persons and 500 acres by an August 1652 patent assigned to him by **Clement Thresh** in 1656.[34] Thresh had purchased this land from land speculator, Bartholomew Hoskins.[35] In Clement Thresh's will written 16 Feb 1656/7 and probated 1659, he left to Thomas[1] and Anne Goodrich tobacco which was the currency of the day and to his godson, Benjamin[2] Goodrich, he left a heifer.[36]

On 16 Mar 1657, Major Thomas[1] Goodrich patented 400 acres on the south side of the Rappahannock River "in the freshes" for transporting 8 persons, which included four Negroes.[37] He sold this land "Opposite New Newcocke" to **Anthony Stevens** 30 Jan 1659/60.[38] Thomas's wife Ann Goodrich made her mark, but not the typical "X", 24 Feb 1660 consenting to the sale. Her marks on other documents show a creative touch.

On 20 Sep 1661 a 219 acre tract was granted to Lt. Coll. Thomas[1] Goodrich and Thomas Button for transporting five persons. In 1662 Thomas[1] and Ann Goodrich assigned the land to **Thomas Button**,[39] and in 1663/4 Button made a deed of gift of this tract to Charles[2], son of Lt. Coll. Thomas[1] Goodrich.[40] Thomas Button had married **Jane**, the widow of **John Gillet**.[41] Also on 20 September 1661 Lt. Col. Thomas Goodrich received a patent for 1,134 acres on the south side of the Rappahanock River, 650 acres of which were purchased from **Robert Armstrong** 17 Jan 1660/1[42] and the rest for transporting ten persons.[43] In 1674 he sold the 1,134 acre tract to **Thomas**

---

[33] Essex (Old Rappahannock) Co VA Deed Book 1656-1664, 2:28, 223.
[34] Nugent, *Cavaliers and Pioneers*, 1:347 (Patent Book 4:99).
[35] Nugent, *Cavaliers and Pioneers*, 1:259 (Patent Book 3:98).
[36] Sweeney, *Wills, Rappahannock Co VA*, 10. Sparacio, *Old Rappahannock Co VA - 1656-64 (I) - RK.DB-01/89*, 50-1.
[37] Nugent, *Cavaliers and Pioneers*, 1:362 (Patent Book 4:159).
[38] Sparacio, *Old Rappahannock Co VA - 1656-64 (I) - RK.DB-01/89*, 97-8.
[39] Sparacio, *Old Rappahannock Co VA - 1656-64 (II) - OR.DB-02/89*, 26-7.
[40] Sparacio, *Old Rappahannock Co VA - 1665-77 - OR.DW-04/89*, 19.
[41] Nugent, *Cavaliers and Pioneers*, 1:363 (Patent Book 4:163).
[42] Sparacio, *Old Rappahannock Co VA - 1656-64 (I) - RK.DB-01/89*, 108.
[43] Nugent, *Cavaliers and Pioneers*, 1:397 (Patent Book 4:302).

Bowler. The document quotes the original grant and sales.[44] Ann Goodrich's mark:

Thomas[1] Goodrich patented 1,800 acres on the south side of the Rappahannock River on the branches of the Puscatna (Piscataway) Creek in Rappahannock County on 15 Oct 1669 for transporting 36 persons, one of whom was **Thomas Hobbs**,[45] who was listed as transported in the *Assurance* 24 Jul 1635 along with a Tho: Gudderidge.[46] This land appears to be made up of the following entries: 2 Mar 1667/8, **Thomas Cooper** sold to Lt. Coll: Thomas Goodrich 1110 acres "called by the name of Old Matapony ..... lands where formerly ... the Matapony Indians did Inhabite" and for "a Mare in hand by me received" and payment to be made of 50 Matchcoats (mantles made of skins) to the Indian King,[47] and 3 Mar 1667/8 **Francis Browne** sold 700 acres "formerly belonging to the Indians of Matapony" to Thomas Goodrich for over 5000 lbs. of tobacco and also for paying the Match Coat due to the Indian King.[48] In 1671 Thomas Goodrich gave an estimated 140 acres to **Richard Jones** for "his seating and saving .... land called Pattipany Indian Towne."[49] The law required, after a tract was surveyed and patented, that it be settled within 3 years.[50] In 1708 Goodrich[3] Lightfoot sold "half ... of the 1800 acres granted to Lt. Col. Thomas Goodrich by patent 15 Oct. 1669", the line of inheritance and a 100 acre exclusion for Jones stated in the document.[51]

On 2 Mar 1670/1 Thomas[1] Goodrich bought "fower" hundred acres from **Henry Clarke**.[52] In his will he left this land, described as adjoining Buttons Range, to his son Charles[2] Goodrich[53] who sold it in 1683 to **Robert Parker**.[54]

---

[44] Sparacio, *Old Rappahannock Co VA - 1672-6 (I) - OR.DB-07/89*, 86-88.

[45] Nugent, *Cavaliers and Pioneers*, 2:64 (Patent Book 6:254). Nugent's date 1659 is probably a transcription error.

[46] Hotten, *Original Lists*, 110-13.

[47] Sparacio, *Old Rappahannock Co VA - 1663-8 - OR.DB-03/89*, 103.

[48] Sparacio, *Old Rappahannock Co VA - 1663-8 - OR.DB-03/89*, 93.

[49] Sparacio, *Old Rappahannock Co VA - 1672-6 (I) - OR.DB-07/89*, 4.

[50] Nugent, *Cavaliers and Pioneers*, 2:ix.

[51] Dorman, *Essex Co VA D&W 1707-1711*, 42.

[52] Sparacio, *Old Rappahannock Co VA - 1670-2 - OR.DB-06/89*, 43.

[53] Sparacio, *Old Rappahannock - 1677-1682 (I) - RK.DW-09/90*, 36-7.

[54] Sparacio, *Old Rappahannock - 1682-6 - RK.DB-13/90*, 41.

The 4 Mar 1680 settlement of Thomas[1] Goodrich's estate included a copy of the 4 Oct 1672 grant for 4626 acres: [55]

"To all to whom etc. I Sr: **William Berkeley** Knt. Lt. Governr. & Capt. Generall of Virginia .... doe with the consent of the Councell of State ...... give unto Coll. Thomas Goodrich fower thousand Six hundred & twenty six acres of land lying in Rappa. County & on the South side of the River; 2876 acres of which was formerly granted to coll. Thomas Goodrich by Pattent dated the 24th of Octobr: 1669 & bounded according as is exprest in the sd Pattent, 1200 acres of the sd Quantity formerly granted to **Thomas Gouldman** by pattent bearing date the 4th of Aprill 1667 & by him sould to the sd Goodrich as by record appeareth. The Residue of the aforesd 4626 acres begin: 550 acres is bounded as followeth Vizt. ....to a red Oake by Rappae: Indian Path near the Poquotion ....due to the sd Goodrich for the transportacon of Ninety three persons into this Collony whose names are on the records mentioned underneath the above recited Pattents To have & to hold the sd land with his due share of all mines & mineralls therein contained with rights of hunting hawking fishing & fowling with all woods waters & rivers .... paying to our sd Soveraigne Lord the King ... for every fifty acres of land hereby granted yearly at the Feast of St. Michaell ..... the fee rent of one Shilling .... if sd Thomas Goodrich do not seat or plant upon the sd land within three yeares next ensuing it shall be lawfull for any Adventeror or Planter to make choice to seat thereupon. Given at James Citty undr: my hand & the Seale of the Collony this 4th Octobr: 1672.

Coll Gutteridge Rappae   William Berkeley
   4626 acres
Recordatr Test Phill Ludwell Cl Off
Recordatr 4 die Martii 1680/1"

The details of the four patents are given below and above, showing 50 acres for each person transported:[56]

    1664 Mar 28 - 2,000 acres on the South side of the Rappahannock for transporting 40 persons for land adjacent to **Clement Thresh**'s estate.

    1669 Oct 24 - 876 acres for transporting 18 persons for land adjacent to Hoskins Creek.

---

[55] Sparacio, *Old Rappahannock - 1677-82 (II) - RK.DW-10/90*, 69.

[56] Nugent, *Cavaliers and Pioneers*, 1:517, 2:64, 2:116 (Patent Books 5:379, 6:254, 424).

1671/2 Mar 4 - 1200 acres south side of the Rappahannock he acquired from **Thomas** and **Alice Gouldman** which was granted to Gouldman on 4 April 1667 (24 headrights).

1672 Oct 4 - 550 acres adjoining the 1200 acres (11 headrights).

Col. Thomas[1] Goodrich also patented 2200 acres on 5 Oct 1672 in New Kent County, "... near the north side of the Indian path from Mattapony town that was at the head of Piscataway Creek onto the new town now planted by those Indians on Mattapony River for transporting 44 persons." After his death this tract was taken up by Col. **Edward Hill** 23 Apr 1681 as it was declared deserted by Col. Thomas Goodrich.[57]

George Nangle, of Dublin, Ireland, named Col. Thomas Goodrich an executor in his will which was written 4 Jan 1675/6 and proved 3 Jan 1677/8. It is possible that Nangle was one of the many who were killed in the Indian raids during the summer and fall of 1676.[58]

Col. Thomas Goodrich provided a school on his plantation which he opened to his friends.[59]

On 3 Nov 1665 Thomas Goodrich, **Thomas Button**, **Anthony North** and others were sworn in as vestrymen for Farnham Parish. On the same day these vestrymen along with **John Catlet**, **John Weir**, **Humphrey Booth**, **William Moseley**, and others of the parishes of Sittingbourne and Farnham, agreed that Mr. **Francis Doughty**, minister, for two years "shall receive yearly of each parish ... 60 pounds sterling to be paid in tobacco."[60]

In 1668 **Thomas Jenkins** appeared in court asking for pardon. He confessed that he had "wrongfully wronged & absurdly abused Lt. Collo. Thomas Goodrich without any reason or Cause .... provoked .... by the overflowing of my Welch Blood the operating of wch hath many times heretofore ... caused my tonge to Ruun at randome and ... Exceed the Bounds of reason & civillity ....."[61]

---

[57] Nugent, *Cavaliers and Pioneers*, 2:116, 222 (Patent Books 6:425, 7:96).
[58] Sweeney, *Wills, Rappahannock Co VA*, 64.
[59] Warner, *History of Old Rappahannock*, 117.
[60] Sparacio, *Old Rappahannock Co VA - 1665-77 - OR.DW-04/89*, 14, 39. Warner, *History of Old Rappahannock*, 137-9.
[61] Sparacio, *Old Rappahannock Co VA - 1663-8 - OR.DB-03/89*, 116.

Indian Troubles and Bacon's Rebellion

Early treaties with the Matapony and Rappahannock Indians are found in the Essex County records. Probably in 1657, along with Coll. **Moore Fantleroy**, Mr. **Andrew Gilson**, Mr. **Humphrey Booth** and others, Major Thomas Goodrich accepted at court a treaty for "continuance of a Stable peace & union" with "the King and great Men and Governor of the Matapony Indians." For the return of an English runaway the Indian would be paid "five arms length of Roanoacke or the vallue thereof." For "hogstealing" the Indians would submit to English law, etc.[62] In 1658 the Rappahannock Indians confirmed a treaty with Col. Moore Fantleroy apparently concerning the boundaries of his land.[63]

On 14 Mar 1661/2 it was "ordered by the assembly that lieutenant colonel Goodridge be summoned to appear before the honourable governour and council .... to answer the complaint of the king of the Mattapony Indians concerning the burning of his English house ..."[64] Then on 20 Jul 1662 Lt. Coll. Goodrich and **George Marsh** were assigned as agents to see that the orders of the court were performed: "50 matchcoats be paid unto the King (of Mattapony)..." by **Thomas Cooper, Francis Browne**, and **James Vaughan** concerning removal of Indians from "their old towne."[65] By 29 Sep 1664 at a Generall Court in James City, Sir **William Berkeley** ordered that guns that had belonged to the Indians, be valued and payment be made to the Indians.[66]

On 22 Jun 1666 Gov. **William Berkeley** wrote a letter to Major General **Robert Smith**, commander of the district of which Rappahannock was a part, expressing his sympathies with the settlers regarding the murders by the northern Indians and the need to "destroy" them. A letter "To my most honr'd friend Majr. Genll. Smyth" from **John Catlett**, Tho: Goodrich, **John Weire**, and **Hum: Booth** agreed with this decision to eradicate the "Northerne Indians, particularly the Doagge."[67]

In July 1675 the Doegs and **Thomas Matthew** had an exchange regarding their claim that Mathew owed them for goods and his reaction to their taking his hogs in payment, resulting in Matthew or his men killing or beating several Indians. They responded by killing one of Matthew's servants. An

---

[62] Sparacio, *Old Rappahannock Co VA - 1656-64 (I) - RK.DB-01/89*, 10, 16-7.
[63] Warner, *History of Old Rappahannock*, 35 (DB2:39-40).
[64] Hening, *Statutes*, 2:155.
[65] Warner, *History of Old Rappahannock*, 33 (DB 2: 249-250).
[66] Sparacio, *Old Rappahannock Co VA - 1656-64 (II) - OR.DB-02/89*, 86.
[67] Sparacio, *Old Rappahannock Co VA - 1663-8 - OR.DB-03/89*, 15.

attack on the Indians in retaliation included some Susquehannas by mistake.[68]

In 1675 Thomas Goodrich wrote a letter about the Indians burning his houses and robbing his wife and family.[69] In March 1675/6 the Assembly at James City passed "an act for the safeguard and defence of the country against the Indians."[70] On May 13 Gov. Berkeley was "at the falls of the James River, expecting the enemy." He wrote "to Colonel Goodrick and Captain **Hawkins**" to "raise as many men as they can to destroy the enemies."[71] Colonel Thomas Goodrich reported "that the tributary Indians had turned against the English." Berkeley replied May 15, "I believe all the Indians, our neighbours are engaged with the Susquahannoes and therefore I desire you to spare none that has the name of an Indian for they are now all our Enemies."[72]

Gov. Berkeley was inconsistent about supporting the solution to the complaints; he and those to whom he granted licenses, profited from trade with the Indians and supplied the Indians with arms.[73] Governor Berkeley was "moved to heare that the people ... Abuse him in thear murmering that it is through his love to the Beavor that he doth not take a speedye course and destroy the Indeans."[74] The expensive, ineffective frontier forts and delays in response to Indian attacks gave no protection to the settlers.[75]

Besides the frustration in the frontier over repelling Indian raids, the increasing burden of excessive taxes led the colonists to rebel against the government.[76] The Rebellion was led by the charismatic leader, General **Nathaniel Bacon, Jr.** who was a member of the "establishment." Bacon had been assigned to frontier duty, had suffered as had others, the loss of crops, stock, even the life of his overseer but was denied a commission to

---

[68] Morgan, *American Slavery, American Freedom*, 251.

[69] Goodrich, *A Great-Grandmother and her People*, 78.

[70] Hening, *Statutes*, 2:326-330.

[71] Neville, *Bacon's Rebellion*, 49.

[72] Washburn, *Governor and Rebel*, 42, 192.

[73] "Bacon's Rebellion", "Mr. Bacon's acct..... June 18th, 1676", Wm & M Qrtrly 9(1)6.

[74] Washburn, *Governor and Rebel*, 42.

[75] Morgan, *American Slavery, American Freedom*, 252-4.

[76] Webb, *1676, The End of Independence*, 21. Webb calls this Bacon's Revolution., xxvi.

lead the defense of these frontier settlers.[77] He then formed his own companies of volunteers "to march out upon the Enemy."[78]

Thomas[1] Goodrich, his eldest son Benjamin[2] and probably **John Taylor**, the foreman of the Goodrich quarter at Hobbs His Hole[79] participated in Bacon's Rebellion. "A unit of the old northern force under Colonel Thomas[1] Goodrich of Hobbs Hole" fought on after the sudden death of Bacon from fever in October 1676. It was late in 1676 before the English warships and troops crushed the rebellion.[80] The rebellion failed because of the lack of economic development, the loss of the support of the middle class men who returned to their own property in order to protect it, and the lack of a navy. However it sowed the "seeds ... that would germinate in 1776."[81]

Governor William Berkeley exacted a very heavy price upon those whom he considered traitors or his personal enemies. Many were hanged; many lost their citizenship and/or property. The change in his personality from the glory years of his first governorship (1641-1652) to his erratic behavior on his return as governor in 1660 is well recorded. It has been speculated that it was caused by ill health or his young wife, **Frances (Culpeper) Berkeley**, "the vindictive goddess of Berkeleyan revenge."[82]

On 10 Feb 1676/7 Berkeley proclaimed that **Gyles Bland**, Thomas Goodrich, **Anthony Arnold**, **John Rutherford** "notorious rebells being now in prison" would not be pardoned.[83] In the 29 Feb 1676/7 "Act of indemnitie and free pardon", two of the exceptions to the pardon were Colonel Thomas[1] and Benjamin[2] Goodrich who were to "suffer ... punishments not extending to life." In Berkeley's "act inflicting paines and penalties upon greate offenders" it was enacted " ... that coll. Thomas Goodrich doe with a rope about his neck, on his knees, begg his life of the governor and councell, and in like posture acknowledge his crimes of rebellion and treason in Rappahannock county court, and that he be fined .... 50,000 pounds of merchantable tobacco and caske, to be paid ....before the 20th day of January next (1677/8)."[84] Colonel Thomas[1] Goodrich of Hobbs

---

[77] Wertenbaker, *Torchbearer of the Revolution*, 59, 90-2. Morgan, *American Slavery, American Freedom*, 258-9.
[78] "Bacon's Rebellion", "Mr. Bacon's acct..... June 18th, 1676", Wm & M Qrtrly 9(1)7.
[79] Warner, *History of Old Rappahannock*, 68.
[80] Slaughter, *Settlers .... of Essex Co VA*, 13.
[81] Webb, *1676, The End of Independence*, 10-11, xxi.
[82] Webb, *1676, The End of Independence*, 5, 138.
[83] Neville, *Bacon's Rebellion*, 61.
[84] Hening, *Statutes*, 2:366, 370-1, 378.

His Hole did finally appear in Rappahannock County court with a Manchester cord about his neck to fulfill Berkeley's order. A Manchester cord is the equivalent of a modern shoestring, which met with the approval of the local court and populace as they strongly favored Goodrich's actions.[85]

Historical marker N-18 at Caret on US Highway 17, west of Tappahannock, states, "About half a mile northeast stood the old courthouse and clerk's office of Rappahannock County, 1665-1693. To this courthouse Thomas Goodrich and Benjamin Goodrich, ordered to appear with halters around their necks, came to express their penitence for taking part in Bacon's Rebellion in 1676."[86]

The royal commissioners sent by King Charles II with the first arrival of the royal squadron 29 Jan 1676/7 imposed direct royal government on Virginia and carried orders which voided all the Virginia laws of 1676, issued a royal pardon to all parties excluding only **Nathaniel Bacon**, and requested statements of grievances from the Virginia counties.[87] On 29 Mar 1677 **William Sherwood** who had lost his own estate in the rebellion, wrote to the secretary of state, **Joseph Williamson**, that had not the King's commissioners arrived, Berkeley would have brought the country to a desperate condition.[88] The commissioners emphasized to Berkeley that the king's pardon was fully in effect and that Berkeleyan confiscations made since December were unlawful, but Berkeley continued his revenge until May 1677 when he sailed for England.[89] In the 8 Jun 1680 General Assembly "act of free and generall pardon, indemnitie and oblivion", in reference to the king's proclamation of 27 Oct 1676, those who took part in the rebellion were restored their real and personal estates, with certain persons excepted. The Goodriches were not among those named as exceptions to that pardon.[90]

Considering the major role of Colonel Thomas[1] Goodrich and the unknown role of his son Benjamin[2] it is surprising they did not lose their lives as did **William Drummond**, the former governor of Albemarle, the northern section of Carolina. Drummond, who "fired" his own house in the attack on

---

[85] Warner, *History of Old Rappahannock*, 69.
[86] Salmon, *Historical Markers*, 107.
[87] Webb, *1676, The End of Independence*, 101-2, 127-134. Hening, *Statutes*, 2:458, 460.
[88] VA Colonial Records Project, Survey Report 00660
[89] Webb, *1676, The End of Independence*, 155-6, 163.
[90] Hening, *Statutes*, 2:458-464.

Jamestown led by Bacon on 20 Sep 1676, saved the records of the land patents for posterity. He was hanged by Berkeley.[91]

Certainly the excessive fine of 50,000 pounds of tobacco meant that the governor wanted to destroy them financially. Even so, it should be noted that Colonel Thomas[1] Goodrich's second son, Joseph[2], married **Francelia Danby**, the niece of Mrs. **Frances (Culpeper) Stephens** who married as her second husband Governor **William Berkeley**. Francelia's mother, Anne and her sister Frances were daughters of **Thomas Culpeper**. **Christopher Danby** married **Anne Culpeper**. Their nephew was **Warham Horsmanden** whose daughter **Mary** married as his second wife, **William Byrd**.[92] Byrd purchased Westover plantation in Charles City County 4 Feb 1688/9 which is near Shirley plantation owned by Colonel **Edward Hill**, who married the widow Mrs. Anne Goodrich in 1680/1. Ironically, Col. Edward Hill was a strong Berkeley supporter.[93]

Colonel Thomas[1] Goodrich died after 15 Mar 1678/9 when he wrote his will and prior to 3 Apr 1679 when the will was probated.[94] He left his land as follows: Benjamin[2], 200 acres which he had bought from **Clement Thresh** and half of the land "I now live on"; Joseph[2], 900 acres of the 1800 acres of the Mattapony land; Charles[2], 400 acres adjoining Buttons Range and the profits of 600 acres of adjoining land he formerly settled on Hoskins Pocosan; Anne[2], 900 acres, one half of the Mattapony land when she married or reached the age of 21; Peter[2], 800 acres which was a part of the 4,000 acres "being upon Hoskins Pocosan"; Katherine[2], 800 acres, also part of the 4,000 acre tract; and to his wife Anne the remainder of his holdings. He also left 19 negroes, cattle, and household furnishings to his children and wife.

The location of some of the Goodrich land holdings was shown in a 1680 survey by **George Morris**, described in a 1722 land trial in a dispute between **Henry Reeves** and Majr. **William Dangerfield**.[95]

---

[91] Webb, *1676, The End of Independence*, 64-5, 98.
[92] Meyer and Dorman, *Adventurers of Purse and Person*, 525-528. On page 528 "**brother** Benjamin Goodrich" should read "**nephew** Benjamin Goodrich."
[93] Webb, *1676, The End of Independence*, 100.
[94] (Old) Rappahannock Co VA Wills No. 2 1677-1682, 116-121. Sparacio, *Old Rappahannock - 1677-1682 (I) - RK.DW-09/90*, 36-37. (See appendix).
[95] Essex Co VA Land Trials 1715-1741, 145-6. Sparacio, *Essex Co VA - Land Trials 1711-41 - EX.LT-28/92*, 72-3. Copies of the survey in Warner, *Origin.... of Tappahannock* and Sweeney, *Wills, Rappahannock Co VA*. (See appendix).

Anne Goodrich gave her son Benjamin[2] the land "I now dwell on" left her by her husband's will.[96] On 28 Jan 1680/1, Benjamin[2] Goodrich sold Edward Hill of Charles City County " ... all my right of this within mentioned patent for 4,626 acres of land for and in consideration of being fully discharged by the sd Hill of all Tobaccoe whatsoever may become due from Coll: Thomas Goodrich dec'd unto **William Cleaton**, orphant, alwaies provided that what is given to Charles, Peter and Catherine Goodrich - out of the sd Pattent as is bequeathed them be delivered to them by the said Hill ... "[97]

Anne married (2) **Edward Hill** before 2 Mar 1680/1, when her sons Joseph[2] and Charles[2] acknowledged their inheritance, "rec'd of Edward Hill as Marrying Ann, the executrix of Coll. Thomas Goodrich deced."[98]

Anne died prior to 31 Aug 1696 when Colonel Hill signed a marriage precontract regarding his third wife, Mrs. **Tabitha (Scarburgh) Smart Brown Custis**.[99] Edward died 30 Nov 1700 at "Shirley", Charles City County, Virginia.[100]

- - - - - - - - - - -

2. **Benjamin[2] Goodrich** <See pg. 157> (1.Thomas[1]). He married **Alice** ____.
    ISSUE:
+ 3.   m   i.   **Benjamin Goodrich**, born before 29 Feb 1676/7, died 29 Apr 1710 <See pg. 175>.

Benjamin[2] Goodrich was born probably about 1647, eldest son of Thomas[1] and Anne (Sherwood?) Goodrich.[101] On 16 Feb 1656/7 he received "one black heifer" as godchild of **Clement Thresh**, in whose will it was also requested that daughter-in-law (probably step-daughter) **Ann Harris** have schooling with "Tho. Goodrichs Children where they do go." This implies that at least Benjamin[2] and Joseph[2] were of school age.[102] On 3 Mar 1667/8 Benjamin[2] was a witness to a land record of his father and **Francis Browne** concerning 1100 acres on the south side of Puscatacon (Piscataway)

---

[96] Sparacio, *Old Rappahannock - 1677-82 (II) - RK.DW-10/90*, 53.
[97] Sparacio, *Old Rappahannock - 1677-82 (II) - RK.DW-10/90*, 69.
[98] Sparacio, *Old Rappahannock - 1677-82 (II) - RK.DW-10/90*, 70.
[99] Northampton Co VA Deeds & Wills 12: 94.
[100] Meyer and Dorman, *Adventurers of Purse and Person*, 544-545. "Old Tombstones of Charles City County", *Wm & M Qrtrly*, 4(1)147.
[101] Sparacio, *Old Rappahannock Co VA - 1677-1682 (I) - RK.DW-09/90*, 36.
[102] Sweeney, *Wills, Rappahannock Co VA*, 10. Sparacio, *Old Rappahannock Co VA - 1656-64 (I) - RK.DB-01/89*, 50-1.

Creek.¹⁰³ **George Nangle** in his Rappahannock County will, which was written 4 Jan 1675/6, left Benjamin² "my best perriwig."¹⁰⁴

Benjamin² Goodrich participated with his father in Bacon's Rebellion, 1676. Among those excepted from the pardons on 29 Feb 1676/7 were "Thomas Goodrich, senr. Benjamin Goodrich, ... **Thomas Gordon**, ..."¹⁰⁵ Historic marker N18 at Caret, on US highway 17 west of Tappahannock, says, "About half a mile northeast stood the old courthouse and clerk's office of Rappahannock County, 1665-1693. To this courthouse Thomas Goodrich and Benjamin Goodrich, ordered to appear with halters around their necks, came to express their penitence for taking part in Bacon's Rebellion in 1676."¹⁰⁶

Benjamin² was married before 29 Feb 1676/7 when he was named "senr. Benjamin Goodrich" indicating that his son Benjamin³ was born by then. On 15 Mar 1678/9 he and "Alice my wife" sold back to Thomas¹ Goodrich for 500 lbs. sterling the 1,800 acres known as Old Matepony and "all those Negroe slaves men and women specified and nominated therein." Alice and Benjamin both signed their names to the document. On the same date Thomas Goodrich wrote his will, which named his "Eldest sonne Benjamine."¹⁰⁷

Benjamin² Goodrich and his mother Anne were named executor and executrix of Thomas Goodrich's will which was probated 3 Apr 1679. Benjamin² inherited 200 acres of land on the River side which Thomas had bought of Clement Thresh and "half the ... land I now live upon wth: all the profits, commodities and emoluments: thereunto belonging" and five Negroes.

Anne Goodrich "out of love I beare to Benjamin Goodrich, my sonn," and for other considerations, gave him the land left to her by her husband with the proviso that she would have the right of use during her lifetime. She appointed Mr. **Thomas Gouldman** as her attorney.¹⁰⁸

On 28 Jan 1680/1 Benjamin² Goodrich sold **Edward Hill** of Charles City County all of his right in the patent of 4,626 acres which had been granted to

---

¹⁰³ Sparacio, *Old Rappahannock Co VA - 1663-8 - OR.DB-03/89*, 115-6.
¹⁰⁴ Sweeney, *Wills, Rappahannock Co VA*, 64. Sparacio, *Old Rappahannock Co VA - 1677-1682 (I) - RK.DW-09/90*, 20.
¹⁰⁵ Hening, *Statutes*, 2:370.
¹⁰⁶ Salmon, *Historical Markers*, 107.
¹⁰⁷ Sparacio, *Old Rappahannock Co VA - 1677-1682 (I) - RK.DW-09/90*, 35-7.
¹⁰⁸ Sparacio, *Old Rappahannock Co VA - 1677-1682 (II) - RK.DW-10/90*, 53.

his father by Gov. **William Berkeley** on the 4 Oct 1672. Hill assumed the responsibility of paying the tobacco due the orphan William Cleaton. The deed specified "that what is given to Charles, Peter, and Catherine Goodrich, the orphans of the said Colonel Thomas Goodrich out of the sd patent as is bequeathed them be delivered to them by the sd Hill."[109]

On 2 Mar 1680/1 Benjamin^2 Goodrich as executor and Edward Hill as the husband of Anne Goodrich, the executrix of Thomas^1 Goodrich's estate, turned over to Joseph^2 and Charles^2 their inheritance.[110]

Benjamin^2 received a patent on 20 Apr 1684 for 930 acres on the South side of the Rappahannock River near the 1,350 acre tract patented by **Bartholomew Hoskins**. This was made up of:

> 600 acres beginning on Hoskins's Creek, parallel to **John Gillett**; granted to Lt. Coll. Thomas Goodrich 18 Sept 1663, and

> 330 acres below the mouth of Tickner's Creek, adjacent to **Reeves** land, which in turn was made up of 200 acres Colonel Thomas Goodrich bought of **Clement Thresh** in 1656 and 130 acres "newly taken" for transporting three persons.[111]

A survey done by **George Morris** 15 Jul 1680 shows the lines for the Goodrich and other property, labels property and land features, and gives a legend for the lettered boundaries.[112]

Founding of Tappahannock

On 18 Oct 1680, "at the request of the Gent: of Rappa: Court", **George Morris**, surveyed the plot for New Plymouth Towne, dividing the 50 acres into 100 lots.[113] By 1705 the town was called Tappahannock, but it often went by the name Hobbs His Hole or Hobbs Hole.[114]

The 25 Mar 1682 deed in which Benjamin^2 and Alice Goodrich sold 50 acres for 10,000 pounds of Tobacco in Cask to the Justices of Rappahannock County, Col. **John Stone**, Lt. Col. **William Loyde**, Henry

---

[109] Sparacio, *Old Rappahannock Co VA - 1677-1682 (II) - RK.DW-10/90*, 69-70.
[110] Sparacio, *Old Rappahannock Co VA - 1677-1682 (II) - RK.DW-10/90*, 70.
[111] Nugent, *Cavaliers and Pioneers*, 2:276 (Patent Book 7:365).
[112] Essex Co VA Land Trials 1715-1741, 145-6. Copies in Warner, *Origin .... of Tappahannock* and Sweeney, *Wills, Rappahannock Co VA*. (See appendix).
[113] Sparacio, *Old Rappahannock Co VA- 1682-6 - RK.DB-13/90*, 1.
[114] Slaughter, *Settlers .... of Essex Co VA*, 14. (See appendix).

Awbrey, Gent. and **Thomas Gouldman**, Gent., refers to the 1680 Morris survey and the 8 Jun 1680 General Assembly "Act for Cohabitation and encouragement of Trade and Manufacture wherein it was enacted that there should be fifty acres of land purchased by the Feoffees of the severall Counties at the rates therein expressed .... for a Towne for Store Houses etc." The deed states that the land was bequeathed to "Benjamin Goodrich by his father Thomas Goodrich, Gent. deceased, who ... purchased the same from Clement Thresh" who purchased it from **Bartholomew Hoskins** who held it and more by patent. The witnesses to this deed were **Robert Synock**, **Joseph² Goodrich**, and **Edmund Crask**.[115]

Col. **Edward Hill** of Charles City County and Capt. **William Howle**, Mariner, purchased two of the first ½ acre lots for 120 pounds of tobacco each: the qualification for these purchases being " ... erect and build upon the said allotment one Store House and Dwelling House according to the Act of Assembly."[116]

James City County

Benjamin² Goodrich had moved to James City County by 6 Apr 1685 when he, **Bridges Freeman** and others were listed as justices in that county.[117] "Mr. Benjamine Goodrich" was noted as being near the plantation in James City County that **Sarah Goddin** inherited from her father in 1688.[118]

In March and June of 1688 Mr. Benjamin² Goodrich, Gent. of James Citty County, served as administrator of the estate of Mr. **John Fry** in Rappahannock County, appointing **James Boughan** his attorney for a sale of Fry's land to **Richard Hall** and also for a sale to **Elizabeth Linch**.[119] Evidently Fry had sold several parcels of land but possibly died before acknowledging them in court. On 31 Jan 1688/9 a deed states "I Benja. Goodrich of James Citty County and Admirst. of the Will annexed of John Fry late of New Kent County deced do by virtue of an order of the Genll. Court dated the 28th of 8ber ano. Dom. 1688 giving me the same powere and authoritie as Mr. Geo. Morris had in and by the last Will and Testament of the sd Fry ....."[120] On 2 Oct 1688, the transaction concerning land John Fry had sold to **William Linch** which went to Elizabeth Linch, admrx. of

---

[115] Sparacio, *Old Rappahannock Co VA- 1682-6 - RK.DB-13/90*, 1-2. Hening, *Statutes*, 2:471-3.
[116] Sparacio, *Old Rappahannock Co VA- 1682-6 - RK.DB-13/90*, 2.
[117] "List of Colonial Officers", *VA Mag Hist*, 8:327-8.
[118] Dorman, *York Co VA Deeds* ....., 1:59.
[119] Sparacio, *Old Rappahannock Co VA - 1686-8 - RK.DB-14/90*, 82-3, 89.
[120] Sparacio, *Old Rappahannock Co VA - 1688-92 - RK.DB-11/90*, 10.

William Linch, refers to a 1687 power of attorney given to Benjamin Goodridge.[121]

Benjamin[2] was present as a justice at James City County court on 18 Dec 1690,[122] and Captain Benjamin[2] Goodrich was appointed sheriff of James City County by 3 Mar 1692/3.[123]

"Mr. **Edward Bland** confessed judgement to Mr. Benj[2] Goodrich assignee of **Nath. Bacon**, Esq. for 671 lbs. tobacco" in the 3 Aug 1691 Charles City County court held at Westopher; **Capt. (Charles) Goodrich** was present.[124] Benjamin[2] Goodrich's move to James City County could have been for several reasons. Economically, it may have been to remove from the unstable frontier, as Indian raids remained a problem until several years after the turn of the 18th century. Politically, it could have been for opportunities in James City County, the seat of the colony's government. After his father's death, Benjamin's mother had married Col. **Edward Hill** of "Shirley" plantation in Charles City County. Also Benjamin[2]'s sister Anne[2] married **John Lightfoot**, brother of **Phillip Lightfoot** of Sandy Point which was located on the Charles City County side of the Chickahominy River at the junction with the James River. John Lightfoot Esqr. was listed in the 1704 Virginia quit rents with 250 acres in James City County.[125]

On 18 Jul 1694 a warrant was ordered by the Councill held at James Citty: for "Ms. Alice Goodrick Applying for making a partition in the Secretary's Office Ordred 03.10."[126] Perhaps this is the widow of Benjamin[2].

Benjamin[2] Goodrich died prior to 27 Apr 1695, by which date **Alice** ( ) Goodrich had married (2) **Edward Sorrell**. This was shown in the 10 Dec 1696 sale of 200 acres adjoining Daingerfield and Reeves between **John Griffin** and **William Ayres**. It refers to the 27 Apr 1695 sale of 830 acres in Essex County to John Griffin by "Edward Sorrell of James City county & Alice his wife, Exex. of the last will & testament of Benja: Goodrich, late of the said County."[127] In court on 10 Apr 1696 the 1691 suit of Captain

---

[121] Sparacio, *Old Rappahannock Co VA - 1686-8 - RK.DB-14/90*, 99.

[122] Dorman, *York Co VA Deeds* ....., 2: 88.

[123] *Calendar of Virginia State Papers*, 1:33.

[124] Weisiger, *Charles City Co VA Orders, 1687-1695*, 107.

[125] Smith, *Quit Rents of Virginia, 1704*, 56.

[126] McIlwaine, *Executive Journals - Colonial VA*, 1:315. Probably £ 03.10.

[127] Sparacio, *Essex Co VA - 1695-7 - EX.DW-23/91*, 59. Essex Co VA Deeds & Wills, 11:2-3.

Edward Thomas vs Mr. **Benjamin²** Goodrich was renewed against Edward Sorrel and Alice his wife, executrix of the said Goodrich.[128]

There is conjecture that **Robert Goodrich** of James City County was a son of Benjamin² Goodrich.[129] Robert had land nearby, but no proof of any relationship has been found.[130] If he was related, it seems unusual that he was not named as "next friend" in 1719 when **Thomas Ravenscroft** was the "next friend" to Anne⁴ and Elizabeth⁴, the orphans of Benjamin³ Goodrich, in their suit against **Philip Ludwell**.[131]

- - - - - - - - - - -

3. Benjamin³ Goodrich <See pg. 170> (2.Benjamin², 1.Thomas¹).
ISSUE:
+ 4. f   i. **Anne Goodrich**, born about 1700, died before 1735 <See pg. 177>.
+ 5. f   ii. **Elizabeth Goodrich**, born about 1707 <See pg. 178>.

Benjamin³ Goodrich was born in (Old) Rappahannock County, today Essex County, Virginia, around 1675. His father Benjamin² Goodrich was named "senr. Benjamin Goodrich" 29 Feb 1676/7[132] in his involvement in Bacon's Rebellion, indicating that his son Benjamin³ was born by then. The family was living in James City County by 6 Apr 1685 when Benjamin² Goodrich was named a justice in that county.[133]

Edward Sorrel and his wife Alice ( ) Goodrich Sorrel, the executrix of the estate of Benjamin² Goodrich, on 27 Apr 1695 sold **John Griffin** 200 acres. Griffin sold it to **William Ayres** of Essex County, planter, 10 Dec 1696.[134] On 10 Jun 1703 Benjamin³ Goodrich of James City County, gentleman, "son and heir apparent" of Benjamin² Goodrich late of said County deceased, affirmed the 1695 and 1696 Essex County deeds for the 200 acres, a part of 830 acres in Essex, adjacent to the line of **William Tomlin**, **John Dangerfield**, Tignor's Creek and **Joseph Reeves**.[135] Benjamin signed with his seal.

---

[128] Sparacio, *Essex Co VA - 1695-9 - EX.OB-19/91*, 8. In 1692, Richmond and Essex counties were created from (Old) Rappahannock.
[129] Tyler, "The Goodrich Family", *Tyler's Quarterly*, 12:69.
[130] Lee Family Papers (1638-1867), Mss1:L51:f:618, 620.
[131] Lee Family Papers (1638-1867), Mss1:L51:f:66.
[132] Hening, *Statutes*, 2:370.
[133] "List of Colonial Officers", *VA Mag Hist*, 8:327-8.
[134] Sparacio, *Essex Co VA - 1695-7 - EX.DW-23/91*, 59-60.
[135] Essex Co VA Deeds & Wills No 11 1702-1704, 2-6.

Also on 10 Jun 1703, Benjamin[3] sold **Elizabeth Lowes**, widow, of Essex County for £25 sterling the 830 acres "near Miles end of a patent of 1350 acres taken up by **Bartholomew Hoskins**", excepting the 200 acres sold to William Ayres. A tract of 230 acres was described as adjoining Reeves, **Robert Coleman**, and the Rappahannock River.[136] 600 acres of this tract was patented by Lieutenant Colonel Thomas[1] Goodrich in 1657.[137]

On 8 Dec 1703 Benjamin[3] Goodrich, gentleman of James City County, sold to **William Aylet**, gentleman of King William County, 200 acres in Essex County,[138] part of the tract taken up by Joseph[2] Goodrich, **William Batt** (Ball) and **John Price**."[139] It adjoined Mr. **John Lightfoot** and Mr. **Edward Chilton**'s land and was known as Mount Maple. It was "sold to said Joseph Goodrich on February 2, 1691 by **John Clark** then of Rappahannock County, and is now vested in Benjamin Goodrich by act of law 'as heir to the said Joseph Goodrich some time since deceased'."

On the following days, December 9 and 10, Benjamin[3] sold Aylet for £84, 700 acres, part of 900 acres in Essex County, which was one-half of the 1,800 acres granted to Lt. Coll. Thomas[1] Goodrich on 15 Oct 1669 and willed on 15 Mar 1678/9 to his son Joseph[2]. At Joseph's death, the land was left to his son Danby[3] who died in his minority. Then the land came by inheritance to Joseph's nephew Benjamin[3] Goodrich. "The land bound according to a division made 15 Nov 1681 between Joseph Goodrich, in his lifetime, and John Lightfoot, gentleman, who married Anne Goodrich, sister to said Joseph."[140] An exception from the 900 acres was stated regarding 100 acres sold in 1680 to **Jno Ferguson**[141] and 100 acres sold in 1685 by Joseph[2] Goodrich to **Thomas Wood**."[142]

Benjamin[3] Goodrich of Wimbleton (should be Wilmington) Parish, James City County, was named " nephew and heir at law" to Joseph[2] Goodrich in an agreement drawn up on 23 Oct 1705 between Benjamin and "**John Danby** of London, now resident in Virginia, Gent., ... lawful attorney" of Sir **Abstrupus Danby**.[143]

---

[136] Essex Co VA Deeds & Wills No 11 1702-1704, 7-11.
[137] Nugent, *Cavaliers and Pioneers*, 1:347 (Patent Book 4:99).
[138] Fleet, *VA Col Abs, Essex Co*, 2:101.
[139] Nugent, *Cavaliers and Pioneers*, 2:282 (Patent Book 7:406).
[140] Fleet, *VA Col Abs, Essex Co*, 2:100-1.
[141] Sparacio, *Old Rappahannock Co VA - 1677-1682 (II) - RK.DW-10/90*, 67.
[142] Sparacio, *Old Rappahannock Co VA- 1682-6 - RK.DB-13/90*, 112-3.
[143] Hamlin, "Goodrich Family", NGSQ, 51:69.

Goodrich Families

In March 1702 Benjamin[3] Goodrich was named in the James City County militia list,[144] and he was listed on the James City County 1704 quit rent rolls with 1,650 acres. **Thomas Parker**, who married the widow of Benjamin[3]'s uncle Joseph[2] Goodrich, was also listed in James City County with 1,650 acres.[145]

Benjamin[3] Goodrich's children Anne[4] and Elizabeth[4] were identified 7 Nov 1719 as infants, orphans of Mr. Benjamin Goodrich when **Thomas Ravenscroft** was named their "next friend" in response to a petition by **Philip Ludwell** regarding 1 acre of land on the Checkerhouse Creek.[146]

Benjamin[3] Goodrich died 29 Apr 1710 probably in James City County. **William Byrd** wrote in his diary April 30 of his death: "Colonel Duke told me that Ben Goodrich died at night and was well that morning two days since."[147]

- - - - - - - - - - -

4. Anne[4] Goodrich <See pg. 175> (3.Benjamin[3], 2.Benjamin[2], 1.Thomas[1]) was born about 1700 in James City County, Virginia. She married **Samuel Boush. (See Samuel Boush number 27 - pg. 202). (See also number 32 - pg. 109).**

ISSUE:[148]

- f   i.   **Ann Boush**, born about 1721, died after 24 Mar 1779.
- m ii. **Samuel Boush**, born about 1722, died before 20 May 1784.
- m iii. **Goodrich Boush**, born about 1724, died before 22 May 1779.
- m iv. **John Boush**, born before 18 Oct 1733, died before 10 Jun 1735.
- m v. **William Boush**, born after 18 Oct 1733, died before 6 Nov 1756.

In James City County on 7 Nov 1719 **Thomas Ravenscroft** brought suit against **Philip Ludwell** regarding an acre of land on the Checkerhouse Creek as the "next friend" of Anne[4] and Elizabeth[4], "orphans of Benjamin Goodrich dec'd."[149] Fleet explains the term next friend: "As an infant cannot legally sue in his own name, the action must be brought by ..... some friend

---

[144] Bockstruck, *Virginia Colonial Soldiers*, 215-6.
[145] Smith, *Quit Rents of Virginia, 1704*, 36, 68.
[146] Lee Family Papers (1638-1867), Mss1:L51:f65, :66.
[147] Wright, *Byrd Diary 1709-1712*, 75.
[148] The documentation on this family is in the Boush chapter.
[149] Lee Family Papers (1638-1867), Mss1:L51:f:66.

(not being his guardian) who will appear as plaintiff."[150] Thomas Ravenscroft had married **Elizabeth Hamlin**, the sister of **John Hamlin** who had married Anne[3] Goodrich.[151]

By 17 May 1722 Anne[4] married Samuel Boush indicated when Samuel Boush Jr. and Anne Boush were witnesses to a deed by Samuel Boush "the elder" to **Peter Malbone**.[152] The marriage between Anne and Samuel is also mentioned in the family Bible of a descendant of her sister Elizabeth[4] Goodrich: "Benjamin Goodrich ... left two daughters Elizabeth the wife of Willis Wilson and the wife of Samuel Boush of Norfolk."[153]

Samuel Boush's father, Samuel Boush Sr., had two wills;[154] the first was written 18 Oct 1733, proved 17 Dec 1736, and named wife Alice, son Samuel, grandsons Samuel, Goodrich, and John. "Daughter" Anne was left only a suit of mourning clothes. In wills, the terms "daughter" and "son" were frequently used for what we today call sons or daughters- in-law. Also her position in a clause in the will, between "son Samuel" and "grandson Samuel", suggests a family unit. Since Anne[4] was not named in the second will, it is highly probable that she had died before it was written in 1735.[155]

Samuel married (2) **Frances Sayer** before 7 Jun 1738. Another point supporting Anne[4]'s being the first wife of Samuel Boush was his bequest to their son Goodrich, to whom he left his Chickahominy land in James City County. This must have been Anne[4]'s dowry. Also Samuel's will states: "the rest to be equally divided among the children now alive each child by each wife to have equal shares.........my desire they have a tender regard for her she being a tender mother in law" (step-mother).[156]

- - - - - - - - - - -

5. Elizabeth[4] Goodrich <See pg. 175> (3.Benjamin[3], 2.Benjamin[2], 1.Thomas[1]) was born about 1707 in James City County, Virginia. She married **Willis Wilson. (See number 97 - pg. 38)**.
ISSUE:
    m i. **Benjamin Wilson, Sr.**, born 6 Jan 1733, died 27 Oct 1814.

---

[150] Fleet, *VA Col Abs, Essex Co*, 2:115.
[151] Hamlin, *They Went That Away*, 2:111.
[152] Norfolk Co VA Deed Book F:23a 24.
[153] "Wilson Family", *VA Mag Hist*, 25:199-200.
[154] McIntosh, *Norfolk Co Wills 1710-1753*, 139-140 (Original will), 247 (Book I:32).
[155] Boush, "The Identity of the 1st wife of Sam. Boush II, Norf. Co", Misc Reel 520, pp. 16-7.
[156] Norfolk Co VA Will Book 1:37-39.

Elizabeth[4] Goodrich was born around 1707 in James City County, Virginia. She and her older sister Anne[4] were infant orphans of Benjamin[3] Goodrich as noted in their suit in 1719 against **Philip Ludwell** brought by their "next friend" **Thomas Ravenscroft**, who was married to **Elizabeth Hamlin**. He was close to the family by in-law relationship with Benjamin[3]'s cousin Anne[3] Goodrich who married **John Hamlin**, Elizabeth Hamlin's brother.[157]

Since an infant can't legally sue in his own name, a friend, not a guardian, was required to appear as plaintiff.[158] Philip Ludwell wrote to Mr. **Joseph Egglestone** in September asking him to meet him at Mr. Ravenscroft's about viewing an acre of land for a watermill on the land of Mr. Goodrich's orphans at the head of Checkerhouse Creek. At James City County court 7 Nov 1719 Thomas Ravenscroft offered to verify that the land belonged to Anne and Elizabeth. He explained the damage a mill would do to their land and told how it would dam up two landings on their land used for shipping; he said there were already two mills nearby.[159]

Elizabeth[4] Goodrich was probably living with her sister Anne[4], wife of **Samuel Boush**, when the marriage bond was issued to Willis[4] Wilson on 7 Jun 1728 in Norfolk. The bond of £50 sterling was posted by Willis[4] Wilson and his uncle **Solomon[3] Wilson** "both of Norfolk County."[160] Both Elizabeth and Willis must have been born before 7 Jun 1707 since consents were not required.[161]

The family Bible of Willis[6] Wilson states that the estate of Benjamin Goodrich was "near the mouth of the Chickahominy" and that he left two daughters, Elizabeth Goodrich, wife of Willis Wilson and the wife of Samuel Boush of Norfolk.[162]

Elizabeth[4]'s great-great grandson **Willis[8] Wilson Hobson** born 1826 and died in 1917 at "Vernon", Powhatan County, Virginia,[163] had an old trunk

---

[157] Hamlin, *They Went That Away*, 2:111.

[158] Fleet, *VA Col Abs, Essex Co*, 2:115.

[159] Lee Family Papers (1638-1867), Mss1:L51:f:65, 66. 1719 Ludwell, Ravenscroft next friend ....

[160] James, *Lower Norfolk Antiquary*, 3:75. Norfolk Co VA Marriage Bonds 1706-1768.

[161] Hening, *Statutes*, 1:181. Hening's Statutes, ACT V states: "1632...no ...lycense.....to be maryed yf they be under age of twenty one yeares" before parents signify their consent.

[162] "Wilson Family", *VA Mag Hist*, 25:199-200.

[163] McClendon, DAR application.

which was brought over from England and contained the wedding trousseau of Elizabeth[4] Goodrich.[164]

After their marriage, they soon settled on the Chickahominy River in James City County, Virginia. Willis[4] was appointed a Justice of the Peace for James City County on 24 Apr 1731 and sheriff in 1732-33. He was appointed again as Justice along with **Robert Goodrich**, and **Philip Ludwell** on 15 Dec 1737.[165]

On 18 Jan 1731/2 Willis[4] and Elizabeth[4] Wilson sold to his uncle, Solomon[3] Wilson, the 400 acre plantation which Willis[4] had inherited from his grandfather, Colonel James[2] Wilson.[166] In the deeds Willis[4] was described as a gentleman of Chickahominy and Solomon[3] as "of the town and county of Norfolk, merchant."[167]

Willis[4] Wilson died "the representative of his county at Williamsburg in the year 1740."[168] It is not known whom his widow, Elizabeth[4] (Goodrich) Wilson, married second nor when and where she died.[169]

- - - - - - - - - - -

14. Joseph[2] Goodrich <See pg. 157> (1.Thomas[1]) was born about 1650. He married **Francelia Danby**. She was the daughter of **Christopher Danby** and **Anne Culpeper**.[170]

ISSUE:
15. m i. **Danby Goodrich**, born about 1687, died before 9 Dec 1703.[171]
16. m ii. **Thomas Goodrich**, born about 1689, died before 20 Nov 1703.[172]

In the 16 Feb 1656/7 will of **Clement Thresh**, he requested that daughter-in-law **Ann Harris** have schooling with "Tho. Goodrichs Children where

---

[164] DAR, Patriot file of Benjamin Wilson.
[165] McIlwaine, *Executive Journals - Colonial VA*, 4:235-6, 273, 297, 410-13.
[166] Norfolk Co VA Deed Book 9:220-222. (See appendix).
[167] Norfolk Co VA Deed Book 11:15-16.
[168] Woodson Family, *Papers, 1740-1945*, Accession 29437-40, LVA. He was probably Justice in the county court.
[169] "Wilson Family", *VA Mag Hist*, 25:199-200.
[170] Meyer and Dorman, *Adventurers of Purse and Person*, 528. This says that this Benjamin of the 1703 sale is a brother of Joseph, instead of nephew. Sparacio, *Old Rappahannock Co VA- 1682-6 - RK.DB-13/90*, 112-3.
[171] Fleet, *VA Col Abs, Essex Co*, 2:100.
[172] "Proprietors of the Northern Neck", *VA Mag Hist*, 33:349.

Goodrich Families

they do go", which implies that Benjamin² and Joseph² were of school age.¹⁷³

On 29 June 1674 his father, Thomas¹ Goodrich, gave Joseph a mare filly and increase,¹⁷⁴ and in his will on 15 March 1678/9 Thomas¹ Goodrich left his son Joseph² 900 acres of land which was one half of the 1,800 acre tract called Matepony. He gave him "his first choice and if my sonne make choice of that Moyetie which contains the Plantation and Houses, then my will is that my son Joseph shall build halfe soe much housing upon the other Moyetie of the said land as is now upon that part he now lives upon for those to whom hereafter I shall bequest it (Anne²)" and three Negroes and all the stock on the land.¹⁷⁵

Joseph² acknowledged the receipt of his inheritance 2 Mar 1680/1,¹⁷⁶ and on 15 November 1681 Joseph² Goodrich and **John Lightfoot** signed an agreement dividing the 1800 acre tract, "the sd John Lightfoot, now the Husband of the sd Anne .... shall imediately or at his pleasure seat and make as a Plantacon upon the sd Divident on the South side of a Branche ..... called ....Western Branch of the old Indian Towne" making the Western Branch the boundary. It was recorded 11 Jun 1696, probably during the settlement of Joseph's estate.¹⁷⁷

On 5 Nov 1680 Joseph² Goodrich sold to **John Ferguson** a parcel "... South side of Pisscatacon (Piscataway) Pocoson at Western Branch adjoining **Francis Browne**, an Indian Field, First Branch of the Indian Towne formerly patent of Coll. Thomas Goodrich."¹⁷⁸ The 1703 release by his nephew Benjamin³ Goodrich states that this tract consisted of 100 acres.¹⁷⁹ In 1684 he, **William Ball**, and **John Price** patented 629 acres in Rappahannock County adjoining **Thomas Harper**, **Col. Hill**, the Indian path, **John Jones**, and Wilson's path. This patent was deserted and granted to **Hugh Bawden** 21 Oct 1687.¹⁸⁰

---

¹⁷³ Sweeney, *Wills, Rappahannock Co VA*, 10.
¹⁷⁴ Sparacio, *Old Rappahannock Co VA - 1672-6 (II) - OR.DB-08/89*, 30.
¹⁷⁵ Sparacio, *Old Rappahannock Co VA - 1677-1682 (I) - RK.DW-09/90*, 36.
¹⁷⁶ Sparacio, *Old Rappahannock Co VA - 1677-1682 (II) - RK.DW-10/90*, 69-70.
¹⁷⁷ Sparacio, *Essex Co VA - 1695-7 - EX.DW-23/91*, 40-1.
¹⁷⁸ Sparacio, *Old Rappahannock Co VA - 1677-1682 (II) - RK.DW-10/90*, 67.
¹⁷⁹ Fleet, *VA Col Abs, Essex Co*, 2:100-1.
¹⁸⁰ Nugent, *Cavaliers and Pioneers*, 2:282, 317 (Patent Book 7:406, 620).

Joseph[2] was given power of attorney by his brother and sister-in-law, **Charles**[2] and **Elizabeth**, on 19 Dec 1683 for their sale to **Robert Parker**, 400 acres which Charles had inherited from his father.[181]

Before 1686 Joseph had moved, as had his brothers Benjamin[2] and Charles[2], to James City County and married Francelia Danby.[182] On 22 Jan 1685/6 Joseph[2] Goodrich "of James City County, Gent.", made a deed to **Thomas Wood** Sr., selling him 100 acres, part of the land left him by his father, Joseph appointing **Thomas Edmondson** of Rappahannock as his attorney. His wife Francelia appointed **William Glover** of Rappahannock to acknowledge "my right or Thirds of all such lands as my loving Husband hath made to Thomas Wood Sr."[183]

A deed dated 3 Mar 1690/1 stated that "Joseph Goodrich of James Citty County" sold **John Powell** 100 acres, part of a devident taken up by Price, Ball, and sd Goodrich "binding on John Harper & Lightfoot and the sd Goodrich", Joseph[2] appointing Mr. **Jonathan Fisher** his attorney.[184]

Joseph[2] Goodrich died by 10 May 1694, as his wife Francelia had by then married (2) **Thomas Parker**.[185] On 11 Jun 1696 Thomas Parker was appointed guardian of Danby[3] Goodrich by the Essex County Court.[186]

Records of the two sons, Thomas[3] and Danby[3], of Joseph[2] and Francelia are shown by the following: Sir **Abstrupus Danby** of Farnley, Yorkshire was granted administration on the estate of Thomas[3] Goodrich, late of Virginia, infant, as uncle on the mother's side and next of kin, on 20 Nov 1703,[187] an inventory for Danby[3] and Thomas[3], infants, deceased, to be exhibited before 31 May 1704 and an account to be rendered before 30 Nov 1704.[188] Joseph[2] Goodrich's estate reverted to Benjamin[3] Goodrich as the oldest male heir of Benjamin[2] Goodrich, Joseph[2]'s elder brother.[189]

---

[181] Sparacio, *Old Rappahannock Co VA- 1682-6 - RK.DB-13/90*, 41-2.

[182] Meyer and Dorman, *Adventurers of Purse and Person*, 528. This article states that Joseph was a brother to Benjamin Goodrich of the 1703 Essex record. This Benjamin is Joseph's nephew.

[183] Sparacio, *Old Rappahannock Co VA- 1682-6 - RK.DB-13/90*, 112-3.

[184] Sparacio, *Old Rappahannock Co VA - 1688-92 - RK.DB-11/90*, 109.

[185] Sparacio, *Essex Co VA - 1693-4 - EX.DW-17/91*, 49-50.

[186] Sparacio, *Essex Co VA - 1695-9 - EX.OB-19/91*, 20.

[187] Withington, *Virginia Gleanings*, 14, 20 (P.C.C. Admon Act Book folio 211).

[188] PROB 6/79 fo. 211 transcriptions done by Simon Neal, records agent, e-mail sn014i4785@blueyonder.co.uk.

[189] Fleet, *VA Col Abs, Essex Co*, 2:100-1.

Joseph² Goodrich's wife Francelia Danby was the daughter of **Anne Culpeper** and **Christopher Danby** who was the son of Sir **Thomas Danby** and **Catherine Wandesford**. Christopher's aunt, **Alice (Wandesford) Thornton** complained in her diary around 1668 of the ingratitude of her nephew's wife Anne: "I was forced to give of my disbursements for maintaining of herself, her husband, and children.... they being cast out of favor by Sir Thomas Danby on her inveighling his son to marry her in Virginia ......"[190]

- - - - - - - - - - -

17. **Charles² Goodrich** <See pg. 157> (1.Thomas¹) was born about 1652. He married **Elizabeth** ____.

ISSUE:

+ 18. m   i.   **Edward Goodrich**, born about 1684, died before 10 Jan 1720/1 <See pg. 185>.
  23. m   ii. **Charles Goodrich, Jr.**, born about 1686, died about 1722 in Charles City County, Virginia. He was named in the Charles City County 1722 Accounts Current of Colonel **Edward Hill**, dec'd, which credited the executors of Charles³ Goodrich.[191] There was an order for the return of the inventory and appraisement of "Charles Goodrich junr, dec'd" in the Oct 1723 Docket book of the Virginia General Court, naming his executor, **Henry Harrison**.[192]
+ 24. f   iii. **Anne Goodrich**, born about 1688 <See pg. 187>.
  32. f   iv. **Lucy (Elizabeth) Goodrich**.
  33. f   v.   **Sarah Goodrich**.

On 5 Jan 1663/4 Charles² received a deed of gift from **Thomas Button** of 219 acres on the South side of the Rappahannock River.[193] "For naturall love & affection" **Jane Button**, widow of Thomas Button gave him a mare 9 Aug 1670.[194] Jane was the widow of **John Gillet** when she married Thomas Button. Charles² Goodrich inherited 300 acres of Buttons Range in Sittingbourne Parish from Thomas Button which was noted in the exclusion of 300 acres in the 1678 deed by Thomas and Jane ( ) Gordon when they sold Buttons Range to **Edmund Crask**.[195] Jane's many marriages, John

---

[190] "Proprietors of the Northern Neck", *VA Mag Hist*, 33:349.
[191] Weisiger, *Charles City Co VA W&D, 1725-31*, 7.
[192] Lee Family Papers (1638-1867), Mss1:L51:f:185.
[193] Sparacio, *Old Rappahannock Co VA - 1665-77 - OR.DW-04/89*, 19.
[194] Sparacio, *Old Rappahannock Co VA - 1670-2 - OR.DB-06/89*, 19-20.
[195] Sparacio, *Old Rappahannock Co VA - 1677-1682 (II) - RK.DW-10/90*, 1.

Gillet, Thomas Button, ... Watts, and **Thomas Gordon**, are well documented.[196]

As recorded in his father's 1679 will, Charles[2] inherited 400 acres adjoining Buttons Range with "all the profits and commodities thereof", all of the profits from 600 acres of land on Hoskins Pocoson, and three negroes.[197] On 28 Jan 1680/1 Benjamin[2] Goodrich, son and heir of Col. Thomas[1] Goodrich, sold to **Edward Hill** 4626 acres excepting from the tract the portions due to "orphans of the sd. Thomas Goodrich", Charles, Peter and Catherine. Charles[2] acknowledged his father's bequest on 2 Mar 1680/1.[198] By 1680 Charles's mother had married Col. Edward Hill of "Shirley", Charles City County, and Charles evidently went to the area to them.[199]

Charles[2] married Elizabeth ____ by 19 Dec 1683 when they assigned a power of attorney to Joseph[2], Charles's brother, for the sale of 400 acres on the South side of Gilsons Creek, adjoining **Thomas Button** and **George Morris**, to **Robert Parker** for 4,200 lbs. of tobacco. Charles[2] had inherited this land from his father, who bought it from **Henry Clark** in 1672.[200]

Charles[2] Goodrich patented 550 acres in Westover Parish on the south side of the James River on 20 Apr 1687 for transporting 11 persons, but he evidently did not get it settled, so it was granted to **John Hamlyn** 2 May 1705.[201] A court in Charles City County Jun 1690 was held at "Capt. Goodrich house," then at "Westopher." On 3 Oct 1690 Collo. Edward Hill and Capt. Cha: Goodrich were present as justices, and at "Westover" on 15 Oct 1695 Capt. Ch: Goodrich and Capt. Hamblin were present.[202] Charles was a justice along with Capt. John Hamlin at a court held at Westover 3 March 1696.[203]

At a court held at Westover 4 Jun 1688, Capt. Cha. Goodrich was sworn in as high sheriff of the county, Col. Hill giving bond.[204]

---

[196] Sweeney, "Thomas Button of Button's Range." *Genealogies, Tyler's Quarterly*, 1:301-5.
[197] Sparacio, *Old Rappahannock Co VA - 1677-1682 (I) - RK.DW-09/90*, 36.
[198] Sparacio, *Old Rappahannock Co VA - 1677-1682 (II) - RK.DW-10/90*, 69-70.
[199] Wilkerson, *Marriages Old Rapp and Essex Cos VA 1655-1900*, 114.
[200] Sparacio, *Old Rappahannock Co VA- 1682-6 - RK.DB-13/90*, 41-2.
[201] Duvall, *VA Col Abs, Pr George Co, 1666-1719*, 19, 47.
[202] Charles City Co VA Orders .... 1687-1695, 290, 304, 595.
[203] Fleet, *VA Col Abs, Charles City Co*, 3:362.
[204] Weisiger, *Charles City Co VA Orders, 1687-1695*, 18.

Charles[2] Goodrich was a burgess from Charles City County from 1695 through 1698.[205] The 1698 militia returned for Charles City County listed Col. **Edward Hill**, Capt. **Edward Hill** with troop of 54 men, and Capt. Charles[2] Goodrich with troop of 71 men;[206] the 1699 officers appointed were "Edward Hill Esqr., Collonell and Comander in Cheif, Edward Hill Junr., Lieutenant Colonell, and Charles Goodrich Majr.[207] Charles[2] served as sheriff and justice of Charles City County in 1702.[208]

Prince George County was created from Charles City County in 1702/3. Major Goodrich was shown in 1704 as owning 900 acres of land in Prince George County,[209] and in 1714 Charles Goodrich and John Hamlin were listed as justices of Prince George County.[210]

Charles[2] Goodrich's will was dated 6 Dec 1725[211] and recorded 14 Jun 1726. He left his daughter Ann[3], who had married John Hamlin, "all my personal estate (because of debt I owe to her deceased husband) except one bed and furniture to daughter Sarah Goodrich." He also named daughter Lucy[3] regarding "one negro now in dispute between her and **Peter Wynne**." The will was witnessed by **John Irby** and **William Goodrich**. Ann[3] was the executrix of her father's will; the inventory was recorded on 9 Aug 1726 for a value of £11/9/00.[212]

- - - - - - - - - - -

18. Edward[3] Goodrich <See pg. 183> (17.Charles[2], 1.Thomas[1]) was born about 1684. He married **Margaret Wynne** about 1710. She was born about 1690. She was the daughter of **Joshua Wynne** and **Mary Jones**.[213]

ISSUE:
- 19. f i. **Mary Goodrich**. She married **Roger Tillman**.
- 20. f ii. **Elizabeth Goodrich**.
- + 21. m iii. **Benjamin Goodrich**, died about 1761 <See pg. 186>.
- + 22. m iv. **Edward Goodrich**, died before 27 Jan 1791 <See pg. 186>.

---

[205] Leonard, *General Assembly of Virginia*, 54-58.
[206] Bockstruck, *Virginia Colonial Soldiers*, 231.
[207] McIlwaine, *Executive Journals - Colonial VA*, 1:443.
[208] Hamlin, "Major Charles Goodrich", NGSQ, 46:130.
[209] Smith, *Quit Rents of Virginia, 1704*, 36.
[210] des Cognets, *English Duplicates*, 22, 28.
[211] Tyler, "The Goodrich Family", *Tyler's Quarterly*, 12:69.
[212] Weisiger, *Prince George County, 1713-1728*, 118, 120.
[213] Boddie, *Southside Virginia Families*, 1:219-21.

Edward³ Goodrich, who married Margaret Wynne,²¹⁴ was a burgess from Prince George County from 1711 until his death.²¹⁵ In his Prince George County will which was written 7 Oct 1720 and proved 10 Jan 1721, he named his daughters Mary⁴ and Elizabeth⁴, sons Benjamin⁴ and Edward⁴ and mentioned but did not name his father, two sisters and brother; nor did he name his wife. His wife and Capt. **Henry Harrison** were to be executors. Capt. Harrison was also executor for Edward's brother Charles. His wife evidently died soon after; the inventories of Edward³ and his wife Margaret were presented to court 10 Dec 1723 by **Peter Wynne**, administrator.²¹⁶

- - - - - - - - - - -

21. Benjamin⁴ Goodrich <See pg. 185> (18.Edward³, 17.Charles², 1.Thomas¹).
ISSUE:
   f   i. **Elizabeth Goodrich**.
   f ii. **Frances Goodrich**.

The orphans of Benjamin Goodrich, Elizabeth and Frances, chose their guardian in the Dec 1761 court of Charles City County ²¹⁷

- - - - - - - - - - -

22. Edward⁴ Goodrich <See pg. 185> (18.Edward³, 17.Charles², 1.Thomas¹). He married **Anne Briggs**.
ISSUE:²¹⁸
  m   i. **Briggs Goodrich**, died before 28 Apr 1788.
   f ii. **Mary Goodrich**.
   f iii. **Dorothy Goodrich**.
   f iv. **Sarah Goodrich**.
  m   v. **Edward Goodrich**.
  m vi. **Benjamin Goodrich**, died before 15 Jan 1803.

Anne died after 1790. Edward died before 27 Jan 1791 in Greensville County, Virginia.

---

²¹⁴ Boddie, *Southside Virginia Families*, 1:219-21. Boddie links Charles Goodrich, father of this Edward, to the Isle of Wight Goodrich family. There was a Charles Goodrich, apparently the son of John Goodrich, in the 1687 Surry Co militia and with 80 acres of land in Isle of Wight Co in 1704. Crozier, *VA Colonial Militia*, 102. Boddie, *Historical Southern Families*, 1:7.
²¹⁵ Leonard, *General Assembly of Virginia*, 65-71.
²¹⁶ Weisiger, *Prince George County, 1713-1728*, 56, 81.
²¹⁷ Weisiger, *Charles City Co VA Records, 1737-1774*, 145-6.
²¹⁸ Boddie, *Southside Virginia Families*, 1:222-5 - gives all names and dates.

- - - - - - - - - - -
24. Anne³ Goodrich <See pg. 183> (17.Charles², 1.Thomas¹) was born about 1688. She married **John Hamlin** about 1705. He was the son of **John Hamlin** and **Elizabeth Taylor**.[219]

ISSUE:
- 25. f   i.   **Mary Hamlin**, born about 1706. She married **John Irby** before 11 Nov 1724, the date of her father's will.
- 26. m ii.   **John Hamlin**.
- 27. m iii. **Peter Hamlin**.
- 28. m iv.   **Charles Hamlin**.
- 29. m v.   **Hubbard Hamlin**.
- 30. m vi.   **William Hamlin**.
- 31. f vii. **Ann Hamlin**.

The will of John Hamlin, dated 11 Nov 1724 and recorded 11 May 1725, named sons John, Peter, Charles, Hubbard, and William, daughters Ann and Mary, wife of John Irby. His brothers **Thomas Ravenscroft** and **William Hamlin** were asked to be trustees until his son John came of age; his wife Ann³ was named as executrix. The will was witnessed by **Peter Wynne**.[220]

In 1727 John⁴ Hamlin the grandson of Charles² Goodrich owned land from his estate.[221] This family is of special interest because Thomas Ravenscroft who married **Elizabeth**,[222] the sister of John Hamlin, lived in James City County[223] and was "next friend" to the orphans of Benjamin³ Goodrich in a 1719 suit.[224]

- - - - - - - - - - -
34. Anne² Goodrich <See pg. 157> (1.Thomas¹) was born after 1658; she was less than 21 in her father's 1679 will.[225] She married **John Lightfoot**, the son of **John Lightfoot**.[226]

ISSUE:
- + 35. m i.   **Goodrich Lightfoot**, born about 1682, died 14 Apr 1738 <See pg. 190>.
- + 42. m ii. **Sherwood Lightfoot**, died 20 Apr 1730 <See pg. 192>.

---

[219] Hamlin, *They Went That Away*, 2:111.
[220] Weisiger, *Prince George County, 1713-1728*, 104-5.
[221] Weisiger, *Prince George County, 1713-1728*, 132.
[222] Hamlin, *They Went That Away*, 2:111.
[223] Weisiger, *Prince George County, 1713-1728*, 74.
[224] Lee Family Papers (1638-1867), Mss1:L51:f:66.
[225] Sparacio, *Old Rappahannock Co VA - 1677-1682 (I) - RK.DW-09/90*, 36-7.
[226] Tyler, "The Lightfoot Family", *Genealogies, Wm & M Qrtrly*, 3:416-7, 420-1.

+ 48. m iii. **Thomas Lightfoot** <See pg. 193>.
   54. f iv. **Alice Lightfoot,** born 25 Sep 1698 in St. Peter's Parish, New Kent County, Virginia.[227]

In July 1672 her father, Thomas[1] Goodrich, gave Ann[2] a heifer, and on 23 Apr 1673 he gave her a bay mare filly and half the increase of the mare,[228] the other half of the increase being given to her sister Katherine[2].

By her father's will in 1679, Anne[2] Goodrich inherited 900 acres of the 1800 acres of land known as Matepony and four Negroes "upon her Marriage Day or at the age of one and Twenty." She also inherited one feather bed and furniture.[229]

She married John Lightfoot by 15 Nov 1681 when her brother, Joseph[2] Goodrich, and John Lightfoot signed an agreement dividing the 1800 acre tract, "the sd John Lightfoot, now the Husband of the sd. Anne .... shall immediately or at his pleasure seat and make as a Plantacon upon the sd Divident on the South side ... Western Branch of the old Indian Towne." This was recorded 11 Jun 1696, probably when the estate of Joseph[2] Goodrich was settled.[230]

On 3 Dec 1681 Anne[2]'s husband, John Lightfoot of the parish of Piscataway in (Old) Rappahannock County created a trust for the "competent Subsistance & Mayntaynance" of his wife Anne, daughter of Tho: Goodridge deceased, selling to **Phillip Lightfoot** of the parish of Petso, Gloucester County, five Negroes, 12 head of cattle, three mares, "one feather bed, bowlster, pillow and one paire of sheets, one paire of blankets, one rugg, one suite of flowered damask curtaines, vallans, counterpaine and testar....goods and estate of my said wife before .... intermarriage." This property was to be "in trust ... for the use and advantage of my said Wife." John reserved the right to dispose of the male cattle age 10 and the female cattle age 14. This deed was "signed, sealed and delivered to **Edward Hill** of Charles City County who received it in behalfe of Lt. Coll. Phillip Lightfoot for the uses it in wrighting expressed." It was recorded 5 Jul 1682.[231]

---

[227] Chamberlayne, *Vestry Book and Register of St. Peter's Parish*, 366.
[228] Sparacio, *Old Rappahannock Co VA - 1672-6 (I) - OR.DB-07/89*, 17, 51.
[229] Sparacio, *Old Rappahannock Co VA - 1677-1682 (I) - RK.DW-09/90*, 36-7.
[230] Sparacio, *Essex Co VA - 1695-7 - EX.DW-23/91*, 40-1.
[231] Sparacio, *Old Rappahannock Co VA - 1677-1682 (II) - RK.DW-10/90*, 106.

Captain John Lightfoot and his brother Phillip were in Virginia around 1670-1.[232] Their ancestor was the Rev. **Richard Lightfoot**, of Stoke Brewer, Northamptonshire, who stated in his will probated the 6th of December 1625 that he left his son **John** "my house at Northon and all other things hereunto appertaining purchased of Thomas Gutteridge, cordwiner."[233] It is not known if this Thomas Goodrich was connected to Anne[2] Goodrich's father.

The 1625 will of Richard Lightfoot, the 1647 will of his son John with 13 children listed, and the 1681 will of John's wife **Elizabeth** suggest an intervening generation. An item dated 7 Mar 1687 concerns **William Lightfoot**, uncle of "John & Philip Lightfoot living in parts beyond the seas, sons of **John Lightfoot** widower who lately died at Surinam" administering "the goods etc. of the said deceased."[234]

On 25 Nov 1686 the vestry of the church for St. Peter's Parish in New Kent County "ordered that Mr. John Lightfoots ffamily be added to the Surveyer of the highway of the Lower Road between Lower Church and Black Creek Mill."[235]

John Lightfoot was listed as a member of the Virginia Council of State from 1697 to 1706.[236] In 1699 John Lightfoot was Colonel and Commander in Chief of the New Kent County militia.[237] John Lightfoot Esqr. was listed in the 1704 Virginia quit rents with 3600 acres in New Kent County, 900 acres in New Kent County with tax due Essex County, and 250 acres in James City County. Phil. Lightfoot was listed with 1650 acres in James City County.[238]

The home of John and Anne[2] Lighfoot was White House Plantation on the south side of the Pamunkey (York) River which John evidently purchased from **William Bassett** and left to his son Goodrich[3] Lightfoot.[239]

---

[232] Tyler, "The Lightfoot Family", *Genealogies, Wm & M Qrtrly*, 3:416.
[233] Tyler, "The Lightfoot Family", *Genealogies, Wm & M Qrtrly*, 3:411-3, 414-5, 420-1.
[234] Tyler, "The Lightfoot Family", *Genealogies, Wm & M Qrtrly*, 3:422.
[235] Chamberlayne, *Vestry Book and Register of St. Peter's Parish*, 9.
[236] Leonard, *General Assembly of Virginia*, xx.
[237] Crozier, *VA Colonial Militia*, 105-6.
[238] Smith, *Quit Rents of Virginia, 1704*, 55-6.
[239] Harris, *Old New Kent Co .... Planters*, 121-2.

Collo Jno Lightfoot died 28 May 1707.[240]

Anne[2] died before 5 Nov 1708 when Goodrich[3] Lightfoot of New Kent County sold 900 acres to **William Aylett** of King William County, Gent. Goodrich[3] had received this land as "heir by right of inheritance", which was the land his mother Anne[2] inherited from her father.[241]

It has been suggested that John Lightfoot had a second wife Mary, who was listed in St. Peters Parish as Madam Mary Lightfoot with **Watt** a Negro born 1709. She was also listed with Mr. Sherwood[3] Lightfoot, their tithables in 1711.[242]

- - - - - - - - - - -

35. Goodrich[3] Lightfoot <See pg. 187> (34.Anne[2], 1.Thomas[1]) was born about 1682. He married **Mary** ____.

ISSUE: [243]

36. f   i.   **Anne Lightfoot**, born 22 Sep 1708 in St. Peter's Parish, New Kent County, Virginia.
37. m   ii.   **John Lightfoot**, born 17 Feb 1711 in St. Peter's Parish, New Kent County, Virginia. John[4]'s will, proved 17 Jun 1735 in Orange County, lists brother William[4] and sister Elizabeth[4].[244]
+ 38. m   iii.   **Goodrich Lightfoot**, baptized 14 Feb 1713, died before 15 Jun 1778 <See pg. 191>.
39. f   iv.   **Mary Lightfoot**, born 2 Oct 1717 in St. Peter's Parish, New Kent County, Virginia.
40. m   v.   **William Lightfoot**. William Lightfoot was a vestryman of St. Mark's Parish 1752-1758 in Culpeper Co.[245]
41. f   vi.   **Elizabeth Lightfoot**.

In 1708 Goodrich[3] Lightfoot of New Kent County sold "half ... of the 1800 acres granted to Lt. Col. Thomas Goodrich by patent 15 Oct. 1669", the line of inheritance and a 100 acre exclusion for Jones stated in the document. [246]

---

[240] Chamberlayne, *Vestry Book and Register of St. Peter's Parish*, 434.
[241] Dorman, *Essex Co D&W 1707-1711*, 42.
[242] Tyler, "The Lightfoot Family", *Genealogies, Wm & M Qrtrly*, 3:417. Chamberlayne, *Vestry Book and Register of St. Peter's Parish*, 368, 145.
[243] Chamberlayne, *Vestry Book and Register of St. Peter's Parish*, 369-370, 470. Tyler, "The Lightfoot Family", *Genealogies, Wm & M Qrtrly*, 3:417.
[244] Tyler, "The Lightfoot Family", *Genealogies, Wm & M Qrtrly*, 3:430.
[245] Finley, Walter S., "Bass and Allied Families", *Americana*, 19:218.
[246] Dorman, *Essex Co VA D&W 1707-1711*, 42.

William Byrd II wrote in his diary of staying in the home of Goodrich³ Lightfoot on the Pamunkey River on 23 Sep 1712, about a mile from the home of his brother Sherwood³ when Byrd was to meet the Governor at the Pamunkey Indian town.²⁴⁷

Goodrich³ Lightfoot moved to Spotsylvania County by 1725 when he was shown as a captain in the militia; he was sheriff in 1726 and Major in 1729.²⁴⁸ His 400 acre patent in St. George Parish was located in the fork of the Rappahannock River, corner of **Harry Beverley**'s patent.²⁴⁹ Goodrich³ was a vestryman of St. George Parish in Spotsylvania County in 1727.²⁵⁰ His death was reported 14 Apr 1738 in the *Virginia Gazette* in Orange County which was created from Spotsylvania County in 1734.²⁵¹

- - - - - - - - - - -

38. Goodrich⁴ Lightfoot <See pg. 190> (35.Goodrich³, 34.Anne², 1.Thomas¹) was baptized 14 Feb 1713 in St. Peter's Parish, New Kent County, Virginia.²⁵² He married **Susanna** ____.

ISSUE:
- m i. **John Lightfoot**.
- f ii. **Elizabeth Lightfoot**.
- f iii. **Ann Lightfoot**.
- f iv. **Mary Lightfoot**.
- f v. **Fanny Lightfoot**.
- f vi. **Susanna Lightfoot**.
- m vii. **Philip Lightfoot**, born after 1757.
- m viii. **Goodrich Lightfoot**, born after 1757.
- f ix. **Priscilla Lightfoot**.
- f x. **Martha Lightfoot**.

The will of Goodrich⁴ Lightfoot of St. Mark's Parish, Culpeper County, Virginia, dated 24 Apr 1778 and proved 15 Jun 1778, named his sons John, Philip (under 21) and Goodrich (under 21), daughters **Elizabeth James**, **Ann Grasty**, **Mary Hubbard**, **Fanny Hackley**, **Susanna Brooks**, Priscilla and Martha, and his wife Susanna.²⁵³

- - - - - - - - - - -

---

²⁴⁷ Wright, *Byrd Diary 1709-1712*, 246.
²⁴⁸ des Cognets, *English Duplicates*, 117, 32, 39. Crozier, *VA Colonial Militia*, 122.
²⁴⁹ Nugent, *Cavaliers and Pioneers*, 3:310 (Patent Book 12:484).
²⁵⁰ Tyler, "The Lightfoot Family", *Genealogies, Wm & M Qrtrly*, 3:417.
²⁵¹ Headley, *18ᵗʰ-Century Newspapers*, 208.
²⁵² Chamberlayne, *Vestry Book and Register of St. Peter's Parish*, 370.
²⁵³ Tyler, "The Lightfoot Family", *Genealogies, Wm & M Qrtrly*, 3:430.

42. Sherwood³ Lightfoot <See pg. 187> (34.Anne², 1.Thomas¹).
ISSUE:²⁵⁴
- 43. f   i. **Mary Lightfoot**, born 9 Sep 1707.
- 44. f   ii. **Frances Lightfoot**, born 31 Oct 1708, died 19 Feb 1725/6 in St. Peter's Parish, New Kent County, Virginia.
- +45. m iii. **John Lightfoot**, born 13 Nov 1711 <See pg. 192>.
- 46. m iv. **Sherwood Lightfoot**, born 1 May 1714.
- +47. f   v. **Elizabeth Lightfoot**, born 23 Nov 1716, died 28 Aug 1759 <See pg. 192>.

Sherwood³ Lightfoot lived at Rickahock in St. Peter's Parish.²⁵⁵ In the diary of **William Byrd** II, he wrote of visiting the home of Sherwood³ Lightfoot on the Pamunkey River on 22 Sep 1712. "He received us very courteously .... lives in a good plantation and seems to be very industrious."²⁵⁶ Major Sherwood Goodrich died 26 Apr 1730.²⁵⁷

- - - - - - - - - - -

45. John⁴ Lightfoot <See pg. 192> (42.Sherwood³, 34.Anne², 1.Thomas¹) was born 13 Nov 1711 in St. Peter's Parish, New Kent County, Virginia. He married **Mary** ____.
ISSUE:²⁵⁸
- m   i. **Sherwood Lightfoot**, born 14 Feb 1733.
- m ii. **Francis Lightfoot**, born 9 Feb 1736/7.
- f iii. **Frances Lightfoot**, born 30 Jul 1738.

- - - - - - - - - - -

47. Elizabeth⁴ Lightfoot <See pg. 192> (42.Sherwood³, 34.Anne², 1.Thomas¹) was born 23 Nov 1716 in St. Peter's Parish, New Kent County, Virginia. She married **Richard Meaux**. He was baptised 31 Mar 1711.²⁵⁹
ISSUE:²⁶⁰
- f   i. **Ann Meaux**, born 3 Mar 1736/7.
- m ii. **Thomas Meaux**, born 17 Oct 1738.

---

²⁵⁴ Chamberlayne, *Vestry Book and Register of St. Peter's Parish*, 369-370,435, 470.
²⁵⁵ Harris, *Old New Kent Co .... Planters*, 122.
²⁵⁶ Wright, *Byrd Diary 1709-1712*, 246.
²⁵⁷ Chamberlayne, *Vestry Book and Register of St. Peter's Parish*, 436.
²⁵⁸ Chamberlayne, *Vestry Book and Register of St. Peter's Parish*, 519, 536, 553.
²⁵⁹ Chamberlayne, *Vestry Book and Register of St. Peter's Parish*, 378.
²⁶⁰ Chamberlayne, *Vestry Book and Register of St. Peter's Parish*, 535, 548.

Elizabeth[4] married Richard Meaux after the death of his first wife Frances, 13 Apr 1735.[261] Elizabeth[4] died 28 Aug 1759. On her tombstone it was recorded that she was the youngest daughter of Mr. Sherwood Lightfoot.[262]

- - - - - - - - - - -

48. Thomas[3] Lightfoot <See pg. 188> (34.Anne[2], 1.Thomas[1]).
ISSUE:[263]
49. f   i.   **Frances Lightfoot,** born 8 Oct 1717.
50. f   ii. **Ann Lightfoot,** born 7 Aug 1720.
51. m iii. **Frayser Lightfoot,** born 30 Mar 1723, died 30 Mar 1723.
52. m iv. **Henry Lightfoot,** born 30 Mar 1723.
53. f   v.   **Mary Lightfoot,** born 24 May 1725.

---

[261] Chamberlayne, *Vestry Book and Register of St. Peter's Parish,* 520.

[262] Harris, *Old New Kent Co .... Planters,* 180-1.

[263] Chamberlayne, *Vestry Book and Register of St. Peter's Parish,* 470- 473, 435.

CHAPTER 5 - Boush Families

Early generations of this Boush family are shown by the 1728 will of Maximillian[3] Boush, in which he named his uncle Col. Samuel Boush, cousin Capt. Samuel Boush, his sons Samuel and Maximillian Boush and his granddaughter Mary.[1]

1. ____ [1] **Boush**.
        ISSUE:
+ 2. m i. ____ **Boush**.
+ 26. m ii. **Samuel Boush**, born about 1668, died before 17 Dec 1736 <See pg. 201>.

- - - - - - - - - - -

2. ____ [2] **Boush** (1. ____ Boush[1]).
        ISSUE:
+ 3. m i. **Maximillian Boush**, born about 1678, died before 3 Apr 1728.

- - - - - - - - - - -

3. **Maximillian**[3] **Boush** (2. ____ Boush[2], 1. ____ Boush[1]) was born about 1678. He married **Mary Bennett** before 1 Jul 1702 when he was named "as marrying with Mary , relict of Jonathan Saunders deceased."[2] She was the daughter of **Thomas Bennett** and **Anne Snayle**.[3]
        ISSUE:
+ 4. m i. **Maximillian Boush**, born after 1700, died before 2 Feb 1736/7 <See pg. 195>.
+ 15. m ii. **Samuel Boush**, died about 1769 <See pg. 200>.

Maximilian was the Queen's Attorney for Norfolk and Princess Anne counties[4] and was named "Councill in behalf of our Soveraign Lady the Queen" at a Lower Norfolk County court 6 Jun 1706.[5] He served as burgess

---

[1] Maling, *Princess Anne Co VA Deed Books 1-7*, 54 (4DB158).

[2] James, *Lower Norfolk Antiquary,* 1:63.

[3] McIntosh, *Norfolk Co Wills 1637-1710*, 19 (C:203 - will of Henry Snaile), 29 (E:51 - will of Charles Edgerton). Norfolk Co VA Deed Book 5:74a.

[4] Cross, *County Court... Norfolk*, 36.

[5] James, *Lower Norfolk Antiquary,* 3:35.

Boush Families 195

from Princess Anne County from 1710 through 1726[6] and was a witness to the will of Col. **James Wilson** in 1712.[7]

Maximillian's will, dated 15 Aug 1727 and proved 3 Apr 1728, named his sons Samuel and Maximillian, uncle Col. **Samuel Boush**, godson **Maximillian Calvert**, and son Maximillian's daughter Mary. The executors were Maximilian and cousin Capt. **Samuel Boush**.[8]

Mary married (1) **Thomas Ewell**.[9]
Mary married (2) Rev. **Jonathan Saunders**, rector of Linnhaven Parish in Princess Anne County, Virginia, by 4 May 1699. Jonathan died before 6 Mar 1700/1.[10]

- - - - - - - - - - -

4. Maximillian[4] **Boush** <See pg. 194> (3.Maximillian[3], 2. ____ Boush[2], 1. ____ Boush[1]) was born after 1700. He married (1) **Sarah Woodhouse** after 17 Feb 1719/20.[11] She was born about 1700. She was the daughter of **Horatio Woodhouse** and **Lucy Keeling**.[12]

ISSUE:

   5. m i. **Lemuel Boush**, born after 1726, died after 21 Mar 1751. A suit at court in 1745 by his brothers and sisters implies that Lemuel received more than his share of his inheritance. He chose Josias Butt (probably his brother-in law Josiah Butt) as his guardian in 1747.[13] In 1751 he sold land to his uncle Samuel Boush.[14]

+ 6. f ii. **Mary Boush**, died before 20 Oct 1794 <See pg. 197>.

   7. m iii. **Maximillian Boush**. In his will, dated 4 Nov 1771 and proved 14 Feb 1782, he named his sister Mary, wife of Josiah Butt of Norfolk County, and his brother Capt. Frederick Boush.[15]

---

[6] Leonard, *General Assembly of Virginia*, 65-72.
[7] Norfolk Co VA Deed Book 9:220-2. (See appendix).
[8] Maling, *Princess Anne Co VA Deed Books 1-7*, 54 (4DB158).
[9] Norfolk Co VA Deed Book 5:74a (Mary Ewell daughter of Anne Bennett), 78a.
[10] Withington, *Virginia Gleanings*, 25. James, *Lower Norfolk Antiquary*, 1:63.
[11] Maling, *Princess Anne Co VA Deed Books 1-7*, 41 (3DB303 - will of Lucy Woodhouse).
[12] Maling, *Princess Anne Co VA Deed Books 1-7*, 10 (1DB121), 41 (3DB278 - will of Horatio Woodhouse).
[13] Walter, *Princess Anne Co VA Deed and Minute Books*, 56 (6MB11), 59 (6MB111).
[14] Maling, *Princess Anne Co VA Deed Books 1-7*, 90 (7DB260).
[15] Maling, *Princess Anne Co VA Deed Books 8-18*, 90 (17DB38).

In Sarah's will, dated 13 Mar 1732/3 and proved 5 Sep 1733, she left her son Lemuel land that had belonged to her brother **Horatio Woodhouse**. She named her son Maximillian, daughter Mary, and her husband Maximillian as executor.[16]

Maximillian married (2) **Elizabeth Wilson** after Jun 1733. **(See number 28 - pg. 16)**.

ISSUE:

+ 8. f ix. **Elizabeth Boush**, born about 1734, died before 7 Jan 1811 <See pg. 18, 198>.
+ 9. m x. **Frederick Wilson Boush**, born before 2 Feb 1736/7, died before 1 Dec 1806 <See pg. 19, 199>.

On 2 Mar 1736/7, the division of part of the estate of Coll. Maximilian Boush was recorded: Elizabeth Boush, the widow's dower, other portions to his children Lemuel, Mary, Maximilian, Elizabeth and Frederick. A division of more property was ordered 4 May 1737.[17]

Elizabeth married (1) **Lazarus Sweny** 14 Feb 1728/9.[18] In his will, dated 21 Oct 1732 and proved 15 Dec 1732, he named his wife Elizabeth, and sons Daniel and James.[19]

ISSUE:

10. m iv. **Daniel Sweny**, born about 1730. His will, dated 25 Oct 1761 and proved Nov 1761, named his mother Elizabeth Thelaball, his brother Frederick Boush and his sister Elizabeth Nimmo.[20]
11. m v. **James Sweny**, born about 1732, died before 25 Oct 1761.

Elizabeth also married (3) **Thomas Thelaball. (See pg. 136)**. Thomas died before Jun 1751, when "Elizabeth Tenaball, Thomas's widow" was listed in tithables lists.[21]

ISSUE:[22]

12. f vi. **Abigail Thelaball**, born Jan 1745/6. She married **Matthew Godfrey** 24 Feb 1784 in Norfolk County, Virginia. He was the son of **Matthew Godfrey** and **Abigail Porter**. Abigail

---

[16] Maling, *Princess Anne Co VA Deed Books 1-7*, 59 (4DB457).
[17] Princess Anne Co VA Deed Book 5:169, 201.
[18] Wingo, *Marriages of Norfolk Co VA, Vol 1*, 63.
[19] McIntosh, *Norfolk Co Wills 1710-1753*, 129.
[20] Wingo, *Norfolk Co VA Will Book 1*, 48 (f 72).
[21] Wingo, *Norfolk Co VA Tithables 1751-1765*, 16.
[22] Dorman, *Adventurers of Purse and Person*, 2:620, 622-3, 609.

died before 26 Mar 1805, the date of her brother Frederick Boush's will.
13. f vii. **Prudence Thelaball**, born 25 Nov 1747. She married **Charles Sayer Boush (See number 58)** 14 Jul 1796 in Norfolk County, Virginia. Prudence died 22 Dec 1807.
14. m viii. **Lemuel Thelaball**, born 22 Dec 1749, died young.

In Elizabeth's will, dated 31 Jan 1778 and proved Jul 1783, she named her son Frederick Boush, daughters Elizabeth Hunter, Abigail Thelaball, Prudence Thelaball, grandson Gershom Nimmo, and granddaughter Elizabeth Jacamine Boush. She appointed her son Frederick Boush and Matthew Godfrey executors.[23]

Elizabeth died 20 Apr 1783 in Norfolk County, Virginia.[24]

- - - - - - - - - - -

6. **Mary^5 Boush** <See pg. 195> (4.Maximillian^4, 3.Maximillian^3, 2. ____ Boush^2, 1. ____ Boush^1). She married **Josiah Butt** 12 Jan 1743/4.[25]
ISSUE:[26]
m i. **Josiah Butt**, died before 21 Apr 1800.[27]
f ii. **Sarah Butt**.
f iii. **Olive Butt**.
f iv. **Prudence Butt**.
m v. **Nathaniel Butt**.
m vi. **Horatio Boush Butt**.

Mary was named in the 1737 division of her father's estate.[28] The 1771 will of Maximilian^5 Boush named his sister Mary, wife of Josiah Butt of Norfolk County [29] The will of Josiah Butt Sr., dated 16 May 1780 and proved Dec 1781, named his son Josiah Butt, daughters **Sarah Murden**, **Olive Tooley**, Prudence, grandson Horatio Boush (probably a transcription error and should be son), and son Nathaniel Butt. His wife Mary and son Josiah were named executors.[30]

---

[23] Norfolk Co VA Will Book 2:212-3/181-2.
[24] Boush Family Bible, Accession 22246, LVA.
[25] Wingo, *Marriages of Norfolk Co VA, Vol 1*, 11.
[26] Norfolk Co VA Will Book 2:175-6/142-3.
[27] beth@TidewaterTapestry.com, (Brewster, *Norfolk Co VA Will Book 3*, 148 - will of Josiah Butt).
[28] Princess Anne Co VA Deed Book 5:169.
[29] Maling, *Princess Anne Co VA Deed Books 8-18*, 90 (17DB38).
[30] Norfolk Co VA Will Book 2:175-6/142-3.

Mary died before 20 Oct 1794 in Norfolk County, Virginia.[31]

- - - - - - - - - - -

8. Elizabeth⁵ Boush <See pg. 17, 196> (4.Maximillian⁴, 3.Maximillian³, 2. ____ Boush², 1. ____ Boush¹) was born about 1734. **(See number 31 - pg. 18).** She married (1) **Gershom Nimmo**. He was the son of **James Nimmo** and **Mary Johnson**.[32]

ISSUE:

m i. **James Nimmo**.
m ii. **William Nimmo**.
m iii. **Gershom Nimmo**, born before 17 Sep 1764, died 7 Jul 1817.[33]

In his will, dated 17 Sep 1764 and proved 20 Nov 1764, Gershom named his sons James, William and Gershom and his brother William Nimmo, Jr. He mentioned his wife, but he did not name her.[34]

Elizabeth was named as Elizabeth Nimmo in the 1761 will of Daniel Sweny.[35] Her mother, in her 1778 will, named her daughter Elizabeth Hunter and grandson Gershom Nimmo.[36]

Elizabeth Nimmo married (2) **Jacob Hunter** 5 Dec 1766.[37] He was born about 1715. He was the son of **John Hunter** and **Jacomine Johnson**.[38]

ISSUE:

m iv. **James Hunter**, born about 1767.
m v. **Jonathan Hunter**, born about 1769.
m vi. **Josiah Wilson Hunter**, born about 1770.
m vii. **William Hunter**, born about 1775.

Jacob married (1) **Susannah Moore**. She was the daughter of **Henry Moore** and **Mary Moseley**, shown by the 21 Sep 1756 suit concerning Jacob

---

[31] beth@TidewaterTapestry.com, (Brewster, *Norfolk Co VA Will Book 3*, 66 - will of Mary Butt).
[32] Maling, *Princess Anne Co VA Deed Books 1-7*, 95 (7DB448 - will of James Nimmo), 29 (2DB38 - will of Jacob Johnson), James, *Lower Norfolk Antiquary*, 1:86-7.
[33] Henley, *Marriage/Obituary Index* - Gershorn Nimmo.
[34] Maling, *Princess Anne Co VA Deed Books 8-18*, 26 (9DB430).
[35] Wingo, *Norfolk Co VA Will Book 1*, 48 (f 72).
[36] Norfolk Co VA Will Book 2:212-3 (181-2).
[37] Wingo, *Marriages of Princess Anne Co VA*, 2:1.
[38] Maling, *Princess Anne Co VA Deed Books 1-7*, 95 (7DB439). Walter, *Princess Anne Co VA Deed and Minute Books*, 87 (7DB449 - will of John Hunter).

Hunter and Susannah his wife and **Anthony Moseley**, administrator of Mary Moore, deceased widow and executrix of Capt. Henry Moore.[39]

The will of Jacob Hunter was dated 24 Jan 1780 and proved 11 May 1780. He first named John, Jacob and Elizabeth Hunter, possibly the children from his first marriage He then named his four youngest sons, James, Jonathan, Josiah Wilson, and William Hunter, requesting that his wife Elizabeth educate them.[40]

In the will of Elizabeth Hunter, dated 8 Jun 1809 and proved 7 Jan 1811, she named her sons, Jonathan and Josiah Wilson Hunter, and several grandchildren.[41]

- - - - - - - - - - -

9. Frederick Wilson⁵ Boush <See pg. 17, 196> (4.Maximillian⁴, 3.Maximillian³, 2. ____ Boush², 1. ____ Boush¹) was born before 2 Feb 1736/7, when he was named in the division of his father's estate.[42] He married (1) **Jacomine Hunter**.[43] She was the daughter of **John Hunter** and **Jacomine Johnson**.[44]

ISSUE:[45]
- m   i.   **William Boush**, died before 3 Feb 1834.[46]
- m   ii.   **Caleb Boush**, born after 1765.
- f   iii.   **Elizabeth Jacomine Boush**, born 9 Jan 1775, died 13 Aug 1861.[47]

Jacomine died 7 Nov 1791.[48]

Frederick married (2) **Elizabeth Wilson** 14 May 1795.[49] **(See number 59 - pg. 27).**

ISSUE:[50]
- f   iv.   **Jacomine Boush**, born 23 Mar 1796, died 5 Mar 1797.

---

[39] Walter, *Princess Anne Co VA Deed and Minute Books*, 110 (7MB249).
[40] Princess Anne Co VA Deed Book 17:1.
[41] Maling, *Princess Anne Co VA, Wills*, 101.
[42] Princess Anne Co Va Deed Book 5:169.
[43] Boush Family Bible, Accession 22246, LVA.
[44] James, *Lower Norfolk Antiquary*, 1:85-7.
[45] Maling, *Princess Anne Co VA, Wills*, 92.
[46] Princess Anne Co VA Will Book 4:160 (Will of William Boush).
[47] Boush Family Bible, Accession 22246, LVA.
[48] Boush Family Bible, Accession 22246, LVA.
[49] Wingo, *Marriages of Princess Anne Co VA*, 2:2.
[50] Boush Family Bible, Accession 22246, LVA.

Frederick Boush was granted "Liberty to keep an Ordinary for one year" (a tavern).[51] He was elected to the Princess Anne County Committee of Safety 17 Aug 1775.[52]

His will, dated 26 Mar 1805 and proved 1 Dec 1806, mentioned wife Elizabeth, son William, land inherited from sister Abigail Godfrey, son Caleb, daughter **Elizabeth Jacomine Smith** and among others, grandson **William Frederick Wilson Boush** son of William.[53]

Elizabeth died 30 Jan 1816.[54]

- - - - - - - - - - -

15. **Samuel⁴ Boush** <See pg. 194> (3.Maximillian³, 2. ____ Boush², 1. ____ Boush¹). He married (1) **Elizabeth Hancock** before 28 Jan 1738/9, when she was named Elizabeth Boush in her father's will. She was the daughter of **Simon Hancock, Jr. and Ann** ____.[55]

ISSUE:
- 16. f   i.   **Elizabeth Boush**.
- 17. m   ii.   **Maximillian Boush**. His will, dated 27 Apr 1761 and proved May 1761, named his father Samuel Boush, his sisters Elizabeth Boush and Affia Boush, and his brother Bennet.[56]
- 18. f   iii.   **Affiah Boush**.
- 19. m   iv.   **Bennett Boush**, died after 26 Dec 1801.

In the will of Simon Hancock, dated 28 Jan 1739/40 and proved 7 Nov 1739, he named his daughter Elizabeth Boush and grandchildren Elizabeth Boush and Maximillian Boush.[57]

Samuel and Elizabeth sold land to **William Hunter** in 1755.[58]

In the 1761 will of Maximillian, the phrase "brothers and sisters" supports the probability of the other siblings mentioned in their father's will.

Samuel married (2) **Ann** ____.

---

[51] Walter, *Princess Anne Co VA Deed and Minute Books*, 114 (7MB375).
[52] Turner, *Gateway to the New World*, 173.
[53] Maling, *Princess Anne Co VA, Wills*, 92.
[54] Wilson Bible 1742-1896, Accession 29076, LVA.
[55] Maling, *Princess Anne Co VA Deed Books 1-7*, 68 (5DB421).
[56] Wingo, *Norfolk Co VA Will Book 1*, 42 (f 63).
[57] Maling, *Princess Anne Co VA Deed Books 1-7*, 68 (5DB421).
[58] Walter, *Princess Anne Co VA Deed and Minute Books*, 100 (7DB677).

In his will, dated 19 Sep 1769 and proved 5 Jan 1770, Samuel named his wife Ann, his sons **Samuel,** Bennet, and **Jonathan,** daughters **Mary Ann Thelaball, Elizabeth Roberts, Anne Stewart** and **Aphia Bowser.**[59]

- - - - - - - - - - -

26. Samuel² Boush <See pg. 194> (1. ____ Boush¹) was born about 1668. He married **Alice Mason. (See number 26 - pg. 105).**

ISSUE:

+ 27. m i. **Samuel Boush,** born about 1694, died before Nov 1759 <See pg. 109, 202>.
  64. f ii. **Mason Boush.** On 15 May 1702 Samuel made a gift to his daughter Mason.[60]

Alice married (1) **Robert Hodge.** Robert died before 18 Oct 1681.[61]

Alice married (2) **William Porten.** William died before 15 Mar 1692/3.[62]

In a suit concerning the estate of William Porten, dated 17 Jul 1694, Samuel Boush was named as married to Alice Porten.[63]

Samuel Boush was listed as one of the owners of the ship *William and Mary* in 1700. He held the various offices of justice, sheriff, coroner, and tobacco agent for Norfolk County during the years 1702 to 1726[64] and served as burgess from Norfolk County from 1728 possibly until 1735.[65]

Samuel was named in the county militia in 1702 and 1715, listed as county lieutenant in 1726.[66] Major Samuel Boush was running ferries from Norfolk in 1715. In 1716 the first ducking stool (a chair suspended over water used as punishment for such as a "good wife who gossiped too much") was erected on Major Boush's wharf.[67]

Samuel Boush was a feofee (trustee) for lots in Norfolk Town from 1697-1729. His land was next to the town boundary, so when all town lots were

---

[59] Maling, *Princess Anne Co VA Deed Books 8-18*, 41 (11DB39).
[60] Norfolk Co VA Deed Book 6:244a.
[61] McIntosh, *Norfolk Co Wills 1637-1710*, 79-80(Book 4:106).
[62] Norfolk Co VA Deed Book 5, pt. 2 Orders:284-5.
[63] Norfolk Co VA Deed Book 5, pt. 2:328.
[64] des Cognets, *English Duplicates*, 288, 11-37.
[65] Leonard, *General Assembly of Virginia*, 74-75.
[66] Bockstruck, *Virginia Colonial Soldiers*, 218, 234. des Cognets, *English Duplicates*, 37.
[67] Wertenbaker, *Norfolk*, 33, 11.

sold, he divided some of his land into lots creating "Norfolk's first suburban development."[68] Samuel Boush was selected the first Mayor of the Borough of Norfolk in 1736, but died before taking office.[69]

Samuel wrote two wills, the first dated 18 Oct 1733 and proved 17 Dec 1736. In it he named his son Samuel, grandsons Samuel, Goodrich and John as male heirs of son Samuel Boush, daughter Anne Boush (who was actually, daughter-in-law, the wife of son Samuel), and his wife Alice Boush. In his second will, dated 10 Jun 1735 and proved 16 Feb 1738/9, he named his "loving wife", his son Major Samuel Boush, and grandson Samuel. He also named Mrs. Mary Miller and Mrs. Margaret Haire, Alice's daughters from her prior marriages, and grandsons Goodrich Boush, and William Boush.[70]

The wills above show that Alice died after 10 Jun 1735. Samuel died before 18 Nov 1736, when at a council meeting in the Borough of Norfolk, it was recorded "..... Samuel Boush Esqr. lately deceased who was appointed mayor....."[71]

- - - - - - - - - - -

27. Samuel³ Boush <See pg. 106, 201> (26.Samuel², 1. ____ Boush¹) was born about 1694. He married (1) **Anne Goodrich** after 7 Nov 1719.[72] **(See number 4 - pg. 177).**

ISSUE:

+ 28. f i. **Ann Boush**, born about 1721, died after 24 Mar 1779 <See pg. 204>.

+ 33. m ii. **Samuel Boush**, born about 1722, died before 20 May 1784 <See pg. 206>.

+ 40. m iii. **Goodrich Boush**, born about 1724, died before 22 May 1779 <See pg. 207>.

  47. m iv. **John Boush**, born before 18 Oct 1733, died before 10 Jun 1735. He was named in the 1733 will of his grandfather, but not in the 1735 will.

  48. m v. **William Boush**, born after 18 Oct 1733. He was not named in the first will of his grandfather; he was named in the second, dated 1735. He was not named in his father's 1756 will.

---

[68] Whichard, *History of Lower Tidewater VA*, 1:352.
[69] Tarter, *Order Book ... Borough of Norfolk*, 36, 45.
[70] McIntosh, *Norfolk Co Wills 1710-1753*, 139-140 (Original Will), 247 (Book I:32). Norfolk Co VA Wills & Deeds I:32 is legible enough to add more details.
[71] Tarter, *Order Book ... Borough of Norfolk*, 45.
[72] Lee Family Papers (1638-1867), Mss1:L51:f:66.

Samuel Boush Jr. and Anne Boush signed documents as witnesses on 17 May 1722 and 7 Jun 1728.[73] The family group was named in the 1733 will of Samuel Boush Sr.: "Son Sam'l Boush, my daughter Anne Boush, my Grandson Sam'l Boush to each of them a mourning Suit of Cloaths."[74] They named a son Goodrich, to whom Samuel Jr., in his 1756 will, left Chickahominy land in James City County. This was very likely the land from Anne's father's estate. Anne apparently died before Samuel Boush Sr.'s second will, 10 Jun 1735.[75]

Col. Samuel Boush married (2) **Frances Sayer** before 7 Jun 1738.[76] She was the daughter of **Charles Sayer** and **Margaret Lawson**.[77]

ISSUE:

+ 49. m ix. **Arthur Boush**, born before 1740, died after Sep 1779 <See pg. 208>.
  56. f x. **Mary "Molly" Boush**, born before 1740, died about 1763.[78]
  57. m xi. Capt. **Nathaniel Boush**. He died 6 Jan 1813, age 54.[79]
  58. m xii. **Charles Sayer Boush**, born after 1740, the date of his grandfather's will. He married (1) **Martha Sweny** 6 May 1774.[80] She was the daughter of **Charles Sweny** and **Ann Wythe**.[81] Martha died 17 Jun 1792.[82] Charles married (2) **Prudence Thelaball (See number 13)** 14 Jul 1796.[83] She was born 25 Nov 1747. She was the daughter of **Thomas Thelaball** and **Elizabeth Wilson**. Charles died before 25 Apr 1809.[84]
+ 59. f xiii. **Margaret "Peggy" Boush**, born before 1754 <See pg. 209>.

---

[73] Norfolk Co VA Deed Books F:23a-24, G:131-131a.

[74] McIntosh, *Norfolk Co Wills 1710-1753*, 139-140.

[75] Boush, "The Identity of the 1st wife of Sam. Boush II, Norf. Co", Misc Reel 520, p. 16-7.

[76] Hart, "Princess Anne Marriages 1737-44", 3:27.

[77] Princess Anne Co VA Deed Book 5:514 - 1740 will of Charles Sayer. Maling, *Princess Anne Co VA Deed Books 1-7*, 103 (7DB661 - will of Margaret Sayer).

[78] Boush, "Samuel Boush Family Chart", Misc Reel 520, p. 10.

[79] Henley, *Marriage/Obituary Index*.

[80] Wingo, *Marriages of Norfolk Co VA, Vol 1*, 6.

[81] Dorman, *Adventurers of Purse and Person*, 2:609.

[82] Dorman, *Adventurers of Purse and Person*, 2:609.

[83] Wingo, *Marriages of Norfolk Co VA, Vol 2*, 16.

[84] Dorman, *Adventurers of Purse and Person*, 2:609 (Norfolk City Order Book 17:153).

Boush Families

Frances Sayer married (1) **Thomas Lawson** about 1730. He was born after 27 Oct 1703. He was the son of **Thomas Lawson** and **Rose Thorowgood**. Thomas died before 7 May 1735.[85]

Col. Samuel[3] Boush married the widow of Thomas Lawson dec'd, shown in the 7 Jun 1738 Princess Anne County court.[86] The will of Thomas Lawson, dated 18 Mar 1731/2 and proved 7 May 1735, named his wife Frances and father-in-law Charles Sayer. In the 1740 will of her father, she was named "daughter Frances Boush."[87]

Samuel[3] Boush was a burgess from Norfolk County from 1736 to 1747.[88] He served as a justice for the Lower Norfolk court with his father in 1726 and 1729.[89] Samuel was a vestryman for Elizabeth River Parish and sheriff of the county.[90] He was elected as the first Town Clerk of Norfolk Borough in 1736, serving until 1737. He requested to be admitted to resign as councilman in 1744, because he planned to "leave the Town."[91]

In his will, dated 6 Nov 1756 and proved Nov 1759, he left his wife Frances the use of the plantation called Sewell's Point. He named his sons Samuel, Goodrich, Arthur, Nathaniel, and Charles Sayer Boush, giving the Chickahominy land in James City County to Goodrich. He also named his daughters Peggy and Molly. The remainder of his estate was to be divided among his children "now alive, each child by each wife to have equal share."[92]

- - - - - - - - - -

28. Ann[4] Boush <See pg. 202> (27.Samuel[3], 26.Samuel[2], 1. ____ Boush[1]) was born about 1721. She married (1) **John O'Sheal**.[93]
ISSUE:
29. m   i.   **John O'Sheal**.[94]

---

[85] Dorman, *Adventurers of Purse and Person*, 2:583. Meyer and Dorman, *Adventurers of Purse and Person*, 620.
[86] Princess Anne Co VA Minute Book 5:22.
[87] Maling, *Princess Anne Co VA Deed Books 1-7*, 62 (4DB549), 70 (5DB504).
[88] Leonard, *General Assembly of Virginia*, 76-9.
[89] des Cognets, *English Duplicates*, 37, 50.
[90] Cross, *County Court... Norfolk*, 36.
[91] Tarter, *Order Book ... Borough of Norfolk*, 45, 51, 64.
[92] Norfolk Co VA Will Book 1:37-39.
[93] Norfolk Co VA Minute Book 1:2.
[94] beth@TidewaterTapestry.com (Wingo, *Guardian Bonds of Norfolk Co VA*, 58).

30. m ii. **David O'Sheal**. He married **Catherine Veale** 17 Feb 1773. She was the daughter of **George Veale**.[95]
31. m iii. **Samuel O'Sheal**, died before 5 Jan 1779, the date of his step-father's will.
+ 32. f iv. **Elizabeth O'Sheal** <See pg. 205>.

John died after 28 Oct 1748, when he was named executor of the will of **William Moseley**[96] and before 16 Nov 1750, when Ann O'Sheal filed suit as administrator of John O'Sheal's estate.[97]

Ann married (2) **James Holt** 29 Sep 1753.[98] He was the son of **Thomas Holt** and **Frances Mason**.[99] James died before 12 Jun 1779.[100] His will was dated 5 Jan 1779; he named his wife Ann and her son Samuel O'Sheal,, son-in-law (step-son) David O'Sheal and daughter-in-law (step-daughter) Elizabeth Shepherd. He left a niece money, provided "she does not Marry a Scotchman." He named his wife Ann also in the 24 Mar 1779 codicil to the will.[101]

- - - - - - - - - - -

32. **Elizabeth**[5] **O'Sheal** <See pg. 205> (28.Ann[4], 27.Samuel[3], 26.Samuel[2], 1. ____ Boush[1]). She married **Solomon Shepherd** 20 Jan 1769.[102]

ISSUE:[103]
 f i.   **Frances Shepherd**.
 m ii. **Samuel Shepherd**.
 f iii. **Anne Boush Shepherd**.
 f iv. **Elizabeth Shepherd**.

In the 1779 will of James Holt, her step-father, he named daughter-in-law Elizabeth, wife of Solomon Shepherd, and their children Samuel Shepherd and Ann Boush Shepherd.[104]

---

[95] Wingo, *Marriages of Norfolk Co VA, Vol 1*, 50.
[96] McIntosh, *Norfolk Co Wills 1710-1753*, 299 (Book I:296).
[97] Norfolk Co VA Minute Book 1:2.
[98] Wingo, *Marriages of Norfolk Co VA, Vol 1*, 34.
[99] Dorman, *Adventurers of Purse and Person*, 2:313-4
[100] Henley, *Marriage/Obituary Index*.
[101] McVey, *Norfolk Co VA Will Book 2*, 94-7.
[102] Wingo, *Marriages of Norfolk Co VA, Vol 1*, 59.
[103] beth@TidewaterTapestry.com (Tucker, *Abstracts from Norfolk City Marriage Bonds (1797-1850)*, 15, 17).
[104] McVey, *Norfolk Co VA Will Book 2*, 94-7.

Solomon married (2) **Ann Boush (See number 44)** 15 Nov 1792.[105] She was born 1762[106]. She was the daughter of **Goodrich Boush** and **Mary Wilson**. Solomon died before 24 Dec 1794.[107]

- - - - - - - - - - -

33. **Samuel[4] Boush** <See pg. 202> (27.Samuel[3], 26.Samuel[2], 1. ____ Boush[1]) was born about 1722. He married **Catherine Ballard** about 1748. She was the daughter of **John Ballard**.[108]

ISSUE:[109]

34. m i. **John Boush**. He married (1) **Ann "Nancy" Waller** 22 Apr 1773.[110] She was born 29 Feb 1756. She was the daughter of **Benjamin Waller**. Ann died 10 Nov 1778. John married (2) **Frances Moseley Munford** 25 Jan 1787.[111] John's will, dated 24 Jul 1790 and proved 28 May 1792, named his wife Frances, brother Robert and mentioned two sisters.[112]

35. m ii. **Robert Boush**. He married **Catherine Ballard** 31 Oct 1784 in Norfolk County, Virginia. She was the daughter of **Robert Ballard** and **Anne Newton**.[113] Robert Boush died 15 Oct 1809.[114]

36. f iii. **Elizabeth Boush**. She married **Champion Travis** 29 Nov 1772.[115] Champion died 22 Aug 1810.[116]

37. m iv. **William Boush**. He married **Margaret Taylor** 21 May 1783 in Norfolk County, Virginia. She was born about 1764. She was the daughter of **James Taylor** and **Alice Smith**.[117] William died before 28 Jun 1787, the date of his wife's second marriage.[118]

---

[105] Henley, *Marriage/Obituary Index* (Solomon Sheperd to Nancy Boush).
[106] Dorman, *Adventurers of Purse and Person*, 2:606.
[107] Headley, *18th-Century Newspapers*, 306.
[108] "Ballard Notes", *Genealogies, VA Mag Hist*, 1:221. Maling, *Princess Anne Co VA Deed Books 8-18*, 43 (12DB56 - will of brother Robert Ballard).
[109] Dorman, *Adventurers of Purse and Person*, 2:604-5.
[110] Headley, *18th-Century Newspapers*, 34.
[111] Wingo, *Marriages of Norfolk Co VA, Vol 1*, 6.
[112] Crozier, *Williamsburg Wills*, 9.
[113] Dorman, *Adventurers of Purse and Person*, 2:603, 605-6.
[114] Henley, *Marriage/Obituary Index*.
[115] Dorman, *Adventurers of Purse and Person*, 2:360.
[116] Henley, *Marriage/Obituary Index*.
[117] Dorman, *Adventurers of Purse and Person*, 2:594.
[118] Dorman, *Adventurers of Purse and Person*, 2:594, 605.

38. f v. **Catherine Boush**. She married (1) **William Nivison** 25 Apr 1787 in Norfolk County, Virginia. William died before 2 Mar 1799. Catherine married (2) **Littleton Tazewell**. Catherine died 8 Dec 1823.
39. m vi. **Samuel Boush**, died 25 Apr 1771 in Williamsburg, Virginia.

Samuel Boush Jr. was burgess from Norfolk County in the 1752-1755 General Assembly, until he became clerk of the Norfolk County Court.[119] He was recommended "as fit for Lieutenant" in 1744. He served as clerk to the Council of Norfolk Borough from Jun 1749 until at least 1772.[120]

The will of Samuel[4], was dated 3 Apr 1779, codicil dated 4 May 1782, and proved 20 May 1784. "Samuel Boush late of the Borough of Norfolk but at present of the county of Brunswick" named sons John and Robert, leaving Robert his plantation called Sewell's Point bought from **Daniel Sweny**. He also named daughter Elizabeth Travis, son William, daughter Catherine, his Travis grandsons and niece Catherine Ballard. He mentioned his wife but did not name her.[121] The codicil reflects the situation after the Revolutionary War: "Whereas by the cruel hand of oppression the fortune that God was pleased to bestow me is much decreased and whereas also the money is daily depreciating so that I am at a loss to make provision for my daughter Catherine in such a certain manner that I could wish........."

- - - - - - - - - - -

40. **Goodrich**[4] **Boush** <See pg. 202> (27.Samuel[3], 26.Samuel[2], 1. ____ Boush[1]) was born about 1724. He married **Mary Wilson** 25 Jan 1759.[122] **(See number 21 - pg. 15)**.

ISSUE:[123]

41. m   i. **Wilson Boush**, born about 1761. He married **Frances Loyall** 18 Sep 1794 in Norfolk County, Virginia. She was the daughter of **Paul Loyall** and **Frances Newton**.[124] **(See number 139 - pg. 54)**. Wilson died 1 Dec 1829.[125]
42. m ii. **Samuel Boush**, born about 1763.
43. m iii. **James Boush**, born about 1765.
+ 44. f iv. **Ann Boush**, born 1762, died 1835 <See pg. 208>.
45. f   v. **Mary Boush**, born about 1769.

---

[119] Leonard, *General Assembly of Virginia*, 83-4.
[120] Tarter, *Order Book ... Borough of Norfolk*, 64, 76, 171.
[121] Norfolk Co Will Book 2:232-5/194.
[122] Wingo, *Marriages of Norfolk Co VA, Vol 1*, 6.
[123] Dorman, *Adventurers of Purse and Person*, 2:606.
[124] Headley, *18th-Century Newspapers*, 34.
[125] Henley, *Marriage/Obituary Index*.

46. f vi. **Elizabeth Boush**, born about 1771.

Goodrich was a councilman for the Borough of Norfolk as early as 1761 until 1774, when he "removed out of the Borough."[126] Capt. Goodrich Boush commanded the warship *Washington* during the Revolutionary War. He died "in service" 22 May 1779.[127]

His will was written 17 Aug 1778 and proved Dec 1782. "Goodrich Boush of the Borough of Norfolk but now living in James City County" named wife Mary, sons Wilson, Samuel, James, daughters Ann, Mary, and Elizabeth Boush. He specified that his plantation in James City County be sold. This was probably the land that his mother, Anne Goodrich, received from her father's estate.[128]

- - - - - - - - - - -

44. Ann⁵ Boush <See pg. 207> (40.Goodrich⁴, 27.Samuel³, 26.Samuel², 1. ____ Boush¹) was born 1762.[129] She married (1) **Solomon Shepherd** 15 Nov 1792.[130]

Solomon married (1) **Elizabeth O'Sheal (See number 32)** 20 Jan 1769 in Norfolk County, Virginia. Solomon died before 24 Dec 1794.[131]

Ann married (2) **Robert Brough** 24 Dec 1806 in Norfolk, Virginia. Robert died 6 Oct 1823 in Norfolk, Virginia. Ann died 1835.[132]

- - - - - - - - - - -

49. Arthur⁴ Boush <See pg. 203> (27.Samuel³, 26.Samuel², 1. ____ Boush¹) was born before 18 Aug 1740, the date of his grandfather's will.[133] He married **Ann Sweny** 8 Feb 1763. She was born about 1745. She was the daughter of **Charles Sweny** and **Ann Wythe**.[134]

---

[126] Tarter, *Order Book ... Borough of Norfolk*, 127, 177.

[127] Boush, "Captain Goodrich Boush (c. 1724-1779) Va. State Navy, Revolutionary War", Misc Reel 306. Headley, *18th-Century Newspapers*, 34.

[128] Norfolk Co VA Will Book 2:206/176-8.

[129] Dorman, *Adventurers of Purse and Person*, 2:606.

[130] Henley, *Marriage/Obituary Index* (Solomon Sheperd to Nancy Boush).

[131] Headley, *18th-Century Newspapers*, 306.

[132] Dorman, *Adventurers of Purse and Person*, 2:606.

[133] Maling, *Princess Anne Co VA Deed Books 1-7*, 70 (5DB504 - will of Charles Sayer).

[134] Wingo, *Marriages of Norfolk Co VA, Vol 1*, 6.

Boush Families

ISSUE:[135]

50. m i. **Samuel Boush**.
51. m ii. **Charles Boush**.
52. f iii. **Ann Boush**.
53. m iv. **Thomas Wythe Boush**.
54. m v. **Daniel Boush**.
55. m vi. **Nathaniel Boush**.

In the will of Arthur Boush, dated 5 Sep 1779, he named his wife Ann, sons Samuel, Charles, Thomas Wythe, Daniel, Nathaniel and daughter Ann.[136]

- - - - - - - - - - -

59. Margaret "Peggy"[4] **Boush** <See pg. 203> (27.Samuel^3, 26.Samuel^2, 1.____ Boush^1) was born before 18 May 1754, the date of her grandmother's will.[137] She married **Christopher Calvert** 27 Oct 1762.[138]

ISSUE:

60. m i. **Samuel Calvert**. He married **Mary Bassett Moseley** 6 Apr 1789. She was the daughter of **Bassett Moseley** and **Rebecca Newton**. (See pg. 53).

- - - - - - - - - - -

---

[135] Dorman, *Adventurers of Purse and Person*, 2:607.

[136] McVey, *Norfolk Co VA Will Book 2*, 111.

[137] Maling, *Princess Anne Co VA Deed Books 1-7*, 103 (7DB661 - will of Margaret Sayer).

[138] Dorman, *Adventurers of Purse and Person*, 2:608.

Appendix

(The following documents are not indexed.)

1679 Will of Thomas Goodrich
Dated 15 Mar 1678/9 - Proved 3 Apr 1679 - (Old) Rappahannock (now Essex) County, Virginia[139]

In the name of God Amen, I Thomas Goodrich of the County of Rapp^{ae}. being weak of Body but of sound and perfect memory, make this my last Will and Testam'^{t}. First I bequeath my Soule to the Almighty, and my body to the Earth to be Decently and Christian like interred. And my Estate Reall and personall in manner and Forme Following:

Impris. I give and bequeath unto my Eldest Sonne Benjamine and to his heires for ever two hundred acres of Land upon the River Side which I formerly bought of Clem^{nt} Thresh and half the Devident of Land I now Live upon wth all the profits, Commodities and Emolum'^{ts} thereunto belonging, I likewise give and bequeath unto my Sonne Benjamine and to his heires For Ever these five Negroes whose names ensue (Viz't) Will, Jenimine, Nan and her Daughter Mall, and her Sonne Ben, and one Mulatto Boy called Will Brandy.

I likewise give and bequeath unto my Sonne Joseph halfe the Devident of Land Called Matepony to him and his heires for Ever, the whole Devident Conteyning Eighteene hundred acres which I will to be Equally Devided into two Moyeties, and my Sonne Joseph to have his first choice and if my Sonne make choice of that Moyetie which Containes the plantation and houses, then my Will is that my Sonne Joseph shall build halfe soe much housing upon the other Moyetie of the said Land as is now upon that part he now Lives upon for those to whom hereafter I shall bequest it. I likewise give unto my Sonne Joseph one Negro call'd Saw, one Negro Woman Called Cutchenah and her Child that now Sucks, wth all the Stock that is now upon the land wth all their increase for Ever.

I likewise give and bequeath unto my Sonne Charles one Tract of Land Conteyning Foure hundred acres adjoyning to a Devident of Land Called Buttons Rang, and to his heires For Ever wth all the profits and commodities thereof and likewise three Negro Slaves by name, Mary and her son George, and one boy Mannall, and Likewise I give and bequeath unto my said Sonne Charles and his heires for Ever wth all the profits thereof Six hundred Acres

---

[139] Will No. 2 (Old) Rappahannock Co VA (1677-1682) pp. 118-122. Sparacio, *Old Rappahannock Co VA - 1677-1682 (I) - RK.DW-09/90, 36-7.*

of land Joyning upon a Devident which I Formerly Settled upon Hoskins Pocoson.

I likewise give and bequeath unto my Daughter Anne nine hundred Acres of Land with the profits, it being the one Moyetie of a Devident of Eighteene hundred acres Called Matapony as abovesaid and to her heires for Ever and likewise I give unto my said Daughter these foure Negroes following (Viz't) Betty Watts, Tho: Evans, Fuller and her now Sucking Child to be delivered to my said Daughter upon her Marriage Day or at the age of one and Twenty yeares which shall First Come.

I likewise bequeath unto my Sonne Peter and to his heires for Ever Eight hundred acres of Land it being a part of a Devident of foure thousand acres, Scituate and being upon Hoskins Pocoson and Likewise Six head of Catle, the one half male, the other Female, with all their Increase and I likewise give unto my said Sonne Peter two Mulatto boys, one named Isaack, the other Toby, to be deliv'd when my said Sonne attaines the age of one and Twenty yeares.

I likewise give and bequeath unto my Daughter Katherine and to her heires for Ever Eight hundred acres of land, it likewise being a part of the Devident of Foure thousand acres as abovesaid and likewise two Negro boys, the one called Kyette, and the other James, to be deliv'd to my said Daughter upon her marriage Day or at the age of one and twenty yeares which first shall happen.

I doe hereby likewise give and bequeath unto my three Eldest Sonnes (Viz't) Benjamine, Joseph and Charles, Each one feather bed and Furniture and likewise the same unto my Eldest Daughter Anne, and I give and bequeath unto my Deare and well beloved wife all the Rest of my Estate Reall and personall who I likewise ordaine and appoint together with my Eldest Sonne Benjamine, Executrix and Executor of this my Last Will and Testam^{rt}.

And lastly, It is my Will & my mind and (blotted out) that this Court or Justices whatsoever, shall (blot) Concerned with any part of my Estate or Cause (blot) Executrix or Executor to give Security or any wise be concerned therein. It is likewise my Will that the Crop which shall be made upon my Plantacions this next Ensuing yeare be at the disposall of my Executrix and Executor for the paym^{rt} of my Debts and (blot)ply of my Family. In Witness whereof I have hereunto Sett my hand and Affixed my Seale this 15th day of March Ano. Dom. 1678/9.

Signed Sealed

in the presence of	Thomas Goodrich (Seale)
Christopher Hargill	
Dennis Connyers, Tho. Edmondson	

The within named Dennis Conniers and Christopher Hargill d(blot) that they see the within named Coll Thomas Goodrich Signe Seale & publish the within mentioned to be his last Will and testament and that he was in perfect sence & memory at the Signing Sealing and publishing thereof to the best of yor: Deponts: Judgmts: and further saith not
Christopher Hargill
     Dennis Conniers

Jurati sunt Hargill et Conniers in Cur Com Rappae: 3th die April Ano 1679

1680 Morris Survey and Tappahannock Plat
(Old) Rappahannock (now Essex) County, Virginia

Survey done by George Morris 15 Jul 1680[140]

The descriptions on the survey (upper left corner, somewhat counter clockwise):

Hoskins Creek
Mr Benia: Goodrich, his Land Bounded with P: O: E: D: N: & River
Mr Benia: Goodrich plant - Towne - Col^o Goodrich Quarter in Towne
Hobb His Hole Harbor - Tickners Creeke
M: N: C: B & River, Mr Reeves
Mr. Reeves plantacon
Rappahanock River - Jelsons Creek Mouth
Mr John Dangerfield - Area 680
Mr Anth^o North's - Mr North's 200 Acres
W B S seg. - old field, Tobo House
old Bounds of M^r ... To Mr Tigners Land ...terly ... to the old devident for Mr Thomalins
Q. R. F. G. H. Mr Thomalin's Bounds Joyneing on Mr Anthony North
Mr. Buttons now Mr Thomalin's - Th. Hills
C^{oll} Goodrich old dwelling house

The legend in the lower right corner:

The Table (The Black lines the Devident it Selfe
    A the begining Hickory on Coupers poynt by the River
    B A white Oake belonging to this Devident & Mr. Reeves
    C is at corner Oake of Mr. Reeves Devident
    D is a branch of Tyckners Creek E. A Poplar another corner
      & from D to E along the branch the bounds of this Devident
    F Three Small Sapplings by Mr.Button's old field
    G is a white Oak in A Small Branch beweene the hills
    H. a corner tree of Mr. Anthony North's: Two Hundred Acres;
    J, K & L: 64 Acres Bounding on Jelsons Creek; July 15: 1680
      Surveyed per George Morris - Surveyor

---

[140] Essex Co VA Land Trials 1715-1741, 145-6. Copies in Warner, *Origin .... of Tappahannock* and Sweeney, *Wills, Rappahannock Co VA*.

Appendix

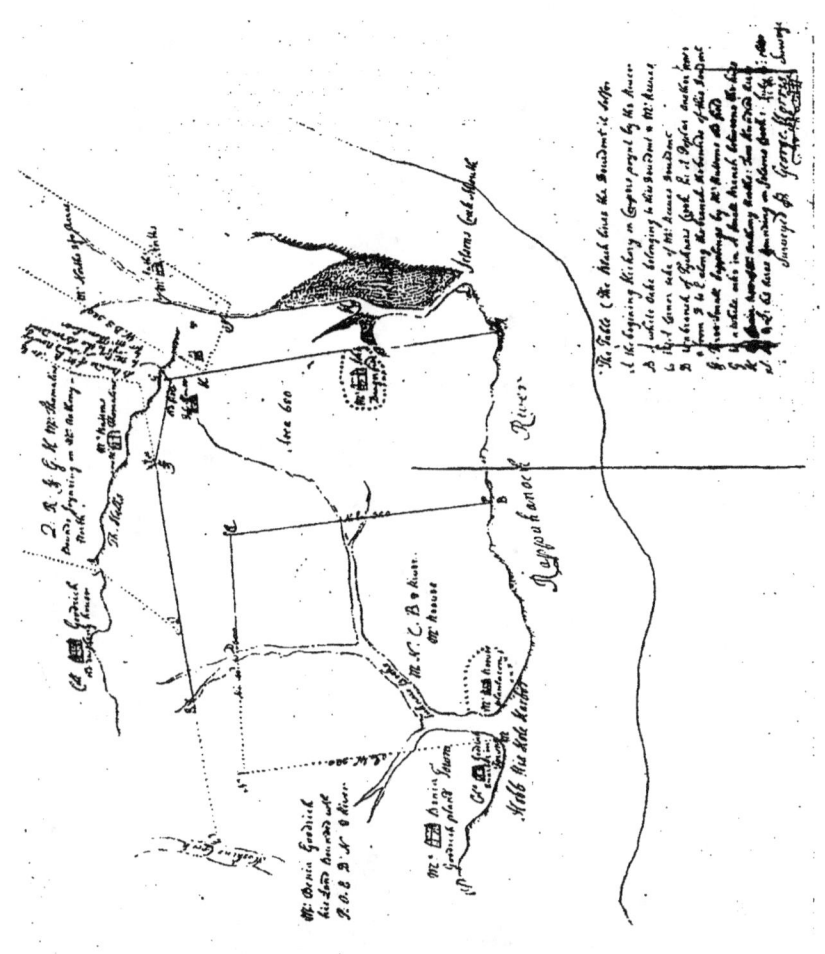

Plat of Tappahannock Town

This plat of Tappahannock Town is labeled both 1706 and 1709.[141] The street labeled "C" between blocks 32 and 36 at the Rappahannock River has been identified as Marsh Street by Mr. Harold Van Arsdale of the Essex County Museum and Historical Society. He also located Tappahannock Town as down river from (southeast of) what is labeled Tickners Creeke on the Morris survey shown on the page before this one.

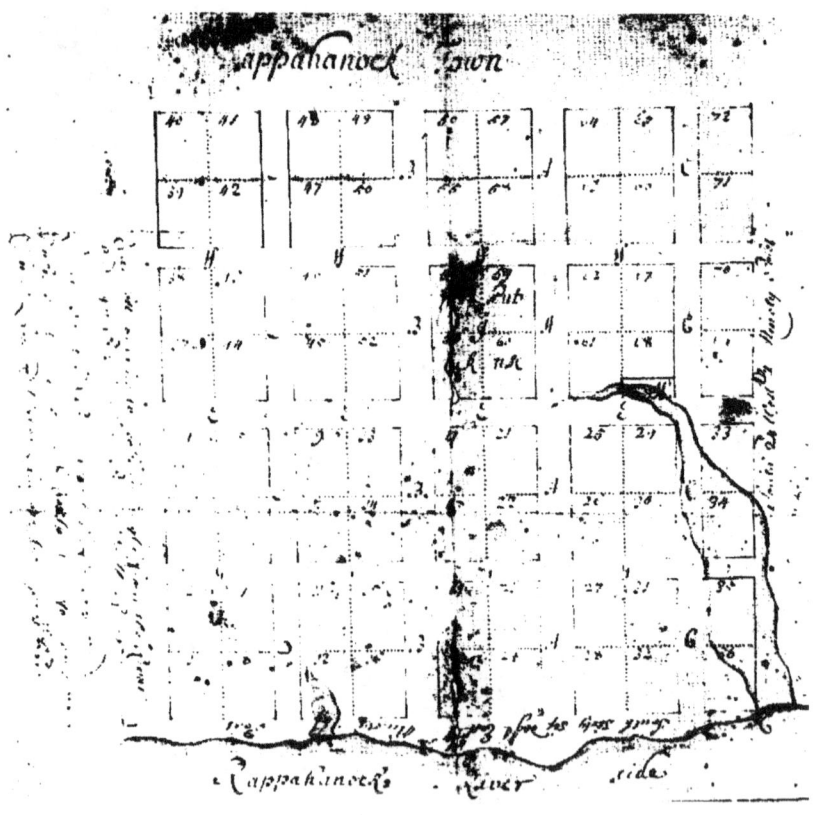

---

[141] Middle Peninsula Planning District Commission. Saluda, VA. http://www.mppdc.com/historical/Tappahannock.htm (accessed 25 Feb 2007).

1680 Will of Margaret (Ganey) Cheesman
Dated 15 Jan 1679/80 - Proved 21 Jul 1680 - County of Surrey, England[142]

In the Name of God Amen
this Fifteenth day of January in the yeare of our Lord Christ One Thousand
six hundred Seaventy and Nyne I Margarett Cheeseman of the parish
of St Mary Magdalen Bermondsey in this County of Surrey Widdow being
sicke in body but of sound and perfect minde and memory thanks be Given
to Almighty God for this same But Considering the frailtye of this present
Life And that all Flesh must yeild unto Death when it shall please God to
Call doe therefore by divine permission make and ordeyne this my last
Will and Testament in manner and forme following (that is to say) First
and principally I Comend my Soule unto Almighty God my maker believ-
-ing to receive free pardon and Comission of all my Sinnes by and through
the pretious death and Meritts of my Saviour and Redeemer Jesus Christ
And my body I Committ unto the Earth from whence it was taken to bee
decently buried according to the discretion of my Overseers hereunder nam-
-ed And as touching the disposeing of such Worldly Estate as the Lord in
mercy hath been pleased to bestow upon me my Will and true meaning
Is that the same shall be disposed of in such manner and forme as here-
-after is declared **Item** my Will and minde is That my Overseers here-
-after named shall disbure expend and lay out for my funerall Expences and
Charges Fifty poundes of good and lawfull money of England as they shall
thinke most decent and fitting **Item** I give and bequeath unto the poore
Inhabitants of the parish of St Mary Magdalen Bermondsey (wherein I now
dwell) the sum[m]e of Five poundes of lawfull money of England to bee
paid to the said poore people of the said parish then in being within three
moneths next after my Decease As my Overseers shall see most needful I
and wanting thereof **Item** I give unto all the Children of my very loveing
Kinsman Mr Lemuell Mason the elder in Virginia That shall be liveing in
Virginia at this Tyme of my Decease unto every one of them severally Ten
poundes a peece of good and lawfull money of England which I will shall be
and remayne in the handes of my Executor hereafter named to be Improved
for their best advantage untill they shall Attaine to their severall Ages of
One and Twenty yeares or dayes of Marriage which shall first happen And if
in Case any of them shall happen to dye (in their Minori--tyes) before
paym[en]t thereof shall be unto him her or them made Then my will
mind and Intent is That the Legacye or Legacyes of him her or them soe
dyeing shall be paid to the Survivor or Survivors of them respectively share
and share alike **Item** I Give and bequeath unto my Cozen Elizabeth
Theleball nowe liveing in Virginia five poundes of good and lawfull money

---

[142] Will of Margaret Cheesman, PROB 11/363 [92 Bath].

of England to be paid her on demand **Item** I give and bequeath unto all the
Children of the said Elizabeth Theleball that shall be liveing at the tyme of
my Decease unto every one of them seaverally the sum[m]e of Five poundes
a peece of lawfull money of England And if it shall happen That any
of them shall dye before payment thereof shall be made unto him her or
them soe dyeing Then my will and minde is that the share or Legacye
of him her or them soe dyeing shall be paid unto'the Survivor or Survivors
of them share and share alike **Item** I give and bequeath unto John
Mathews liveing in Virginia who was brother by the Mothers side to my
late Grandaughter Anne Cheeseman deceased Five poundes of good and
lawfull money of England And also a Dyamond Ring which formerly
was his Sisters to be paid and Delivered unto him on demand **Item** I
give and bequeath unto my Kinswoman Anne Gayney Twelve pence
to be paid her on demand **Item** I give and bequeath unto my Godaughter
Margarett Mason who lives with me the sum[m]e of One hundred and Fifty
poundes of good and lawfull Money of England and all my household
Goodes Lynnen and Apparell and the lease of my house And all the
plate I had of John Harrison All the rest of my plate I give and bequeath
unto seaverall of the Children of my said Cozen Lemuel Mason as followeth
(that is to say) to Alice Mason a greate Beaker to Elizatbeth a Tankard
to Anne a Tankard And to Abigail Mary and Dynah all the rest of my
plate to be equally divided among them as neere as may be share and
share alike and to each one of them a Ring And to Lemuell Mason
the younger my best greate Ring **Item** I give and bequeath unto
Mr John Samuell Mr Thomas Gladwin my said Cozen Margarett Ma-
-son and Mrs Mary Childe widdow to every one of them severally five
poundes a peece of lawfull money of England And I doe hereby
Authorize desire and appointe tbe said John Samuell Thomas Gladwin
Margaret Mason and Mary Childe to be Overseers of this my last Will
and testam[en]t And in the absence of my Executor for him and on his
behalfe to Actt doe and performe soe much of this my said Will
And testam[en]t as they can or may Conveniently doe and performe And
to give a true and just accompt unto my Executor hereafter named of
all such their Actings and doeings in aboute or Concerning this my said
Will **Item** I give and bequeath all the rest residue and remainder of
my Estate Goodes and Chattells whatsoever unto my s[ai]d loveing
Kinsman Mr Lemuell Mason in Virginia And I doe hereby make ordeyne
and appointe the siad Lemuell Mason to be Executor of this my last Will
and testam[en]t And my Will and Minde further is That my said Godaughter
Margarett Mason (by and with the advice and Consent of the rest of my
Overseers) shall be Executor in truste only for the use benefitt and behoofe
of the said Lemuell Mason her Father And to take Care and preserve
secure and Keepe all such parte of my Estate Goodes and Chattell as of
right by vertue of this my will belongeth unto him untill such tyme as he

Appendix 219

or his Assignes shall come and receive the same And in the meane tyme
she shall have power to pay of my funerall and other Charges And all such
Legacyes as I have given away and bequeathed to any person or persons
liveing here in England In Testimony whereof I the said Margarett
Cheesman have hereunto sett my hand and Seale the day and yeare first
above written :*//*: Margarett Cheesman her marke Read published declared
Signed Sealed and delivered by the said Margarett Cheesmand the Tes-
-tatrix for and as her last Will and Testament in the presence of Sarah
Gladwin Jonath[a]n Scott./

Probatum fuit hu[ius]mo[d]i Testamentum apud London
vicesimo primo die Mensis Julij Axmo D[omi]ni Millesimo sexcentesimo
et Octogesimo coram ven[era]b[i]li viro Guilielmo Trumbull Legum
D[o]c[t]ore Surr
Prerogative Cantuariensis Magistri Custodis sive Com[m]issarij l[egi]time
constituti juramento Margarete Mason Executricis iuxta tabulas
testamentarias in hujusmodi testam[en]to nominat' Cui Com[m]issa fuit
Administrac[i]o
omnium et singulorum bonorum jurium et creditorum dicti defuncti De
bene et fidel[ite]r administrando eadem ad S[anc]ta Evangelia Jurat' etc

Translation of the probate

This will was proved at London on the twenty-first day of the month of July
in the year of the Lord 1680 before the venerable master William Trumbull,
doctor of laws, surrogate of the venerable and excellent master Lord Lionel
Jenkins, knight and doctor of laws, master, guardian or commissary of the
Prerogative Court of Canterbury, lawfully constituted, on the oath of
Margaret Mason, the executrix, named according to the testamentary tables
in this will. To whom was committed the administration of all and singular
the goods, rights and credits of the said deceased, sworn on the holy gospels
to administer well and faithfully the same.

1695 Will of Lemuel Mason
Dated 17 Jun 1695 - Proved 15 Sep 1702 - Norfolk County, Virginia[143]

[In the name of God Am]en I Lemuell Mason of Elizabeth
[………………………] Norfolk Gent' Being at this writing
[………………………] of good health p[er]fect sence and
[………………………] calling to minde the
[………………………] life doe therefore think fitt for
[………………………]all estate which it hath pleased God
[……………………….] pronounce and declare this and this
only [………………….] and testament and that in manner
and form[……………fi]rst and principally I comitt my soul
into […………………al]mighty and my body to the earth from
whence [……………….] to be buried in decent and christian
burial [………………….]on of my Executrix hereafter named

It[em] I give […………u]nto my loveing wife Ann the plantation
and [……………………] I now live for and during her naturall
li[fe………………………] with all priviledges and appurtenances
[……………………………] that is to say, that one hundred acres of
[…] former[ly……………]sed by my father Francis Mason deceased
excepting [……………..]rt of the produce of the orchard on the
abovesaid [……………..] where I now live which said third part
of the orchard [………..] I bequeath to my sonn Thomas Mason
immediately […………..] decease

It[em] I give unto my […..] pounds sterling […..] out of my
estate and [……………..] due […] the same at […..] unto which
of my childr[……………..]
doe [……………………..] Ann, all and whatsoever
[…………………………..] of what nature or quality
[………………………….]

Item I giv[e…………………..] Ann all the stock of cattle, sheep
and […………………….]ing to the plantation where I now
live […………………….] dureing life to make use of
[…………………………..]d noe other wife (otherwise), and after her
dec[ease……………..……..] on the said plantation, I
give [………………………..]mas Mason his heires and assignes

---

[143] Norfolk Co VA Deed Book 6:258-260. Though badly torn, a few more details of the will other than given in an abstract in 1914 are legible. Transcription done by Simon Neal, records agent, e-mail sn014i4785@blueyonder.co.uk. His insertions are indicated by [ ] Comments by PSM ( ).

for e[............................] and hoggs that shall be left
on [...................................] of Ann my
wife [................................] sonns Thomas # my three sonns#[144]
Lem[................................] heires or assignes   {Lemuel}[145]

Item I give [........................] a negro girle named
Betty [.............................] her decease to fall and decende
to my [...........................]rge Mason or to either of   {son George}
their [......................]

Item I give [........................] Mason the land above
men[............................] wife, and alsoe all [....]
my l[............................] w[i]th all priviledges and
appurt[enances....................] the said Thomas
Mason [..........................]

Item I give and [...................] Thomas Mason all the
right title [........................] the timber upon a p[ar]cell
#terrest that I have to#
of land [..................(Thelaball)] and my selfe lying at   #By Mr James#
(Wolves Neck) [...] also twenty cutts of good b[(oard)]d timber from
of my land [whi]ch I purchased of George [Kemp)] deceas[e]d at the head
of the East[....................] of Elizabeth River which said timber I
give unto the said Thomas and [........................]

Item I give and bequeath to my sonn [..................]
of what nature or quallity [..............................]
or assignes for ever [.................]

Item I give and bequeath unto my [.................]
cattle and hoggs runing [(on)................]
excepting six cowes w[hi]ch ca[...................]
Mason, to be delivered him [.................]
Lemuell at Machapongo [.................]
afores[ai]d stock of cattle run[...............]
Lemuell, it shall and be law[..............]
during her naturall life to [.................]
shall have occasion for the u[...............]

---

[144] McIntosh, *Norfolk Co Wills 1637-1710*, 1:182. Insertions in # #.

[145] *New England Historical and Genealogical Register*, 47 (1893) 65, 70. Insertions in { }

Appendix

wast, w[i]thout molestation or [..............]
order

Item I give and bequeath unto my [..............]
head of the Eastern-br[....................]
(give)] the said George his heires [............]

Item I give and bequeath to [...................]   {Frances, wife (widow) of
                                                    George Newton}
shillings at fall (in full) of her [....................]
Item I give and bequeath unto [..................]   {Alice, wife of
                                                    Samuel Boush,
daughter Alice the widdow [(of).....................]   widow of William
                     Porten}
portion of my estate [............................]
I give and bequeath to M[aste]r [..................] daughter {Mr T Cocke,
                     husband of}
Elizabeth one (sh)[..](te)

Item I give and [................................dau]ghter
Margar[et..] of my estate {wife of Mr
              (torn)}*in England*[146]

Item I give and [...................................] my daughter
Ann tenn [(sh)..]   {wife of (torn)}

Item I give and [(Beq)............................] daughter Mary
one silver wine [.................................] estate   {wife of Mr. Walter
                                                              Gee (sic)}

Item I give and bequeath [.......................]
money, and one small [..........................]her estate   {daughter Dinah}
as may equal[...] her [............................] the times of
their marriages, excep[..........................] my sonn
Thomas Mason since[......................] settled
a plantation, and by [........................]d hundred
acres of land given to [....................] is that he may
not be disturbed on th[.........................] but if my said
wife should want [..........................]es on the
southeast side of [............................] parts my
brother (Thela)[..................................]

Item I give and be[queath..................] now on

---

[146] *VA Mag Hist*, 4 (1896) 84.

Appendix

the plantati[on..............................]ture to [...]
[........] at he[..........................] noe other intent
or purpose [.............................(ter)] the decease
of my wife, to my [......................] for ever

Item all the rest of my esta[te ....] give unto my
loveing wife Ann my [...........................] to be equally
divided amongst them [...........................] appoint and
ordaine my two sonns Th[.......................] to be overseers of
          Thomas and Lemuel
this my will to see the sa[..........................] lastly I doe hereby
nominate appoint [.................................] wife Ann Mason my
whole and sole execut[..........................wi]tnesse whereof I have
[...................................] this 17 day of June 1695

[......................................] doe hereby further order and it is my will
[......................................] if I the said Lemuell Mason doe
[......................................] my sister Elizabeth Thel[...] the[..]
[......................................] give and bequeath unto my said sister
[......................................] good black se[(erge)]e as will
[......................................] her a morning gowne My will is
[......................................] wife that if my man James doe faithfully
[......................................]ly serveing my wife soe longe as shee
[......................................] live, after my decease, then my
[......................................] the said James shall be free and
[......................................] noe longer
          Lemuell Mason and seale
[....................................] the oaths
[....................................] this 15th of Sep[tembe]r 1702

1702 Will of Elizabeth (Mason) Thelaball
Dated 12 May 1702 - Proved 15 Mar 1707 - Norfolk County, Virginia[147]

In the name of God Amen I Elizabeth Thelaball of Elizabeth River Parish in the County of Norfolk Gentw^{on} being at this present in perfect health of body & of sound & perfect Memory, but being now well stricken in years & know not how suddenly it may please God to Call me out of this world into his Mercy and for the according of all further contentions as may hereafter arise about what small estate that it hath pleased God in his mercy to leave me, doe therefore think fitt & convenient to make this my last will & testam^t & hereby to make void & null all other manner of Will or Wills testam^t or testaments by me heretofore made & doe ordain & appoint this only to be my last Will and Testam't in manner & form following.

Imprimis I give & bequeath my Soule into the hands of my Creator Jesus Christ my redeemer through whose death & passion I hope to have a joyful resurrection at the last day. I give & bequeath my body to the Earth from whence it came, there to be buried in Christian manner according to the direction of my two Sons Francis & James Thelaball & that the s^d Francis & James be at equal charges towards my funeral & likewise in proving my will & as for my worldly goods afores^d I give & bequeath Them as follow'g.

Viz I give & bequeath unto my loving Son Francis Thelaball one great Chest which commonly Standeth in my Entry, Six pewter plates broad brimmed, One Iron pessil one frying pan, one writing Slate & all the Stock of hoggs that I shall have belonging to me at the time of my decease, & the halfe of my Stock of Sheep which I shall have at the time of my decease excepting Six Ewes which I as I shall after herein direct.

Imp^r I give & bequeath unto my loving Son James Thelaball one great trunk with lock & key to it Standing in the Shade, one plank Cupboard, one Small round Table, one looking Glass the frame thereof black-wood, one small trunk to keep writing in, one Iron pessil, one Iron ...... two wooden Chairs, & eight pewter plates & one small flock Couch bed & also the half of my Stock of Cattle & also the half of my Stock of Sheep, excepting what I have above excepted & also all my right & title to the increase of a Negro girl named Rose, now in the possession of my Said Son James given him by the last will & testament of my aforesaid husband, Mr James Thelaball.

---

[147] James, *Lower Norfolk Antiquary*, 3:144-6.

Imp^r I give and bequeath unto my Son in law Wm Langley who formerly married my daughter Margaret One Shilling in full of his portion as marrying my said daughter Margaret.

Imp^r I give & bequeath unto my loving daughter Elizabeth Langley now wife of Thomas Langley one trunk with drawers in it, & a little black box that Stands on the top of it, & two turkey work Chairs One Iron Pott one paire of fire tongs one pewter Candlestick & small stoned Ring of Gold, & one hoop ring of ditto, & one large brass skillett with a frame & one great Chest which was my mothers & one small Deske & all my right & title to the increase of a Negro Girl named Nanny now in the possession of my Son in law Thomas Langley & my daughter Elizabeth, given my Said daughter Elizabeth Langley by the last will and testam^t of my dear husband Mr James Thelaball.

Imp^r I give and bequeath unto my loving daughter Mary Mason now wife of Lemuell Mason one long Chest which goeth by the name of the Clothes Chest one iron Pott one Gridiron, one paire of fire Tongs of Iron, One great chafing dish, one Small looking Glass & two wooden Chairs, one pewter Candlestick, one great blue Cushion which standeth on the Cupboard & one small feather bed, with Bolsters, & a Small green wollen Rugg, & one red Mohaire petty coat.

Imp^r I give & bequeath unto James Thelaball my grand Son now Sonn^d to Francis Thelaball two Ewes to be delivered him immediately after my decease.

Imp^r I give & bequeath unto Thomas Langley my GrandSon now eldest son to Thomas Langley two Ewes to be delivered him immediately after my decease.

Imp^r I give and bequeath unto my great Grandson Wm Ivy now Sonn to George Ivy two Ewes to be delivered him within Six months after my decease, but if it should So happen at my decease that I should not have so many Sheep as is above given to my three grandchildren, that what is remaining may be equally divided between my said three grand Children as to quality.

Imp^r I give & bequeath unto my loving daughters Elizabeth and Mary all my wearing apparel woollen & Linning excepting w^t is before given to be equally divided between my said two daughters & in case either one should die before my Self the same to fall to the Survivor.

Imp^r I give & bequeath all my pewter and Table Linen & Sheets money or other Sort of goods of w^t nature or quality soever not before bequeathed wch I shall have at the time of my death to be equally divided between as many of my own sons & daughters, as at the same time shall be living & doe hereby nominate & appoint my son Francis Thelaball my whole & Sole Executor of this my last will and testament.

In witness whereof I have hereunto set my hand this 12 day of May 1702 & fixt my Seal to the Confirmation of the within premises.

     Elizabeth Thelaball & Seale
Signed & Sealed & delivered
by Elizabeth Thelaball as her
last will in presence of us
Geo. Mason
Rich Sayer
Lemuel Newton

Proved by Richard Sayer & Capt. George Mason two of the witnesses aforesaid March the 15th, 1707 in open Court & ordered to be Recorded
    Test. Jno Ferebee D C Cur.

 A Copy

    Teste Alvah H Martin C. C
    By W^m. H. Barnes D. C.

1705 Will of Ann (Seawell) Mason
Dated 30 Oct 1705 - Proved 15 Mar 1705/6 - Norfolk County, Virginia[148]

In the Name of God Amen, I Ann Mason of Elizabeth river Parish in the County of Norfolk, Gentlewoman, being at this writing, Signing & sealing hereof in perfect Sense of mind & Memory, praised be god for the same & calling to mind the Uncertainty of this transitory life doe therefore thinke fitt for the settlem^t of what small estate wch it hath pleased God to bestow upon mee by the death of my dec'd husband Colo. Lemuel Mason, do make Pronounce & declare this and this only to bee my last will & testam^t & that in Manner & forme following

Viz^t, first and principally I committ my soule into the hands of God Almighty and Jesus Christ my Redeemer & my body to the earth from whence it came, there to be buried in decent & Christian burial at the discretion of my executors hereafter named or the discretion of my three sonnes Thomas, Lemuel & George Mason.

Imp^r I give & bequeath unto my Loving Daughter Frances Sayer the sum of seven pounds ten shillings in money to be paid her within two Months of my decease by my three Sonns & my will is that she dispose of the same at her owne pleasure without being accountable to her husband for the same in any Respect.

It^m I give & bequeath unto my loving daughter Alice Boush the sum of seven pounds ten shillings in Money to be paid her within two months after my decease & my will is that she dispose of the same at her owne pleasure wthout being accountable to her husband for the same in any respect.

It^m I give & bequeath unto my loving daughter Mary Cock the sum of seven pounds ten shill' in money to be paid her within two months after my decease & my will is that she dispose of the same at her owne pleasure without being accountable to her husband for the same in any respect.

It^m I give & bequeath unto my loving daughter Dinah Thorowgood seven pounds ten shill' in money to be paid her within two months after my decease by my three sons aforesaid provided the said Dinah Thorowgood take nor receive anything more by virtue of the will of my dec'd husband Coll. Lemuel Mason than what is there directly mentioned in money it being twenty shill'. If claiming anything more by my husbands dec'd will than the

---

[148] Norfolk Co VA Deed Book 7 1:117-118.

twenty shill', my will is that she the said Dinah receive one shilling in full of her portion of my Estate & noe more.

It^m I give and bequeath unto my Sonne Thomas Mason & his heirs for ever the paire of andirons that are in the Chimney where I commonly are my Selfe, my dec'd husband promising the same to my said son Thomas above twenty yeares past.

It^m I give and bequeath unto my Loving Daughter Frances Sayer my seale skinned trunke with all woolling lining ... silke apparel wh^{ch} hath been worne on my body or properly for that use to bee delivered her within a Month after my decease.

It^m I give and bequeath unto my Sons Thomas Mason, Lemuel Mason & George Mason all the other part of my estate w^{t}Soever not before bequeathed, be it of w^t nature or quality Soever, either by deed of gift made to mee by my dec'd husband Colo. Lemuel Mason as Negroes, Plate, household goods or anything else to me appertaining .... or belonging, to my said three Sonnes Thomas, Lemuel & George Mason to them their heirs, executors & adm^{rs} & assignes forever to be equally divided between them. And lastly, I doe hereby nominate, appoint & ordaine my said three Sonns Thomas, Lemuel & George Mason my whole & sole Executors of this my will. In witness whereof I have hereunto Sett my hand & Seale this 30th day of October 1705

      Ann Mason (seal)

Signed, Sealed and delivered by Mrs Ann
Mason as her last will & testam^t in
presence of us

Tho: Willoughby
Elizabeth Newton
Ann Porten

Proved in open Court this 15th of March 1705/6 by the oath of Colo. Thomas Willoughby & Mrs Ann Porten, two of the witnesses thereunto subscribed & ordered to be recorded.

      Test: Jno Ferebee D C C
Recorded the 22th of M'ch 1705/6 Test J F..... D C C

1712 Will of James Wilson
Dated 12 Nov 1712 - Proved 19 Dec 1712 - Norfolk County, Virginia[149]

In the Name of God Amen I James Wilson of the County of Norfolk in virginia being Very Sick and weak of body but of sound and perfect Memory, thanks be to the almighty god I Doe make this to be my last will and testament in manner and forme following

First - I recommend my Soule to almighty god that gave it my body to the Earthe from whence it came etc.

And as for my whole worldly estate it hath pleased god to grant me, I Dispose of it as followeth.

Imp's my will is that all my Just Debts be first paid of what Nature soever. I Give to my Son John Wilson two hundred acres of land which land I bought of John Fulford. I give it to him and his heirs for Ever with all the Stock thereon both Cattle and hogs and I give to my Said Son all my Land and houses being and Lying on the westermost Side of the land at the bridge at the head of the Southerne branch to him & his heirs for Ever.

I Give to my Son Willis Wilson all the land and the New Store Standing the Eastermost Side of the wroade by the bridge to him and his heirs for Ever.

I Give and bequeath to my said son Willis Wilson my plantation where on I now live being about four hundred acres to him and his heirs for Ever.

I Give to my Said Son all the stock both Cattle and hoggs being on the said plantation allowing my Dear and Loveing wife Elizabeth Wilson to have the use of the Said plantation and Stock during her natural Life for her better Suport and Maintainance. I also give to my Loving Son Willis the feather bed and furniture that he Lyes one with the one halfe of my plate. I give to my Loveing Son John Wilson one feather bed and furniture.

I give to my Loveing Son John Wilson my Negroes Called by the name of Peter and Bossman.

And my will is that my Son John have the use of the Negroes which he has now in possession till he recover his Negroes of Capt. Robert Bolling or a Determination of the Suite.

---

[149] Norfolk Co VA Deed Book 9:220-222.

I give and bequeath unto my Grandson James Wilson Son of my Son Thomas Wilson Dec'd the plantation whereon my Negro Sambo Lives one beginning on the South Side of Sambo's plantation at the Swamp Called the Sypress Swamp and runing into the woods upon a Northerly Course one hundred and fifty poles then thence a north East Course to my westermost Line. I give the said land to him and the heirs of his body Lawfully begotten and in Default of Such heirs Then I give and bequeath the said land to my Loveing Son Solloman Wilson and his heirs forever.

I give and bequeath unto my Grandson Willis Wilson Son of my dec'd Son, Sam[ll] Wilson four hundred acres of land known by the name of poplar Neck beginning at the Northerly Line of James Wilson and running Such a Course that shall Include the Land whereon the poplars Grow and thence to the Cypress Swamp to him and the heirs of his body lawfully begotten for Ever, to be Delivered Into his possession at the age of twenty one years and in Default of Such heirs then I Give and bequeath the said Land unto my Loveing Son Solloman Wilson and his heirs for Ever.

I Give to my Grandson Willis, Son of my Dec'd on Sam[ll] Wilson one Negro man & Stock that Shall be on the aforesd plantation to be Delivered to him, my Said Grandson at the age of Twenty one years.

I Give and bequeath unto my Son Solloman Wilson the plantation or tract of land I bought of Henry Bright being two hundred acres be it more or be it Less to him and his heirs for Ever. I give unto my Said Son my land Called the western Ridge and his heirs for Ever.

I give and bequeath unto my son James Wilson one hundred acres of land lying and being over the Gumme Swamp in the back woods to him & his heirs for ever.

I give and bequeath unto my son Jno. Wilson one hundred acres of Land Lying and being over the Gumme Swamp in the back woods to him and his heirs for Ever

And all the rest of my Land not already bequeathed I give and bequeath unto my Son Willis Wilson and his heirs for Ever.

I give to Capt. George Newton one I hundred acres of Land called the Cowpens to him and his heirs forever.

I Give to my son Solloman Wilson to be Delivered to him at the age of Twenty one years Two Negroes Jonas and Dragoone. All the rest of my personal Estate not before given, I will and Desire that it be Equally Divided between my Sons Willis, John and Soloman and my Daughters Affiah and

Mary, my Loving wife Elizabeth to have the use of it During her Naturale Life.

I Give to my Daughter Elizabeth the wife of Mr Henry Trigany of Philadelphia five pounds Current Money In full of her part of my Estate She have had her part before.

I Give to my Son Lem[ll] Wilson five Shillings in full of his portion he haveing had a Sufficient part already.

I Give to my Son James Wilson my pistols and Sword and Lastly I Doe nominate and appoint my Dear and Loveing wife Elizabeth Wilson and my Loveing Son Willis Wilson my whole and sole Executor and Exex of this my Last will and Testament Revoking and Disavowing any former will by me made in wittness whereof I have hereunto sett my hand and Seale the 12th day of November 1712.

Signed, Sealed and Delivered
in the presence of us   James Wilson and Seale
M. Boush
Wm Armistead
Thomas Walke
Francis Flourney
Nich° Curle

Norfolk County at a Court held for the Said county the 19th of December 1712 the above will was presented in Court by Mrs. Elizabeth Wilson and Willis Wilson Exec^{rs} therein named who made oath thereto and on their Motion was proved in Court by the oaths of. Thomas Walk and Maximillian Boush and admitted to record.
                Test Lemuel Wilson Cl Cur

I Doe further give and bequeath unto my Grandson Soloman Wilson Son of my Sonn James Wilson two hundred Acres of Land being the land I purchased of Joele Martain known by the name of Canew Necke to him and his heirs for Ever.
                James Wilson and Seal
Signed Sealed and Published
in the presence of
Nich° Curle
Wm Armstead
M Boush
Thomas Walke
Francis Flournoy

Norfolk County at a Court held for the Said county the 19th of December 1712 the above Codicil was proved in Court by the oaths of Thomas Walke and Maximillian Boush and admitted to record.
                Teste... Lemuel Wilson Cl Cur

Appendix

1812 Will of Benjamin Wilson
Dated 1 Feb 1812 - Proved 28 Nov 1814 - Cumberland County, Virginia[150]

In the name of God, amen, Benjamin Wilson of Cumberland
now nearly four score years old tho of sound & disposing
mind makes & declares this his last Will & Testament.
My soul is resigned to the bountifull Grace with a firm
trust of a happy resurrection thro my mercifull Redeemer.
Of the property with which we have been blessed & of that
of which we are now posse^d I give & dispose to my aged
wife for life
To son Benj^a I give Jim, Abby & Charles
To son Saml I give Mongo, Melley & Charles
To son Mat^w I give Samson, Necy, Mary & children
To son Alex^r I give Moses, Phillis & Arreanna
To son Goodrich I give Sam, Cate & Tom
To daughter Mason I give Will, Amy, Daphne, & her children
To daughter Martha I give Mat, Archer, ...
To daughter Unity I give Phil ..... Stephen, John, Fan..... & Ch..
To grand daughter Hobson I give Aggy & her children & Bob (to be ....
To grand daughter Maria Willis I give Leddy
To grand daughter Ann daug^h of James I give Ned
To my sons Willis & James I assign my debt & interest due
from Jas Meredith in satisfaction their debts & accounts.
All the rest of my property both real & personal (except
a negro boy Davy son of Anny) I give & devise to my
sons Willis, James, Saml & Goodrich who are hereby appointed my executors, who, the surviving or qualifying
part of whom are directed to di-
vide the same by sale of other ways or by both means
among all my children or their legal Representatives
including G'daughter Hobson. - And I do further direct
that proportion of my residuary estate which shall
be so alloted to my son Alex^r together with the said
negroe boy Davy be secured in Trust by my ex^{ors}
to my sons Ben, James & Goodrich to the ... annually
of son Alex^r & his legal representatives in ....
I consider an Inventory of my estate sufficient without
an appraisement & require no security of my
executors to the ... part of whom or all of qualify
to allow two Lbs?6^d each on the amount of my estate

---

[150] Will of Benjamin Wilson, LVA.

... settled & divided. In Witness whereof I hereunto
set my hand and affix my seal this 1ˢᵗ Feby 1812
....
& ...... in presence of

George W Jones   Ben: Wilson (Seal)
Thomas Bradley
Smith Criddle

I Do direct that my exe^{trs} heretofore Named
in this my Will Sel my Land being 870...
acres for the payments of my Debts to son Saml witness my hand
& seal this 20 day of September 1814

Teste
Paul C Venable   Ben:Wilson (seal)
Thos Nixon
....

Cumberland November Court 1814
This last Will and Testament of Benjamin Wilson dec^d was exhibited
in court and proved by Thomas Bradley one of the Witnesses
thereto. And on the motion of Willis Wilson, James Wilson,
Goodrich Wilson, and Samuel Wilson the Executors named in
said will who made oath according to law, certificate is granted
them for obtaining probate thereof in due form they haveing
entered into bond according to law. and at a Court held for the
said county the   day of   18

Order Book 1811-15, page 464

At a Court held for Cumberland County the 28ᵗʰ day of November 1814

Present

John Holeman Sen'r
Willis Wilson
Francis B. Deane   Gentlemen Justices
Daniel A. Allen
Charles Womack

The last will and testament of Benjamin Wilson dec'd was exhibited
in Court and proved by Thomas Bradley a witness thereto. And on
the motion of Willis Wilson, James Wilson, Goodrich Wilson and

Samuel Wilson Executors named in said will who made oath according to law certificate is granted them for obtaining probat thereof in due form they haveing entered into bond according to law.

                Miller Woodson Jr. D. C.
                Willis Woodson J. P.

A copy - teste
Carol O. Henshaw, Deputy Clerk
Circuit Court of Cumberland Co., Va.

1728 Marriage Bond of Willis Wilson and Elizabeth Goodrich
7 Jun 1728 - Norfolk County, Virginia[151]

Know all men by these presents that wee Solomon Wilson & Willis Wilson, both of Norfolk County do Owe and stand Justly Indebted unto our Sovereign Lord King George the Second, his heirs and Successors in the Sum of fifty pounds Sterling and for the Just and true paym't thereof we bind our Selves and Either of us and Either of our heirs, Exe[rs] Joyntly and Severally firmly by these presents In Witness whereof we have hereunto Sett our hands & Seals this 7 day of June 1728.

The condition of the above Obligation is such that whereas the above bounden Willis Wilson is by Gods grace Intended to Intermarry with Eliz[a] Goodrich. Now in Case there shall be no lawfull Impedim[t] nor obstruction to hinder the said Marriage and that the said Willis Shall from time to time Save harmless and Indemnified all persons Concerned in granting the said Licence from all Costs and Damages Whatsoever that then this obligation to be Voide or Else to Remain in full force Power and Virtue.

Sealed and Delivered
Presents of us:
John Smith
                  Willis Wilson (seal)
                  Solo. Wilson (seal)

---

[151] Norfolk Co VA Marriage Bonds 1, 1706-1759. Reel 218. Library of Virginia, Richmond.

Appendix

1754 Marriage Bond of Benjamin Wilson and Anne Seay
25 Mar 1754 - Cumberland County, Virginia[152]

CONSENT:
I Do agree and Consent to the marige
Betwen Anne Seay & Benj^a Wilson
as Witness my hand this 20th Day march 1754.

        James Seay
Wittness
John Seay
Lucy Coleman

MARRIAGE BOND:
Know all men by these Presents that We Benjamin
Wilson & Thomas Tabb are held & firmly bound unto
our Sovereign Lord the King in the full & Just sum
of fifty Pounds Current money to them which
Payment well & truly to be made over and our
selves our heirs Excers & Admers jointly &
severally firmly by these Presents Sealed with our
Seals & dated this xxvth Day of March 1754.

The Condition of the above obligation is such that
Whereas there is a marriage intended to be had &
Solemnized between the s^d.Wilson & Ann Seay now if there
shall be no lawfull Cause to obstruct the s^d Marriage
then this Obligation to be void.
        Benj^a Wilson
        Thomas Tabb.

---

[152] Cumberland Co VA Marriage Bonds 1749-1788. Reel 39. Library of Virginia, Richmond.

Bibliography

Abercrombie, Janice L and Richard Slatten. *Virginia Revolutionary Publick Claims.* Athens GA: Iberian Publishing Co, 1992.

Abstracts of Philadelphia Co PA Wills, 1682-1726. Broderbund Software's Family Archives (www.genealogy.com), Pennsylvania Wills, 1682-1834 - CD #209.

"Ancestry of George Wythe, LL. D." *Genealogies of Virginia Families from William and Mary College Quarterly Historical Magazine* 5:612. Baltimore: Genealogical Publishing Co, 1982.

"Armistead Family." *Genealogies of Virginia Families from William and Mary College Quarterly Historical Magazine* 1:105-164. Baltimore: Genealogical Publishing Co, 1982.

"Bacon's Rebellion." Eggleston MSS containing "Mr. Bacon's acct. of their troubles in Virginia by the Indians, June 18th, 1676". William & Mary Quarterly. Series 1, 9:1-10 (1901).

"Ballard Notes." *Genealogies of Virginia Families from The Virginia Magazine of History and Biography.* 1:221. Baltimore: Genealogical Publishing Co, 1981.

Barnes, Robert. "Henry Sewell and Some of His Descendants." Anne Arundel Readings. Vol 5:1- (2002). Pasadena MD: Anne Arundel Genealogical Society.

Barton, R T, ed. *Virginia Colonial Decisions, The Reports by Sir John Randolph and by Edward Barradall of the Decisions of the General Court of Virginia, 1728-1741.* 2 vols. Boston MA: Boston Book Co, 1909.

Bell, Landon C. *Charles Parish, York County, Virginia, History and Registers.* Richmond: The VA State Library Board, 1932.

Benjamin Wilson Papers 1785-1916, 97MS439. Special Collections and Archives Department, Margaret I King Library, University of Kentucky, Lexington KY. Transcriptions of papers from 1785-1849, see McCrary, *Wilson Families ... Correspondence .... 1785-1849.*

"Blair." *Genealogies of Virginia Families from William and Mary College Quarterly Historical Magazine* 1:361-2. Baltimore: Genealogical Publishing Co, 1982.

Blomquist, Ann Kicker. *The Vestry Book of Southam Parish, Cumberland County, Virginia, 1745-1792.* Westminster MD: Willow Bend Books, 2002.

Bockstruck, Lloyd DeWitt. *Virginia Colonial Soldiers.* Baltimore: Genealogical Publishing Co, 1988.

Bibliography

Boddie, John Bennett and Mrs. John Bennett Boddie. *Historical Southern Families*. 23 vols. 1959-80. Reprint, Baltimore: Genealogical Publishing Co, 1993-95.

Boddie, John Bennett. *Southside Virginia Families*. 2 vols. Redwood City CA: 1955-6.

Boush Family Bible Record, 1775-1903. Accession 22246. Archives & Manuscripts, Library of Virginia, Richmond, VA.

Boush, Kenneth C, comp. *Boush Family Genealogical Notes*. Library of Virginia, Miscellaneous Reel 306.

Boush, Kenneth C, comp. *The Boush and Allied Families*. Library of Virginia, 1961, Miscellaneous Reel 520.

Brandow, James C. *Omitted Chapters from Hotten's Original Lists* ..... Baltimore: Genealogical Publishing Co, 1983.

Brewster, Ethel W, Comp. *Norfolk County, Virginia Will Book 111, 1788-1802*. Fredericksburg VA:1986.

Brock, Robert A. *The Official Letters of Alexander Spotswood, Lt-Gov of the Colony of Virginia, 1710-1722*. 2 vols. Collections of the Virginia Historical Society. New Series (Series 3). Richmond:Virginia Historical Society, 1882-85.

Broderbund Software's Family Archives (www.genealogy.com)/ Genealogical Publishing Company, (www.genealogical.com). The following books reproduced on Family Archive CD-ROM are listed also under the author or title heading:

    Bockstruck - CD #503 Virginia Colonial Records, 1600s-1700s.
    Boddie, *Historical Southern Families* - CD #191 Southern Genealogies #1, 1600s-1800s.
    Crozier - CD #503 Virginia Colonial Records, 1600s-1700s.
    des Cognets - CD #503 Virginia Colonial Records, 1600s-1700s.
    Fleet - CD #503 Virginia Colonial Records, 1600s-1700s.
    Genealogies, Tyler's Quarterly - CD #187 Virginia Genealogies, 1600s-1800s, #3.
    Genealogies, Virginia Magazine of History and Biography - CD #162 Virginia Genealogies, 1600s-1800s, #1.
    Genealogies, William and Mary Quarterly Historical Magazine, - CD #186 Virginia Genealogies #2.
    Headley - CD #510 Colonial Virginia Source Records, 1600s-1700s.
    Meade - CD #550 Virginia Genealogies and Biographies, 1500s-1900s.
    National Genealogical Society Quarterly - CD #210 Vols 1-85 1600's-1900s.
    Nugent, Vol 1- CD #503 Virginia Colonial Records, 1600s-1700s.
    Pennsylvania Wills, 1682-1834 - CD #209.
    Sanders, Barbados Records - CD #22 English Settlers in Barbados.
    Smith, Quit Rents - CD #503 Virginia Colonial Records, 1600s-1700s.

Bibliography

Stanard - CD #503 Virginia Colonial Records, 1600s-1700s.
Torrence - CD #510 Colonial Virginia Source Records, 1600s-1700s.
Virginia Vital Records #1, 1600s-1800s. CD# 174 - Vital, Marriage, Will, Land, Military, and Tax vols .
Withington - CD #503 Virginia Colonial Records, 1600s-1700s.
Wulfeck - CD #510 Colonial Virginia Source Records, 1600s-1700s.

Brown, Alexander. *The First Republic in America.......from Records then (1624) Concealed by the Council rather than from the Histories then licensed by the Crown.*. Boston: Houghton, Mifflin and Co, 1898.

Butt, Marshall Wingfield. *An Account of Some of the Descendants of Robert Butt* .... Portsmouth VA: 1967.

Butt, Marshall Wingfield. *Colonel James Wilson (1651-1712) of Norfolk County, Virginia, and Some of His Descendants.* Portsmouth VA: 1968.

Calendar of Virginia State Papers and Other Manuscripts Preserved in the Capitol at Richmond. 11 vols. New York: Kraus Reprint Corp., 1968.

Cary, Wilson Miles. "The Dandridges of Virginia." *Genealogies of Virginia Families from William and Mary College Quarterly Historical Magazine* 2:117-131. Baltimore: Genealogical Publishing Co, 1982.

Cary, Wilson Miles. "Wilson Cary of Ceelys, and His Family." *Genealogies of Virginia Families from The Virginia Magazine of History and Biography* 1(1901-1902):689-701. Baltimore: Genealogical Publishing Co, 1981.

Chamberlayne, C. G. *The Vestry Book and Register of St. Paul's Parish, Hanover County, Virginia, 1706-1786.* Richmond: Library of Virginia, 1973.

Chamberlayne, C. G. *The Vestry Book and Register of St. Peter's Parish, New Kent and James City Counties, Virginia, 1684-1786.* Richmond: Library of Virginia, 1937, reprint 1997.

Chapman, Blanche Adams, *Wills & Administrations of Elizabeth City County, 1688-1800*, Baltimore: Genealogical Publishing Co, 2000, originally published 1941.

Creecy, John Harvie. "Thorowgood Family of Princess Anne County , Virginia." *The Virginia Genealogist* 17:277-280 (1973).

Cross, Charles B Jr. *The County Court, 1637-1904, Norfolk County, Virginia.* Portsmouth: Printcraft Press, 1964.

Crozier, William Armstrong. *Virginia County Records, Vol. II, Virginia Colonia Militia 1651-1776.* Baltimore: Genealogical Publishing Co, 1986.

Bibliography

Crozier, William Armstrong. *Williamsburg Wills*. Baltimore: Southern Book Co, 1954.

Cumberland County Virginia and Its People. Cumberland VA: Cumberland County Historical Society, 1983, 1991.

Cumberland County, Virginia Historical Bulletin. Cumberland VA: Cumberland County Historical Society.

DAR. Daughters of the American Revolution, National Society. Washington DC. Willis Wilson Hobson Bible and Meredith Family Bible located in Benjamin Wilson Patriot File.

des Cognets, Louis. *English Duplicates of Lost Virginia Records*. Princeton: 1958. Reprint, Baltimore: Genealogical Publishing Co, 1981.

Dorman, John Frederick, ed., comp. *Adventurers of Purse and Person Virginia 1607-1624/25*. 4th edition. Baltimore: Genealogical Publishing Co, 2004.

Dorman, John Frederick, abs. *Essex County, Virginia, Deeds and Wills No. 13: 1707-1711*. Washington DC: 1963.

Dorman, John Frederick, abs. *York County, Virginia, Deeds, Orders, Wills, etc., No. 8, 1687-1691*. 2 vols. Washington: 1974-5.

Dumont, William H. "Some Virginia Revolutionary Veterans and their Heirs." *Virginia Genealogist* 1:47, 2:115.

Duvall, Lindsay O. *Virginia Colonial Abstracts, Series 2, Vol 6, Prince George Co, Vol 1 Land Patents 1666-1719*. Irvington VA: 1962.

"Elizabeth City County Families." *Genealogies of Virginia Families from William and Mary College Quarterly Historical Magazine* 5:647-662. Baltimore: Genealogical Publishing Co, 1982.

Ellis, Thomas Harding. "The Thorowgood Family of Princess Anne County, Va." *The Richmond Standard*, 26 Nov., 3, 10, 17 Dec. 1881.

Fauntleroy, Juliet and Mary Hope West. "Foxall-Vaulx-Elliott." *Virginia Magazine of History and Biography*. 44:151-4 (1936).

Finley, Walter S. "Bass and Allied Families". *Americana*, 19:216-220 (1925).

Fleet, Beverley, abs. *Virginia Colonial Abstracts*. Original 34 volumes reprinted 3 vols. Baltimore: Genealogical Publishing Co, 1988.

Fretwell, Shela S. *Abstracts of the Cumberland County, Virginia, Court Order Books from June 1749 to May 1756*. 1987.

Bibliography 243

Fretwell, Shela S. *Abstracts of the Cumberland County, Virginia, Court Order Books from May 1756 to June 1762.* 1988.

Forrest, William S. *Historical and Descriptive Sketches of Norfolk and Vicinity* ..... Philadelphia: Lindsay and Blakiston, 1853.

Gardner, Virginia. *Index to Wills and Estate Settlement Commencing 1608 - Williamburg, James City, York County, Virginia.* Gardner, 1977.

Genealogies of Virginia Families from Tyler's Quarterly Historical and Genealogical Magazine. 4 vols. Baltimore: Genealogical Publishing Co, 1981.

Genealogies of Virginia Families from The Virginia Magazine of History and Biography. 5 vols. Baltimore: Genealogical Publishing Co, 1981.

Genealogies of Virginia Families from William and Mary College Quarterly Historical Magazine. 5 vols. Baltimore: Genealogical Publishing Co, 1982.

Goodrich, Percy E. and Calvin Goodrich. *A Great-Grandmother and her People.* Winchester IN: Privately printed, 1950.

Gwathmey, John H. *Historical Register of Virginians in the Revolution.* Baltimore: Genealogical Publishing Co, 1987.

Hall, Jean P. and Kathryn P. Hall, contributors, "Legislative Petitions: Cumberland County 1776-1786", *Magazine of Virginia Genealogy,* Vol. 30, No.2, p. 88-89.

Hall, Wilmer L. *Journals of the Council of the State of Virginia.* Richmond: 1952.

Hamlin, Charles Hughes. "Goodrich Family of Virginia". National Genealogical Society Quarterly 51:67-70 (1963).

Hamlin, Charles Hughes. "Major Charles Goodrich of Charles City County, Virginia". *National Genealogical Society Quarterly* 46:128-131 (1958).

Hamlin, Charles Hughes, comp. *They Went That Away.* 3 vols. Richmond: 1964-.

Hargroves, Abigail Langley Granbery. *Commonplace Book, 1694-1818.* Often referred to as "Journal of Abigail Langley." Mss5:5 H2244:1. Virginia Historical Society, Richmond.

Harris, Malcolm Hart. *Old New Kent County, Some Account of the Planters, Plantations, and Places in New Kent County.* Vol. I. West Point VA: Harris, 1977.

Harrison, Fairfax. *The Virginia Carys, An Essay in Genealogy.* Privately printed, New York: DeVinne Press, 1919.

Hart, Lyndon H. and J. Christian Kolbe, ed. "Princess Anne Marriages 1737-44". *Southside Virginian.* 3:27-9 (1984).

Hart, Lyndon H. *Surry County, Virginia, Wills, Estate Accounts and Inventories 1730-1800.* Easley SC: Southern Historical Press, 1983.

Headley, Robert K. Jr. *Genealogical Abstracts from 18th-Century Virginia Newspapers.* Baltimore: Genealogical Publishing Co, 1987.

Hening, William Waller, ed. *The Statutes at Large, Being a Collection of All the Laws of Virginia.* 13 vols. 1809-23. (Volumes 1-7 transcribed as of Jan 2007 at http://vagenweb.org/hening/index.htm).

Henley, Bernard J. *Marriage/Obituary Index to Virginia Newspapers.* Online database, Library of Virginia. http://www.lva.lib.va.us/siteindex/index.htm.

Hiden, Mrs. P. W. "Boxley." *Genealogies of Virginia Families from William and Mary College Quarterly Historical Magazine* 1:404-9. Baltimore: Genealogical Publishing Co, 1982.

Hildeburn, Charles Swift Riché. *Baptisms and Burials from the Records of Christ Church, Philadelphia, 1709-1760.* Baltimore: Genealogical Publishing Co, 1982.

Holtzclaw, Benjamin C. "The Ivy-Ivey Family of Norfolk Co VA." *Historical Southern Families* (edited by Mrs. John Bennet Boddie). 16:158-166. 1971.

Hopkins, William Lindsay. "Selected Wills from the Burned Record Counties." Magazine of Virginia Genealogy. 31:353-4 (1993).

Hotten, John Camden. *The Original Lists of Persons of Quality ..... 1600-1700.* New York: G A Baker & Co Inc, 1931.

Hutton, Mary Louise Marshall, comp. *Seventeenth Century Colonial Ancestors of Members of the National Society Colonial Dames XVII Century 1915-1975.* Baltimore: Genealogical Publishing Co, 1987.

"James, Edward Wilson - In Memoriam." *Virginia Magazine of History and Biography.* 15:229-232 (1908).

James Edward W. "Abstracts from Princess Anne County Marriage Licenses." *Virginia Marriage Records.* Baltimore: Genealogical Publishing Co, 1984.

James, Edward W. *Lower Norfolk Antiquary.* 5 vols. New York: Peter Smith, 1900; reprint, 1951.

Kennedy, Mary Selden. *Seldens of Virginia and Allied Families.* 2 vols. New York: F. Allaben Genealogical Co, 1911.

"Langley Family." *Genealogies of Virginia Families from William and Mary College Quarterly Historical Magazine.* 3:303-306 (1911).

Lawrence-Dow, Elizabeth. *Autographs 1701/2 Charles City/Prince George and Surry Counties.* Richmnd VA: Dietz Press, 1976.

Lee, Francis Bazley. *Genealogical and Memorial History of the State of New Jersey.* Vol II. New York: Lewis Historical Publishing Co, 1910.

Lee Family Papers (1638-1867). Mss1:L51. Virginia Historical Society, Richmond.

Leonard, Cynthia Miller, comp. *The General Assembly of Virginia, July 30, 1619 - January 11, 1978, A Bicentennial Register of Members.* Richmond: Published for the General Assembly of Virginia by the Virginia State Library, 1978.

"List of Colonial Officers." *Virginia Magazine of History and Biography.* 8:327-8 (1900).

"List of the American Graduates in Medicine in the University of Edinburgh." *New England Historical & Genealogical Register* 42:159-162 (1888).

Littleton Parish (Cumberland County, Va.). *Records, 1840-1899.* Accession 29330, Church Records Collection, Library of Virginia, Richmond.

Maling, Anne E. *Princess Anne County, Virginia, Land and Probate Records Abstracted from Deed Books One to Seven, 1691-1755.* Bowie MD: Heritage Books, 1992. Available on cd from Heritage Books, Inc., 65 E. Main St. Westminister, MD 21157-5026. http://www.heritagebooks.com/

Maling, Anne E. *Princess Anne County, Virginia, Land and Probate Records Abstracted from Deed Books Eight to Eighteen, 1755-1783.* Bowie MD: Heritage Books, 1993. Available on cd from Heritage Books, Inc., 65 E. Main St. Westminister, MD 21157-5026. http://www.heritagebooks.com/

Maling, Anne E. *Princess Anne County, Virginia, Wills, 1783-1871.* Bowie MD: Heritage Books, 1994. Available on cd from Heritage Books, Inc., 65 E. Main St. Westminister, MD 21157-5026. http://www.heritagebooks.com/

Marshall, James Handley, comp. *Abstracts of the Wills and Administrations of Northampton County, Virginia 1632-1802.* Camden ME: Picton Press, 1994.

McClendon, Margaret Hobson. Application National number 564990. Daughters of the American Revolution, National Society. Washington DC.

McCrary, Patti Sue. *Cumberland County Tithable Lists for 1759.* Westminster MD: Heritage Books, in production 2006.

McCrary, Patti Sue. *Cumberland County Virginia, Historical Inventory, Subject and Owner Indexes.* Westminster MD: Heritage Books, 2006.

McCrary, Patti Sue. *Wilson Families: Descendants of Colonel Benjamin Wilson (1733-1814).* Westminster MD: Heritage Books, in production 2007.

McCrary, Patti Sue. *Wilson Families in Cumberland County Virginia and Woodford County Kentucky with Correspondence and Other Papers 1785-1849.* Westminster MD: Heritage Books, 2005.

McIlwaine, H R, ed. *Executive Journals of the Council of Colonial Virginia.* 6 vols. Richmond: Virginia State Library, 1925.

McIlwaine, H R, ed. *Journals of the House of Burgesses of Virginia 1659/60-1693.* Richmond: Virginia State Library, 1914.

McIlwaine, H R, ed. *Legislative Journals of the Council of Colonial Virginia.* 3 vols. Richmond: Virginia State Library, 1918.

McIlwaine, H R, ed. *Minutes of the Council and General Court of Colonial Virginia.* Richmond: Virginia State Library, 1924.

McIlwaine, H R, ed. *Proceedings of the Committees of Safety of Cumberland and Isle of Wight Counties Virginia 1775-1776.* Richmond: Davis Bottom, Superintendent of Public Printing, 1919.

McIntosh, Charles F. "Ages of Lower Norfolk County People". *William and Mary Quarterly.* Series 1, 25:36-40 (1916).

McIntosh, Charles Fleming. *Brief Abstract of Lower Norfolk County and Norfolk County Wills 1637-1710.* Colonial Dames of America in the State of Virginia. 1914. Reprint 2 vols. in one, Genealogical Publishing Co, 1998.

McIntosh, Charles, Fleming. *Brief Abstracts of Norfolk County Wills 1710-1753.* Colonial Dames of America in the State of Virginia. 1922. Reprint 2 vols. in one, Genealogical Publishing Co, 1998.

McLean, Harry Herndon. *The Wilson Family - Somerset and Barter Hill Branch.* Charlotte NC: Observer Printing House, 1950.

McVey, Pamela W, comp. *Norfolk County, Virginia, Will Book 11, 1772-1788.* Virginia Beach VA: 1986.

Meade, William. *Old Churches, Ministers, and Families of Virginia.* 2 vols. 1857. Reprint, Baltimore: Genealogical Publishing Co, 1966.

Meyer, Virginia M. and John Frederick Dorman, eds. *Adventurers of Purse and Person Virginia 1607-1624/25.* 3rd edition. Richmond: Order of First Families of Virginia, 1987.

Middle Peninsula Planning District Commission. Saluda, VA. http://www.mppdc.com/historical/Tappahannock.htm.

Moorshead, Halvor. "Reading Old Handwriting." *The Family Chronicle Collection* Sept 1996-Aug 1997, p. 62.

Morgan, Edmund S. *American Slavery, American Freedom, The Ordeal of Colonial Virginia.* New York: W W Norton, 1975.

Neal, Rosemary Corley, comp. *Elizabeth City County, Virginia, Deeds, Wills, Court Orders, Etc. 1634, 1659, 1688-1702.* Bowie MD: Heritage Books, 1986.

Neal, Rosemary Corley, comp. *Elizabeth City County, Virginia, Deeds, Wills, Court Orders, Etc. 1715-1721.* Bowie MD: Heritage Books, 1988.

Neville, John Davenport, comp. *Bacon's Rebellion: Abstracts of Materials in the Colonial Records Project.* Jamestown VA: Jamestown Foundation, 1976.

Newton, Virginius. "Newton Family of Norfolk." *Genealogies of Virginia Families from The Virginia Magazine of History and Biography* 4(1921-2):538-549. Baltimore: Genealogical Publishing Co, 1981.

Noël Hume, Ivor. *The Virginia Adventure, Roanoke to James Towne: An Archaeological and Historical Odyssey.* New York: Alfred A Knopf, 1994.

Nugent, Nell Marion, abs. *Cavaliers and Pioneers, Abstracts of Virginia Land Patents and Grants.* 8 volumes. Vol 1 originally published Richmond: Dietz Press, 1934. Reprint, Genealogical Publishing Co, 1963.

"Old Kecoughtan". *William and Mary Quarterly.* Series 1, 9:130 (1900). Williamsburg VA: The College.

"Old Tombstones of Charles City County." *William and Mary Quarterly.* Series 1, 4:143-150 (1896). Williamsburg VA: The College.

"Organization of Rappahannock County, 1656". *Virginia Magazine of History and Biography.* 8:176-7 (1900). Richmond: Virginia Historical Society.

Pecquet du Bellet, Louise. *Some Prominent Virginia Families.* Baltimore: Genealogical Publishing Co, 1976.

"Proprietors of the Northern Neck". *Virginia Magazine of History and Biography.* 33:349 (1925). Richmond: Virginia Historical Society.

Reynolds, Katherine, abs. *Abstracts of Cumberland County, Virginia, Will Books 1 and 2 1749-1782.* Easley, SC: Southern Historical Press, 1985.

Robinson, Conway. "Acts of the General Assembly, Jan. 6, 1639-40". *William and Mary College Quarterly Historical Magazine.* Series 2, 4:16-26 (1922).

Robinson, Morgan Poitiaux. *Virginia Counties: Those Resulting from Virginia Legislation.* Reprint, Baltimore: Genealogical Publishing Co, 1992.

Rosen, Carl Coleman Sr. *History of Maysville Presbyterian Church, Buckingham Court House, Virginia 1824-1996*. Buckingham VA: Maysville Presbyterian Church, 1997.

Rountree, Helen C. *Pocahontas's People, The Powhatan Indians of Virginia through Four Centuries*. Norman: Univ of Oklahoma Press, 1990.

Salmon, John S., comp. *A Guidebook to Virginia's Historical Markers*. Charlottesville: Univ Press of VA, 1994.

Sanders, Joanne McRee. *Barbados Records, Baptisms 1637-1800*. Baltimore: Genealogical Publishing Co, 1984.

Sanders, Joanne McRee. *Barbados Records, Marriages, 1643-1800*. 2 vols. Baltimore: Genealogical Publishing Co, 1982.

Sewell, Worley Levi Sewell. *History of the Sewell Families in America*. Privately printed, 1955.

Slaughter, James B. *Settlers, Southerners, Americans: the History of Essex County, Virginia, 1608-1984*. Essex County Board of Supervisors, 1985.

Smith, Annie Laurie Wright. *The Quit Rents of Virginia, 1704*. Baltimore: Genealogical Publishing Co, 1977.

Southall, James C. "Genealogy of the Cocke Family in Virginia."*Genealogies of Virginia Families from The Virginia Magazine of History and Biography* 2:185-192. Baltimore: Genealogical Publishing Co, 1981.

Sparacio, Ruth & Sam, eds. *Virginia County Court Records, Deed Abstracts of (Old) Rappahannock County, Virginia, (Part I of 1656-1664, Transcript), RK.DB-01/89*. McLean, VA: The Antient Press, 1989.

Sparacio, Ruth & Sam, eds. *Virginia County Court Records, Deed Abstracts of (Old) Rappahannock County, Virginia, (Part II of 1656-1664 Transcript), OR.DB-02/89*. McLean, VA: The Antient Press, 1989.

Sparacio, Ruth & Sam, eds. *Virginia County Court Records, Deed Abstracts of (Old) Rappahannock County, Virginia, 1663-1668, Deeds, etc. No. 3, OR.DB-03/89*. McLean, VA: The Antient Press, 1989.

Sparacio, Ruth & Sam, eds *Virginia County Court Records, Deed & Will Abstracts of (Old) Rappahannock County, Virginia, (1665-1677, Deeds & Wills No. 1, OR.DW-04/89*. McLean, VA: The Antient Press, 1989.

Sparacio, Ruth & Sam, eds. *Virginia County Court Records, Deed Abstracts of (Old) Rappahannock County, Virginia, (1670-1672), Part II Deed Book 4, OR.DB-06/89*. McLean, VA: The Antient Press, 1989.

Bibliography

Sparacio, Ruth & Sam, eds. *Virginia County Court Records, Deed Abstracts of (Old) Rappahannock County, Virginia, (Part I of 1672-1676 transcript), Deeds, Wills No. 5 (Part I) 7 March 1671/2 - 4 February 1673/4, OR.DB-07/89*. McLean, VA: The Antient Press, 1989.

Sparacio, Ruth & Sam, eds. *Virginia County Court Records, Deed Abstracts of (Old) Rappahannock County, Virginia, (Part II of 1672-1676 transcript), Deeds, Wills No. 5 (Part II) 4 March 1773/4 -10 May 1676, OR.DB-08/89*. McLean, VA: The Antient Press, 1989.

Sparacio, Ruth & Sam, eds. *Virginia County Court Records, Deed & Will Abstracts of (Old) Rappahannock County, Virginia,(1677-1682) (Part I), RK.DW-09/90*. McLean, VA: The Antient Press, 1990.

Sparacio, Ruth & Sam, eds. *Virginia County Court Records, Deed & Will Abstracts of (Old) Rappahannock County, Virginia, (1677-1682) (Part II), RK.DW-10/90*. McLean, VA: The Antient Press, 1990.

Sparacio, Ruth & Sam, eds. *Virginia County Court Records, Deed Abstracts of (Old) Rappahannock County, Virginia, 1688-1692, Deed Book No. 8, RK.DB-11/90*. McLean, VA: The Antient Press, 1990.

Sparacio, Ruth & Sam, eds. *Virginia County Court Records, Deed Abstracts of (Old) Rappahannock County, Virginia, 1682-1686, Deed Book no. 7, RK.DB-13/90*. McLean, VA: The Antient Press, 1990.

Sparacio, Ruth & Sam, eds. *Virginia County Court Records, Deed Abstracts of (Old) Rappahannock County, Virginia, 1686-1688, RK.DB-14/90*. McLean, VA: The Antient Press, 1990.

Sparacio, Ruth & Sam, eds. *Virginia County Court Records, Orders of (Old) Rappahannock County, Virginia, 1687-1689, RK.OB-17/90*. McLean, VA: The Antient Press, 1990.

Sparacio, Ruth & Sam, eds. *Virginia County Court Records, Order Book Abstracts of Essex County, Virginia 1695-1699, EX.OB-19/91*. McLean VA, The Antient Press, 1991.

Sparacio, Ruth & Sam, eds. *Virginia County Court Records, Deed & Will Abstracts of Essex County, Virginia 1695-1697 (Part I of Deed & Will Book 1695-1699), EX.DW-23/91*. McLean VA, The Antient Press, 1991.

Sparacio, Ruth & Sam, eds. *Virginia County Court Records, Abstracts Land Trials of Essex County, Virginia 1711-1741, EX.LT-28/92*. McLean VA, The Antient Press, 1992.

Stanard, William G. and Mary Newton, comp. *Colonial Virginia Register*. Albany: 1902.

Stanard, Wm. G. "Harrison of James River." *Genealogies of Virginia Families from The Virginia Magazine of History and Biography* 3:687-844 (1895). Baltimore: Genealogical Publishing Co, 1981.

Stanard, William G, comp. *Some Emigrants to Virginia*, 2nd ed. Richmond, 1915.

Stauffer, W. T. "The Old Farms Out of Which the City of Newport News Was Erected, With Some Account of the Families Which Dwelt Thereon." *Genealogies of Virginia Families from William and Mary College Quarterly Historical Magazine* 5:789-839. Baltimore: Genealogical Publishing Co, 1982.

Sweeney, Mrs. William Montgomery. "Thomas Button of Button's Range, Rappahannock County, Virginia." *Genealogies of Virginia Families from Tyler's Quarterly Historical and Genealogical Magazine.* 1:297-305 (1952).

Sweeney, William Montgomery. *Wills of Rappahannock County, Virginia 1656-1692*. Lynchburg, VA:1947.

Tarter, Brent. *The Order Book and Related Papers of the Common Hall of the Borough of Norfolk, Virginia, 1736-1798*. Richmond: Virginia State Library, 1979.

Thelaball Family Bible Record, 1684-1777. Accession 35231. Archives & Manuscripts, Library of Virginia, Richmond, VA.

Tinling, Marion, ed. *The Correspondence of the Three William Byrds of Westover, Virginia, 1684-1776*. 2 vols. Charlottesville: Univ Press of VA, 1977.

Today and Yesterday in the Heart of Virginia. Farmville VA: Farmville Herald, 1935.

Torrence, Clayton, comp. *Virginia Wills and Administrations 1632-1800, An Index.....* Originally published 1930. Reprint, Genealogical Publishing Co, 1972.

Torrence, Clayton, comp. *Winston of Virginia and Allied Families.* Richmond VA: Whittet & Sheperson, 1927.

Trout, W. E. *The Slate & Willis's Rivers Atlas: Rediscovering Historic Waterways in the Heart of Virginia*. Virginia Canals and Navigation Society, 1994.

Tucker, George Hulbert. *Abstracts from Norfolk City Marriage Bonds (1797-1850)*. Baltimore: Genealogical Publishing Co, 2001.

Tucker, George Holbert. *Norfolk Highlights 1584-1881*. Norfolk VA: Norfolk Historical Society, 1972. http://www.norfolkhistorical.org/highlights/03.html.

Turner, Florence Kimberly. *Gateway to the New World, A History of Princess Anne County, Virginia, 1607-1824*. Easley SC: Southern Historical Press, 1984.

Tyler, Lyon G. "The Goodrich Family." *Tyler's Quarterly Historical and Genealogical Magazine.* 12:66-70 (1930).

Tyler, Lyon G. "The Lightfoot Family." *Genealogies of Virginia Families from William and Mary College Quarterly Historical Magazine.* 3:409-430. Baltimore: Genealogical Publishing Co, 1981.

Virginia Colonial Records Project at the Library of Virginia in Richmond contains images that survey and describe documents relating to colonial Virginia history that are housed in repositories in Great Britain and other European countries, http://www.lva.lib.va.us/index.htm.

Virginia Land Office Patents . Library of Virginia. (http://www.lva.lib.va.us/).

Virginia Land Records. Comprised of articles that originally appeared in *The Virginia Magazine of History and Biography*, *William and Mary College Quarterly*, and *Tyler's Quarterly*. Reprint, Baltimore: Genealogical Publishing Co, 1982.

Virginia Magazine of History and Biography. Richmond: Virginia Historical Society.

Virginia Marriage Records. Comprised of articles that originally appeared in *The Virginia Magazine of History and Biography*, *William and Mary College Quarterly*, and *Tyler's Quarterly*. Reprint, Baltimore: Genealogical Publishing Co, 1982.

Virginia Military Records. Comprised of articles that originally appeared in *The Virginia Magazine of History and Biography*, *William and Mary College Quarterly*, and *Tyler's Quarterly*. Reprint, Baltimore: Genealogical Publishing Co,1983.

Virginia Tax Records. Comprised of articles that originally appeared in *The Virginia Magazine of History and Biography*, *William and Mary College Quarterly*, and *Tyler's Quarterly*. Reprint, Baltimore: Genealogical Publishing Co, 1983.

Virginia Vital Records. Comprised of articles that originally appeared in *The Virginia Magazine of History and Biography*, *William and Mary College Quarterly*, and *Tyler's Quarterly*. Reprint, Baltimore: Genealogical Publishing Co, 1982.

Virginia Will Records. Comprised of articles that originally appeared in *The Virginia Magazine of History and Biography*, *William and Mary College Quarterly*, and *Tyler's Quarterly*. Reprint, Baltimore: Genealogical Publishing Co, 1982.

Walker, Emily L. *General Index to Deeds, 1646-1780, Norfolk County, Virginia.* Norfolk VA: Emily L. Walker, 1998.

Walter, Alice Granbery. *Genealogical Abstracts of Princess Anne County, Va. Court Records from Deed Books 6 & 7 and Minute Books 6 & 7, 1740-1762.* Virginia Beach VA: 1975. Reprint, Baltimore: Genealogical Publishing Co, 1981.

Walter, Alice Granbery. *Genealogical chart of Adam Thorowgood 1603 - 1640 & His Descendants in Lower Norfolk & Princess Anne Counties, Va.* 3 sheets. Virginia Beach VA: Mrs. Alice Granbery Walter, n.d.

Walter, Alice Granbery. *Lower Norfolk County, Virginia, Court Records, Book "A" 1637-1646 & Book "B" 1646-1651/2.* Baltimore: Clearfield Co, 1994.

Walter, Alice Granbery. *Vestry Book of Elizabeth River Parish 1749-1761.* New York: A G Walter, 1967.

Walter, Alice Granbery. *Virginia Land Patents of the Counties of Norfolk, Princess Anne, and Warwick for Patent Books "O" and "6" 1666 to 1679.* Lawrence NY: 1972.

Warner, Charles Willard Hoskins. *Hoskins of Virginia and Related Families.* Tappahannock VA: Privately Published, 1971.

Warner, Charles Willard Hoskins. *The Origin and Establishment of Tappahannock with sketches of Its Founders, Bartholomew Hoskins, Thomas and Benjamin Goodrich, Thomas Gouldman, and Harry Beverley.* Mss7:2 T1655:1. Virginia Historical Society, Richmond.

Warner, Thomas Hoskins. *History of Old Rappahannock County, Virginia 1656-1692 with Introduction 1608-1656.* Tappahannock, VA: Pauline Pearce Warner, 1965.

Washburn, Wilcomb E. *The Governor and the Rebel: A History of Bacon's Rebellion in Virginia.* New York: Norton & Co, 1957.

Waters, Henry F. *Genealogical Gleanings in England.* 2 vols. Baltimore: Genealogical Publishing Co, 1969.

Webb, Stephen Saunders. *1676, The End of Independence.* Syracuse Univ Press, 1984, 1995.

Weisiger, Benjamin B, abs. *Charles City County, Virginia, Court Orders, 1687-1695.* Richmond: 1980.

Weisiger, Benjamin B, abs. *Charles City County, Virginia, Records, 1737-1774.* Richmond: 1986.

Weisiger, Benjamin B, abs. *Charles City County, Virginia, Wills & Deeds 1725-1731.* Richmond: 1984.

Weisiger, Benjamin B, abs. *Prince George County, Virginia: Wills and Deeds 1713-1728.* Richmond: 1973.

Wertenbaker, Thomas and Marvin W Schlegel. *Norfolk, Historic Southern Port.* Durham NC: Duke Univ Press, 1962.

Wertenbaker, Thomas Jefferson. *Torchbearer of the Revolution.* Princeton: Princeton Univ Press, 1940.

Whichard, Rogers Dey. *The History of Lower Tidewater Virginia.* 2 vols. New York: Lewis Historical Publishing Co, 1959.

Will of Benjamin Wilson, 1812-1814. Cumberland County VA Lodged Wills, Box 1, 1790-1825, Feb. 1814. Archives & Information Services Division, Library of Virginia, Richmond.

Will of James Seay 1752, King William Co VA. Burned County Records Collection, Library of Virginia, Richmond.

Will of Margaret Cheesman. PROB 11/363 [92 Bath]. Records of the Prerogative Court of Canterbury. Transcription done by Simon Neal, records agent, e-mail sn014i4785@blueyonder.co.uk .

Will of Nicholas Curle, 1714. Accession 30881. Archives and Manuscripts Division. Library of Virginia, Richmond.

Will of Thomas Goodridge, PROB 11/155. Records of the Prerogative Court of Canterbury. http://www.nationalarchives.gov.uk/default.htm

William and Mary College Quarterly Historical Magazine. 3 Series. Williamsburg VA: The College.

Willis Wilson Bible. Wilson vertical file, Francis M. Manning History Room, Martin Community College, Williamston NC. Very similar to "Wilson Family", *VA Mag Hist*, 25:199-200. Transcription in McCrary, *Wilson Families: Descendants of Colonel Benjamin Wilson.*

Wilkerson, Eva Eubank. *Index to Marriages of Old Rappahannock and Essex Counties, Virginia, 1655-1900.* Baltimore: Genealogical Publishing Co, 1976.

Wilson Family Bible Record, 1742-1896. Accession 29076. Bible Records Collection. Library of Virginia, Richmond, VA.

"Wilson Family of Princess Anne, Norfolk, &c." *Virginia Magazine of History and Biography* 25:199-200 (1917).

Wingo, Elizabeth B, comp. *Collection of Unrecorded Wills, Norfolk County, Virginia 1711-1800.* Norfolk: 1961.

Wingo, Elizabeth B, comp. *Guardian Bonds of Norfolk County, Virginia 1750-1800.* Athens GA: Iberian Publishing Co, 1993.

Wingo, Elizabeth B, comp. *Marriages of Norfolk County Virginia 1706-1792, Vol 1.* Originally published 1961. Reprint, Easley SC: Southern Historical Press, 1988.

Wingo, Elizabeth B, comp. *Marriages of Norfolk County Virginia 1788, 1793-1817, Vol 2.* Norfolk: 1963.

Wingo, Elizabeth B, comp. *Marriages of Princess Anne County Virginia 1749-1821.* Norfolk: 1961.

Wingo, Elizabeth B, comp. *Marriages of Princess Anne County Virginia 1799-1821.* Vol. II. Norfolk: 1968.

Wingo, Elizabeth B, comp. *Norfolk County, Virginia Tithables 1730-1750.* Norfolk: 1979.

Wingo, Elizabeth B, comp. *Norfolk County, Virginia Tithables 1751-1765.* Norfolk: 1981.

Wingo, Elizabeth B, comp. *Norfolk County, Virginia, Will Book 1, 1755-1772.* Originally published 1986. Reprint Athens GA: Iberian Publishing Co, 1996.

Wirt, William. *The Life of Patrick Henry.* 9th ed. Freeport, New York: Books for Libraries Press, 1836 (reprinted 1970).

Wise, Bel Hubbard, abs. *Amelia County, Virginia Will Book 4 1786-1792.* Signal Mountain TN: Mountain Press, 1991?.

Withington, Lothrop. *Virginia Gleanings in England Abstracts of 17th and 18th Century English Wills and Administrations relating to Virginia and Virginians.* Baltimore: Genealogical Publishing Co, 1980.

Woodson Family. *Papers, 1740-1945.* Accession 29437. Personal Papers Collection, Archives Branch, Library of Virginia, Richmond.

Wright, Louis B and Marion Tinling, eds. *The Great American Gentleman, William Byrd of Westover in Virginia, His Secret Diary for the Years 1709-1712.* New York: G P Putnam's Sons, 1963.

Wright, Louis B, ed. *The Prose Works of William Byrd of Westover.* Cambridge MA: Belknap Press, 1966.

Wulfeck, Dorothy Ford, comp. & ed. *Marriages of Some Virginia Residents, 1607-1800.* Original 7 volumes reprinted 2 vols. Baltimore: Genealogical Publishing Co, 1986.

Index of Names

(No Surname)
  Alice [-aft 1696], 170
  Alice [-bef 1748], 10, 143
  Alice [abt 1612-1644], 83, 147
  Ann, 20, 76, 121, 200
  Ann [-aft 1722/1723], 135
  Anne [-bef 1708/1709], 6
  Blandinah, 121
  Charity [-1797], 20
  Elizabeth, 8, 12, 46, 57, 97, 111, 183
  Frances [-aft 1754], 11
  Hannah, 134
  Hannah [1652-bef 1691], 127, 134
  Jane [abt 1655-1713], 59
  Joyce [abt 1621-bef 1680], 128, 141
  Judith [-aft 1718/1719], 140
  Katherine, 31
  Katherine , 152
  Katherine [-aft 1750], 142
  Lydia [-1803], 13
  Margaret, 22, 34, 142
  Margaret [-aft 1699], 117
  Margaret [-aft 1712], 100
  Margaret [-bef 1784], 23
  Margery, 127
  Martha, 25
  Martha [-aft 1775], 77, 78
  Mary, 57, 69, 76, 190, 192
  Mary , 151
  Mary [-aft 1704], 62
  Mary [-aft 1719], 138
  Mary [-aft 1768], 12
  Mary [-bef 1624/1625], 79
  Prudence, 29
  Sarah, 8, 11, 20
  Sarah [-1742], 130
  Sarah [-aft 1712], 140
  Sarah [-aft 1756], 25
  Sarah [-bef 1715], 73
  Sarah [-bef 1764], 14
  Susanna, 191
  Thomas , 87
  Watt, 190

Alkin
  Susanna, 73, 74
Allen
  Archer, 45
  Benjamin, 45
  Edmund, 117
  Elizabeth (Bassett), 68
  John , 68
  Thomas , 86
Allit
  John , 89
Alston
  Elizabeth (Wright) [-1823], 50
  Euphan [1761-], 50
  Euphan (Wilson) [-aft 1758], 50, 105
  Henry [1753-], 50
  John [-1758], 48, 50
  Joseph John [-bef 1781], 48, 50, 105
  Joseph John [1767-1841], 50
  Martha [-bef 1755], 48
  Martha (Kearny) [1771-1852], 50
  Mary [1756-], 50
  Sarah (Hill), 50
  Willis [1752-1819], 50
Ambler
  Edward [1758-1775], 69
  Edward, of Jamestown [1732-1768], 69
  Elizabeth (Jaquelin), 69
  John [1762-1836], 69
  Mary (Cary) [1732-1781], 69
  Richard, 69
  Sarah [1760-1782], 69
Anderson
  George, 45
  Robert, 44
Archer
  Dinah (Godfrey) [-aft 1772], 139
  Edward, 139
Armistead
  Ann (Wallace) [-aft 1739], 77
  Hannah, 72
  Mary, 77

Index of Names

Mary Latham (Curle) [-aft 1799], 78
Robert, 77
William [-bef 1799], 77, 78
Armstrong
   Robert , 161
Arnold
   Anthony , 167
Ashall
   Mary [-bef 1710], 132
Awbrey
   Henry , 173
Aylet
   William , 176, 190
Ayres
   William , 174, 175
Bacon
   Nathaniel, 174
   Nathaniel, Jr , 166, 168
Ball
   William , 176, 181
Ballard
   Anne (Newton) [bef 1740-bef 1773], 206
   Catherine, 206
   Catherine [-aft 1779], 206
   John [-1745], 206
   Robert [-bef 1770], 206
Barrett
   Basil, 37
Barrington
   Benjamin, 37
Bartee
   Lemuel, 27
   Letitia (Butt) [abt 1735-aft 1772], 27
   Lydia (Wilson), 27
   Rebecca (Wilson), 27
   Samuel , 130
   Signa (Langley) [-aft 1771], 130
   Thomas , 26
   William, 27
Bassett
   Elizabeth , 68
   Joanna (Burwell) [abt 1675-1727], 68
   Lucy [1699-aft 1755], 68
   Mary [1716-1755], 53
   Priscilla, 70
   William , 189
   William, III [abt 1671-1723], 68
Baum
   Elizabeth , 61
Bawden
   Hugh, 181
Belgrove
   Dinah (Godfrey) [-aft 1772], 139
Benbow
   Edward, 51
   Elizabeth (Newton) [1707-], 51
Bennett
   Anne (Snayle), 194
   Mary, 194
   Thomas, 194
Berkeley
   Frances (Culpeper), 167, 169
   William , 89, 163, 165, 169, 172
Beverley
   Harry, 191
Blair
   Archibald [-1734], 67, 72
   James , 66
   John [1687-1771], 67, 70, 72
   Mary (Monro) [1708-abt 1768], 70, 72
   Mary (Wilson) [1675-1741/1742], 67
   Sarah [1739-1799], 70, 73
Bland
   Edward, 174
   Giles, 167
Bolton
   Jane ( ), 34
   Richard, 34
Booth
   Humphrey , 164, 165
Boswell
   Grace, 77
Boughan
   James , 173
Boush
   _____, 194
   Affiah, 200
   Alice (Mason) [abt 1659-aft 1735], 106, 177, 201
   Ann, 209
   Ann [1762-1835], 15, 206-208

Index of Names

Ann [abt 1721-aft 1779], 109, 177, 202, 204
Ann "Nancy" (Waller) [1756-1778], 206
Ann (--), 200
Ann (Sweny) [abt 1745-], 208
Anne, 201
Anne (Goodrich) [abt 1700-bef 1735], 39, 109, 177, 202
Arthur [bef 1740-aft 1779], 110, 203, 208
Bennett [-aft 1801], 200
Caleb [aft 1765-], 19, 199
Catherine [-1823], 207
Catherine (Ballard), 206
Catherine (Ballard) [-aft 1779], 206
Charles, 209
Charles Sayer [aft 1740-bef 1809], 17, 110, 136, 197, 203
Daniel, 209
Elizabeth, 200, 206
Elizabeth [abt 1734-bef 1811], 17, 18, 132, 196, 198
Elizabeth [abt 1771-], 15, 208
Elizabeth (Hancock), 200
Elizabeth (Wilson) [1749-1816], 19, 28, 199
Elizabeth (Wilson) [abt 1704-1783], 16, 196
Elizabeth Jacomine [1775-1861], 19, 199
Frances (Loyall), 54, 207
Frances (Sayer) [-aft 1756], 109, 178, 203
Frances Moseley (Munford), 206
Frederick Wilson [bef 1736/1737-bef 1806], 17, 19, 28, 132, 196, 199
Goodrich [abt 1724-bef 1779], 13, 15, 54, 109, 177, 202, 206, 207
Jacomine [1796-1797], 19, 28, 199
Jacomine (Hunter) [-1791], 19, 132, 199
James [abt 1765-], 15, 207
John [-bef 1792], 206
John [bef 1733-bef 1735], 109, 177, 202
Jonathan , 201
Lemuel [aft 1726-aft 1751], 195
Margaret "Peggy" [bef 1754-], 110, 203, 209
Margaret (Taylor) [abt 1764-], 206
Martha (Sweny) [-1792], 203
Mary [-bef 1794], 58, 195, 197
Mary [abt 1769-], 15, 207
Mary "Molly" [bef 1740-abt 1763], 110, 203
Mary (Bennett), 194
Mary (Wilson) [abt 1739-aft 1778], 15, 54, 206, 207
Mary Anne, 137, 201
Mason [-aft 1702], 106, 201
Maximillian [-bef 1761], 200
Maximillian [-bef 1782], 195
Maximillian [abt 1678-bef 1728], 37, 104, 194
Maximillian [aft 1700-bef 1736/1737], 16, 194, 195
Nathaniel, 209
Nathaniel [aft 1740 -1813], 110, 203
Prudence (Thelaball) [1747-1807], 17, 136, 197
Robert [-1809], 206
Samuel, 209
Samuel , 201
Samuel [-1771], 207
Samuel [-abt 1769], 137, 194, 200
Samuel [abt 1668-bef 1736], 5, 32, 35, 93, 95, 106, 194, 195, 201
Samuel [abt 1694-bef 1759], 39, 106, 109, 177, 179, 195, 201, 202
Samuel [abt 1722-bef 1784], 109, 177, 202, 206
Samuel [abt 1763-], 15, 207
Sarah (Woodhouse) [abt 1700-bef 1733], 195
Thomas Wythe, 209

William [-bef 1787], 206
William [-bef 1834], 19, 199
William [aft 1733-bef 1756], 109, 177, 202
William Frederick Wilson, 200
Wilson [abt 1761-1829], 15, 54, 207

Bowler
  Thomas , 162
Bowser
  Affiah (Boush), 201
Bradley
  George , 62
  Mary (--) [-aft 1768], 13
  William [-bef 1785], 13
Branker
  Narthaniel, 87, 102, 145
Branton
  Jno, 37
Briant
  Mary (Langley) [abt 1716-aft 1750], 142
Bridge
  Thomas , 88
Briggs
  Anne [-aft 1790], 186
Bright
  Henry , 54
Brooks
  Susanna (Lightfoot), 191
Brough
  Ann (Boush) [1762-1835], 208
  Robert [-1823], 208
Brown
  Tabitha (Scarburgh) , 170
Browne
  Francis , 162, 165, 170, 181
Bruce
  Alexander [1718-1764], 14
  Margaret [1755-1827], 14
  Sarah (Tucker), 14
  Susanna, 30
Bryan
  Ben, 43
Burgess
  Anne (--) [-bef 1708/1709], 6
  Elizabeth, 7
  Emanuel, 7
  Emanuel [- 1745], 6
  George, 7
  Isabella [abt 1675-bef 1740], 6
  Rachel, 7
  Robert, 7
  Robert [-aft 1714], 6
  Sarah, 6
  Thomas, 7
Burke
  Mary (Freeman), 56
  Thomas, 56
Burrowes
  Christopher, 149
Burton
  John, 44
  Robert, 42
Burwell
  Joanna [abt 1675-1727], 68
Butt
  Abigail [1694/1695-aft 1741], 136
  Caleb [abt 1728-bef 1772], 16
  Edward [abt 1732-], 16
  Elizabeth (--), 8, 57
  Elizabeth (Fairfield), 58
  Henry, 3
  Horatio Boush, 58, 197
  James [abt 1723-1762], 10, 57
  Jane, 12
  Jane (Wilson), 12
  John [abt 1739-], 58
  Josiah [-1800], 197
  Josiah [abt 1720-bef 1781], 58, 197
  Letitia [abt 1735-aft 1772], 27
  Mary [abt 1725-], 57
  Mary (Boush) [-bef 1794], 58, 197
  Mary (Wilson) [abt 1697-bef 1772], 57
  Mary (Wilson) [abt 1700-aft 1760], 16
  Nathaniel, 58, 197
  Nathaniel [1695-bef 1750], 57
  Nathaniel [abt 1721-1788], 12, 57
  Olive, 197
  Prudence, 58, 197
  Prudence [abt 1678-bef 1724], 8
  Richard, 92
  Richard, the elder [1645-bef 1727], 16

Index of Names

Sarah, 197
Sarah [abt 1730-], 16
Sarah (Sayer) [-aft 1724], 16
Sarah (Wilson), 10
Theresa [abt 1730-], 58
Thomas [1650-1710], 8, 13, 57
Thomas [abt 1735-], 58
William, 8
William [abt 1699-1751], 16
Wilson [abt 1737-], 58
Button
   Jane ( ), 161, 183
   Thomas , 161, 164, 183, 184
Byrd
   Mary (Horsmanden), 169
   William [1652-1704], 63, 169
   William [1674-1744], 51, 62, 65, 93, 177, 191, 192
Calvert
   Christopher, 209
   Elizabeth (Newton) [1761-1791], 52
   Jonathan [1752-1792], 52
   Margaret "Peggy" (Boush) [bef 1754-], 209
   Mary Bassett (Moseley), 209
   Maximillian , 195
   Samuel, 209
Campbell
   Hugh, 34
   Jane ( ), 34
   John, 77
   Priscilla (Meade) [-bef 1785], 77
Carrington
   George, Jr, 44
   Joseph, 45
   Mayo, 45
Carron
   Lydia [-aft 1796], 26
Cary
   Anne [1706-bef 1749], 67
   Anne [1735-1786], 69, 70
   Anne (Taylor) [-aft 1682], 66
   Elizabeth [1738-1778], 69, 71
   Elizabeth Blair [abt 1770-], 70
   Hannah (Armistead), 72
   Mary [1704-bef 1775], 66, 71
   Mary [1732-1781], 69
   Mary (--), 69
   Mary (Wilson) [1675-1741/1742], 66
   Mary Monro [1764-1836], 70
   Miles [1655-1708/1709], 66
   Miles [1708-1756], 67
   Miles [abt 1766-], 70
   Miles, of Peartree Hall [1701-1766], 72
   Miles, of Windmill Point [1623-1667], 66
   Rebecca [1728-], 72
   Rebecca (Dawson) [1755-1823], 70
   Sally [1762-1779], 70
   Sarah "Sally" [1730-1811], 69
   Sarah (Blair) [1739-1799], 70, 73
   Sarah (Pate) [abt 1710-1783], 68
   Wilson [1702-1772], 66, 68
   Wilson [1760-1793], 70
   Wilson Miles [1734-1817], 69, 70, 73
Catlet
   John , 164, 165
Catlin
   Henry , 81
Cawson
   Christopher [-1757], 23
   Jonas, 35, 55
   Margaret [1749-], 23
   Margaret (--) [-bef 1784], 23
Cheesman
   Margaret (Ganey) [-1680], 80, 83, 101, 105, 106, 110, 116, 118, 119, 121, 125
Cheshire
   _____, 139
   Elizabeth (Godfrey) [abt 1713-aft 1741/1742], 139
   John, 34
   Margaret (Wilson), 34
   Richard [-bef 1725], 34
   Sarah (Thruston) [aft 1683-], 34
Chichester
   James [abt 1681-bef 1711/1712], 101, 145
   John [abt 1683-], 101, 145
   Mary [abt 1688-bef 1758], 46, 101, 104, 145

Mary (Thelaball) [abt 1662-bef 1714], 99, 101, 104, 145
Thomas [abt 1685-], 101, 145
William [-bef 1698], 98, 101, 104, 145
William [abt 1679-bef 1711/1712], 101, 145
Chilton
　Edward , 176
Church
　_____, 20
　Abiah (Corprew), 25
　Ann (--), 20
　Anne [1678-bef 1743], 123
　Joseph, 13
　Joseph [-bef 1768], 25
　Richard, 91
　Richard [-bef 1743], 25
　Sarah (--) [-aft 1756], 25
Clark
　Henry , 162, 184
　John , 176
Cleaton
　William , 170
Coats
　Caseby, 8
　Isabel ( ) , 9
　John, 8, 9
Cocke
　Anne, 119
　Anne [bef 1694-], 110
　Christopher, 98
　Elizabeth, 121
　Elizabeth (Mason) [abt 1662-bef 1697], 110
　Hannah (Hamlin) [-bef 1752], 121
　John, 119
　John [aft 1729-], 121
　Lemuel [-bef 1751], 121
　Mary [bef 1695-], 110, 111
　Mary (Mason) [abt 1675-bef 1735], 119
　Mary (Pearse), 110, 119
　Thomas , 98, 110, 118, 119, 121
　Thomas [-1750], 119, 121
　Thomas [1652-bef 1697], 98, 110, 122

　Walter [1657-bef 1738/1739], 98, 110, 118, 119
　William , 98, 120
Cole
　Martha (Lear) [-1704], 68
　Mary (Roscow) [-1752], 68
　William [1638-1693/1694], 68
　William [1692-aft 1729], 68
Coleman
　Daniel, 42, 43
　Daniel, Jr., 42
　Robert , 176
Collier
　Anne (Mason) [abt 1668-bef 1703], 116
　Mary, 116
　Peter [-bef 1703], 116
Collins
　Elizabeth (Thelaball), 128
　Giles, 81
Conner
　Abigail (Crawford) [abt 1690-bef 1774], 118
　Crawford [1717-1757], 119
　Elizabeth [abt 1717-aft 1766], 119
　Elizabeth ( ), 97
　Elizabeth (Daines) [-bef 1742], 118
　John [1716-bef 1750], 119
　Keader [-bef 1722], 118
　Lewis [1707-bef 1749], 97, 118
　Lewis [abt 1649-bef 1697/1698], 118
　Margaret [1710-1763], 118
　William [1711-1775], 118
Conquest
　Richard, 86
Cook
　_____, 53
　Ann (Newton) [1720/1721-1749], 53
　George, 53
　John, 42
Cooper
　_____, 140
　Abigail, 140
　Euphan (Alston) [1761-], 50
　John, 50
　John [-bef 1718], 140

Thomas, 162, 165
Corbin
   Gawin [1669-1744], 62, 64, 65
   Jane (Lane) [-bef 1716/1717], 62, 64
   Joanna [-aft 1765], 52
Cornick
   Elizabeth T (Moseley), 50
   James, 50
Corprew
   Abiah, 25
   Elizabeth [bef 1762-], 31
   Euphan (Wilson) [aft 1734-], 31
   James [bef 1762-], 31
   John, 31, 92
   John [bef 1762-], 31
   Sally [bef 1762-], 31
Costen
   Walter, 3
Craig
   James, 91
Craigdallie
   Hugh [-bef 1774], 49, 138
   Janet, 49
   Mary (Thorowgood) [1753-1819], 49, 138
Crask
   Edmund, 173, 183
Crawford
   Abigail [abt 1690-bef 1774], 118
   Abigail (Mason) [abt 1671-bef 1691], 117
   George [-bef 1691], 117
   Margaret (--) [-aft 1699], 117
   William, 112
   William [-1699], 117
   William [abt 1689-1762], 93, 117
Cullington
   _____, 74
   Elizabeth (Ricketts), 74
Culpeper
   Anne [1630-], 169, 180, 183
   Frances, 167, 169
   Lord, 169
   Thomas, 169
Cummings
   James, 34, 37
Curle
   Andrew [-bef 1762], 76

Ann (--), 76
David Wilson [-abt 1767], 76, 77
Elizabeth (Gutherick) [-bef 1705], 74
Elizabeth Kello, 78
Euphan (Wallace) [-bef 1774], 77
Hamilton [-bef 1760], 76
Jane, 73, 76
Jane (Wilson) [-bef 1758], 73
Mary, 77
Mary [aft 1714-bef 1775], 73
Mary (--), 76
Mary (Armistead), 77
Mary (Kello), 78
Mary Latham [-aft 1799], 76, 78
Nicholas [-1714], 60, 73
Nicholas Wilson [-abt 1771], 76
Pasco [-bef 1731/1732], 66, 73
Pasco [aft 1646-bef 1714], 73
Priscilla, 77
Priscilla (Meade) [-bef 1785], 76
Sarah [-bef 1715], 65
Sarah (--) [-bef 1715], 73
Sarah (Hancock), 78
William Roscow Wilson [aft 1729-bef 1782], 76, 77
Wilson, 77
Wilson [-aft 1784], 76
Wilson [1709-bef 1748], 73, 76
Curling
   Daniel, 58
Custis
   Ann (Kendall) [abt 1692-1760], 117
   Edmund, 117
   Elizabeth, 117
   Henry, 117
   John, 62, 65
   John, III [1653-bef 1714], 117
   Margaret (Michael) [1658-], 117
   Sorrowful Margaret [-1750], 117
   Tabitha (Scarburgh), 170
   Tabitha Scarburgh (Whittington), 117
   Thomas, 117
Daines
   Elizabeth [-bef 1742], 118
Danby

Index of Names

Abstrupus, 176, 182
  Anne (Culpeper) [1630-], 169, 180, 183
  Catherine (Wandesford), 183
  Christopher, 169, 180, 183
  Francelia, 169, 180
  John , 176
  Thomas , 183
Dandridge
  Euphan (Wallace) [1695-1717], 65
  William [-1743], 65, 73
Dangerfield
  John , 175
  William , 169
Dawson
  Priscilla (Bassett), 70
  Rebecca [1755-1823], 70
  Thomas, 70
Deane
  James, 45
Dey
  Lewis, 57
  Martha (Waller), 57
Doughty
  Francis , 164
Douglas
  William , 152
Drummond
  William , 168
Duke
  Grace [abt 1722-1795], 8
Dunnock
  Katherine , 142
  Thomas , 142
Dyer
  Sarah [-bef 1694], 126
  Thomas, 126
Edmondson
  Thomas , 182
Egerton
  Charles , 154, 156
Eggleston
  Joseph , 179
Elcock
  Mary , 154
Ellegood
  Abigail (Mason) [-aft 1757], 103, 114
  Fernelia [-aft 1768], 114

  Jacob [-bef 1768], 114
  John [-bef 1740], 55, 95, 103, 111, 113, 114
  John [-bef 1760], 114
  Mary (Pallett) [-bef 1732], 114
  Mason [-bef 1753], 114
  Rebecca [-bef 1779], 52, 114
  William [-aft 1753], 114
  William [-bef 1726], 114
Ellerson
  Richard, 9
Ellison
  Mary (Mason), 98
  William, 98
Ervin
  Katherine ( ), 110
  William, 110
Esten
  Frances (Newton), 52
  John [-bef 1788], 52
Ewell
  Mary (Bennett), 195
  Thomas, 195
Fairfax
  Bryan, 8th Lord [1736-1802], 71
  Elizabeth [abt 1770-], 71
  Elizabeth (Cary) [1738-1778], 71
  Ferdinando [1766-1820], 71
  George William, of Belvoir [1724-1787], 69
  Henry, 71
  Robert [-aft 1787], 71
  Sally [1760-bef 1779], 71
  Sarah "Sally" (Cary) [1730-1811], 69
  Thomas, 9th Lord [1762-1846], 71
  William [1765-abt 1782], 71
  William, of Belvoir [1689-1781], 69, 71
Fairfield
  Elizabeth, 58
Faulconer
  Elizabeth (Newton) [1707-], 51
  James [-bef 1728], 51
Fauntleroy
  Moore, 165
Fazakerly
  Ann, 7
Fenwick

Index of Names

Mary , 87
Ferebee
  John , 91
Ferguson
  John , 176, 181
Fielding
  Frances, 62
  Henry , 62
Fife
  John, 28
Finiken
  William , 95
Fisher
  Jonathan, 182
Foreman
  Alexander , 92
Foster
  Richard, 150
Fowler
  Frances ( ), 87
  George , 87, 88
Freeman
  Bridges, 173
  Frances, 57
  John, 57
  Mary, 56
  Robert, 57
  Tabitha (Wilson) [aft 1728-aft 1789], 56
  William [-bef 1782], 56
Fry
  John , 173
Fulford
  John, 35
Furlong
  Anne (Porten) [abt 1688-bef 1717], 109
  Mary [abt 1705-bef 1737], 109
  Richard [-bef 1713], 109
  William [aft 1691-], 109
Gaines
  Katherine, 157
Ganey
  Alice [abt 1599-aft 1655], 79, 80
  Ann (--), 80
  Anna, 79
  Anna, Jr., 79
  Henry , 79

  Margaret [-1680], 79, 80, 83, 101, 105, 106, 110, 116, 118, 119, 121, 125
  William , 79, 80, 82
Gilham
  John , 159
Gillet
  Jane ( ), 161, 183
  John , 160, 161, 172, 183
Gilson
  Andrew , 165
Glascocke
  Robert, 149
Glenn
  Nathan, 43
Glover
  William , 182
Goddin
  Sarah , 173
Godfrey
  Abigail (Cooper), 140
  Abigail (Porter), 17, 139, 196
  Abigail (Thelaball) [1745/1746-bef 1805], 17, 136, 139, 196
  Affiah [abt 1715-aft 1780], 139
  Amy, 52
  Anne [-aft 1739], 20, 28
  Anne [abt 1709-bef 1754], 139
  Dinah [-aft 1772], 139
  Dinah (Thelaball) [abt 1688-bef 1765], 138
  Elizabeth [abt 1713-aft 1741/1742], 139
  Elizabeth (Thelaball) [aft 1691-aft 1722], 140
  Isabella (Burgess) [abt 1675-bef 1740], 7
  John, 7
  John [-bef 1710], 138
  Keziah [-bef 1777], 139
  Leddy, 140
  Lemuel, 140
  Mary [abt 1711-bef 1754], 139
  Mary (--) [-aft 1719], 138
  Mathew [-bef 1717], 7
  Mathew [-bef 1755], 138
  Matthew, 5, 17, 136, 139, 196
  Peter [-bef 1723], 140

Index of Names

Sarah (--) [-aft 1712], 140
Warren [-bef 1712], 140
Godwin
  Devorax [-bef 1726/1727], 115
  Susanna (Kendall) [abt 1683-bef 1758], 115
Goodrich
  Alice (--) [-aft 1696], 170
  Anne [abt 1688-], 183, 187
  Anne [abt 1700-bef 1735], 39, 109, 175, 177, 202
  Anne [aft 1658-bef 1707], 157, 187
  Anne (Briggs) [-aft 1790], 186
  Anne (Sherwood) [abt 1625-bef 1696], 157
  Benjamin [-1761], 185, 186
  Benjamin [-bef 1803], 186
  Benjamin [abt 1647-bef 1695], 157, 170
  Benjamin [bef 1676/1677-1710], 38, 170, 175
  Briggs [-bef 1788], 186
  Charles [abt 1652-bef 1726], 157, 174, 182, 183
  Charles, Jr [abt 1686-abt 1722/1723], 183
  Danby [abt 1687-bef 1703], 180
  Dorothy, 186
  Edward, 186
  Edward [-bef 1791], 185, 186
  Edward [abt 1684-bef 1720/1721], 183, 185
  Elizabeth, 185, 186
  Elizabeth [abt 1707-], 38, 124, 175, 178
  Elizabeth (--), 182, 183
  Francelia (Danby), 180
  Frances, 186
  Joseph [abt 1650-bef 1694], 157, 173, 180
  Katherine [abt 1663-], 157
  Lucy (Elizabeth), 183
  Margaret (Wynne) [abt 1690-By 10 dec 1723], 185
  Mary, 185, 186
  Peter [abt 1662-], 157
  Robert , 175, 180
  Sarah, 183, 186
  Thomas [abt 1614-aft 1679], 85, 157
  Thomas [abt 1689-bef 1703], 180
  William , 185
Goodricke
  Henry , 158
Goodridge
  Thomas , 158
Gookin
  John , 149
  Mary [1642-], 7
  Sarah (Offley), 82, 149
Gooscott
  John , 87, 98, 102, 112
Gordon
  Jane ( ), 184
  Thomas , 171, 184
Gottridge
  Thomas , 158
Gouldman
  Alice ( ), 164
  Thomas , 163, 164, 171, 173
Granbery
  Abigail (Langley) [abt 1702-1763], 144
  John [1699-1733], 144
  John [1730-], 144
  Josiah [1728-1772], 144
  Margaret [1733-], 144
  Mary [1726-1814], 144
  Thomas [1724-bef 1782], 144
  William [1731/1732-], 144
Grasty
  Ann (Lightfoot), 191
Griffin
  Abigail (Thelaball) [-bef 1774], 128
  James , 128
  John , 128, 174, 175
Groughere
  Joseph, 120
Grundy
  Charles, 88
Grymes
  John , 65
Gutherick
  Anne (Sheppard) [-bef 1739/1740], 74
  Elizabeth [-bef 1705], 74

Index of Names

Quintillian [-1689], 74, 158
Gutteridge
   John, 158
Gwyn
   Alexander [-bef 1721], 127
   Sarah (Thelaball), 127
Hackley
   Fanny (Lightfoot), 191
Haire
   James, 108
   John, 96, 108
   Margaret (Porten) [abt 1682-aft 1740], 108
   Porten, 108
   Samuel, 108
Halbert
   Lucy, 63
Hall
   Richard, 173
Hamilton
   Alexander, 116
   Alexander [-bef 1746], 73
   Mary (Curle) [aft 1714-bef 1775], 73
Hamlin
   _____, 119
   Ann, 187
   Anne (Cocke), 119
   Anne (Goodrich) [abt 1688-], 187
   Charles, 187
   Elizabeth, 178, 179, 187
   Elizabeth (Taylor) [-bef 1720], 121, 187
   Hannah [-bef 1752], 121
   Hubbard, 187
   John, 187
   John [-1725], 178, 179, 184, 187
   John [-bef 1719], 121, 187
   Mary [abt 1706-], 187
   Peter, 187
   William, 187
Hancock
   Ann (--), 200
   Elizabeth, 200
   Sarah, 78
   Simon, Jr [-bef 1739], 200
Happer
   Mary [-bef 1772], 14
   Nancy [abt 1770-], 26

   Sarah (--) [-bef 1764], 14
   William [-bef 1757], 14
Hargrave
   Ruth, 153, 155
Hargroves
   Abigail (Langley) [abt 1702-1763], 144
   Abigail Langley [1738-1747], 145
   Hilary [1736/1737-1743], 145
   Margaret [1740-1740], 145
   Robert, 144
   Willis [1741-], 145
Harper
   Thomas, 181
Harris
   Ann, 170, 180
Harrison
   Benjamin, 63
   Cary, 45
   Henry, 183, 186
   John, 83
   Prudence, 22
   Sarah, 66
   Thomas, 149
Hart
   Thomas, 82
Hawkins, 166
Hayes
   Robert, 149
Heslett
   William, 106
Hicks
   _____, 57
   Martha (Waller), 57
Hill
   Anne (Sherwood) [abt 1625-bef 1696], 170
   Edward, 63, 185
   Edward [1637-1700], 157, 164, 169-171, 173, 174, 181, 183-185, 188
   John, 148, 152
   Sarah, 50
Hobbs
   Thomas, 158, 162
Hobson
   Elizabeth (--), 111
   Peter, 111
   Phillis [aft 1681-bef 1760], 111

Index of Names

Willis Wilson [1826-1917], 179
Hodge
    Alice (Mason) [abt 1659-aft 1735], 105, 201
    Mary [aft 1681-bef 1743/1744], 105, 107
    Robert [-bef 1681], 105, 201
Hodges
    Elizabeth (Burgess), 7
    Frances ( ), 11
    Richard, 11
    Robert, 7
    Thomas, 89
Hodgson
    Ann (Newton), 52
    John [-bef 1777], 52
Holland
    John, 42
Holloway
    James, 42
Holmes
    John, 81, 85, 86, 152, 153
Holstead
    Elizabeth [-bef 1754], 10, 57
    Henry, 10, 16
    Jacomine N (Thorowgood), 50
    Richard, 50
    Sarah (Butt) [abt 1730-], 16
Holt
    Ann (Boush) [abt 1721-aft 1779], 205
    Frances (Mason), 205
    James [-aft 1779], 205
    Thomas [-bef 1730/1731], 205
Horner
    George, 86
Horsmanden
    Mary, 169
    Warham, 169
Hoskins
    Bartholomew, 88, 160, 172, 173, 176
Howell
    John, 62
    Mary, 62
Howle
    William, 173
Howson
    William, 22

Hubbard
    Mary (Lightfoot), 191
Hunter
    Elizabeth (Boush) [abt 1734-bef 1811], 18, 198
    Euphan (Wilson), 24, 132
    Jacob [abt 1715-bef 1780], 18, 24, 132, 198
    Jacomine [-1791], 19, 132, 199
    Jacomine (Johnson) [-aft 1753], 18, 19, 198, 199
    James [-bef 1774], 138
    James [abt 1767-], 18, 198
    John [-bef 1753], 18, 19, 132, 198, 199
    John [abt 1758-aft 1794], 24, 132
    Jonathan [abt 1769-], 18, 198
    Josiah Wilson [abt 1770-], 18, 198
    Josiah Wilson [abt 1785-], 24
    Keziah (Thelabll [-bef 1774], 138
    Susannah (Moore) [aft 1721-bef 1766], 24, 132, 198
    Thomas, 138
    William, 200
    William [abt 1775-], 18, 198
Hutchings
    Amy, 52
    Amy (Godfrey), 52
    John [-bef 1768], 52
Irby
    John, 185, 187
    Mary (Hamlin) [abt 1706-], 187
Ives
    James, 7
    Rachel (Burgess), 7
Ivey
    Alexander [abt 1668-bef 1694], 127
    Alice (Miller) [-abt 1772], 108
    Ann (Thelaball) [aft 1693-aft 1769], 134, 141
    Elizabeth [-bef 1769], 141
    Elizabeth (Langley) [abt 1682-], 134
    George [-aft 1740], 135
    George [abt 1640-bef 1688/1689], 88, 127, 134
    George [abt 1669-bef 1710], 134

Index of Names

Hannah (--), 134
Hannah (--) [1652-bef 1691], 127, 134
James [abt 1702-bef 1752], 134
John, 141
Joseph [abt 1704-abt 1754], 134
Margaret [abt 1706-], 134
Margery (--), 127
Thomas , 152, 159
William [abt 1700-bef 1769], 134, 141

James
Elizabeth (Lightfoot), 191
Jamieson
Fernelia (Ellegood), 114
Neil, 114
Jaquelin
Elizabeth, 69
Jarvis
Thomas , 88
Jenkins
Thomas , 164
Jennings
Edmund, 60
Elizabeth, 71
Jermy
William , 86, 102
Johnson
Jacob, 133
Jacob [-bef 1710], 132
Jacomine [-aft 1753], 18, 19, 132, 198, 199
Margaret (Langley) [abt 1677-bef 1749/1750], 132
Mary [-bef 1761], 18, 132, 198
Mary (Ashall) [-bef 1710], 132
William [-bef 1727], 133
Jones
Evan, 37
John , 181
Mary, 185
Richard, 162
Roger, 63
Julian
William , 80, 149
Kean
Henry, 57
Martha (Waller), 57
Kearny

Martha [1771-1852], 50
Keeling
Ann [-bef 1744], 121
George, 44
Leonard, 42, 43
Lucy [-bef 1722], 195
Keith
Ann, 73
Kello
Mary, 78
Kelsall
John [aft 1698-], 31
Katherine (--), 31
Roger [-1709], 5, 31
Kemp
George , 88
Richard, 88
Kendall
Ann, 117
Ann [abt 1692-1760], 116, 117
Anne (Mason) [abt 1668-bef 1703], 115
Custis, 117
George Mason, 117
John [abt 1689-bef 1738], 99, 116
Leah, 117
Littleton, 117
Mary (Taylor), 116
Mason [abt 1690-], 116
Peggy, 117
Sorrowful Margaret (Custis) [-1750], 117
Susanna [abt 1683-bef 1758], 115
Tabitha (Watts), 116
William, 117
William [-1686], 115
William [1687-bef 1720], 116, 117
Kirkpatrick
Priscilla (Sweny) [-bef 1756], 75
Knott
William , 106
Lambard
Thomas , 152
Lane
Jane [-bef 1716/1717], 62, 64
John, 62
Mary (--) [-aft 1704], 62
Thomas , 63

Index of Names

Langley
  Abigail [abt 1702-1763], 142, 144
  Abigail [bef 1746-], 144
  Abraham [abt 1671-aft 1740], 129
  Absalom [-bef 1760], 130
  Affiah (Wilson) [abt 1729-aft 1767], 29, 143
  Anna, 131
  Betty, 144
  Elizabeth, 130
  Elizabeth [abt 1682-], 129, 134
  Elizabeth (Thelaball) [1660-1738], 141
  Euphan [abt 1764-], 30
  Frances, 131
  Frances [abt 1718-1775], 21, 22, 143
  George, 130
  George [abt 1690-aft 1748], 142
  Jacob [-bef 1747], 130
  Jacob [abt 1673-bef 1741], 129
  James , 144
  James [-bef 1777], 130
  James [abt 1669-bef 1752], 129, 131
  James [abt 1756-bef 1785], 30
  Jeremiah [abt 1675-bef 1749], 129
  John [abt 1685-1753], 141, 143, 144
  John [abt 1718-aft 1750], 142
  Jonathan, 130
  Joseph [-bef 1750], 130
  Josiah , 144
  Josiah [abt 1760-bef 1766], 30
  Joyce [abt 1680-], 129, 133, 137
  Joyce [bef 1724-bef 1742], 130
  Joyce (--) [abt 1621-bef 1680], 128, 141
  Katherine [abt 1720-bef 1750], 142
  Katherine (--) [-aft 1750], 142
  Kezia [aft 1724-bef 1753], 131
  Lemuel, 144
  Lemuel [abt 1683-bef 1748/1749], 22, 30, 56, 141, 142
  Lemuel [abt 1716-bef 1772], 143
  Letitia , 144
  Letitia [aft 1750-], 30
  Lydia, 144
  Margaret [abt 1677-bef 1749/1750], 129, 132
  Margaret (--), 22, 142
  Margaret (Thelaball) [abt 1648-bef 1702], 128, 137
  Mary [-aft 1750/1], 143
  Mary [abt 1698-], 142
  Mary [abt 1716-aft 1750], 142
  Mary [abt 1762-], 30
  Mary (Nicholson) [-bef 1761], 30, 143
  Moses, 131
  Nathan [abt 1667-bef 1742], 129, 130
  Nathaniel [-bef 1752], 143
  Samuel [-bef 1771], 143
  Sarah (--) [-1742], 130
  Sarah (Nicholson) [-bef 1755], 131
  Sarah (Vaughan), 130
  Signa [-aft 1771], 130
  Susanna (Bruce), 30
  Tabitha [abt 1714-aft 1750], 142
  Thomas [1654-1747], 56, 141
  Thomas [abt 1681-bef 1750/1751], 56, 141, 142
  Thomas [abt 1712-bef 1753], 142
  Thomas [abt 1714-bef 1761], 143
  William [-1676], 128, 141
  William [-bef 1755], 130
  William [abt 1665-aft 1740], 129, 130
  William [bef 1650-bef 1718], 98, 128, 137
  Willis [-bef 1767], 29, 143
  Willis Wilson [abt 1753-], 30, 143
Latham
  Mary [-1739], 76
Laurence
  Michael, 98, 102
Lawson
  Anne [abt 1694-], 95
  Anthony, 5, 87
  Elizabeth (Daines) [-bef 1742], 119
  Frances (Sayer) [-aft 1756], 204
  Margaret [-bef 1754], 203

Index of Names

Rose (Thorowgood) [abt 1672-bef 1709], 95, 204
Thomas [aft 1703-bef 1735], 204
Thomas [bef 1672-bef 1703], 95, 204

Leachley
Eleanor, 25

Lear
Martha [-1704], 68

Lee
Joseph, 5
Thomas , 62

Leigh
William , 63

Lightfoot
Alice [1698-], 188
Ann, 191
Ann [1720-], 193
Anne [1708-], 190
Anne (Goodrich) [aft 1658-bef 1707], 187
Elizabeth, 190, 191
Elizabeth [1716-1759], 192
Elizabeth (Phillips), 189
Fanny, 191
Frances [1708-1725], 192
Frances [1717-], 193
Frances [1738-], 192
Francis [1736/1737-], 192
Frayser [1723-1723], 193
Goodrich [1713-bef 1778], 190, 191
Goodrich [abt 1682-1738], 187, 190
Goodrich [aft 1757-], 191
Henry [1723-], 193
John, 191
John [1598-1649], 189
John [1711-], 192
John [1711-bef 1735], 190
John [abt 1622-1687], 187, 189
John [abt 1648-1707], 174, 176, 181, 187
Martha, 191
Mary, 191
Mary [1707-], 192
Mary [1717-], 190
Mary [1725-], 193
Mary (--), 190, 192
Philip [abt 1650-aft 1708], 174, 188
Philip [aft 1757-], 191
Priscilla, 191
Richard [-1625], 189
Sherwood [-1730], 187, 192
Sherwood [1714-], 192
Sherwood [1733-], 192
Susanna, 191
Susanna (--), 191
Thomas, 188, 193
William , 189
William [-aft 1758], 190

Linch
Elizabeth , 173
William , 173

Littleton
Nathaniel, 115

Lloyd
William , 172

Love
Frances [-bef 1730], 96

Lowery
Ann, 140
Ann (Thelaball) [aft 1693-aft 1769], 140
James [-aft 1736], 140
James [-bef 1716], 140
Judith (--) [-aft 1718/1719], 140
Sarah [-bef 1741], 141
Sophia [-bef 1752], 48, 140
Tabitha [-bef 1762], 140

Lowes
Elizabeth , 176

Lownes
John , 159

Loyall
Frances, 54, 207
Frances (Newton) [1728/1729-1793], 54, 207
George, 54
Paul [1722-1807], 54, 207

Ludwell
Philip , 175, 177, 179, 180

Lyon
Walter [-bef 1775], 78

MacNary
Gilbert, 31
Mary (Wilson) [abt 1711-], 31

Index of Names

Malbone
    Margaret (Porten) [abt 1682-aft 1740], 108
    Peter [-bef 1738], 94, 108, 178
    Sarah (Burgess), 6
Marsh
    George , 165
    Margaret (Mason) [abt 1652-bef 1697], 83
    Susannah (Thomas), 84
    William, 83
Martin
    Joel, 2, 32
Mason
    Abigail [-aft 1757], 103, 112, 114
    Abigail [abt 1671-bef 1691], 84, 117, 154
    Alice [abt 1659-aft 1735], 84, 105, 154, 177, 201
    Alice (Ganey) [abt 1599-aft 1655], 80
    Ann, 79
    Ann (Seawell) [abt 1635-bef 1705/1706], 36, 83
    Ann (Snale), 113
    Anne [-bef 1758], 97, 100
    Anne [abt 1668-bef 1703], 84, 115, 154
    Dinah [abt 1678-bef 1713/1714], 36, 84, 121, 154
    Elizabeth , 86
    Elizabeth [1701-1764], 55, 101, 104
    Elizabeth [abt 1630-bef 1706/1707], 80, 83, 124
    Elizabeth [abt 1662-bef 1697], 84, 110, 154
    Elizabeth (--), 97
    Frances, 112, 115, 205
    Frances [abt 1650-aft 1708], 83, 90, 154
    Francis [abt 1595-bef 1648], 79, 149
    Francis [bef 1624/1625-], 79
    George, 55
    George [-aft 1733], 111
    George [abt 1666-bef 1710/1711], 84, 93, 107, 111, 154
    Lemuel [-bef 1713/1714], 97
    Lemuel [abt 1629-bef 1702], 4, 80, 83, 151, 153, 154, 159
    Lemuel [abt 1657-bef 1711], 54, 84, 101, 145, 154
    Margaret, 98
    Margaret [abt 1652-bef 1697], 83, 154
    Mary, 72, 98
    Mary [abt 1675-bef 1735], 84, 119, 154
    Mary (--) [-bef 1624/1625], 79
    Mary (Newton) [-aft 1740], 113
    Mary (Thelaball) [abt 1662-bef 1714], 54, 101, 145
    Nathaniel Newton, 113
    Phillis (Hobson) [aft 1681-bef 1760], 111
    Tabitha [abt 1699-aft 1736], 54, 101, 103
    Thomas , 86, 99
    Thomas [-bef 1740], 94, 111, 113
    Thomas [abt 1654-bef 1711], 84, 97, 127, 154
    Trustram, 86, 99, 159
Mathias
    Edward, 42
Matthew
    Thomas , 165
Matthias
    Frances (Wilson) [abt 1774-1833], 22, 24
    Joshua, 24
Mayo
    William, 42
McCariel
    Frances (Freeman), 57
    John, 57
McCreife
    John , 122
McRae
    Christopher, 43
Meade
    Andrew [-1745], 76
    Mary (Latham) [-1739], 76
    Priscilla [-bef 1785], 76
Meares
    Thomas , 149

Index of Names

Meaux
    Ann [1736/1737-], 192
    Elizabeth (Lightfoot) [1716-1759], 192
    Richard [1711-], 192
    Thomas [1738-], 192
Michael
    Margaret [1658-], 117
Miller
    Alice [-abt 1772], 107
    Elizabeth (Godfrey), 139
    Henry , 139
    Henry [-bef 1741/1742], 107
    Lemuel, 55
    Mary (Hodge) [aft 1681-bef 1743/1744], 107, 112
    Mason [-bef 1775], 107
    Matthias [-bef 1767], 107
    Solomon , 55
    William, 36, 55, 107, 112
    Willis, 55
Millner
    _____, 142
    Mary , 67
    Mary ( ) , 67
    Mary (Langley) [abt 1698-], 142
    Thomas , 67
Monro
    Mary [1708-abt 1768], 70, 72
Moodie
    James , 66
Moore
    Ann (Sweny) [-aft 1801], 75
    Anna (Langley), 131
    Augustine, 75, 76
    Francis , 131
    Henry [-bef 1745], 132, 198
    Mary (Moseley) [-bef 1745], 198
    Susannah [aft 1721-bef 1766], 24, 132, 198
Morris
    George , 169, 172, 184
    Robert, 89
    Thomas, 80
Moseley
    Abigail (Butt) [1694/1695-aft 1741], 137
    Anthony [bef 1697-bef 1771], 137, 199
    Bassett [1745-bef 1789], 53, 209
    Edward [abt 1661-bef 1736], 7, 37
    Edward Hack [1716-1782], 7, 53
    Elizabeth T, 50
    Frances [1776-1836], 53
    George , 122
    Isabella (Burgess) [abt 1675-bef 1740], 7
    Mary [-bef 1745], 198
    Mary (Bassett) [1716-1755], 53
    Mary (Gookin) [1642-], 7
    Mary Bassett, 53, 209
    Rebecca [1769-1812], 53
    Rebecca (Newton) [1749-1794], 53, 209
    William , 164, 205
    William [abt 1634-bef 1671], 7, 159
Munford
    Frances Moseley, 206
Murden
    Edward [-bef 1735], 57
    Mary (--), 57
    Mary (Butt) [abt 1725-], 57
    Maximillian, 57
    Sarah (Butt), 58, 197
Nangle
    George , 164, 171
Narne
    William , 98
Nash
    Dinah [-aft 1771], 28
    John [-1776], 73
    Mary (Curle) [aft 1714-bef 1775], 73
    Thomas, 28
Newton
    Affiah (Wilson) [1689-aft 1753], 50, 92
    Amy (Hutchings), 52
    Ann, 52
    Ann [1720/1721-1749], 51, 53, 92
    Ann [abt 1680-bef 1708], 90
    Anne, 96
    Anne [bef 1740-bef 1773], 206
    Anne (Lawson) [abt 1694-], 95
    Anthony, 96
    Elizabeth [1707-], 51, 92
    Elizabeth [1761-1791], 52

Index of Names

Elizabeth [abt 1682-], 90
Elizabeth (Sayer), 95
Elizabeth (Sims), 97
Frances, 52
Frances [1728/1729-1793], 51, 54, 92, 207
Frances (Love) [-bef 1730], 96
Frances (Mason) [abt 1650-aft 1708], 90
Frances Sims [1741-], 97
George [-bef 1762], 52
George [1678-1762], 50, 90, 92
George [1711/1712-1719], 51, 92
George [1722/1723-], 51, 92
George [1735-], 97
George [abt 1637-bef 1694/1695], 90
Katherine [1733-], 97
Lemuel, 96
Lemuel [1715-], 51, 92
Lemuel [bef 1687-bef 1721], 90, 95, 108
Margaret (Porten) [abt 1682-aft 1740], 96, 108
Martha (Tucker) [1748-1816], 52
Mary [-aft 1740], 94, 113
Mary [1725-], 96
Nathaniel [abt 1684-bef 1737], 37, 90, 94, 113
Nathaniel [abt 1714-bef 1767], 95
Rebecca [1749-1794], 52, 53, 209
Rebecca (Ellegood) [-bef 1779], 52, 114
Thomas [1713/1714-1794], 51, 52, 92
Thomas [1737-], 97
Thomas [aft 1687-], 90, 96
Thomas, Jr [1742-1807], 52
William [1726-], 51, 92
William [1731-], 97
Wilson [1718-bef 1762], 51, 52, 92, 114
Nicholas
   Anne (Cary) [1735-1786], 70
   Elizabeth [1753-1810], 70
   George [1754-1799], 70
   John [abt 1756-1819], 70
   Judith [1765-], 70
   Lewis, 70
   Mary [abt 1772-], 70
   Philip Norborne [1775-1849], 70
   Robert [1768-], 70
   Robert Carter, of Williamsburg [1728-1780], 70
   Sarah [1752-], 70
   Wilson Cary [1761-1820], 70
Nicholson
   _____, 29
   _____ (Wilson) [-bef 1749/1750], 29
   Alice (--) [-bef 1748], 10, 143
   Dinah [-bef 1771], 9
   Dinah (Wilson) [abt 1727-bef 1762], 29
   Francis , 60
   James [abt 1747-aft 1762], 29
   John [-aft 1762], 29
   Joshua, 29, 140
   Mary [-bef 1761], 30, 143
   Prudence (--), 29
   Sarah [-bef 1755], 131
   Tabitha (Lowery) [-bef 1762], 140
   William, 29
   William [-bef 1728], 10, 143
   William [-bef 1731], 29
   William [abt 1745-aft 1762], 29
   Wilson [abt 1735-aft 1780], 29
Nimmo
   Elizabeth (Boush) [abt 1734-bef 1811], 18, 198
   Gershom [-bef 1764], 18, 198
   Gershom [bef 1764-1817], 18, 132, 198
   James , 18, 198
   James [-bef 1753], 18, 132, 198
   Mary (Johnson) [-bef 1761], 18, 198
   William , 18, 198
Nivison
   Catherine (Boush) [-1823], 207
   William [-bef 1799], 207
North
   Anthony , 164
O'Sheal
   Ann (Boush) [abt 1721-aft 1779], 204
   Catherine (Veale), 205

Index of Names

David, 205
Elizabeth, 205, 208
John, 204
John [-bef 1750], 204
Samuel [-bef 1779], 205
Offley
    Sarah , 82
Opechancanough, 79, 82
Page
    Robert, 148
Pallett
    Mary [-bef 1732], 114
Palmer
    Mary (Alston) [1756-], 50
    William, 50
Parker
    Francelia (Danby), 182
    Robert, 162, 184
    Thomas, 177, 182
Parsons
    John, 75, 76
    Mary (Sweny) [-aft 1787], 75
Pasteur
    James, 30
    Letitia (Langley) [aft 1750-], 30
Pate
    Sarah [abt 1710-1783], 68
Patton
    Susannah, 97
Pearse
    Mary, 110, 119
Perry
    Micajah, 63
    Richard, 63
Peters
    Simon , 153, 155
Phillips
    Anne ( ), 150-152, 155
    Elizabeth , 189
    Grace [-abt 1725], 9
    Matthew, 150-152, 155
Phripp
    Ann [-1796], 115
    Frances (Mason), 115
    John [-1766], 115
    John [1683-1776], 113-115
    Matthew, 115
Pilkinton
    Sarah (Porter) [abt 1695-], 48

    Seth [abt 1690-1751], 48
    Winifred [abt 1730-], 48
Porten
    Alice (Mason) [abt 1659-aft 1735], 106, 201
    Anne [abt 1688-bef 1717], 106, 109
    Craddock [-young], 108
    Daniel [abt 1684-1714], 106, 108
    Elizabeth (Vaulx) [-1744], 108
    Margaret [abt 1682-aft 1740], 96, 106, 108
    Sarah ( ), 91
    William [-bef 1692/1693], 87, 106, 201
    William [abt 1686-bef 1722], 106
Porter
    Abigail, 17, 139, 196
    Sarah [abt 1695-], 48
Portlock
    John , 24
Powell
    John , 182
    William, 45
Prescott
    Moses, 12
Price
    John , 181
Pugh
    Edward, 114
Purdy
    Elizabeth [-aft 1688], 130
Querke
    William, 79
Randolph
    Thomas, 45
Ravenscroft
    Elizabeth (Hamlin), 178, 179, 187
    Thomas , 175, 177, 179, 187
Reeves
    Henry , 169, 172
    Joseph , 175
Reid
    Alice (Wilson), 26
    William, 26
Ricketts
    Elizabeth, 74
    James [-bef 1724/1725], 74
    Jane (Wilson) [-bef 1758], 74

Roberts
    Butts, 25
    Elizabeth (Boush), 201
    Sarah (--) [-aft 1756], 25
Robinson
    John, 79
Roe
    William, 36
Rogers
    Phillis (Hobson) [aft 1681-bef 1760], 113
    Samuel [-bef 1719], 95, 113
    William , 113
Ronald
    Ann (Waller) [-bef 1788], 57
    William [-bef 1793], 57
Roscow
    Euphan (Wallace) [1695-1717], 65
    James, 68
    James [-bef 1721/1722], 62, 64
    Jane (Wilson) [abt 1700-], 62, 64
    Lucy (Bassett) [1699-aft 1755], 68
    Mary [-1752], 68
    Mary (Wilson) [1675-1741/1742], 64
    William [1664-1700], 63, 64
    William [abt 1695-1752], 65, 68
    Willis, 64
    Wilson, 68
    Wilson [-1713/1714], 65
Rouviere
    George, 131
Russell
    Joseph, 12
    Richard, 127
Rutherford
    John , 167
Sanderson
    Elizabeth (--), 100, 113
    Richard, 100, 113
Saunders
    Jonathan [-abt 1700], 195
    Mary (Bennett), 195
Sayer
    Charles [abt 1686-aft 1740], 95, 203
    Elizabeth , 95
    Frances [-aft 1756], 109, 178, 203
    Frances (Mason) [abt 1650-aft 1708], 92
    Francis [abt 1640-bef 1708], 89, 92
    Margaret (Lawson) [-bef 1754], 203
    Sarah [-aft 1724], 16
Scapes
    William , 85, 153
Scarburgh
    Tabitha , 170
Scott
    Thomas , 111
Scruggs
    Drury, 42
Seawell
    Alice (--) [abt 1612-1644], 83, 147, 150, 151
    Ann [abt 1635-bef 1705/1706], 36, 83, 147, 154
    Henry [-1644], 81, 83, 147
    Henry [1639-bef 1672], 85, 147
    Thomas , 147
Seay
    Anne [1735-1814], 40
    James, Sr [abt 1695-bef 1757], 40
Selden
    Ann, 72
    Cary [-1822], 72
    Cary [abt 1723-], 71
    Elizabeth [-1825], 72
    Elizabeth [1761-1815], 72
    Elizabeth (Jennings), 71
    Grace (Boswell), 77
    Hannah [1762-1813], 72
    John [-aft 1742], 77
    Joseph, 71
    Joseph [-1807], 72
    Joseph [-bef 1727], 71
    Joseph [-bef 1776], 77
    Mary, 71, 72
    Mary (Armistead), 77
    Mary (Cary) [1704-bef 1775], 71
    Mary (Mason), 72
    Mary Mason [1754-1787], 72
    Miles, 72
    Miles [abt 1726-1785], 71, 72
    Miles Cary [-bef 1833], 72
    Nathaniel [-bef 1833], 72

Index of Names

Rebecca, 72
Rebecca [-bef 1833], 72
Rebecca (Cary) [1728-], 72
Rebecca (Yeo) [-1736], 71
Samuel [-1720], 71
Samuel [abt 1725-], 71, 72
Sarah, 72
Wilson Cary [1761-1835], 72
Sewell
   Henry , 154
   Joanna (Warner) , 154
Sexton
   Peter , 158, 159
Shepherd
   Ann (Boush) [1762-1835], 208
   Anne Boush, 205
   Elizabeth, 205
   Elizabeth (O'Sheal), 205
   Frances, 205
   Samuel, 205
   Solomon [-bef 1794], 205, 208
Sheppard
   Anne [-bef 1739/1740], 65, 74
Sherwood
   Anne [abt 1625-bef 1696], 157
   Philip [-bef 1685], 158
   Philip [abt 1585-], 157, 158
   William , 168
Sibsey
   John , 81, 147, 149, 159
Sikes
   Costen, 3
   Thomas, 3, 36
   Walter, 3, 9
Simmons
   Ann [-1749], 111
   Benjamin, 111
   Charles [1722-bef 1771], 111
   Elizabeth, 111
   Henry [-bef 1766], 111
   John [-bef 1738], 111
   John [-bef 1749], 111
   Lucy [-bef 1799], 111
   Mary (Cocke) [bef 1695-], 111
   Sarah, 111
   William, 111
Sims
   Elizabeth, 97
Slack
   Winnie (Wilson), 11
Smart
   Tabitha (Scarburgh) , 170
Smith
   Abigail (Mason) [-aft 1757], 114
   Alice [1743-1787], 115, 206
   Alice [abt 1780-], 27
   Charles [1712-1773], 114
   Charles [abt 1776-], 27
   Elizabeth [abt 1772-], 27
   Elizabeth (Wilson) [1749-1816], 27
   Elizabeth Jacomine (Boush) [1775-1861], 200
   Henry, 32
   James, 27
   James [abt 1770-], 27
   John [abt 1766-], 27
   Margaret, 142
   Mary [abt 1774-], 27
   Prudence , 28
   Robert, 165
   Samuel, 34, 95
   Samuel , 56
   Solomon [-bef 1785], 27
Smythairs
   Thomas , 151
Snale
   Ann, 113
   Ann , 141
   William Ivy, 141
Snayle
   Anne, 194
Sorrell
   Alice ( ) [-aft 1696], 174, 175
   Edward, 174, 175
Southerland
   William, 33
Stafford
   William, 79
Starnell
   Richard, 160
Stephens
   Frances (Culpeper), 169
Stevens
   Anthony , 161
Stewart
   Anne (Boush), 201
Stone

Index of Names

John , 172
Summersall
   Ruth, 97
Swann
   _____, 20
   Samuel [-bef 1787], 20
   Sarah (--), 20
Sweny
   Ann [-aft 1801], 75
   Ann [abt 1745-], 208
   Ann (Wythe) [aft 1719-], 203, 208
   Charles [abt 1720-], 203, 208
   Daniel [abt 1730-bef 1761], 16, 196, 207
   Elizabeth (Wilson) [abt 1704-1783], 16, 196
   James [abt 1732-bef 1761], 16, 196
   Jane , 76
   Jane (Wilson) [-bef 1758], 74
   Lazarus [-bef 1732], 16, 196
   Martha [-1792], 203
   Martha [-aft 1757], 75
   Mary [-aft 1787], 75
   Merritt [-bef 1752], 66, 74
   Priscilla [-bef 1756], 75
   Roscow [-aft 1765], 74
   Samuel, 16, 100
   Sarah , 76
   Sarah [-bef 1768], 75
Synock
   Robert , 173
Tanner
   Daniel , 83, 86, 125, 155
   William , 88
Tatem
   Anne (Godfrey) [-aft 1739], 20, 28
   Dinah (Nash) [-aft 1771], 28
   James, 28
   Love, 20
   Nathaniel [-bef 1739], 20, 28
   Nathaniel [-bef 1771], 28
   Prudence (Wilson) [aft 1722-], 28
Taylor
   Abigail, 115
   Alice (Smith) [1743-1787], 115, 206

Anne [-aft 1682], 66
Elizabeth [-bef 1720], 121, 187
James, 115, 206
John , 167
Margaret [abt 1764-], 115, 206
Mary, 116
Tazewell
   Catherine (Boush) [-1823], 207
   Littleton, 207
Thelaball
   Abigail [-bef 1774], 128
   Abigail [1745/1746-bef 1805], 17, 136, 196
   Abigail (Butt) [1694/1695-aft 1741], 136
   Ann [aft 1693-aft 1769], 135, 140
   Ann (--) [-aft 1722/1723], 135
   Dinah [abt 1688-bef 1765], 135, 138
   Dyer [-bef 1714/1715], 126
   Elizabeth, 128
   Elizabeth [1660-1738], 124, 141
   Elizabeth [aft 1691-aft 1722], 135, 140
   Elizabeth (Mason) [abt 1630-bef 1706/1707], 83, 124
   Elizabeth (Wilson) [abt 1704-1783], 17, 136, 196, 203
   Francis [1684/1685-1726/1727], 135, 136
   Francis [abt 1646-bef 1704/1705], 124, 126
   Francis [aft 1684-], 127
   Francis [bef 1715-bef 1758], 128
   James, 128
   James [1714-bef 1741/1742], 136
   James [abt 1628-bef 1693], 82, 84, 120, 124
   James [abt 1655-bef 1711/1712], 124, 135
   James [abt 1677-bef 1767], 126, 128
   Joyce (Langley) [abt 1680-], 133, 137
   Keziah [-bef 1774], 133, 138
   Lemuel [-bef 1718], 127
   Lemuel [1720-bef 1746/7], 137
   Lemuel [1749-young], 17, 197

Index of Names

Lemuel [abt 1652-bef 1677], 124
Lemuel [abt 1686-bef 1727], 133, 135, 137
Lewis [1722-bef 1767], 137
Margaret, 133, 137
Margaret [abt 1648-bef 1702], 124, 128, 137
Margery (--), 127
Martha [aft 1707-], 135
Mary [-aft 1758], 49, 133, 138
Mary [abt 1662-bef 1714], 54, 99, 101, 104, 124, 145
Mary Anne (Boush) , 201
Nathaniel [1724-bef 1755], 137
Prudence [1747-1807], 17, 136, 197, 203
Robert [-bef 1737/1738], 133, 137
Sarah, 127
Sarah (Dyer) [-bef 1694], 126
Sarah Dyer, 128
Thomas [1716-young], 136
Thomas [1718-bef 1751], 17, 136, 196, 203

Thomas
  Edward, 175
  Job, 42
  Susannah, 84

Thompson
  Sarah , 83

Thornton
  Alice (Wandesford), 183

Thorowgood
  Adam , 81, 87, 122
  Adam [-bef 1769], 49, 138
  Adam [1603-1640], 149
  Adam [abt 1641-abt 1685], 121
  Ann (--), 121
  Ann (Keeling) [-bef 1744], 121
  Blandinah ( ), 121
  Dinah (Mason) [abt 1678-bef 1713/1714], 37, 121
  Frances (Yeardley), 121
  Jacomine N, 50
  Lemuel, 49, 138
  Mary [1753-1819], 49, 138
  Mary (Thelaball) [-aft 1758], 49
  Mary (Trevethan) [-bef 1733], 123

  Mary Anne, 124
  Priscilla [abt 1695-bef 1713/1714], 121
  Robert [abt 1669-1702], 37, 38, 87, 121
  Robert [aft 1695-1755], 37, 38, 121
  Rose [abt 1672-bef 1709], 95, 204
  Sarah (Offley), 82, 149
  Thomas [aft 1695-bef 1726/1727], 37, 38, 121, 123
  William , 122

Thresh
  Clement, 161, 163, 169, 170, 172, 180

Thruston
  Edward, 34
  Malachi, 87
  Sarah [aft 1683-], 34

Tillman
  Mary (Goodrich), 185
  Roger, 185

Todd
  Christopher [1690-1743], 104
  Elizabeth [1723/1724-1788], 104
  Elizabeth (Mason) [1701-1764], 104
  Lucy [1721-1791], 104
  Mary [1732-1805], 104
  Thomas [1728-1780], 104

Tomlin
  William , 175

Tooley
  Olive (Butt), 58, 197

Travis
  Champion [-1810], 206
  Elizabeth (Boush), 206

Tregany
  Elizabeth (Wilson) [abt 1673-], 2
  Henry [-bef 1704], 2
  Henry, Jr, 2, 11, 32

Trent
  Alexander , 43, 45

Trevethan
  Anne (Church) [1678-bef 1743], 123
  Dinah (Mason) [abt 1678-bef 1713/1714], 123
  Mary [-bef 1733], 123

Index of Names

Sampson, 123
William, 38, 123
Triniman
  John , 147, 153
Tucker
  Elizabeth (--), 15
  Joanna (Corbin) [-aft 1765], 52
  John, 34
  Martha [1748-1816], 52
  Robert, 15
  Robert [-bef 1769], 52
  Sarah, 14
  Susanna, 15
  William , 147
Vaughan
  Elizabeth (Purdy) [-aft 1688], 130
  James , 165
  Robert, 102
  Sarah, 130
  William [-abt 1688], 130
Vaulx
  Elizabeth [-1744], 108
Veale
  Catherine, 205
  George, 205
Vincent
  William , 160
Wake
  Richard, 86
Walker
  Ann (Keith), 73
  George [abt 1659-aft 1704], 73
  George [abt 1698-1773], 73, 75, 76
  Jane (Curle), 73
Wallace
  _____, 58
  Ann [-aft 1739], 77
  Anne (Sheppard) [-bef 1739/1740], 65
  Euphan [-bef 1774], 77
  Euphan [1695-1717], 65, 73
  James, 77, 78
  James [1667-1712], 63, 65
  Martha (--) [-aft 1775], 77, 78
  Mary Latham (Curle) [-aft 1799], 78
  Robert [-bef 1768], 78
  Theresa (Butt) [abt 1730-], 58

Wilson, 78
Waller
  Ann [-bef 1788], 57
  Ann "Nancy" [1756-1778], 206
  Benjamin, 206
  Martha, 57
  Mason (Wilson) [bef 1737-bef 1794], 57
  Robert [-bef 1787], 57
Wandesford
  Alice , 183
  Catherine , 183
Ward
  Thomas , 63
Warner
  Joanna , 154
Watson
  Ray, 42
Watt
  James [-bef 1716], 116
  Mason (Kendall) [abt 1690-], 116
Watts
  Jane ( ), 184
  Tabitha, 116
Webb
  Affiah (Wilson) [abt 1729-aft 1767], 30
  James, 30
Weir
  John , 160, 164, 165
Welburn
  Mason (Kendall) [abt 1690-], 116
  Samuel [-bef 1728], 116
Westwood
  Elizabeth ( ), 75
  James, 75
  Sarah (Sweny) [-bef 1768], 75
Whiting
  Anne (Cary) [1706-bef 1749], 67
  Peter, 67
Whittakers
  Captain, 80
Whittington
  Tabitha Scarburgh, 117
Wickens
  John, 46
Wilder
  _____, 140
Wilkinson

Index of Names

Cary, 43
Williamson
    Joseph , 168
Willis
    Elizabeth [abt 1651-aft 1714/1715], 2, 6, 35
    John [abt 1621-], 2
Willoughby
    Alice (--) [abt 1612-1644], 147
    Allerton, 100
    Anne (Mason) [-bef 1758], 100
    Elizabeth, 100
    John [-aft 1776], 100
    Lemuel [-1764], 100
    Margaret (--) [-aft 1712], 100
    Ruth, 33
    Sarah (Thompson), 83, 86, 91
    Thomas, 33, 80, 89
    Thomas [1601-bef 1657], 85, 147, 149, 153
    Thomas [1632-1672], 86
    Thomas, III [aft 1655-1712], 88, 100, 102
    Thomas, IV [-bef 1753], 100
    Thomas, V [-1784], 100
    William, 100
Willson
    Richard [-1768], 40
Wilson
    _____ [-bef 1749/1750], 9, 29
    _____ [abt 1615-], 1
    Abiah, 10
    Affiah [1689-aft 1753], 2, 50, 92
    Affiah [abt 1729-aft 1767], 10, 29, 143
    Alexander [1774-aft 1850], 41
    Alice , 26
    Amsey White [abt 1783-1824], 13
    Ann [-aft 1771], 54, 103
    Ann [abt 1695-aft 1750], 8
    Ann [abt 1767-1824], 14
    Ann (--), 20
    Anne [1762-1786], 41
    Anne [abt 1750-], 48
    Anne (Seay) [1735-1814], 40
    Benjamin, Jr [1759-1839], 41
    Benjamin, Sr [1733-1814], 38, 40, 124, 178
    Caleb, 10
    Caleb [-aft 1796], 26
    Caleb [1771-1835], 21, 23
    Caleb [abt 1706-aft 1754], 8, 20
    Charity (--) [-1797], 20
    Charles [-bef 1794], 22, 24
    Charles [bef 1752-], 48
    Charles Wesley [1787-1817], 21, 23
    Charlotte Happer [abt 1769-], 14
    Christopher [abt 1776-], 24
    Daniel Allen, 45
    Deborah, 11
    Dinah [abt 1727-bef 1762], 10, 29
    Dinah (Mason) [abt 1678-bef 1713/1714], 36, 122
    Dinah (Nicholson) [-bef 1771], 9
    Elizabeth, 10, 34
    Elizabeth [-aft 1771], 54, 103
    Elizabeth [1749-1816], 19, 21, 26, 27, 199
    Elizabeth [1756-1808], 40
    Elizabeth [abt 1673-], 2
    Elizabeth [abt 1704-1783], 8, 16, 136, 196, 203
    Elizabeth (--), 12, 46
    Elizabeth (Goodrich) [abt 1707-], 38, 124, 178
    Elizabeth (Holstead) [-bef 1754], 10, 57
    Elizabeth (Willis) [abt 1651-aft 1714/1715], 2, 6, 35
    Elizabeth (Wilson) [1749-1816], 21, 28
    Euphan, 22, 24, 132
    Euphan [-aft 1758], 46, 50, 105
    Euphan [1782-1810], 21, 23
    Euphan [aft 1734-], 10, 31
    Felix [-1646], 1
    Felix [-1662], 1
    Frances [1773-], 21, 23
    Frances [abt 1774-1833], 22, 24
    Frances (--) [-aft 1754], 11
    Frances (Langley) [abt 1718-1775], 21, 22, 143
    Frederick [-aft 1819], 13
    Goodridge [1776-1849], 41
    Grace (Duke) [abt 1722-1795], 8
    Grace (Phillips) [-abt 1725], 9

Henry [abt 1738-], 10
Holt [1779-1845], 14
Isabella (Burgess) [abt 1675-bef 1740], 6
James, 1
James [-aft 1766], 46, 105
James [1671-bef 1756], 2, 8, 143
James [1765-1847], 41
James [1776-1801], 21, 23
James [abt 1648-bef 1712], 1, 2, 85, 89, 92, 93, 195
James [abt 1691-bef 1718], 6
James [abt 1696-1761], 8
James, Sr [1742-1820], 20, 21, 23, 28
Jane, 11, 12, 34, 57
Jane [-bef 1758], 59, 73
Jane [abt 1700-], 62, 64
Jane (--) [abt 1655-1713], 59
Jane (Lane) [-bef 1716/1717], 62
Jeremiah, 12
John, 13, 42
John [1776-1843], 14
John [abt 1677-bef 1728], 2, 34
John [abt 1716-aft 1763], 34
John [abt 1737-bef 1780], 12, 14
John [abt 1750-1826], 43
Josiah [-1778], 15, 22, 23
Josiah [1708-1795], 8, 21, 22, 143
Josiah [abt 1772-abt 1809], 24
Josiah [aft 1777-], 24
Josiah Ashbury [1789-1801], 21, 23
Katherine (--), 31
Lemuel, 22
Lemuel [-aft 1771], 54, 103
Lemuel [1713-bef 1719], 31
Lemuel [abt 1675-1731], 2, 6, 31
Lemuel [abt 1713-1765], 46, 48, 104, 140
Love [-aft 1787], 20
Love [1779-], 21, 23
Love (Tatem), 20
Luce [abt 1716-], 31
Lydia, 13, 27
Lydia (--) [-1803], 13
Lydia (Carron) [-aft 1796], 26
Malachi, 13

Malachi, Jr [abt 1736-1794], 12, 13
Malachi, Sr [abt 1716-bef 1787], 9, 26
Margaret, 34
Margaret (--), 34
Margaret (Bruce) [1755-1827], 14
Margaret (Cawson) [1749-], 23
Martha [1778-bef 1849], 41
Martha (--), 25
Martha (Alston) [-bef 1755], 48, 140
Mary, 43
Mary [-bef 1803], 13
Mary [1675-1741/1742], 59, 64
Mary [1749-1805], 21-23
Mary [1754-1787], 40
Mary [1778-], 21, 23
Mary [abt 1697-bef 1772], 2, 57
Mary [abt 1700-aft 1760], 8, 16
Mary [abt 1711-], 31
Mary [abt 1739-aft 1778], 12, 15, 54, 206, 207
Mary [abt 1746-], 48
Mary [abt 1765-1799], 14
Mary (--) [-aft 1768], 12
Mary (Chichester) [abt 1688-bef 1758], 46, 104
Mary (Happer) [-bef 1772], 14
Mary (Thorowgood) [1753-1819], 49, 138
Mary (Wilson) [1749-1805], 21, 23
Mason [1768-1837], 41
Mason [bef 1737-bef 1794], 54, 57, 103
Matthew [1772-bef 1833], 41
Miles Simmons [abt 1781-], 13
Nancy (Happer) [abt 1770-], 26
Nathaniel [-1803], 26
Nathaniel [1790-aft 1817], 21, 23
Nathaniel [abt 1714-], 9
Peggy, 22
Peggy [1784-], 21, 23
Prudence [aft 1722-], 9, 28
Prudence (Butt) [abt 1678-bef 1724], 8
Rebecca, 27
Richard [1752-1827], 40, 43

Index of Names

Robert [-1793], 13
Robert [-bef 1758], 46, 105
Samuel, 13, 31, 63
Samuel [1770-bef 1842], 41
Samuel [abt 1680-bef 1710/1711], 2, 36, 122
Sarah, 10, 57
Sarah [1756-1779], 48
Sarah [1780-], 25
Sarah [abt 1763-1803], 14
Sarah (--), 8, 11, 20
Sarah (--) [-aft 1756], 25
Seth Pilkinton [1761-1790], 49
Simon [-bef 1801], 10, 11
Solomon [abt 1694-bef 1775], 2, 6, 11, 40, 54, 103, 111, 179
Solomon, Sr [abt 1693-aft 1754], 8, 10, 57
Sophia (Lowery) [-bef 1752], 48, 140
Tabitha [aft 1728-aft 1789], 54, 56, 103
Tabitha (Mason) [abt 1699-aft 1736], 54, 103
Tatem [-1795], 20
Tatem [1774-1831], 21, 23, 24
Thomas [-1655], 1
Thomas [-bef 1766], 46, 105
Thomas [-bef 1797], 26
Thomas [abt 1669-bef 1696], 2, 6
Thomas [abt 1694-1724], 8, 12
Unita [1783-bef 1852], 41
William, 21, 28
William [-1815], 11
William [1646-1713], 1, 3, 59
William [1761-1838], 14
William [1782-], 25
William [abt 1715-1752], 9, 25
William, Jr [aft 1750-1787], 20
Willis [1748-1798], 48, 49, 138
Willis [1758-1822], 41
Willis [abt 1683-bef 1760], 2, 6, 35, 46, 104, 146
Willis [abt 1707-abt 1740], 36, 38, 123, 124, 178
Willis [abt 1744-1804], 25
Willis [abt 1770-], 13

Willis [aft 1671-1701], 3, 37, 59, 62
Willis, Jr [abt 1687-bef 1750], 8, 12
Winifred (Pilkinton) [abt 1730-], 48
Winnie, 11
Wingo
    Elizabeth (Baum) , 61
    William B , 61
Wishart
    James , 153
    John, 134
    Joyce (Langley) [abt 1680-], 134
Woneycutt
    Affiah (Godfrey) , 139
    Nicholas , 139
Wood
    Matthew, 159
    Thomas , 176, 182
Woodhouse
    Henry , 86
    Horatio , 196
    Horatio [-bef 1719], 195
    Lucy (Keeling) [-bef 1722], 195
    Sarah [abt 1700-bef 1733], 195
Woodson
    Stephen, 45
Worthall
    Thomas, 79
Wright
    Elizabeth [-1823], 50
    Mary (Trevethan) [-bef 1733], 124
    Stephen, 124
    Thomas , 81, 86
Wynne
    Joshua, 185
    Margaret [abt 1690-By 10 dec 1723], 185
    Mary (Jones), 185
    Peter, 185-187
Wythe
    Ann [aft 1719-], 203, 208
Yeardley
    Frances, 121
Yeo
    Rebecca [-1736], 71

www.ingramcontent.com/pod-product-compliance
Lightning Source LLC
Chambersburg PA
CBHW062002220426
43662CB00010B/1208